PHILOSOPHICAL PERSPECTIVES ON COMPUTER-MEDIATED COMMUNICATION

SUNY SERIES IN COMPUTER-MEDIATED
COMMUNICATION

TERESA M. HARRISON AND TIMOTHY STEPHEN,
EDITORS

PHILOSOPHICAL PERSPECTIVES ON COMPUTER-MEDIATED COMMUNICATION

EDITED, WITH AN INTRODUCTION BY
CHARLES ESS

STATE UNIVERSITY OF NEW YORK PRESS

Published by
State University of New York Press, Albany

© 1996 State University of New York

Printed in the United States of America

For information, address State University of New York Press,
State University Plaza, Albany, N.Y. 12246

Production by M. R. Mulholland
Marketing by Nancy Farrell

Library of Congress Cataloging-in-Publication Data
Philosophical perspectives on computer-mediated communication /
    edited, with an introduction by Charles Ess.
        p.   cm.—(SUNY series in computer-mediated communication)
    Includes bibliographical references and index.
    ISBN 0-7914-2871-0 (alk. paper).—ISBN 0-7914-2872-9 (pbk.:
alk. paper)
    1. Telematics—Social aspects.   2. Computer networks—Social
aspects.   I. Ess, Charles, 1951–   .   II. Series.
TK5105.6.P55   1996
302.23—dc20   95-12668
                                                            CIP

10 9 8 7 6 5 4 3 2

CONTENTS

III. *Impacts and Implications for Religious Authority,*
Communities, and Beliefs

ACKNOWLEDGMENTS

I am most grateful to Dr. Richard Killough and Dr. Peter Browning, my colleagues in the Philosophy and Religion Department, who took on additional burdens to help see me through the labors of editing. The administration of Drury College graciously arranged release time and computer resources. The good sense and sharp eyes of Dr. Karen Taylor (Drury College), Rabbi Rita Sherwin (United Hebrew Congregations, Springfield, Missouri), and Dr. Susan Herring (University of Texas at Arlington) caught many an errant typo and clumsy phrase. Four anonymous reviewers of the manuscript gave us both encouragement and helpful criticism. Dr. Teri Harrison, the co-editor of this series, first suggested that I take up this venture, and provided constant encouragement through its many phases. Finally, I can only thank my students at Drury College, my spouse Conni, and our children Joshua and Kathleen, for their considerable patience with the many negative artifacts of my attending to this volume.

—*Charles Ess*

Introduction: Thoughts along the I-way: Philosophy and the Emergence of Computer-Mediated Communication

CHARLES ESS

Computer-mediated communication (CMC) and its attendant cyberspace—the peculiar space/time created by literally millions of human beings around the globe communicating with one another via computer networks—have moved rapidly from the status of futuristic dream to exponentially exploding reality. Book-length guides to the mother of all networks, the Internet, proliferate, as software tools for mining its information riches are simply assumed as building blocks of new computer operating systems. The once heady exchange of e-mail now seems staid compared with increasingly sophisticated libraries of materials accessible via the World Wide Web. What was a few years ago largely the cozy club of technology-oriented academics has become a commonplace: the notion of an "Information Superhighway," or I-way, is now an elemental part of American popular culture; being on-line is taken for granted by such diverse cultural mavens as Rush Limbaugh, National Public Radio hosts, and the cartoon strip "Doonesbury"; and stories about pornography on the Internet command front-page attention.

CMC Theory: Disciplinary Boundaries and Their Consequences

A burgeoning literature of analyses and discussions has accompanied these phenomena. From tightly focused academic studies to popular books of diverse musings, enthusiasts and critics see everything promised by the rise of CMC and its virtual communities—from the radical expansion of democracy in a uniquely libertarian cyberspace to the enslavement of whole populations via a perfected technology of deception and surveillance.

To begin with, the essays collected here provide a scholarly overview of this expanding literature. But this overview further makes clear that the starting points of earlier CMC literatures largely have been defined, sensibly enough, by such academic disciplines as computer science, communication theory, and literary theory. These analyses, however, point to typically *philo-sophical* concerns—to the underlying assumptions (and their attendant questions) regarding knowledge (epistemology), reality (ontology or metaphysics), and values, including ethical and political issues. For all of their insights, few of these earlier analyses have made explicit their undergirding philosophical assumptions—and the possible critiques of those assumptions. Fewer still have exploited the riches of philosophical analyses and traditions by taking these up as fruitful and suggestive frameworks within which to consider CMC and its especially philosophical dimensions.

By the same token, few academic philosophers have considered carefully the various technologies, behaviors, and possible consequences of a massive, perhaps inevitable surge toward communication as mediated by computers. But to ignore this domain is to ignore what many see as a technologically mediated revolution, one that promises to reshape radically our fundamental conceptions of—ethics and politics, knowledge and reality.

This disciplinary separation all but condemns theoretical literature in CMC to minimize attention to philosophical issues. But without taking up philosophical issues directly, CMC theories rely on largely implicit philosophical assumptions: Such unexamined assumptions then run the risk of contradiction and incoherence. To borrow a Socratic metaphor: Attempting to navigate the waters of theory on such a vessel is to ride a raft cobbled together from whatever one finds available, whose pieces fit together badly and constantly threaten to fall apart. We could wish for a more coherent and seaworthy craft —especially if we believe we are about to embark on a revolution.

Overcoming the Barriers, Embarking on the Revolution:
The Goals of These Essays

The disciplinary barriers between philosophy and CMC thus leave each incomplete, perhaps dangerously so. In the face of these barriers, the essays in this volume begin with the shared assumption that reflection on CMC from within explicitly articulated philosophical frameworks is crucial for at least two reasons. First, by bringing our philosophical assumptions to the foreground, our resulting reflections on CMC no longer rest on unexamined—and thus potentially contradictory or incoherent—assumptions. Indeed, to bring these assumptions to the foreground is to invite critical attention to these assumptions and thereby to the reflections on CMC which rest upon them. Especially for a technology that appears to promise everything—from the realization of Enlightenment democracy to the demise of print, literacy, and civilization as we know it—such critical scrutiny would seem especially urgent. The second reason is that developed philosophical frameworks often include conceptual elements and implications which are not otherwise obvious when such frameworks operate only implicitly. By taking up reflection on CMC within various philosophical frameworks, the authors of these essays are able to add insight and understanding that might otherwise be overlooked.

Taken together, these essays serve two further purposes. First, as CMC expands and becomes its own discipline within the academy, more and more instruction takes up not only the empirical dimensions of CMC but also reflection on its philosophical dimensions, especially its ethical problems and social and political implications. In fact, in their preliminary form, several of the essays collected here have already found use in courses concerned with such problems and implications. We hope that this collection—to our knowledge, the first of its kind—will serve as a useful textbook for such courses and related research.

Second, much of philosophy sees that *everything* involves some set of philosophical assumptions or foundations. This means, in turn, that there are many "philosophies of *X*"—that is, explicitly developed philosophical frameworks and approaches to, say, the natural sciences, education, technology, and so on. While there are diverse philosophies of technology (and these essays address questions taken up in philosophy of technology per se), there are as yet, to our knowledge, no well-developed philosophies of CMC. We hope the essays in this volume, taken as a whole, begin to sketch out the basic questions, specific issues, and tentative responses that would constitute such philosophies. Indeed, readers who examine these essays with care will see that such philosophies of CMC will include traditional philosophical areas such as epistemology (questions of knowledge), ontology (questions of reality), ethics and politics, and so forth. Readers will further discover that the questions and responses raised in these domains are at moments both similar to traditional questions *and* novel and unique. This suggests that responses from earlier philosophical traditions to similar questions may be appropriate and useful *and* that new responses may emerge here—new responses which may well constitute entirely new chapters in the history of philosophy. (I will summarize my own impression of what these essays suggest by way of conclusion.)

The Essays: Approaches, Issues, Findings

The essays take up a considerable range of philosophical approaches: phenomenology, semiotics, diverse ethical and political systems, Frankfurt School critical theory, and postmodernism. On these foundations they examine a range of specific theoretical issues. Will the new technologies facilitate or undermine critical reflection (David Kolb)? Is communication the transfer of information or the creation of meaning (Gary Shank and Don Cunningham)? What privacy rights do individuals have, and how may these be protected in societies that depend on computerized databases of their citizens (Dag Elgesem)? How can we sustain and expand the ethical sensibilities necessary to protect individuals in cyberspace (Peter Danielson)? What is the future of intellectual property and property rights in cyberspace (John Lawrence)? Do CMC environments achieve egalitarian and democratic forms of communication—communication which accomplishes gender equality as well—or do such environments only reinforce existing social systems of power and hierarchy (Susan Herring, Carol Adams, Sunh-Hee Yoon, Charles Ess)? How will religious discourse and rhetoric change in the new environment of CMC (Stephen O'Leary and Brenda Brasher)? Will textual, specifically biblical, authority survive the promised transition from an age of print to a cyberspace made up of electronic documents (Phil Mullins)?

We begin with David Kolb, who takes a phenomenological approach to the question of how CMC technologies may both preserve and expand the discursive moves of argument and criticism. Kolb introduces a commonly shared theme of several essays to follow—namely, that CMC environments issue in a more oral style of communication, in contrast with the style associated with print. (Lawrence explores more extensively the contrast between electronic and paper media: O'Leary and Brasher and Mullins take up most centrally the "orality" of electronic communication.)

Kolb further introduces a second theme in several of these essays: the debate between modernists, as represented by the German critical theorist Jürgen Habermas, and postmodernists. While postmodernists typically celebrate the episodic and ephemeral characteristics of e-mail as consistent with the themes of deconstruction, *bricolage,* and so on (see especially O'Leary and Brasher), Kolb observes that these characteristics also facilitate the kind of dialogue Habermas takes as foundational for democratic communities. (The democratizing potential of CMC environments is explored more fully in this volume by Herring, Yoon, and Ess.) But Kolb further points out a chief weakness of this medium: Returning to earlier threads of discussion and argument is all but impossible, at least within the framework of current software. Kolb suggests a technological solution—namely, making CMC environments function more like hypertext.

Kolb asks what will happen to argument and criticism in such an environment. He explores how hypertext can facilitate various logical structures, including the dialectical patterns of Hegelian and Nietzschean thought. Kolb further argues that the human realities of finite time and attention, in the face of the dramatically richer environment of continuously expanded hypertexts, will force the emergence of new forms of hypertextual discourse. (Danielson develops more extensively notions of guides and filters, both human and computerized; the *need* for such authoritative gateways is also discussed by Lawrence.) By creating such forms, Kolb concludes, we will move beyond computers as tools for data storage and manipulation, to CMC as a realm of discourse and poetics.

Gary Shank and Don Cunningham take up semiotics as a theoretical framework for understanding CMC. They argue that the unique combination of oral and textual dimensions of communication on the Internet escapes the assumptions and categories of earlier theory. They offer Shank's notion of a "multilogue" (in contrast with a monologue or dialogue), exemplified in a message thread initiated by one person and then rapidly developed through the responses of any number of communicants, as better able to account for these new forms of communication and communicative subjects. After introducing us to semiotics, Shank and Cunningham argue that the semiotic notion of abduction is fundamental to the multilogues characteristic of CMC conversation and to their more egalitarian atmosphere. They conclude that a semiotic conception of the self and communication may lead, via the rapidly expanding technologies of CMC, to an "age of meaning" rather than an information age.

Dag Elgesem explores the central issue of privacy and its protection in connection with research involving personal medical information stored in computerized databases, especially with regard to a Norwegian proposal to use a system of pseudonyms to protect individual privacy. Elgesem draws important distinctions between the *kinds* of privacy we seek to protect and what privacy *means* in the context of computerized information, in order to develop a notion of privacy as fair information processing. He further clarifies how we may think about the trade-offs between individual privacy, now understood primarily in terms of control over information about ourselves, and public benefit, especially in terms of the *risks* we are willing to take in the contemporary world in order to achieve our personal and social goals. His work will be useful especially for ethicists and other theorists who seek both greater conceptual clarity and promising foundational principles for developing ethical guidelines regarding privacy in computer-related contexts. At the same time, his discussion of the Norwegian project, which, by way of pseudonymization, seeks to achieve an ethically acceptable balance between public benefit and a minimal risk of individual loss of privacy, may provide useful suggestions for system designers facing similar ethical dilemmas. (This use of pseudoanonymity to protect privacy, however, should be considered alongside ethical critiques of anonymity by Peter Danielson and Carol Adams.)

Peter Danielson's evolutionary ethics is well suited for addressing the central ethical problems brought about by the rapid development and expansion of open computer networks. Danielson initially proposes the adoption and adaptation of several communicative conventions of the paper world to help users sort more easily through e-mail floods. As well, Danielson exploits CMC technologies to suggest, for example, the use of ethically programmed computational agents both to serve as buffers between humans and their increasingly complicated communication technologies and to issue in more beneficial behaviors.

Danielson's approach also maintains a central emphasis on the traditional focus of ethics—namely, on human choice and responsibility. His many suggestions for ethically moderating network behavior—human list moderators, mailbots designed to minimize the noise of unnecessary messages (e.g., subscribe and unsubscribe messages), and so forth—in part rely on utilitarian and liberal traditions which favor freedom and experiment, so far as these result in no harm. And precisely because the Net constitutes an ideal environment in which to develop and test the sort of evolutionary ethics he favors, Danielson emphasizes a constructive approach of developing and disseminating beneficial conventions, informing users of these conventions, and filtering techniques, instead of attempting to prohibit undesirable behaviors. CMC advocates intent on defending the currently open, even anarchic, environment of the Internet will find in Danielson's approach and suggestions both a strong ethical defense of such an environment and constructive responses to the genuine problems users face on the Net as an open commons.

John Lawrence is an adept traveler in both the paper and electronic worlds and, hence, uniquely qualified to offer an unusually balanced appraisal of paper vs. electronic publishing. Lawrence raises a number of crucial questions: How far may digital communication transform the paper-based system of property and prestige? How might electronic publishing democratize the hierarchies and exclusions of print scholarship? What new structures must accompany cyberdiscourse if it is to replace print? And, what electronic forms of publication are most likely to replace paper? Reiterating Danielson's strategy of drawing on models from the print world, Lawrence strongly argues the need for equivalent levels of indexing, accessibility, and stability in the electronic world, if digital publishing is, in fact, to begin replacing paper-based scholarship. Lawrence also argues that two forms of electronic publishing will prove to be attractive and useful to scholars—namely, publishing large corpora on CD-ROM and providing timely book reviews and critical exchanges.

Linguist Susan Herring reports on her most recent research on communication styles and gender in CMC contexts. Herring's analyses first support the claim that there *are* gender-related differences in communication styles, differences further associated with different value systems. Briefly, women appear to prefer an ethic of politeness, emphasizing attention to positive face (a person's desire to be ratified and liked), while men appear to prefer an ethic of agonistic debate, emphasizing negative face (the desire to be free from rules and other forms of imposition by others). Second, Herring's findings powerfully demonstrate the overwhelming dominance of the male discourse style—both in practice and in various "netiquette" guidelines—in the current Internet environment. These findings argue that if CMC is to realize gender equality as one of its most cherished moral and political goals, changes in communication style will be imperative—primarily on the part of the males who may constitute as much as 95 percent of the current population of cyberspace. Otherwise, Herring suggests, the much-vaunted freedom and equality of cyberspace will only reproduce, and perhaps amplify, existing patterns of male dominance and female subordination.

Carol Adams takes up the work of Catherine MacKinnon, Evelyn Kaschak, Deborah Tannen, and others to articulate a feminist analysis of society and pornography. Adams argues that in a male-dominant society, naming and representation of the world reflect a male view, including a male (hetero)sexuality that reduces the object of its desire—woman—from personhood to an impersonal thing to be manipulated according to the male will. Adams then inventories myriad examples of such sexism in cyberspace, ranging from sexualized computer jargon and adult bulletin board discourse to pornography exchange and real/virtual rape. From a phenomenological perspective, Adams further points out the striking intersection between male dominance of the machine and male dominance via the machine of woman as image. Indeed, Adams argues that computing technologies dramatically expand men's ability to manipulate "woman" as entirely reduced to a computer-generated and user-controlled image. Adams's analysis thus forcefully reiterates Herring's point: The ethically and politically compelling promise of gender equality in CMC is directly contradicted by manifold reflections and amplifications in cyberspace of the sexual domination operating in the larger society.

Adams's findings have implications for both feminist philosophers and philosophers of technology. If the Internet serves as a kind of ethical and social laboratory (so Danielson), lab tests show, in Adams's words, that "cyberspace cannot escape the social construction of gender," because it is constructed and used by gendered individuals whose construction and use reflect social assumptions about gender. This not only confirms feminist analyses of society but further says that technology does not necessarily transform, much less liberate us from, cultural assumptions. Adams thereby directly contradicts more optimistic views (articulated in this volume most carefully by Danielson) that a self-regulated CMC environment will rather naturally develop toward greater equality for women and men. In the face of what seems instead to be the reinforcement and amplification of inequality, Adams concludes by arguing for greater accountability and restrictions on speech. She echoes here the strategies seen in Danielson, Elgesem, and Lawrence, of translating extant social practices, including recognized restrictions in current law on free speech, into the contexts of cyberspace.

Focusing on the centrally planned development of "computer mind" in South Korea, Sunh-Hee Yoon seeks to create a better theoretical foundation for explaining the complex interrelationship between human consciousness and technologies. Rejecting both liberal and Marxist theories of technology, Yoon turns instead to an approach to discourse and power drawn from Michel Foucault. (Yoon's account of Foucault's critique of Habermas will be balanced by my account of Habermas's critique of Foucault and others.)

Yoon takes Foucault's analysis of discourse (one which explicitly rejects, for example, the semiotic theory articulated by Shank and Cunningham) as the foundation for a methodology of discourse analysis and then applies this methodology to the deployment of computer technology in South Korea. This analysis is of compelling interest especially because it applies a Western poststructuralism to a non-Western society and culture. The results, interestingly, are mixed: While Yoon argues that Foucault's conception of power and methodology of discourse analysis are more successful in the Korean example, he also acknowledges that, despite its lip service to democratic intentions, the Korean implementation of CMC in fact accomplishes the instrumental rationality criticized as antidemocratic by Habermas. Yoon also finds that computerization in South Korea has failed to achieve the decentralization of power and communication necessary for democracy.

Charles Ess takes up a central claim made to justify the use of CMC— namely, the claim that such communication environments have a democratizing effect, as they level traditional hierarchical structures of authority. The democratization claim, however, faces several theoretical deficits. A stronger theoretical foundation is hence required if the democratization claim is to retain its justificatory power. To develop such a theory, I turn to Jürgen Habermas's theory of communicative action and discourse ethics. I argue that Habermas's theory overcomes the deficits facing the democratization claim, thus providing it with a stronger theoretical foundation. CMC proponents will also find Habermas useful as he makes explicit the connection between communication and democratic forms of polity and as he defends modern technologies—including the computers and networks of CMC—against important critiques of such technologies as antidemocratic. Finally, I try to show how Habermas's theory, especially the rules and guidelines of his discourse ethics, provide significant guidelines regarding the ethical and political practices required if communication in CMC environments is to live up to its promise of democratization. I close by noting ways in which current and emerging practices largely appear to affirm Habermas's approach, as these emerging practices work both to counter forms of discourse which Habermas's theory would reject as antidemocratic and to encourage forms of discourse which his theory would affirm as democratizing.

If CMC only partially effects the revolutionary transformations of values and social structures envisioned by its enthusiasts, then religion—as humanity's oldest expression of values and community—is likely both to impact and to be impacted by these transformations. Accordingly, a more complete philosophical approach to CMC must include the perspectives of religion scholars. Stephen D. O'Leary and Brenda Brasher introduce us to these perspectives by first showing how religious beliefs and rhetorics of persuasion are transformed by technologies of communication. In particular, they explore the transformations made possible by the peculiar "secondary orality" (so Walter Ong) of CMC which resurrects oral communicative elements of tribal cultures into a new, global context of communication. O'Leary and Brasher then describe the first glimmers of "technologized religion" visible on Internet lists and Usenet groups devoted to religion. Largely optimistic regarding the potentials of new religious possibilities enabled by cyberspace, O'Leary and Brasher further consider the "cyborg humanity" of those who take up CMC as an extension of their communicative interests, speculating on what effects this new form of being human, made possible by CMC technologies, may have on fundamental questions of religious consciousness. (Readers concerned with the questions of gender and CMC so sharply raised by Adams and Herring will also want to look carefully at O'Leary and Brasher's discussion of the negative and positive implications for women of cyborg disembodiment.) O'Leary and Brasher further point out a peculiar danger of cyberspace —namely, of falling victim to a contemporary form of Gnosticism. The cyber-Gnostic cannot distinguish between wisdom and knowledge, on the one hand, and the digitized forms of communication possible in cyberspace, on the other; this epistemological confusion may condemn the cyber-Gnostic to a futile quest for "the knowledge that saves," knowledge that may simply not be found on the Net. Appropriately, O'Leary and Brasher close with a cyberpunk's prayer, completing the rhetorical journey they begin by quoting St. Paul's speech in the Athenian marketplace.

Sharing David Kolb's interest in phenomenology and hypertext, Phil Mullins examines notions of text and textual authority engendered by print culture as these are exemplified by the authority of the Bible in its role as a sacred text in North American culture, and explores how these notions may be fundamentally altered in a new era of electronic communication. Mullins argues that the emergence of secondary orality transforms print-based attitudes toward text—specifically, biblical literalism and historical-critical scholarship. This transformation is exemplified in the American Bible Society's project of creating a multimedia translation of selected portions of the Christian Scriptures, a project which radically reshapes the very form of the Scripture. More generally, Mullins argues that the communicative excess of electronic culture leads to a shift in our rhetorical strategies (thus reinforcing a central point made by O'Leary and Brasher). In this new context, the making of interesting but temporary connections in the electronic medium may override print culture's emphasis on scholarship as the cumulative development of more complex and sturdy argumentative wholes (a point also explored by Kolb).

Mullins likewise parallels Kolb, drawing on scholarly analyses of hypertext to argue that print-culture notions of textual authority and stability will be replaced by "texts" as fluid creations of active author/readers who delight in the play of message construction out of an information-rich environment. In contrast with the literalists' print-bound conception of textual authority, Mullins observes that the new fluidity of text—especially as "text" now becomes the open and continuously revised hypertext of digitized information shared across global networks—in fact recovers a forgotten feature of sacred texts: In earlier communities, the sacred "texts," whether oral or literary in form, remained vital precisely by virtue of their fluidity, as they transformed and were transformed by community experience over time. In this way, Mullins suggests in the domain of religiosity the communitarian promise of CMC, endorsed especially by those who see a democratization potential in CMC (see Yoon and Ess), as a counterweight to the isolated Cartesian self of modernity (see Shank and Cunningham).

Summary 1: What CMC Theory May Gain

As they bring diverse philosophical perspectives to bear on especially the ethical and political choices occasioned by CMC technologies, these essays should help both theoreticians and users from all disciplines understand more clearly the complex issues surrounding such concerns as privacy and the public good, individual rights, intellectual property, sexism, and democratization. We hope these essays thus not only contribute to a crucial interdisciplinary dialogue regarding theories of CMC—assumptions regarding ethical and political values and the nature of knowledge and reality, which underlie the design, implementation, and justificatory arguments for CMC systems—but also contribute to more informed and wiser choices in practice.

Summary 2: What Religion May Gain

In turn, philosophers and scholars of religion can glean new insights as well. Scholars of religion will see that cyberspace offers new forms of religious experience, while it directly challenges print-related notions of textual scholarship and the sacred text as authority. But the promised revolution here is complex. CMC may not only catapult us forward to entirely new forms of religion and religious communities; in addition, precisely as text-based authority and literalism are threatened with extinction by hypertexts and CMC, religious communities may recover an older, but currently forgotten, freedom and autonomy with regard to questions of authority and interpretation.

Summary 3: What Philosophy May Gain;
the Nature of the CMC Revolution

The essays point to both tradition and revolution for philosophers as well. Cunningham and Shank, for example, see CMC as unseating Descartes—but requiring the semiotic theory of the nineteenth-century philosopher C. S. Peirce. Danielson's evolutionary ethics includes modern utilitarianism and rights-based notions, as does Elgesem's notion of privacy rights. Any claims of revolution must face an entrenched sexism which continues, if not expands, in cyberspace (Herring, Adams). And the postmodernist Foucault's realization in Korea (Yoon) is countered by the moderns Habermas and Kant as important sources for understanding how democratization and gender equality might be achieved in cyberspace (Ess).

Finally, both Kolb and Mullins observe that the hypertextual, ephemeral, and ludic qualities of CMC will directly undermine especially one form of philosophical discourse and argument—namely, the carefully crafted, largely linear accumulations of argument and scholarship closely associated with literacy and print culture. Such discourse is likely to disappear, replaced by the playful and the evanescent. But to trumpet the victorious overthrow of a grand philosophical past may be premature. Just as the CMC revolution may catapult religionists both forward and back, so it may cut in more than one temporal direction for philosophers. As especially David Kolb makes clear, the claim that philosophical discourse per se is tied narrowly to print culture is only partially correct. Rather, philosophical thought as practiced especially by Hegel and Nietzsche intentionally moves beyond the alleged linearity of printed texts; such thought may be even more powerfully articulated and critiqued in the fluid and hypertextual spaces of CMC. Again, the CMC revolution clearly threatens to overturn a familiar part of the present—but in doing so, it may return us more powerfully to other elements of our past. Indeed, a Hegelian might observe that the transformations promised by CMC —as going beyond a certain form while incorporating elements of past stages in some promising new synthesis of these two—might constitute simply another dialectical transition, or *Aufhebung,* in the development toward the Absolute.

In a famous metaphor, Hegel also noted that the owl of Minerva flies only at dusk. That is, philosophy, as a reflective activity, can only follow upon act, not guide it. The essays collected here suggest that this view may be only partially true. They argue that CMC will fulfill its revolutionary promise, though in paradoxical and incomplete fashion; but these essays also intend to contribute to that fulfillment by offering prior, philosophically informed critique and insight. We thus hope that these essays will inaugurate and constitute important voices in the dialogues out of which more complete philosophies of CMC will emerge—philosophies that, unlike the owl of Minerva, will continually unfold in dialogue with CMC technologies and their appropriations by diverse human communities.

I

EPISTEMOLOGY AND SEMIOTICS

1

Discourse across Links

DAVID KOLB

Most people's experience of computer-mediated communication starts easily, with e-mail. But it does not stop there. In quick advances we can find ourselves involved in group mailing lists, bulletin boards and Usenet, and hypertext (whether exchanged on disk or "live" on the World Wide Web). Someday we may create virtual environments for communication and persuasion. In a wide-bandwidth future we may find ourselves no longer communicating over distance but "face to face" with the "presence" of our dialogue partners (or their intelligent software agents) yet having in that communication the resources of the network at our virtual fingertips. At that stage, the mediation of the computer would be omnipresent yet invisible. For now, however, we interact with the computer sitting there on the desk, one item among others, which mediates our texts and images to one another over time and distance.

No matter what the bandwidth, if we are going to communicate with one another mediated by the computer, then we will have to do more than shower one another with images and texts. Those images and texts will have to make moves in discourse. This essay will deal with computer-mediated communication (CMC) in terms of the patterns and moves of discourse and argument that it encourages and discourages. I will touch on four topics: the rhythm of communication, its interruptibility and branching, the need for competing metamoves, and the audience/director duality. I close with some thoughts about kinds of text and image linkages that might foster thoughtful discourse.

The Rhythm of Communication

Consider the rhythm of e-mail. It has become something of a commonplace that, while e-mail is a written medium, it has more of the feel and style of oral communication. E-mail messages are typically rapid and short. Topics get developed in several exchanges of shorter messages rather than in one exchange of long position statements. The liveliness of e-mail comes from this rhythm of communication. I do not have to work out my ideas in advance to the last detail, because you will ask questions and I will clarify as we go along. Perhaps we will both discover something unexpected in the process.

This contrasts with the slower rhythm of regular mail. You send me a five-page letter commenting on an article I wrote. I let it sit on my desk for three months, then compose a six-page response. You reply after a while. Such texts tend to be longer, more carefully written in a more reflective way. This is even truer at the next rhythm of exchange, where you write an article about mine, or a book. On this level the turnaround time is often measured in years, but the responses can be immensely detailed and usually comment on a far wider range of topics and writings.

E-mail offers focus and fast turnaround. A written letter unanswered for a month is not a serious matter; an e-mail message unanswered for a month may signal the end of a relationship; the message is almost beyond recall, covered over and bypassed in quickly developing conversations with others. The message can be resurrected, of course, but it may be further in the experienced past than a book published ten years earlier.

Such a rhythm tends to encourage certain patterns of discussion and discourage others. Instead of long argumentative lines developed then presented all at once, we find point-for-point statements and rebuttals. The texts feel more like animated conversation; it is not possible to monopolize attention so as to "unload" a book on people. People protest at long e-mail messages that give too much material at once, and the current e-mail editing programs do not make it easy to respond to large-scale argumentative structures. Most replies consist of quoted portions of the earlier message with some sentences or a paragraph of response. The quoted sections are seldom very long. This is good for disputing summary claims and short arguments, but it does not encourage dealing with argumentative structures that take pages or chapters to develop.[1]

Of course, it is possible to make a booklike (long, linearly organized) text available on the Net. But present-day computer technology does not provide convenient methods for viewing such long texts; they usually end up printed out and read in traditional ways, so that the computer has acted like a remote copying machine. In that case, the computer has not changed the mode of encounter of the long text. Hypertext can alter that encounter.

In terms of argument patterns, the rhythm of e-mail and mailing list exchange encourages opposing manifestos and summaries but also quick movement from what you just said to the arguments and presuppositions behind it. Positions get examined from a variety of angles, and there will be demand for backing on specific points. This makes e-mail a good medium for the kind of dialogue that Habermas speaks of, which demands justification for each speech act and inquires into the validity and sincerity of claims.[2] But there is a problem: the difficulty of return.

Interruptions and Branchings

Discussions by e-mail often branch off without ever returning to bring the contributions or conclusions of the branched discussions into contact with earlier questions and earlier stages of the discussion. This weakens the discourse, but the fault is not inherent in CMC; rather, it is due to e-mail or bulletin board technology that makes lines of discussion present only in their most current stages. What is needed is better database access to previous messages and some provisions for mapping the flow of discussion and the relevance of issues to one another. What is needed, in other words, is a way to make e-mail or bulletin boards more like hypertext.[3]

E-mail encourages interruption; threads of discussion mutate and branch. This resembles the fast-moving ''examine it from many sides and move on'' focus of French intellectual life rather than the patient accumulation we associate with German or English scholarship. Such a rhythm works against conclusive argument and patient discussion. In part this is because so much arrives. Our image of the traditional scholar does not include wading through fifty messages on fifteen topics every morning. Our intellectual life needs a new lightness of touch since we find ourselves doing so many things at once. There will be little room for the patient scholar whose forte was memory, who knew the location of every occurrence of key words in the *Iliad* or in Pindar. Our electronic assistants will find the key words; we need to refine our questions. This should free us for creative thought, but it tempts us with constant distraction. The rhythm and tools provided make difficult the long incubation and unexpected, unasked-for connections that could come to that patient memorious scholar. Nor is it easy, on the Net, to sustain the kind of unrelenting pursuit of single questions or novel visions that led Kant, for instance, to keep silent for ten years while thinking out the *Critique of Pure Reason.* This is why it will remain important that our thinking and writing not all be on the Net.

Competing Metamoves

The wandering topics of computerized discussions are not confined in neat tree structures. Branchings cross; there are multiple origins. Discussion does not stay on one level. Mailing lists or Usenet groups carry on multiple discussions at once, some of which are about the content and process of the others. These discussions do not arrange themselves into a neat hierarchy. For example, last year on a philosophy list an angry discussion developed about the appropriate rules and etiquette for discussing the question of what topics should be on the list itself. The moderator set up a separate "rules" discussion list and asked that the metadiscussion (about the topics) and the meta-metadiscussion (about the rules for deciding the topics) migrate to the higher-level list, but that move itself was discussed and resisted. The resulting meta-meta-metadiscussion (about the process for deciding the rules about deciding the topics to discuss) refused to leave the main list, thus bending the intended hierarchical structure into a circle.

We are most familiar with computer communication in the form of e-mail systems. However, we should distrust the branching-tree structure enforced by the software governing the typical e-mail or computer-conferencing systems. Much more complex discursive patterns are going on, and the software should allow them to be explicitly available. Hypertext provides a better model of what computer-mediated discussion will become. Hypertext can relate its nodes in other ways than in hierarchical or tree structures, and it does not assume that the units of discourse will themselves be linearly ordered text segments. My contribution to the discussion could be a single node analogous to an e-mail message, but it may also be a set of linked nodes, or no new nodes at all but rather a set of links that connect or reuse existing nodes to make a new point or gesture.

In producing these wandering structures that do not separate out into neat levels, CMC is only magnifying a situation that already exists in print. Computer-mediated communication resembles not a large book but the whole library with its web of references, different approaches, and multiple internal references. There is not now and will not be an authoritative metalevel from which discussion and dialogue can be surveyed and legislated. A library catalogue provides access via a physically dominant classification, but the library also contains a thousand competing global and regional overviews that amount to rival classifications. In an electronic library, these competing classifications can all be active at once as ways of "shelving" the material.

There is another crucial difference. Printed books and articles do not contain references to commentaries upon themselves that will have been published years later. But hypertext links can move both ways. When I comment upon your article, I can link from as well as to it. In hypertext, ongoing recontextualization is not a separate work. But also, as in the library, there will be more than one recontextualization going on at once. In the hypermedium, as in the library, there will be as much and more demand for guidance among competing overviews, for landmarks, for the results of skilled sensitivity to context and implications.

Any activity of reading combines searching for relevance and pruning the results of the search. Computer-mediated communication intensifies both. In the environment of electronic information, we users will have more responsibility for constructing or selecting the object of our attention. There will be so many references and paths, so many places to search, so much to discard, so many places where we will have to rely on authority or expertise not just about what is said but about where to look and what to ignore. In the forest of information and opinion, filled with murmuring voices, we will rely on filters: editors and points of view and digests that we feel we can trust. These will be the equivalent of refereed journals or expert editors. Such guides will multiply and compete with one another; soon metadigests and metajournals will appear.

There is no doubt that hypertext and CMC will bring a new freedom. Authority will be more displaced and text more decentered. I say "more" because authority and text are already decentered in the library, though difficulties of access make this less obvious. One of the joys of hypertext and hypermedia is the consummate textual and imagistic play they make possible. But play and the pleasure of the text are not for long the same as arbitrary discontinuity and sheer flood. Structures and overviews will not disappear; they will multiply and turn on one another.

Critical Responsibility

Computer-mediated communication starts with text, but, as bandwidth increases, communication will increasingly employ graphic images, which will lead to complex analogous units and structures that go beyond textual paragraphs. There will also be pointers to whole bodies of images and information. This process has begun today in the documents one finds on the World Wide Web (WWW), where highlighted phrases can lead one to images or to whole families of other documents. We can imagine the creation and "transmission" of whole virtual environments. These will be powerful instruments of communication and persuasion. But we can ask: In the high-bandwidth environment, what will become of argument and criticism? When you can send your "world" to me, what do I do?

How do we maintain dialogue and keep our critical sense alive in high-bandwidth situations? The temptation will be great to limit our reactions to passive absorption or to an aesthetic attitude ("Who would have thought of that combination!") or else to marvel at the amount of work that went into the creation of the communication, without confronting its content or presuppositions. I could emerge from such "communication" knowing your beliefs and desires and dreams, and this would be communication, but would I also find ways to disagree with those beliefs or argue about those desires?

How do we encourage critical gestures and ongoing dialogue when we can enter each other's virtual reality? Perhaps I could structure the communication so that if you want to see what and why I am speaking you would enter this world I will have created. If you want to critically comment on my world, go in and modify it and send it back, or embed it in one of your own that shows mine to be partial. We do this sort of thing now, going "into" a literary or philosophical or political text and evaluating the "world" it creates, and our response frequently embeds texts in "larger" texts. Hypermedia and virtual environments could continue the process; they need not be blocks to dialogue.

The Audience/Director Duality

I keep speaking of critical sensitivity, but there is another way to conceptualize what is needed. We will need to be at once audience and director, immersed and distant, inhabitants and engineers. You can see this happening today: Consider the video and computer game culture. For players of games ranging from shoot-'em-ups to elaborate role-playing simulations there have developed specialized glossy magazines that advertise games and offer tips on how to play them. Recently there have begun to appear magazines on game design and programming. These, too, are glossy magazines, with similar advertisements, available on the same racks in popular book stores. There are also programs on the market that allow you to modify and cheat in popular games. This means that the supposed game addicts who cannot think of anything except the next thrill are being offered a chance to reflect on the construction of their games and to find ways to modify, to reengineer, and to choose between variants (as is happening, for example, with the game Doom). We live in worlds but we also work at changing their structures. This doubled attitude of intimate participation plus awareness of options and choice could become characteristic of CMC.

Consider, too, the way people progress through MUDs and MOOs (multiple user dungeons and multi-user dungeon-object oriented, respectively), moving from adventure roles into programming, from being inhabitants of the virtual world to occupying the mixed role of inhabitant and stage manager. This is one way in which CMC may encourage political awareness. Democracies need citizens with this doubled attitude of inhabitation and reconstruction. How much of our social existence is talk about the rules and roles for social existence? As people are spurred to choose and modify their worlds and experiences, there is more room for reflection and dialogue.

What kind of experience will be chosen? Philosophers from Aristotle to John Dewey have talked about experience as having a temporal unity (beginning-middle-end) with a unified tone and narrative structure. Most computer games and the primitive virtual worlds we have so far created follow this standard paradigm, though the narrative is usually designed to promise a culmination that never arrives, to keep the customer spending. So far, computer-mediated worlds have had rather traditional forms. In fact, there are wider and wilder forms of experience available in print. Think of the experiments with time and narrative and coherence and their permutations and lacks in modernist and postmodernist fiction. Among present CMC media, only hypertext fiction attempts such effects. Virtual worlds will eventually do the same. People will have more choices to make about what they are "living through." Choices of the kind and rhythm of our experience could be new occasions for reflection.

Design Suggestions

But will this reflection happen? That depends on the overall climate and the means available. What facilities can we build into our worlds that will encourage critical discussion and the duality of roles as audience and director? While virtual reality provides an enticing way of posing this problem, we don't yet know enough about how that will develop. So I want to examine what structures might be helpful in the case of hypertext and hypermedia, which are our most "different" computer communication media so far. Undoubtedly, present hypermedia only vaguely foreshadow what will happen in the broadband future. But if CMC is to be more than a mail system or passive entertainment, then linkage and choice will be a crucial feature of what is to come, and today's hypertexts are already showing us some of the possibilities and problems of linkage. So, in what follows, I discuss what kinds of hypertext linkages would facilitate communal discourse and reflection.

Concerning hypertext, Michael Joyce distinguishes two types: constructive and exploratory.[4] Most hypertexts available today are "exploratory": They present a given fixed structure of nodes and links for the reader to explore. The purpose of that exploration varies depending on the type of text, but, in general, the structure has already been set up and cannot be altered. Present-day technology encourages hypertexts that are presented as fixed and finished, delivered on a disk or as files available on the World Wide Web. In such situations, the reader either cannot add to the web or can do so only in one direction. If I have a copy of a hypertext on a disk, the whole web is there for me to read, and even if I can annotate it for myself, there is still an authoritative text from which the disk was copied. The WWW style of hypertext begins to break down the wall between author and reader, because it is not difficult for me to make available a new document containing a link to your older document; so the available web grows through multiple authorship. But WWW hypertext still has a master text I cannot alter: Your document resides on your computer; I can refer to it, but I can't introduce into your document some links to my document. The suggestions below have to do with the possibilities for fully symmetrical "constructive" hypertexts where the text remains open to readers becoming authors and adding links in both directions.

Here are two general principles that can help guide our thinking about hypertext systems. The first principle is that once they become large, hypertexts need to have regions with local form. The second principle is that the hypertext needs to provide ways to return.

By "local form" I mean that a group of text units could be linked in such a way that, within the larger hypertext, the group enacts some discursive gesture. There should be areas or localities within the text that are in between the individual node and the web as a whole. In those local areas, the structure of linked nodes should be able to perform traditional discursive moves as well as new gestures that are not possible (or not easily possible) in single nodes or in linear text.

We are familiar with the moves of argumentation. We have refined techniques for analyzing the logical steps of an argument. An area of a hypertext could present argument in a linear or a tree fashion.[5] But more can be done than present the logical structure. The local area might contain texts linked according to the kinds of speech acts performed rather than the logical steps made. Stephen Toulmin's description of argument could be helpful in suggesting a typology of such links.[6] Or we could find links patterned according to the kinds of questions that Habermas raises about types of validity.[7]

But there are other kinds of links than question and answer or linear argument. Links do not have to form straight paths or branching trees. They can curl around and intersect themselves; they can have connections that fit no patterns we are used to in linear text. We don't yet know how to read or write such connections.

We can get some ideas, though, from thinkers who have resisted the straight line. For example, we could consider the kinds of moves found in dialectical thinkers such as Hegel. He shows how claims and concepts and institutions can, in trying to enact what they "are," turn into something else. This happens not through a linear argument or because of some outside metajudgment but because of inner tensions and contradictions. Related moves show up in Nietzsche and in deconstructive discussions, though without Hegel's emphasis on closure. What is common to these traditions is the gesture of taking a conceptual dichotomy that seems to dominate a field of thought and relocating it within a wider field that it does not dominate and in which it is seen as an effect or a part of something else. Such gestures come naturally to hypertext. Brought up on print, it is difficult for us to avoid thinking in terms of settled units and fixed metalevel comments, but we have to learn to let the text or image units try to be themselves, and then flow and change. What is important for hypertext construction is that the "units" need not be single nodes; they can be gestures and movements themselves performed over a local group of nodes.

Such local units cannot have closed forms. I might come along and use your texts in other ways, linking them into other gestures, other forms and movements, without affecting your form directly. Your forms will be local but porous. There will be places of local decision but without fixed local boundaries. There is always more hyperspace, always another dimension that can intersect any local form.

The second principle concerns return. There needs to be some way to make later additions relevant to earlier ones and available to someone traveling in the earlier region. On the larger scale, "we" need to come together somewhere. It is exciting to contemplate endless dissemination that avoids any even temporary closure, but there is still a need for return. We are not endless readers. There may always be more hyperspace, but there is not always more time or attention. In CMC there are textual and communal labors to be done. We want to be able to have discourse heard and reach conclusions, even if they be only temporary. If hypertext is to be a medium of communication and exchange as well as of play and demonstration, it will need ways to bring its parts and its readers together. Otherwise, like too many e-mail discussions, there will be endless fractionating of ever smaller groups that talk among themselves. Can CMC open up new kinds of discursive gestures and also be a medium of public discourse?

The two principles suggest some design guidelines about the capabilities needed in hypertext systems (and future computer communication systems) that would articulate and enhance thought and shared discourse.

There need to be mechanisms for creating localities within the text. There need to be local gestures that take up more than one node and are linked in more than a linear fashion. The reader needs to have the sense of having entered a zone dedicated to an argument, a discourse, or a discursive gesture with some local form, rather than being within a random cloud of associations and links. These localities will be porous and intersecting, since items in such "places" could be part of other localities as well. Therefore, given limited time and attention, the reader needs ways of organizing and prioritizing.

In hypertext, decisions are unavoidable. Even indulging in the pure play and flow of images and text is a decision exercised for a portion of time. So, in a large hypertext the reader needs some navigational information about intersecting localities and (possibly competing) local gestures. This should be more than a list of the nodes available one step away. The most obvious way to provide such information would be through typed or labeled links, but perhaps these could be supplemented by explicitly navigational nodes that indicated the multiple localities that include the present location and others "nearby." The navigational information might be given in graphic form. Another helpful device would be a way of temporarily privileging a certain kind of link or a certain cluster of links for display or for following a local form.

As readers, we need to know when we cross a boundary. Boundaries allow us to pause and take stock as we gather attention and anticipation. Print has developed many conventions for that purpose. But what is a boundary in hypertext? Movement from one locality to another. Such a boundary would divide interconnected groups, but it could itself be an item discussed and argued over. Even if boundaries intersect and compete, even if they are controversial, we need to sense where they are purported to be or where they are fought over or infolded.

Ideally, these kinds of navigational aids should be built into the software and automatically updated as the web changes. But how would we create programs with enough intelligence to handle flexible contexts and intersecting local areas? Many of the navigation aids are likely to be constructed by reader/authors who declare localities, give links special types, and create summaries and overviews. Such reader-created aids will have no privileged position; they will themselves be discussable and multiple and become outdated as the web grows. The software could facilitate the construction of such aids by having a rich repertory of link types and ways of indicating the date and authorship of nodes and links. There should be a variety of graphical mapping formats that could be annotated by users and presented as nodes in the text. Or users should be able to call up and selectively highlight or annotate maps of the text that will then be automatically updated.

If hypertext is going to sustain communal discourse, it will need machinery to facilitate metamoves and branching but also ways to allow return. Readers need ways to keep lines relevant to one another and to bring later additions to bear on earlier nodes. So a hypertext will need searching tools and ways of tracing paths backward. It will also need cross-time links in both directions, so that a document or a comment can have links created from itself to later comments. The text will have to have ways of remembering its own history.

There is another, perhaps more disturbing, aspect to the text's history. Hyperspace may have no limits other than what current technology imposes, but people have limited time and attention to spend. Decisions made in reading are economic insofar as they distribute attention, a scarce resource. In a constructive hypertext where reader/authors add links and nodes, those localities that are most visible and most accessible will tend to accrete more links and more traffic. They will become more visible and more accessible while other areas fade into a seldom-visited back country. The rich will get richer. This suggests that the software ought to provide some means of accounting that monitors the accretion of links and points out both the areas of intense activity and the unexplored locales.

In sum, large ongoing hypertexts will need mechanisms that facilitate reflection about their own form and its development, although not from any privileged point of view that can define The Form, since there is no The Whole to have that form. Nor is form the whole story; I have been emphasizing local form and communicative discourse, but we want also to be able to avoid form, to have discourse go wild in unexpected hope and openness.

Among the many assumptions that influence people's thinking about CMC, one seems paramount. In an inversion of Mies van der Rohe's famous dictum, in cyberspace, more is more: Let us have more links, more bandwidth, more images, more connections. Yet "more" can also overwhelm and weaken communal thought and reflection. We always live as inhabitants and as stage managers; we are in the flow and keeping an eye on it. So we need more form, albeit temporary and multiple and itself a topic of discussion. We need more space for reflection and self-criticism. In oral and print cultures, that space has been achieved by soliloquy, private notes, withdrawal; it will be harder to find private space on the Net, but not impossible. Imagine the hypertextual or virtual equivalent of nooks in libraries, private studies, personal notebooks, walks in the woods. Sometimes less is more.

I have made some suggestions concerning hypertext, which will be only a part of our wide-bandwidth future. Still, by concentrating on linkage and choice, I have tried to find clues about some capabilities that would help us be and communicate together. Computers, and hypertext in particular, are too often thought of as tools for the storage and manipulation of data. We have to come to understand the ways in which hypertext and CMC move us beyond data access into the realm of discursive gestures and poetics.

Notes

1. For example, a practice called "slow reading" has developed on some e-mail lists. A book-length text is presented by a leader, a few sentences at a time, and messages are exchanged over the current section's meaning and significance in the larger text. While this can allow both microscopic examination and wide-focus discussion of the target book, it has more difficulty with the intermediate-size level inhabited by chapter-length argumentative structures.

2. See, for example, Jürgen Habermas, "What Is Universal Pragmatics?," Trans. Thomas McCarthy, in *Communication and the Evolution of Society* (Boston: Beacon Press, 1979), 1–68.

3. The classic discussion of computer conferencing systems is Starr Roxanne Hiltz and Murray Turoff, *The Network Nation: Human Communication via Computer,* rev. ed. (Cambridge: MIT Press, 1993). Although they concentrate on systems that presume unified linear messages arranged in a tree structure, the database model underlying their discussion could be adapted to more hypertextual "front ends" by increasing the types of attributes attached to text segments. In other ways, such as their discussion of messages that are agents (objects containing executable code that

is exercised under certain conditions), their vision extends beyond current hypertext, which still maintains the separation of data and program. (See especially 503 ff.).

4. Michael Joyce, "Siren Shapes: Exploratory and Constructive Hypertexts," *Academic Computing,* November 1988; reprinted in Michael Joyce, *Of Two Minds: Hypertext Pedagogy and Poetics* (Ann Arbor: University of Michigan Press, 1994).

5. I discuss some of the ways in which hypertext links could be used to present the logical structure of argument, and the ways hypertext goes beyond argument, in my hypertext essay "Socrates in the Labyrinth" (Watertown, MA: Eastgate Systems, 1994).

6. Toulmin's model is presented for classroom use in Stephen Toulmin, Richard Rieke, and Allan Janik, *An Introduction in Reasoning* (New York: Macmillan, 1979).

7. See Habermas, "What Is Universal Pragmatics?"

2

Mediated Phosphor Dots: Toward a Post-Cartesian Model of Computer-Mediated Communication via the Semiotic Superhighway

GARY SHANK AND DONALD CUNNINGHAM

Imagine that René Descartes, father of modern philosophy, has returned to life and is sitting at a computer terminal linked to the Internet. He types:

FTP MRCNEXT.CSO.UIUC.EDU

After logging in as ANONYMOUS and after giving his Internet address, he types the following sequence:

CD ETEXT
CD ETEXT 93
DIR

He then gets a listing of a series of files. Looking them over carefully, he types:

GET DCART10.TXT
QUIT

This file is then shipped to his ftp site, and he downloads it onto his hard disk. He opens the ASCII document and begins to read:

The Project Gutenberg Etext of A Discourse on Method

DISCOURSE ON THE METHOD OF RIGHTLY CONDUCTING
THE REASON, AND SEEKING TRUTH IN THE SCIENCES
by René Descartes

He reads the document with great interest. He is particularly taken with Part II, Paragraph 3:

> The majority of men is composed of two classes, for neither of which would this be at all a befitting resolution: in the first place, of those who with more than a due confidence in their own powers, are precipitate in their judgements and want the patience requisite for orderly and circumspect thinking; whence it happens, that if men of this class once take the liberty to doubt of their accustomed opinions, and quit the beaten highway, they will never be able to thread the byway that would lead them by a shorter course, and will lose themselves and continue to wander for life; in the second place, of those who, possessed of sufficient sense or modesty to determine that there are others who excel them in the power of discriminating between truth and error, and by whom they may be instructed, ought rather to content themselves with the opinions of such than trust for more correct to their own reason.

Descartes unfortunately does not bother to read on, to see that he himself argued that a third type of person exists. After all, it has been over 400 years since he penned those words, and memory can play tricks on you. Instead, he composes a hastily drawn rebuttal, or "flame." He rails against his own judgment of describing people as being either tenacious believers in whatever they happen to believe or else slaves to authority. He champions again, unknowingly, his third type, who seeks to find a consistent foundation for building a coherent worldview. Satisfied with his scathing words, he e-mails his message off to the long-suffering administrator of the e-text archives.

Clearly, Descartes has much to learn about Internet communication. First, you do not flame someone without reading the full message. Second, if you have to flame, you send the flame to the offending individual, not the list or archive manager. Finally, if you really want to grasp the dynamics of Internet communication, you need to move beyond a Cartesian frame. The first two points are simple courtesy. The third point is the focus of this chapter.

Our strategy for this paper is, first of all, to explicate the nature of communication on the Internet as a unique phenomenon. After laying out a brief overview of semiotic concepts, we then hope to show how semiotic theory per se helps capture the unique nature of Internet communication. Finally, we argue that accepting the semiotic approach to understanding Internet communication allows us to move beyond the Cartesian frame. This move beyond Cartesianism is important, as we demonstrate by contrasting in our conclusion the consequences of making such a move with the consequences of staying within a Cartesian perspective.

Communication qua Conversation on the Internet

What is the nature of communication on the Internet? Consider the image of Descartes at his terminal. What does he experience? This is the starting point for any model of communication—namely, the experience of the person who is either sending or receiving the message. In this case, Descartes is the receiver. So what is he receiving? Simply put, phosphor dots. His eyes are picking up the excitations of phosphor dots on the CRT screen that form patterns we call words and sentences and paragraphs and, eventually, statements. This is what is usually meant by communication. According to Jakobson, any act of communication requires a sender, a receiver, and a message (1970, 33ff.). The message travels along some medium from the sender to the receiver.

How is it that communication on the Internet is perceived as something far more powerful than just the experience of reading words on a screen? There are at least two possible answers. The first answer is that the receiver is somehow removed from the process, as a pure Cartesian observer, and therefore is free to react and interact with the flow of information while retaining a great degree of control as an outside agent. The second answer is that the receiver is immersed in the communicative process itself and that the phosphor dots, and even the words they form, cease to be interesting in and of themselves but become a powerful and always emerging semiotic system of which the participant is a key, but certainly not the only, component. The first approach favors the idea of Internet communication as the act of acquiring information (see Shannon and Weaver 1949; Gerbner 1956, as primary examples), while the second approach favors the notion of Internet communication as a large and complex semiotic act of conversation (see Jakobson 1970; Sebeok 1976; Deely 1982).

Three basic semiotic types of conversation can be identified by using the Jakobson (1970) model. The first one is the monologue. A monologue occurs when there is a single sender and one or more passive receivers. The lecture qua lecture is a good example of a monologue. The second type of conversation is called the dialogue. In case of the dialogue, the sender and receiver take turns. This is the basic model of all dyadic oral communication. The third and final type of conversation is the discussion. In the discussion, we have one person who starts as the sender and multiple receivers. While it is important for the receivers to take turns as senders, in the discussion the initial sender still usually retains control of the conversation.

These issues are particularly important for attempting to understand the nature of communication on the Internet. Is Internet communication like conversation? Absolutely. Messages tend to be informal, phrased in conversational form, and often engender a great deal of direct interchange. Is Internet communication also like writing? Absolutely. Messages are written instead of spoken. Nonverbal, gestural, and articulatory cues, so important in speech, are missing. But the linguistic models of lecture, dialogue, discussion, and even text (the written model of communication) do not capture the dynamics of usage that characterize Internet communication.

In the typical Internet communication setting, we have a much different set of circumstances, thereby requiring a model of a different mode of conversation. It starts with a number of players. There is the starter, or the initial sender, who begins the sequence of communication that is eventually called the "thread." A thread, as the computer literati use the term, is a series of computer-generated communications that start on a particular topic but that might lead in many different directions before the discussion is done. Once a thread has been started, though, it is no longer under sender control. This is because the mechanics of Internet response do not require turn taking. From the oral side, it is as if everyone who is interested in talking can all jump in at once, but still their individual voices can be clearly heard. From the written side, it is as if someone had started writing a piece, but, before he/she gets too far, people are there magically in print to add to, correct, challenge, or extend the piece. Therefore, what we have is a written quasi discussion that has the potential to use the strengths of each form. Since the "feel" of Internet communication is still oral, this form of communication has been called multiloguing, to retain the link with its oral heritage (Shank 1994).

Understanding a phenomenon such as the multilogue requires us to go beyond traditional theories of communication that focus on the transfer of information (such as Shannon and Weaver 1949; Gerbner 1956). To forge the appropriate theoretical base for a theory of communication that reflects the nature of the Internet, we turn instead to semiotic theory.

Semiotics in Brief

What is semiotics, and what does it have to do with computer-mediated communication (CMC)?

Semiotics is an enormously broad approach to understanding such matters as meaning, cognition, culture, behavior, even life itself. As a result, there are a number of distinctive theories that go under the heading of semiotics. Any attempt to characterize semiotics, therefore, inevitably involves choices regarding basic assumptions about the phenomena emphasized, preferred methods of inquiry, the philosophical grounding of an approach, and so forth.

What follows represents *our* understanding of semiotics, with particular emphasis on those concepts that offer promise for the exploration of communication per se, especially in relation to CMC issues. We make no pretense to being able to represent semiotics as that term is always used. We believe that most semioticians would agree, however, that semiotic theory offers the position that a wide variety of problems in modern inquiry, taken from a number of different disciplines, are actually special cases of one general set of problems. For example, a linguist trying to analyze a particular word usage, an anthropologist trying to unravel a particular kinship pattern, a biologist trying to show how protein synthesis might be triggered by a certain gene segment, a computer scientist trying to model expert performance, a teacher trying to get a class to read and interpret a short story—all are working on the same general problem: What is a sign? How does it work? How can I use it?

Signs and Sign Types

At the heart of semiotics lies the notion of sign. A sign, according to C. S. Peirce (widely acknowledged to be, along with Saussure, the founder of modern semiotics) is "something which stands to somebody for something in some respect or capacity" (Peirce, from Buchler 1955, 154). In Peirce's theory, the sign stands for something else, called the object, by creating an interpretant, which is itself an additional sign that stands for some aspect of the original object. This interpretant (which can be either physical or mental) represents the object in some fashion but is not itself that object. As far as communication is concerned, our experience of the world (which is ultimately the basis of interpersonal communication) is mediated through signs and can never be strictly isomorphic with the objects of the world. In essence, we create our world of experience by creating signs as we interact with objects in our environment. As a result, the ways that we communicate are governed at the outset by the ways that our semiotic systems interact not only with others but with the world at large.

Peirce and many others (see, for example, Sebeok 1976) have written extensively on the nature of signs. Numerous classifications of signs and sign processes are available, and generating such classifications is a favorite activity of many semioticians. We will mention only one such classification system. This system is linked, for technical reasons beyond the scope of this paper, quite specifically to both the object and the experiential world. Since Internet communication is quite clearly grounded in the experiential world of its users, this system is a good logical starting point. In this system of classification, Peirce proposes three ways in which the sign can stand for its object: as icon, index, or symbol.

An icon is a sign that stands for an object by resembling it, not merely visually but by any means. Included in this category of sign are obvious examples, such as pictures, maps, and diagrams, and some not-so-obvious ones, such as algebraic expressions and metaphors. The essential aspect of the relation of an icon to its object is one of similarity, broadly defined.

Indexes refer to their objects not by virtue of any similarity relation but rather via an actual causal link between the sign and its object: Smoke is an index of fire, a weather vane is an index of wind direction, a mark on a fever thermometer is an index of body temperature, and so forth. The relation between the sign and its object is actual in that the sign and object have something in common; that is, the object "really" affects the sign.

Finally, symbols refer to their objects by virtue of a law, rule, or convention. Words, propositions, and texts are obvious examples in that no similarity or causal link is suggested in the relation between, for example, the word "horse" and the object to which it refers. In this category especially, the potentially arbitrary character of signs comes to the foreground. If symbols need bear no similarity or causal link to their object, then the signs can be considered by the sign user in unlimited ways, independent of any physical relationship to the sign user.

It is obviously not enough to have a system of sign types when we look at the role of signs in the communicative process. We need to consider two additional aspects: the role of codes in combining and using signs and the role of meaning (or, in our terms, semiosis) in the communicative act. Each aspect will be described in turn.

Codes and Meaning

If signs stand for other things, then we have a case where a system of signs acts as some code for some system of objects. It is intuitively obvious that codes play a crucial role in communication, but the dynamics of codes per se are not well understood. Semiotic theory stands to play an important role in helping us understanding the general workings of codes.

The first critical insight from semiotics is that a sign stands for its object not completely but only in terms of some aspect or ground. If the sign and the object were equivalent, the sign would be the object. Therefore, we can say that signs are incomplete acts of equivalence. That is, a sign stands partially and uniquely for some object, but it is not the object. Signs, because they are only incompletely equivalent to their objects, are thereby free to have characteristics of their own. Crucially, these characteristics can include coherence with other signs to form a system of signs that are related, on the one hand, to their objects and, on the other hand, to the other signs in the system. Therefore, what might at first seem to be a liability of a sign system—namely, that it cannot fully represent objects—actually allows sign systems to be quite flexible and useful, particularly as vehicles of communication. In fact, we can say that there can be no communication without signs and systems of signs.

The best example of such a system, as was recognized by such early pioneers in semiotics as Saussure (1959), Jakobson (1970), and Hjelmslev

(1943), is language. In fact, most semiotic inquiry that focuses upon the equivalence relation between signs and objects uses language as a model for other systems of significance; that is, other systems of equivalence codes were treated as if they were linguistic codes (possessing rules of grammar and representation, for example). Two exemplary expressions of such code elucidations are the works of Claude Lévi-Strauss (1966) in anthropology and Roland Barthes (1964) in cultural criticism. Lévi-Strauss dedicated his career to demonstrating that there are underlying systems of order and coherence behind such dazzlingly varied and complex social systems as kinship patterns and myth. Barthes took all of culture as his domain as he mapped out systems of connotation and denotation for such objects as cars, food, and clothing.

Inquiry aimed at uncovering systems of codes has come to be called structuralism (see Hawkes 1977 for a useful summary) and has proved to be a fruitful approach in a wide variety of areas: film, art, music, spectacles, and so on. Ironically, however, structuralism came under the most fire when it was applied to the very system that it took as its basic model: language. When structuralist approaches were applied to linguistic texts, certain assumptions underlying the analysis came under critical scrutiny—in particular, the concept of the meaning of the text. Structuralist models tend to suggest there is a single meaning to a text, a notion attacked forcefully by such poststructuralists as Derrida (1984). The problem arises from the equivalence relationship itself. The meaning of a text cannot reside in the text but only in the signs which represent the text. As such, the signs are only a part of the potential meanings of any text, and alternate equivalence relations lead to alternative meanings. Fiske (1982), in comparing semiotics to information processing, points out that semiotic systems involve not so much the transfer of information as the exchange of meanings. Thus, when meanings are involved, there are meanings for senders and receivers, embedded in particular contexts. To speak of the meaning of a text is nonsense; there will be as many meanings as there are senders, receivers, and/or contexts. But these meanings are nonetheless related to the network of equivalences mapped out by the sign system in question. The relation, as Eco (1984) shows, is one of inference, where

> to walk, to make love, to sleep, to refrain from doing something, to give food to someone else, to eat roast beef on Friday—each is either a physical event or the absence of a physical event, or a relation between two or more physical events. However, each becomes an example of good, bad, or neutral behavior within a given philosophical framework. (Eco 1984, 10)

Again, we can see the power of the notion that signs are arbitrary and can be manipulated in their own right independent of their relation to the object and the sign user. Alternate interpretations of the same object not only are possible; they are an inevitable outcome of the sign relation itself.

This same point can be made another way. Peirce was originally drawn to the study of signs by his search for a model of meaning valid for scientific inquiry. For Peirce, hypotheses are signs, inferred from the world of experience to give meaning to aspects of that world. Imagine, for example, stumbling across some bit of experience that, in itself, is quite puzzling and surprising (e.g., a talking dog). Yet if that bit of experience is treated not for its unique properties but as an example or case or sign of some rule of experience in action (e.g., as a trick), then it is transformed into an ordinary affair. Couple this notion with Peirce's assumption that the things of the world of experience that we claim to be true are at best only more or less plausible and therefore only meaningful hypotheses, and we can begin to understand why Peirce came to equate logic and semiotics. That is, signs can be both the product of and a further source of inference.

The relation of meaning and communicative activity to inference is an area that has hardly been addressed but that is a natural consequence of a semiotic approach. To see this, we need to examine the concept of semiosis, which links inference, meaning, and communication in an interdependent fashion.

Semiosis

The subject matter of semiotics is semiosis, or the building up of structures of experience via signs. Signs are not isolated entities. Rather, we create structures of signs which then serve to mediate our experiences in the world. It is these structures which determine our worldview, the things we notice and ignore, the things that are important to us and not important, the means by which we organize our lives.

Semiosis is a process that characterizes all varieties of life (Anderson et al. 1984). In animals, for instance, semiosis creates structures of experience which organize the environment and determine what is and is not functional for that animal. For example, during breeding season, male goats are especially tuned to attend to certain stimuli in their environment: rapid tail wagging and certain odors emitted by receptive does. Other cues are completely ignored. These signs define a portion of the significant world for male goats, their *Umwelt*, a term borrowed from German ethnologist Jacob von Uexkull (1982). This Umwelt, determined jointly by species-specific factors and the particular experiences of the organism in a given environment, characterizes that organism's behavior.

It is important to distinguish the concept of Umwelt from the more familiar concept of environment. An environment is a physical setting that impacts the person and serves as a source of stimulation. As such, it can be conceived independently of the person in question and, in fact, is usually spoken of as an entity that exists for a multitude of different persons. The Umwelt of a person, however, is not independent of the person; in fact, it exists only in relation to the person. In a famous example, von Uexkull (1982) described the various Umwelten created by a tree: a rough-textured and convoluted terrain for a bug, a menacing form for a young child, a set of limbs for a nesting bird, and so on. In all these cases, the environment of the tree was the same; that is, the bark, the height, and the limbs were "available" to each of the organisms, yet their experience of them was quite different.

Signs can furthermore be created which go beyond the immediate experience of the person. Words, pictures, bodily movements, and the like generate interpretants for objects which need have no basis in the "real" world and which can be manipulated independent of that world. Yet these signs come to form the Umwelt of a human organism as surely as does tail wagging for the male goat. According to Deely (1982), it is the intervention of language which allows humans to engage in this particular type of semiosis. Through language we create culture as manifest in institutions such as religions, governments, armies, schools, marriage rites, and so forth. Culture, in turn, impacts our lives by determining what is important and what is not, what makes sense and what does not.

The arbitrary nature of these sign systems is not readily apparent to the human organism until he is exposed to systems that depart from his own, as when traveling to another culture. For example, marriage customs that are at odds with those of the cognizing person seem "foreign" or just plain wrong.

The fact that humans can utilize signs that are arbitrary and that need have no existence in their immediate experience is what makes thought possible and distinctly human. Ideas can be brought to mind and manipulated without being directly experienced. Meanings can be expressed in various ways, through a variety of sign systems—language, music, gesture, and so forth. In essence, humans can create via signs a world entirely separate from the one of direct experience (e.g., sensation and perception) but that is every bit as "real." We find it hard to imagine a world without traffic regulations, social conventions, basketball games, and so forth. These are as real to us as the trees and rocks. Yet they, as well as our understanding of the trees and rocks, have come about via the interaction of humans individually and collectively through the sign structures that we call culture.

Deely's model is essentially a model of inference drawing upon Peirce's trichotomy of abduction, deduction, and induction. Semiosis is a process of applying signs to understand some phenomena (induction), reasoning from sign to sign (deduction), and/or inventing signs to make sense of some new experience (abduction). These modes of inference are cyclic, characterizing the development of Umwelten throughout life: Signs are invented to account for experience, linked to existing sign structures, and then used to define the Umwelt for that organism. But the world is not infinitely malleable to our sign structures, and the abductive process will be again instigated. Deely is here, in our view, incorporating growth into his model, from the perspectives of both experience and ontology. That is, Deely not only is arguing that growth is an essential concept in describing how we use our experiences to enrich our understanding of the world; he extends that thought further to incorporate the idea that we not only live in reality but that we are partners with reality. In other words, we grow when we do research, but reality also grows as a consequence of our increasingly sophisticated attempts to understand reality as we first find it.

The notion of semiosis demonstrates that, from the perspective of semiotic theory, signs, inferences, meaning, and our understanding of reality are all interdependent, and they are held together by those tools, such as language, that allow us to be able to communicate in the first place. It remains, however, to apply these notions explicitly to the unique form of communication that we call the Internet.

Why the Internet Needs Semiotics

The Internet is all about communication. Semiosis is all about sense making. The link, as we see it, between communication and sense making is the act of inference. If, as semioticians contend, all thought is in signs, then thinking is fundamentally inferential. We infer an object from its sign, and that inference, the effect of the sign, is the interpretant.

Traditional accounts of inference usually describe two processes of logic: deduction and induction. By contrast, Peirce has proposed three irreducibly distinct movements of the mind: abduction, deduction, and induction. Induction and deduction have been well discussed in theories of meaning, but abduction is relatively unknown and needs to be examined in some detail.

Abduction is the inferential move whereby we, when confronted with some experience not accounted for by our existing beliefs, invent a new set of beliefs or revise an existing one. This new structure will provide a context within which the surprising experience is a matter of course, that is, makes sense. Abduction is instigated when we are in a condition of conceptual inadequacy and psychological discomfort that Peirce called ''genuine doubt,'' to distinguish this form of skepticism from the methodological form used by Descartes. Genuine doubt arises from experience. Hence, it is naturally embedded in a relevant context: It is situated or anchored. Being in a state of genuine doubt is unpleasant—the world does not make obvious sense. So it is necessary to create or alter beliefs to move from genuine doubt to some new state of belief.

What do examples of abductive inference look like? Shank (1987) distinguishes between three modes. In detection, our sign serves as a clue to an aspect of experience that is no longer present, as when an archeologist searches for an explanation of the unexpected presence of stone tools at a prehistoric settlement. Diagnosis is involved when our sign stands for something presently occurring, as when a doctor attempts to account for an unexplained swelling in the abdomen of a child. And, finally, divination is an abductive mode in which our sign predicts something in the future, as when we try to predict the consequences of global warming by creating a new set of beliefs about its consequences.

One of the most remarkable aspects of human cognition is the pervasive belief that the world makes perfectly good sense. This sense is a consequence of our ongoing abductive inferences about the world. And we could hardly imagine living in a world that did not make sense—where, for example, the floor might disappear or the meaning of a word changes every time someone uses it. In other words, the sign structures we have developed are perfectly adequate for our everyday functioning. Because abduction is so fundamental to basic sense making, Shank (1993) has contended that abduction is the ground-state, or basic, unreflected, mode of cognition. Therefore, we would expect abduction to play a critical role in understanding the multilogue of communication on the Internet. We can take this a step further, though, and use our understanding of abduction and semiotics to make predictions about the future evolution of Internet communication.

The first thing that an abductive multiloguing perspective predicts is that conversation in the virtual community will continue to be more and more nonlinear and less hierarchical. This is the case for several reasons. First of all, discussions are inclusive rather than exclusive. Credentials are not checked at the door of most discussion lists, and so persons with varying interests are allowed to listen and participate. Therefore, rather than retreating into more and more specialized discussions, we can reasonably expect a topic to expand into wider and wider content realms, as people with different areas of primary expertise bring that expertise and its insights to bear on the discussion at hand.

An example is the case of the "hackers" in the early days of computing, when hacking did not connote illegal activities. These early hackers were respected for what they could do, not for who they were or for what degrees or credentials they could bring to bear. Some of this feeling lives in many, though not all, Internet discussion circles. Furthermore, the very idea of the multilogue helps preserve this egalitarian atmosphere, since there is no "teacher" or primary "discussant" either to lecture or to lead and orchestrate the discussion. Since everyone comes into the discussion sequentially, everyone has equal access to being heard.

Secondly, the multiloguing dimension allows members of the community to pull together disparate arguments and examples, file them electronically, archive and examine them, and pull them up for later reference, all with the perceived immediacy of oral speech. This can allow us to create a broader base of potential abductive "rules" to bring to bear on any relevant discussion.

For example, most discussion lists operating under listserve or listproc software provide the capability of accessing discussion material as selected by date, person, subject matter, or any combination of the above. As a consequence, this multiform availability of information within the overall multilogue form facilitates the hybridization of information, since we are capable of operating within a series of simultaneous and parallel sets of discussion in the typical multilogue setting as a matter of course.

Finally, the virtual community consists of people with wide-ranging interests and areas of expertise, and all members of the community have almost instantaneous access, in principle, to the expertise of each other. This allows for the synthesis of patterns of meaning in often nontraditional ways.

For example, sometimes the pursuit of meaning takes off on its own merry abductive way, leading to strange and unusual fruit. As a recent example, a member of the ERL-L list on educational research accidentally sent a private message, about the need to keep a refrigerator door shut, to the entire list. The person immediately apologized, but several people failed to see the apology and took the note as a cryptic message about the state of educational research today. The metaphor continued to expand, as people considered the significance of the contents of the refrigerator, the fact that the door did not seal easily, and the amount of energy required to keep the food cold.

On one level, this is an exercise in learned silliness; but at a much deeper level, it is an exercise in taking apart and examining the basic metaphors that hold the field together and examining what happens when those fundamental metaphors are replaced. Again, the multilogue form helped to sustain and foster the abductive musings.

Revisiting Descartes via Semiotics

What does Descartes do? Does he prevail, adapt, or go away?

Another way of asking this question is to say, What do the phosphor dots stand for? Are they a way for a disembodied Cartesian self to look at the world of the Internet, or are they signs that direct the immersed Peircean self as guideposts of the emerging reality of multiple and simultaneous patterns of communication with the vast set of others linked via the information superhighway we call the Internet?

If the Cartesian model prevails, then it would predict that Internet communication will move away from the current conversational form into a more cocoonlike phenomenon. In other words, as the individual cognizers begin to realize the distance between themselves and the rest of the people on the Internet, there will be a natural solipsistic turn. In ten years' time, if the Cartesian models are correct, the information superhighway will be a series of convenient off-ramps that allow discrete individuals essentially one-way access to the riches of the Internet.

If the Cartesian model is adapted, then its manifestation will be determined differently by different users. Some users will cling to the straightforward Cartesian model and take the path described above. Other users will move toward a more utilitarian position that preserves the individual Cartesian ego but posits a larger, collective "good" to which individual users should pledge personal allegiance. As a consequence of these contrasting, yet still Cartesian, maneuvers, we would predict a move both toward and away from the cocoonlike, solipsistic turn described above. In other words, the Internet will be a personal and a collective battleground between the ideas of the predominance of the individual vs. the collective will. This will be a schizophrenic scenario, and it argues that those who traverse the information superhighway will do so at the peril of their mental health.

If the Cartesian perspective is replaced with the idea of the semiotic superhighway, then we get the most optimistic scenario. The very nature of communication stands to be changed, just as changes in technology in the past have changed the nature of communication in their day. A good example is the shift from orality to literacy documented by Ong (1982). Ong is correct to point out that this shift was not just a matter of moving from one communication code to another. As he pointed out dramatically in one of his chapter headings, "Writing Restructures Consciousness," the act of communicating via the medium of writing not only changes the parameters of communication; it also changes the writer and the reader. In addition, communicative media, as semiotics has argued, create culture, and we should expect drastic cultural change as a consequence of Internet communicative structures.

An oral culture is fundamentally different from a literate culture, and an Internet culture will be different from both of those. Personal identities are less important, and will be subject to forces of drift and situational shifting pressures. Some of the youngest members of the Internet community are the teenagers and college undergraduates that constitute the bulk of users of Internet Relay Chat systems. Internet Relay Chat, or IRC, is a real-time communication mode that acts like a form of ham radio, in that there are thousands of shifting channels for discussion. Importantly, practically no one takes his/her identity, or his/her real name, into IRC. Instead, they adopt nicknames and alternate persona. It is a cliche that "everyone lies on IRC," but it is not really lying. It is using the ability to create a persona in conjunction with others as a communication medium. We have only begun to attempt to understand these sorts of dynamics, as, for example, Hakim Bey's (1985/1991) groundbreaking work on cyberculture. Bey (who, incidentally, is writing under both a pseudonym and an assumed persona himself!) looks at the Internet in terms of it consisting of TAZs, or temporary autonomous zones. These TAZs are enclaves of created persona where people can use the notions of identity shifting to explore ways of creating new communicative modes and new cultures. All of this suggests that we are not talking not about minor cultural shifts but of a watershed move. Perhaps it signals the end of the Enlightenment, or the Age of Science, which arguably began with Descartes himself.

If it is true that the Age of Science, which has prevailed since the era of the Enlightenment, is on the wane, then its logical successor is an Age of Meaning. If we are venturing into an Age of Meaning, then the information superhighway will be one of our major resources and assets. But it cannot be such an asset if we persist in looking at ourselves and the world, and the ways that we interact with each other, in old, possibly inappropriate forms.

Should we allow Descartes to stay at the terminal? The answer will determine how we see ourselves as rising above the phosphor dots that line the information superhighway.

References

Anderson, M., J. Deely, M. Krampen, J. Ransdell, T. Sebeok, and T. von Uexkull. 1984. A Semiotic Perspective on the Sciences: Steps toward a New Paradigm. *Semiotica* 52: 7–47.

Barthes, R. 1964. *Elements of Semiology.* New York: Hill & Wang.

Bey, Hakim. 1985/1991. *T.A.Z.: The Temporary Autonomous Zone, Ontological Anarchy, Poetic Terrorism.* Brooklyn, NY: Autonomedia.

Buchler, J. 1955. *Philosophical Writings of Peirce.* New York: Dover.

Deely, J. 1982. *Introducing Semiotic.* Bloomington, IN: Indiana University Press.

Derrida, J. 1984. Languages and the Institutions of Philosophy. *Researches Semiotique/Semiotic Inquiry* 4: 91–154.

Eco, U. 1984. *Semiotics and the Philosophy of Language.* Bloomington, IN: Indiana University Press.

Fiske, J. 1982. *Introduction to Communication Studies.* London: Methuen.

Gerbner, G. 1956. Toward a General Model of Communication. *Audio Visual Communication Review* IV(3): 171–99.

Hawkes, T. 1977. *Structuralism and Semiotics.* Berkeley: University of California Press.

Hjelmslev, L. 1943. *Prolegomena to a Theory of Language.* Madison, WI: University of Wisconsin Press.

Jakobson, R. 1970. *Main Trends in the Science of Language.* New York: Harper & Row.

Lévi-Strauss, C. 1966. *The Savage Mind.* Chicago: University of Chicago Press.

Ong, W. 1982. *Orality and Literacy: The Technologizing of the Word.* New York: Methuen.

Saussure, F. 1959. *Course in General Linguistics.* New York: Philosophical Library.

Sebeok, T. 1976. *Contributions to the Doctrine of Signs.* Lisse, the Netherlands: Peter de Ridder Press.

Shank, G. 1987. Abductive Strategies in Educational Research. *American Journal of Semiotics* 5: 275–90.

————. 1993. *The Extraordinary Ordinary Powers of Abductive Reasoning.* Paper presented at the I Conferencia Internacional sobre los Nuevos Paradigmas de la Ciencia. Guadalajara, Mexico: Universidad de Guadalajara.

————. 1994. Abductive Multiloguing: The Semiotic Dynamics of Navigating the Net. *Electronic Journal of Virtual Culture* 11. [Retrievable in electronic form under the file name SHANKV1N1 from EJVC-L@kentvm.kent.edu.]

Shannon, C., and W. Weaver. 1949. *The Mathematical Theory of Communication.* Champaign, IL: University of Illinois Press.

von Uexkull, J. 1982. The Theory of Meaning. *Semiotica* 42: 25–82.

II

ETHICS, GENDER, AND POLITICS

3

Privacy, Respect for Persons, and Risk

Dag Elgesem

Introduction[1]

The conflict between privacy and freedom of information shows itself in different forms. One aspect of this conflict is the question of the protection of privacy in connection with various kinds of research. The problems that I will discuss in this paper are all raised by a recent proposal, made in Norway, for a system that claims both to make possible new kinds of epidemiological research on the basis of medical records and to give an adequate protection of the privacy of those registered (see NOU 1993). The core of the proposal is to give each individual a special pseudonym that is peculiar to the system. This makes it possible to identify uniquely the individual across various registers without revealing her social identity. I will return to a more detailed description and discussion of the suggestion toward the end of the paper.

The proposal raises a series of general questions concerning privacy and its protection. The first question to be discussed is, What is privacy? Privacy protection in the context of computing of personal information is, in some ways, different from other, more traditional ways of protecting privacy. Very little of the philosophical discussion of privacy tries to take into account the principles for the protection of privacy in this area. I will suggest some elements of an account that is able to explain the sense in which principles of "fair information management," such as the principle that information that is collected for one purpose should not be used for a different purpose, are principles for the protection of people's privacy.

The second general issue concerns the *justification* of privacy. Again, I think the question of the justification of privacy in connection with computing of personal information has some new aspects, in spite of strong continuity with the more traditional questions. I will discuss the three lines of justificatory argumentation that I think are the most important in this context. In particular,

I will develop a version of an argument for privacy as respect for persons which emphasizes that rules for the protection of privacy are part of the terms of social cooperation.

The third general question about privacy is related to the question of justification: How should the concern for privacy be balanced against other legitimate interests with which it might be in conflict? This problem presents itself as the problem of how to evaluate and manage the risk of privacy violations as compared to other costs and benefits. I will discuss this question in relation to the proposal for the new system of registers for medical research and administration mentioned above. In the context of this proposal, the question appears, for example, in connection with the discussion of whether the patient could be said to have an *obligation* to contribute information about himself to the register. The standpoint of the committee that makes the proposal is that there is a prima facie obligation to this effect, but that the patient has such an obligation *only if* the risk of violations of his privacy is low enough. I share this view, and I think it suggests that we intuitively feel that considerations pertaining to the protection of privacy should have some sort of priority over other kinds of considerations. It also seems to suggest that there must be some point where the risk of such violations is so well taken care of that it is legitimate to balance the remaining, very low, risk against other costs and benefits.

What Is Privacy?

The very nature of privacy raises controversial questions. There is not room within the scope of this paper to discuss all the questions and the proposed answers in this area. I will try, however, to indicate some of the elements of what I think is the correct characterization of privacy. I will do this by discussing the interesting recent proposal of Jim Moor (1990).[2] His account is clear and suggestive, and is one of the few *philosophical* accounts of privacy that tries to shed light on privacy in the context of computing of personal information as well.[3] I think Moor's account is suggestive; but it also has some important limitations, and my criticism of his proposal will form the basis of my own suggestions.

Moor's account has two central claims. First, he suggests that the notion of a *private situation* is useful in order to get a good grasp of privacy. The kind of private situations in which we are interested are those that are *normatively* private, in contrast to naturally private situations. Being alone in one's home is the best example of the first kind of private situation, and being alone in some deep forest is an example of the latter. When we are alone in our homes, we are protected from the intrusion of others by a set of norms pertaining to the physical boundaries that surround us. The second element in Moor's account is the claim that privacy is a state of *restricted access*. "The core idea of restricted accounts is that privacy is a matter of the restricted access to persons or information about persons" (Moor 1990, 76).[4] These two elements give the following conception of privacy: "By my definition, an individual or group has privacy in a situation if and only if in that situation the individual or group or information related to the individual or group is protected from intrusion, observation, and surveillance by others" (Moor 1990, 79). This is an initially plausible, and not very controversial, account of privacy. But the account runs into problems that show that it is too inflexible.

The first problem is related to Moor's conception of private situations and the way he tries to classify situations as private and nonprivate. Which situations are normatively private and which are not? Moor asks. While it is clearly true that some situations allow for more privacy than others, the classification of situations into classes private and public obscures the fact that most situations do have private aspects. This rigid dichotomy forces him to make the following, implausible claim: "The restricted access view, as presented here, counts intrusions as violations of privacy only as long as they interrupt private situations. Intrusions on public streets are not invasions of privacy" (Moor 1990, 79). It seems clear, however, that to lift a woman's skirt on a public street *is* an intrusion of her privacy. Or, again, to read another person's diary without his consent is a violation of that person's privacy, even if it is done over his shoulder on a public bench.

The solution to this problem, I suggest, is to give up the rigid dichotomy between classes of public and private situations and to acknowledge instead that private situations occur within the scope of larger, public situations.[5] This view results in a more flexible treatment of privacy. Recognizing that private situations occur within larger public situations, we can take into account that privacy comes in degrees. In some situations, such as being in our private homes, there is very restricted access to us, while other situations, such as being in a public street, offer fewer—but still some—restrictions on access to us. The situation of riding in a car seems to be somewhere in between. Furthermore, being in our homes is, of course, not a completely private situation: There are limits to what we can do even there, and we are accessible through various channels.

There is a second reason for emphasizing that private situations may occur within public situations: This point makes sense of the fact that norms pertaining to the protection of privacy themselves are *public*. In order for these norms to be able to restrict access to persons, they have to be part of the public aspects of the situation. Privacy norms are part of "the basis of social cooperation," to borrow a term of Rawls (1993, 16); hence, they are public principles. This is a point to which I will later return.

Two Kinds of Privacy

There is a further way in which Moor's account is too inflexible, I think: There is an important kind of norm that does not fit the situational account very well. For example, there are norms of confidentiality pertaining to the way doctors should manage medical information about their patients. While such norms in some sense can be said to protect the private situation where the doctor examines her patient, it seems more correct to say that these norms protect the integrity of the *patient*. This suggests that there are two senses of "privacy" that are important to keep separate. On the one hand is privacy in the sense of a *state* in which a person can find himself—for example when he is said to enjoy the privacy of his home. I think this is the sense of privacy that lies behind Moor's discussion. I will call this privacy in the *situational* sense. There is, however, as the example suggests, a different sense of privacy in which it is more like a property, namely, the property of having control over the flow of personal information. Taken in this sense, privacy is something that attaches to the person and that is protected more or less well in different situations. I suggest we call this "personal privacy." To have personal privacy is, on my account, to have the *ability to consent* to the dissemination of personal information. This definition involves a notion of informational control in the *negative* sense of being able to prevent others from getting access to information about us. (Privacy does not, of course, involve informational control in the *positive* sense of being able to get others to access us or information about us.)

Interestingly, Moor explicitly rejects a characterization of privacy in terms of informational control. I think this rejection is untenable, and I believe it can be shown that this rejection leads him to an unreasonable position. Consider the way he highlights the contrast between his own restricted access account and the account of privacy as informational control:

> Control of information is important for privacy, but again it is the notion of private situation that makes the difference. Here is an example that contrasts the two theories. Suppose *A* confesses personal information to a priest *B*. Though *A* has no control over what *B* will do with the confessions, confessions are regarded in this culture as a private situation. The loss of control does not entail any loss of privacy. Clearly, if the confessional moment had been recorded clandestinely by someone else, then there would have been an invasion of a private situation and a corresponding loss of privacy. (Moor 1990, 78)

First, it seems implausible to say that A has no control over what B will do with the information. After all, the priest is bound by norms of confidentiality that contribute to the protection of A's privacy, norms by virtue of which the situation is private. Without these norms, A would probably not have confessed to the priest in the first place. It seems strange to deny that A, by virtue of these norms, has some control over the flow of personal information. Moor's account here seems to leave out a set of norms that are an important part of the protection of privacy, norms by virtue of which the person has control over the flow over personal information.

A second point where Moor's refusal to admit the notion of informational control in the account of privacy leads to problems is in the analysis of privacy violations. On his analysis, privacy violations seem to consist *only* in the intrusion into a *state* of privacy. In terms of the example cited above, this means that on Moor's analysis, both the privacy of priest and that of confessor are violated, and to the same degree. But this seems wrong. There is an important difference here that seems difficult to explain without bringing in the notion of control over personal information. Both the situational and the personal privacy of the confessor are violated, while only the situational privacy of the priest is.

It seems clear that norms of confidentiality, like those pertaining to a priest or a doctor, primarily protect their clients' privacy in the sense of giving them control over the flow of personal information. This is even clearer with principles pertaining to the protection of privacy in connection with computers, such as the principle that information that is collected for one purpose should not be used for a different purpose or, to mention another example, that people should know about and have the opportunity to inspect and correct information that is registered about them. Such rules seem to be concerned with nothing but informational control, and an account of privacy that rejects any idea of informational control will have little to say about this kind of privacy protection. This is a problem for Moor's account, since he wants his account to throw light on the question of privacy in connection with computing. So he says, "A feature that is particularly attractive about the restricted access theory of privacy is that it gives technology the right kind of credit for enhancing privacy and the right kind of challenge for protecting privacy" (Moor 1990, 79). I will return to this point in the discussion of the principles of fair information processing.

So far I have argued that we should distinguish situational from personal privacy and that we have to bring in a notion of informational control to make sense of the latter. This invites the idea that situational privacy could be characterized only in terms of restricted access, and personal privacy in terms of informational control. But I do not think this is quite right either. First, it seems to me that while it is true that norms of confidentiality confer control on the part of the client or patient, they also restrict access to him. Second, it also seems that the restricted-access view cannot avoid appeals to informational control. The problem is that there can be restricted access to a person or information about him without the situation being private. Suppose a prisoner is constantly surveyed by her guards but that the guards prevent everybody else from access to her. According to Moor's definition, which says that "privacy is a matter of restricted access to persons or information about persons" (1990, 76), the prisoner has privacy. But, since this is clearly wrong, the kind of restricted access Moor has in mind must be of a different kind. The restricted-access account must therefore be developed in some way, and I cannot see any way to do this that does not bring in the notion of informational control. The reason why the prisoner does not have privacy, it seems to me, is precisely because the restrictions on access to her are not restrictions in virtue of which she can control who has access to her or has information about her.

This suggests that the characterization of both situational and personal privacy needs both kinds of ideas and, therefore, that the distinction between situational and personal privacy does not correspond to the distinction between privacy as restricted access and privacy as informational control. This seems to suggest, more generally, that the alleged conflict between the restricted-access view on privacy and the informational-control account is not a real issue. But this rejection of the alleged conflict between the restricted-access and the informational-control accounts does not make superfluous the distinction between situational and personal privacy. The example of the priest and the confessor, discussed above, illustrates a case of loss of situational privacy without loss of personal privacy. For an example where personal privacy is independent of situational privacy, suppose that the priest after the confession is asked for information about the confessor but that he refuses to do so on the grounds of norms of confidentiality. In this case, the privacy of the confessor is also protected in a situation that does not include him and, hence, in which he does not enjoy situational privacy. This is not to deny, of course, that such norms of confidentiality also contribute to the situational privacy of the confessional situation. In general, the function of situational privacy normally is to protect personal privacy, but that personal privacy, in addition, requires protection of information in situations that are not private.

Before I go on to discuss privacy as fair information processing, let me make one more general point concerning the characterization of privacy. This is that one should also distinguish private situations from *intimate* situations. Several authors have pointed out that there is an important connection between privacy and intimacy. One of the functions of privacy is no doubt to make intimacy possible, and Julia Inness (1992, especially chap. 6) has suggested that this is the primary function—or "core"—of privacy. It is clear, however, that many situations are private without being intimate. To undress in a public bath, for example, is private in the sense that there is restricted access to the person by virtue of which he can control the flow of information about himself.

But there is normally no intimacy involved in the situation—the undressing is not part of an intimate act. The same holds for a situation where a doctor examines a patient. (I would argue that undressing in a public bath is not an intimate situation because the activity is regulated by public rules. By contrast, intimate situations characteristically allow for spontaneity and actions based on emotions, that is, acts that are not rule governed.) We should not, therefore, identify privacy with intimacy.

The upshot of this discussion is that there are three distinctions that should be made in the characterization of privacy. First, we must distinguish situational privacy (i.e., privacy as a state) from personal privacy (i.e., privacy as the property of having informational control). Second, we must distinguish privacy from the way it is protected: Different situations require different forms of protection. Third, we must distinguish privacy and its value. In my view, to have personal privacy is to have the ability to *consent* to the dissemination of personal information. This kind of control can be the basis for achieving other things, such as intimacy, but should not be confused with intimacy or any other desirable state to which it is a means. The same holds for situational privacy: It can also be a precondition for intimacy, but it should not be identified with it.

Privacy as Fair Information Processing

After this discussion of the general question about the nature of privacy, I will turn to the more specific one about the protection of privacy in the context of computing of personal information. Once again, we can see the limitations in Moor's account. He points out two ways in which computers affect the situational aspect of privacy: "A feature that is particularly attractive about the restricted access theory of privacy is that it gives technology the right kind of credit for enhancing privacy and the right kind of challenge for protecting privacy" (Moor 1990, 79). First, he points out that "even computer technology, which is often portrayed as the greatest threat to privacy, can enhance it. Withdrawing money from an automatic teller after banking hours is more private than talking to a human teller in the middle of the day" (1990, 79). Second, he maintains that

> we should ask whether and how specific situations should have restricted access. For example, as library circulation records become more computerized, the resulting circulation databases ought to be regarded as zones of privacy. The issue is not whether a borrower should have control over his or her lending record in the database, but whether there is restricted access to the data so that borrowers feel the freedom to read what they please without scrutiny from the FBI or other outside organizations. (1990, 79)

While both of these points are sound, Moor's rejection of any notion of informational control in the characterization of privacy leaves out some of the most important questions of privacy in this area, namely, those pertaining to the fair processing of personal information. These are the questions with which all of the modern privacy regulation in connection with computing is concerned. And privacy in the personal sense is precisely the issue in such regulation.

The central question that these pieces of legislation address is, I think, the following. In a modern society we have to give up personal information to various institutions all the time, in order to realize our projects. To give up personal information involves some, perhaps small, cost. We choose to give up a little of our privacy in this way, however, in order to achieve other things that we want. The problem now is that with the introduction of modern information technology, the processing of personal information becomes more complex and extensive. As a result, there is an increased cost in the form of increased risk of privacy violations. The point of the principles of modern privacy legislation is, in my view, to relieve the individual of this additional cost.

The principles of fair information processing are nicely summarized by Colin J. Bennett in his book *Regulating Privacy* (1992). Bennett compares the privacy legislation in Britain, Germany, Sweden, and the United States, and finds that all of them are built around six principles pertaining to fair information management. The same principles also underlie the Norwegian regulation in the area, which resembles the Swedish data-privacy legislation. In fact, Bennett claims that we find the same principles at the basis of the legislation in all of the countries that have such laws (1992, 95). The first principle Bennett calls the "principle of openness"; that is, "The very existence of record-keeping systems, registers, or data-banks should be publicly known" (1992, 101). There are differences in the way the information about the existence of the registers are made public in the different countries, but the principle is the same in all of the pieces of legislation. The second is the "principle of individual access and correction," which is the principle that the individual concerned should have the right to access and correct information about herself. Implicit in this principle is the requirement of data quality, that is, that the information should be correct and complete with regard to the purpose for which it is used. The requirement of data quality also involves the procedural ideal that the information should be registered by means of reliable methods, methods that insure that the information is correct and complete. The third principle is the "principle of collection limitation." This is the principle that personal information should be collected for one specific, legitimate purpose and that the collection should be justified by the nature of the activity for which it is collected. The Organization for Economic Cooperation and Development's [OECD] principles, for example, formulate it this way: "There should be limits to the collection of personal data and any such data should be obtained by lawful and fair means and, where appropriate, with the knowledge or consent of the data subject" (Bennett 1992, 106). This is a principle of *relevance*. Some bodies of legislation, like the Norwegian, contain a list of types of information that are considered particularly sensitive and for the collection of which the requirement of relevance is particularly strict.[6] The fourth principle Bennett calls the "principle of use limitations." All of the pieces of legislation articulate the principle that information shall "be used only for purposes that were specified at the time of collection" (Bennett 1992, 108). This is the general principle that information that is collected for one purpose should not be used for another purpose. The notion of relevance that is involved here can be interpreted in different ways, and the principle is open to exceptions in the different legislations. Hence, the practical application of the principle raises problems. This is a problem to which I return below. The fifth principle that seems to be common to modern privacy legislation is the "principle of disclosure limitation." This is the principle that "personal data shall not be communicated externally (to another agency) without the consent of the data subject or legal authority" (Bennett 1992, 109). Again, this is a principle that involves a notion of relevance, though it can be difficult to determine in practice just to what the individual can be said to have consented. The last principle formulated by Bennett is the "security principle." This requires that "personal data should be protected by reasonable security safeguards against such risks as loss or unauthorized access, destruction, use or modification or disclosure of data" (Bennett 1992, 110).

These six principles can plausibly be seen to express an important part of the answer to the question What is privacy? as it arises in the modern, computerized society. The principles no doubt lack precision in certain respects and are open to different interpretations. They are also implemented differently in different countries. Nevertheless, they have a certain content, and an account of privacy in connection with computers has to make sense of them. This is not possible, I will argue, without making use of the notion of informational control.

These principles of "fair information processing" *presuppose* the legitimacy of the activities for the purpose of which information is collected. The aim is to ensure that the individuals are adequately and correctly represented for the purpose of the decision in which the information is used. There is no attempt here to limit the collection of information as such. The legislators did not try, in particular, to define the boundaries of a legitimate "private zone" which the legislation should try to protect (see Selmer 1990). Furthermore, the legislators did not make the erroneous assumption that the individual's primary interest is to stop the flow of personal information. Instead, one recognized that in a modern society there are numerous legitimate interactions that involve the flow of personal information, and that in many situations it is, of course, in our interest to share personal information with the other party with whom we are interacting. The leading idea behind the legislation is, therefore, to protect the integrity of the norms that constitute the activities for which personal information is collected, that is, to make sure that the very processing of personal information does not affect the practice itself. Second, the norms protect the individual's ability to consent to the dissemination of personal information—they give the individuals informational control.[7]

If we look back at the discussion of Moor's account of privacy, it seems clear that his characterization of privacy only in terms of restricted access is not adequate for making sense of the norms of fair information management. The aim of these principles is not to protect a *state* of privacy but rather to protect the personal privacy through the processing of personal information in predominantly public situations. These norms for the protection of privacy show quite clearly that an account of privacy needs a notion of informational control.

Furthermore, if we look at the central example of the paper, concerning the protection of privacy in connection with research involving personal medical information stored in computerized databases, it is the notion of personal privacy that is relevant. The question is, again, how to protect the individual's control over the flow of personal and perhaps sensitive information, not how to create a state of privacy.

As noted above, even if there is broad agreement on the general principles, there are important differences among the countries concerning the procedures and resources they have chosen to employ for the management of the *risk* of privacy violations. I will return to this problem below, after a discussion of some of the justificatory arguments for privacy. I will discuss three such arguments for the importance of privacy. The first is an argument from the value of personal relations; the second rests on the value of a predictable social environment for the realization of our projects; and the third is an argument based on the idea that the respect others show us by respecting our privacy is important for our feeling of self-respect.

The Justification of Privacy

It is useful to start by distinguishing two different kinds of privacy violations (Elgesem, in press). The first we might call the "classical" form of privacy violation: it consists in the dissemination of information of an intimate nature to an interested audience without the consent of the subject. In this case, there is a violation of the person's integrity, even if the information is not used to do anything to the subject. Such uncontrolled flow of intimate information is harmful to the individual because it harms her personal relations. I will return to this point below. Such classical privacy violations, in the form of uncontrolled flow of intimate information, can, of course, also take place in new and more efficient forms with the aid of modern information technology. The six principles of privacy legislation identified by Bennett can be seen as partly motivated by the interest in the protection of and control over the flow of intimate information. If a person gives consent to the disclosure of some intimate information in the context of an activity, then he ought to be able to trust that the information is not disclosed in ways to which he has not consented. The point is, then, that the information-processing practices involved should not falsify this expectation.

The second form of privacy violation is related to the fact that the personal information is used to make decisions concerning the individual. If these decisions are made on the basis of wrong or irrelevant information, then this might harm the individual in illegitimate ways. This form of privacy violation can take effect through two different mechanisms: One is that the information on which the harmful decision is made can be wrong, incomplete, or irrelevant; the other is when the information is correct, complete, and relevant, but the information should not, according to the norms regulating the practice, be used as the basis for the decision in question. In both cases, the individual's right to form legitimate expectations about how she will be treated is violated. I return to this point below. Again, this form of privacy violation does not originate with the computer, but the risk of this form of privacy violation has increased considerably with the introduction of computers in public and private administration, because the complexity of the information processing now has increased considerably. The principles of fair information management can be seen as attempts to raise safeguards against both forms of privacy violations. But why is it important that our privacy is protected in this way?

The first line of justificatory argument focuses on the importance of our personal relations.[8] This argument starts with the observation that a variety of different personal relations is valuable and that it is consequently valuable to be able to control the closeness of our personal relationships. It is a fact, furthermore, that the closeness and degree of intimacy of our personal relations is, to a large extent, a function of the amount and quality of the personal information we share with others. Privacy violations, where intimate information flows without our control, take away some of our legitimate control over our personal relations. In this way, the privacy-protection principles can be seen to help us maintain some of our control over our personal relationships.

In light of this argument, consider our example of the protection of medical information in the context of epidemiological research. I think the argument gives part of the answer to why we do not want everybody to have access to our medical record. The reason why medical information in general is "sensitive" is that such information is *emotionally charged,* in the sense that these are facts about ourselves toward which we can have feelings of loss, helplessness, and vulnerability. Information about our medical condition can therefore give access to our emotional life. This gives a reason for wanting to have control over who has this information: A lack of control in this respect can mean a lack of control over other people's intimate access to us.

The second line of justification is related to the second form of privacy violation mentioned above—that is, cases where features of the information processing cause wrong and harmful decisions. This might happen, first, because the information that is used in some decision concerning the individual is incorrect or incomplete, so that the individual is misrepresented in the decision. A person might be denied a credit card, for example, because he is wrongly represented as a person who does not pay in time. Second, the person might be harmed through a wrong decision if the information is used in a context where it is supposed to be irrelevant. That is, information is abused for illegitimate purposes: For example, someone might be denied a job for which she is qualified because the employer gets access to medical information that is supposed to be irrelevant to the decision.

In cases of this sort, the individuals will fail to realize their projects, and their legitimate expectations concerning how they will be treated by the institutions with which they interact will be frustrated. If the information management of social institutions did not in general conform to the principles of fair information processing, it would be very difficult to form reliable expectations about the behavior of these institutions and, hence, to realize our projects through interaction with them. A relatively stable and predictable social environment is necessary in order to be able to develop and pursue our projects. Some of these projects are important for our whole plan of life. These considerations suggest that privacy protection can be motivated in terms of arguments similar to those pertaining to the rule of law.[9] They resemble principles such as "Similar cases should be treated similarly" and "Laws should be open, prospective, and clear." All of the principles of fair information processing can be seen as providing the individual with control concerning what decisions will be made on the basis of the information.

Consider our central example also in the light of this justificatory argument. This kind of justification is only partly relevant to the justification of privacy in connection with research conducted on personal information registered in computer databases, since the information in this case is not used to make any decisions concerning the individual. The relevance of the argument in this case is that some kinds of medical information—for example, information about psychiatric problems or AIDS—can be used for illegitimate purposes. The point here is not, of course, that such information should never be disseminated to anybody but the doctor (there might be situations where the information is relevant); the point is only that there are many contexts in which such information *should* be irrelevant but where it still might play a role in decisions if it were available, and that the individual should, accordingly, be protected against the dissemination of such information into these situations.

The third kind of justificatory argument that is relevant to our discussion starts from the observation that principles for protecting privacy express respect for persons. This line of argument has been developed by Stanley Benn (1984, 1988), who argues that the notion of respect for persons is essential for an adequate understanding of the value of privacy. Benn articulates the principle of privacy as the claim that ''B should not observe and report on A unless A agrees to it'' (1984, 225). He argues that this principle can be justified by, or ''grounded'' in, a general principle of respect for persons as choosers: ''To *respect* someone as a person is to concede that one ought to take account of the way in which his enterprise might be affected by one's own decisions. By the principle of respect for persons, then, I mean the principle that every human being, insofar as he is qualified as a person, is entitled to this minimal degree of consideration'' (1984, 229). The content of the principle of privacy is, then, to protect against interference with the person's way of realizing and developing her interests.[10]

In Benn's view, the notion of interest has two aspects. First, interests are connected to the goals that the person pursues: ''A person's interests are, in one sense, those things that would be to his advantage'' (1988, 105). Second, there is one sense of interest in which it is not ''merely objects or objectives to which he as subject addresses himself; they provide the strands of his identity over time, through which he is able to see continuity of meaning and pattern in what he does'' (Benn 1988, 107). It is the person as an entity with interests—in both senses—who is the object of respect.

The crux of this part of Benn's argument is that by protecting privacy, one protects the person's ability to develop and realize his own projects in his own way. This same line of justification applies also to privacy in the sense of fair information processing, since the function of this kind of protection precisely is to give the individual control over the development and realization of his own projects and personal relations. Benn then goes on to base his case for privacy on the way intrusions affect the person's relationship to his own projects. I will not follow up this part of his argument, for I do not think it brings us very far. Instead, I will develop a somewhat related version of the argument from respect, one that emphasizes the importance of expressions of respect for our feeling of self-respect.

The first element in this argument is the observation that self-respect is important because it motivates us and is necessary for us to feel that our projects are worth doing. This observation, as well as much of the argument to follow, is heavily inspired by John Rawls (1982; 1993, part 3). The development of a feeling of self-respect depends, furthermore, on the respect that is shown to us by others. Our self-respect depends, therefore, on properties of social institutions and the way people behave on the basis of the norms that regulate such institutions. When social institutions and practices are governed by privacy principles like those reviewed above, we are given the freedom to develop and realize our own projects and our own conception of what goals are worth pursuing. In this way we are shown respect, and our feeling of self-respect is sustained: Through the principles of privacy we express mutual respect for people as trustworthy and sensible individuals with valuable projects and goals.

On this line of argument, the principles that protect privacy are important because they constitute fair terms of social cooperation, terms that everybody can accept ''without humiliation or resentment'' (Rawls 1993, 303). Everybody is interested in privacy in this sense, no matter what particular projects and relationships they are pursuing. Principles of privacy express, therefore, due respect for persons by giving consideration to their interests in developing and realizing their own projects and relationships. Respect for principles of privacy enhances self-respect, once again, since the feeling of self-respect is dependent on the way one is treated by others in the context of various social institutions.

The idea that we show respect for people by respecting their rights is, of course, not new. Joel Feinberg, for example, points to the fact that a right is the basis for making valid claims: ''There is no doubt that their characteristic use and that for which they are distinctively well suited, is to be claimed, demanded, affirmed, insisted upon. They are especially sturdy objects to 'stand upon,' a most useful sort of moral furniture'' (1970, 252). Feinberg further suggests that we show respect for people by recognizing them as potential makers of such claims and that this recognition, in turn, is the basis for proper self-respect:

> To think of oneself as the holder of right is not to be unduly but properly proud, to have that minimal self-respect that is necessary to be worthy of the love and esteem of others. Indeed, respect for persons (this is an intriguing idea) may simply be respect for their rights, so that there cannot be the one without the other; and what is called ''human dignity'' may simply be the recognizable capacity to assert claims. (Feinberg 1970, 252)

The idea is, then, that there is an intimate connection between rights as the basis for making valid claims, respect for persons by recognition of them as issuers of valid claims, and a person's self-respect on the basis of an ability to make valid claims. It is, essentially, the same point that I am making here with respect to privacy.

Note that the respect argument does not show that considerations pertaining to the protection of privacy should *always* outweigh other considerations. The argument emphasizes that rules of fair information processing should be seen as principles for the regulation of social cooperation that give people control over the development and realization of their own projects. Neither the respect argument nor the other two justificatory arguments show that the interest in the protection of privacy should never be balanced against other interests. In fact, the proposed system for pseudonymization in connection with epidemiological research, mentioned above, is a case in point. I now turn to the discussion of this proposal and the procedures for the management of risk of privacy violations that are involved.

Risk and Privacy

As mentioned above, there is broad agreement on the general *principles* of fair information processing, although different countries use different *procedures* for the management of risk in this area. The problem, of course, is that in real life we have to accept *some* level of risk: It is impossible to reduce the risk to zero, and there is a limit to the price it is reasonable to pay to reduce the risk further. Despite the agreement on the general principles, therefore, there is also the potential for differences concerning the costs that one is willing to accept to reduce the risk of privacy violations. The most important procedural instrument in this connection has been the establishment of a Data Protection Commission which is supposed to see to the realization of the principles of fair information processing. This institution, however, has been given very different powers in different countries. Countries such as Sweden and Norway have a licensing system and a Data Protection Commission with the power to stop projects that do not meet the requirements. In other countries, such as Germany, there is a system with an ombudsman, while in the United States there is an even weaker institutional enforcement of the principles, and one relies primarily on citizen initiative and judicial enforcement.[11]

I will not go into a general discussion of procedures for the management of risk in connection with privacy. Instead I will look more closely at the example with which we started: the suggestion for a new system of registers of medical information for epidemiological research. I will start by sketching the main elements of the proposal. I will then go on to argue that this is a case where the interest in privacy is so well taken care of (i.e., the risk of privacy violations is so low) that it is reasonably balanced off against other interests.

Registers with Pseudonyms

The reason for wanting to have central registers with medical information about identifiable individuals is to make it possible to follow the medical history of particular individuals in a systematic fashion. It is assumed that this will create a significantly better basis for epidemiological research and for health administration and, furthermore, that there are no alternative ways to achieve the same results. The point of the proposal is to outline a system that takes care of these interests in epidemiological research and, at the same time, gives adequate protection of the privacy of the individuals concerned. The key to this is the use of a system of pseudonyms that identifies the individuals uniquely in the process of research, without revealing the social identity of the individuals. The main elements of the proposal are as follows.

First, it is suggested that a central medical register be established in each of five regions in the country, rather than one national register, since this will serve the purposes well enough. There will be a national secretariat for the administration of the registers, but there will be no medical information registered with this secretariat. All hospitals within a given region are obliged to supply the register with information about all of their patients. It will be possible, however, to match the information in the regional registers to obtain national data. Second, each patient will have his own pseudonym that can be used to identify him *only within* this system of medical information. This pseudonym, a numeric code, is claimed to be *hard* to break, in the sense that it takes ''all the computing power in the world for several thousand years'' to compute the identity from the pseudonym (NOU 1993, 291). Furthermore, the system is such that if the true identity of one pseudonym is revealed, this does not reveal the identity of other patients. The pseudonymization of the medical information provided by the hospital is not carried out by the hospital itself but by a trusted ''security central'' from outside of the health system (e.g., the Data Protection Commission). Third, the real identity of the individuals shall not be known to the registers or their users—only the pseudonyms and the medical information. The hospitals, on the other hand, of course will know the identity and the medical information but not the pseudonyms. The security central that carries out the pseudonymization will know the identity and the pseudonym but not the medical information that is attached to the pseudonym. It will be possible, however, for the individual to check the information about herself that is registered on the basis of pseudonyms, without revealing her identity and without revealing her pseudonym to the hospital. Fourth, it will be possible to extend the pseudonymization to facilitate matching between the new regional registers and existing registers. The users can obtain statistical and anonymous information about individuals, but they never actually see the pseudonyms. Furthermore, it is not possible to reverse the process of pseudonymization. Fifth, the system is less expensive than a national register, it can be built up gradually, and it is flexible enough to be modified to incorporate new technological solutions. The system will be given a trial period, after which it will be evaluated (NOU 1993, part 3).

This is, of course, only a very brief indication of the main elements of the system, but it is sufficient for the purposes of the present discussion. There is one further aspect that deserves special attention in the evaluation of the proposed system—namely, that it gives the patient the right to refuse to have information about himself registered. This is important for the following, obvious reason. People do not choose to get ill, and they of course seek treatment in a hospital because they *have* to. It would, therefore, be more problematic to impose an additional risk for privacy violations on them without their consent. (It is, of course, not altogether unproblematic to impose such risks on people when they have been given the choice, but it is much less of a problem.)

This question is related to the general problem of risk evaluation, a problem that has been called "the consent dilemma," and concerns the problem that arises from the difference between "consenting *in* a market" and "consenting *to* a market" (Shrader-Frechette 1991, chap. 5). The problem is that in many cases people cannot freely choose whether to consent to a risk or not. This is generally the case with risks of privacy violations in connection with modern information technology, since such technology is used in all of public and private administration. People in a modern society cannot, in many situations, choose not to share personal information with others. In order to function properly in a modern society, we have to accept the risks that come with the information practices of the institutions on which we depend. Given this, it is unreasonable that each individual should bear the costs of the risks imposed by the use of information technology. This seems to be an important general consideration in favor of a powerful institution for the implementation of the principles of fair information management. And it is, again, a consideration in favor of giving people the opportunity to refuse to contribute to the research register.

A question that naturally arises, and that is given attention in the proposal, is whether the patient has an obligation to consent to the further use of information about herself, for purposes of research and administrative planning. After all, the information will be used to improve and distribute more effectively the very same kind of service the person has benefited from. The standpoint of the committee behind the proposal seems to be that there is a prima facie obligation to contribute but that the obligation is contingent on a very low risk for privacy violations. I agree with this, but the question then arises: Given the importance that one attaches to the protection of privacy, how can one legitimately accept any level of risk above zero? As mentioned above, the justificatory account I have developed can accommodate a low level of risk. There is a point where the risk of privacy violations is so low that it is reasonable to accept it in order to achieve other things. Furthermore, the argument from respect and self-respect is also compatible with a very low level of risk. The point of this argument is that we, by abiding by the principles of privacy, express respect for persons and that this is, in turn, an important part of the basis for our feeling of self-respect. But one can, it seems, without humiliation accept terms of cooperation that involve some level of risk.

In the present case, I think the acceptability of the risk depends on a number of features. First of all, it is important to note that the risk is quite low and that it is not higher than necessary. Second, the use of personal information is necessary: There are no other means of achieving the same knowledge. Third, it is important epidemiological research that actually helps to improve treatment: What one sacrifices contributes to the production of some important good. Fourth, the acceptance of the risk involves the fulfilment of a moral obligation, namely, to contribute to the research and services from which one has oneself benefited. Fifth, it is possible for the patient to reject the use of information about oneself. (For a similar line of argument, see Wallace 1982.)

All of these features of the case at hand contribute to the acceptability of the proposed system and of the risk involved. Whether all of them are also necessary in order for research on individual data to be acceptable, is a question I will not try to answer completely. I will, however, make three points. First, it seems clear that the first three conditions are necessary for the research to be acceptable. If the risk is higher than necessary, if the research could be conducted without the data, or if the research is useless, then research on personal data would be an expression of disrespect for persons. Second, Wallace (1982) argues that it is justifiable to *violate* people's privacy to some extent as part of epidemiological research. He thinks that "the duty to respect another's privacy is overridden by duties governed by the principle of beneficence" (279). The violation is only justified, Wallace argues, if it is minimal, necessary, the object of useful research, and not directly harmful to the person's interests. While I am sympathetic to much of what Wallace says, I am here arguing for a weaker claim—namely, that, on conditions like those Wallace suggests, we should accept a very low *risk* of privacy violations in connection with epidemiological research. There is an important distinction between *violating* and *limiting* privacy. My argument concerns the justifiability of the latter, Wallace's the justifiability of the former. Third, I am not arguing that a system of large registers with medical data for purposes of epidemiological research would be *unacceptable* if the technology of pseudonymization were *not* available. If we accept Wallace's arguments, as I am inclined to do, we should perhaps endorse such a system even in the absence of such technology. But my point here is that once this technology exists, we have an obligation to use it, since it reduces the cost associated with giving up personal information.

Conclusion

I have tried to focus on the central aspects of the problem of privacy as it arises in connection with computer-mediated communication. First, I think the central problem here, and the one that modern legislation in the area addresses, is the problem of the distribution of costs that arise in connection with the processing of personal information. In a modern society, we have to give up information about ourselves all the time. To give up information about ourselves can be costly, but we give up parts of our privacy in this way because we thereby achieve something we want. It is unreasonable, however, that we should have to bear additional costs that stem from the way the information is processed. On this account, the principles of fair information processing can be seen as designed to ensure that the costs of giving up privacy, on the part of the individual, are not higher than necessary for the realization of the purposes for which the individual chose to give up information in the first place.

I have further presented what I believe to be three good arguments as to why privacy is important—arguments that rest on identifying the values that are protected by principles of fair information processing. None of these arguments seems to preclude the possibility, however, that, in some cases, it is reasonable to accept a low risk of such violations for the purpose of other important goods. Lastly, I have argued that the proposed system of registers with pseudonyms for the purpose of epidemiological research is one such case of reasonable acceptance of risk. Again, central to this argument is the consideration that the risk of potential privacy violations should be minimal.

Notes

1. The research reported in this paper is supported by the Norwegian Research Council. The paper has benefited from comments by Lee Bygrave, Charles Ess, Thomas Pogge, and members of the seminar of the Research Council's Ethics Programs.

2. See also Moor 1989. In this latter paper, Moor independently suggests and argues for the advantages of a system very similar to the proposed Norwegian system for registers for medical research based on pseudonyms.

3. The philosophical literature in this area is, as far as I have been able to find out, very small. One of the few who has contributed, in addition to Moor, is Deborah

Johnson (1985, chap. 4, "Computers and Privacy"). See also Westin 1967. It is characteristic that two of the most recent general books on privacy in English, Inness 1992 and Schoeman 1992, do not discuss the question of privacy in connection with computers at all.

4. Moor's account is at this point representative of a family of privacy accounts. Other members are Allen (1988, chap. 1), Gavison (1984), and Bok (1983).

5. That situations can be nested in this way is, for example, an important feature in *situation theory*. See Barwise and Perry 1983, and Barwise 1990.

6. According to the Norwegian act, "sensitive" information (i.e. information the registration of which normally requires a license) is information about race, political and religious opinion, suspicion or conviction in criminal cases, health, drug addiction, sexual matters, and private family matters (see Bennett 1992, chap. 4; Selmer 1987).

7. To emphasize this aspect, the Norwegian legislation presents these principles as legitimate *interests* that the individual has in connection with the management of personal information as part of some practice. These interests cover roughly the six principles mentioned above. In addition, the Norwegian act recognizes a trio of "collective interests" (Selmer 1987). A discussion of these falls outside the scope of this paper.

8. This line of argument is developed by James Rachels (1984). For similar arguments for the value of privacy, see Inness 1992. For a related argument, see also Fried 1984.

9. Joseph Raz, for example, characterizes the value of rule of law in this way:

We value the ability to choose styles and forms of life, to fix long-term goals and direct one's life towards them. One's ability to do so depends on the existence of stable frameworks for one's life and actions. The law can help to secure such fixed points of reference in two ways: (1) by stabilizing social relationships which but for the law might disintegrate or develop in erratic and unpredictable ways; (2) by a policy of self-restraint designed to make the law itself a stable and safe basis for individual planning. This last aspect is the concern of the rule of law. (1979, 220)

Raz here follows Hayek, who maintains that "stripped of all technicalities this [rule of law] means that government in all its actions is bound by rules fixed and announced beforehand—rules which make it possible to foresee with fair certainty how the authority will use its coercive powers in given circumstances, and to plan one's individual affairs on the basis of this knowledge" (Hayek cited in Raz 1979, 210).

10. Various questions can be raised concerning the precise relationship between the principle of privacy and the principle of respect for persons. There are, for example, many ways to take people's interest into account without seeking their consent. It is not necessary to go into these difficulties for the purpose of my discussion.

11. See Bennett 1993, chaps. 5 and 6, for a discussion of the history behind this divergence. See Selmer 1990 for a systematic discussion of the possibilities that exist.

References

Allen, Anita L. 1988. *Uneasy Access. Privacy for Women in a Free Society.* Totowa, NJ: Rowman & Littlefield.

Barwise, Jon. 1990. *The Situation in Logic.* Stanford: Center for the Study of Language and Information.

Barwise, Jon, and John Perry. 1983. *Situation and Attitudes.* Cambridge: MIT Press.

Benn, Stanley. 1984. Privacy, Freedom, and Respect for Persons. In *Philosophical Dimensions of Privacy,* ed. F. D. Schoeman, 223–44. Cambridge: Cambridge University Press.

———. 1988. *A Theory of Freedom.* Cambridge: Cambridge University Press.

Bennett, Colin J. 1992. *Regulating Privacy. Data Protection and Public Policy in Europe and the United States.* Ithaca, NY: Cornell University Press.

Bok, Sissela. 1983. *Secrets.* New York: Vintage Books.

Elgesem, Dag. In press. Data Privacy and Legal Argumentation. In *Communication and Cognition,* special issue, ed. Ghita Holmstrom-Hintikka.

Feinberg, Joel. 1970. The Nature and Value of Rights. *Journal of Value Inquiry* 4: 243–57.

Fried, Charles. 1984. Privacy. In *Philosophical Dimensions of Privacy,* ed. F. D. Schoeman, 203–22. Cambridge: Cambridge University Press.

Gavison, Ruth. 1984. Privacy and the Limits of Law. In *Philosophical Dimensions of Privacy,* ed. by F. D. Schoeman, 346–402. Cambridge: Cambridge University Press.

Inness, Julia. 1992. *Privacy, Intimacy, and Isolation.* Oxford: Oxford University Press.

Johnson, Deborah. 1985. *Computer Ethics.* Englewood Cliffs, NJ: Prentice-Hall.

Moor, Jim. 1989. How to Invade and Protect Privacy with Computers. In *The Information Web: Ethical and Social Implications of Computer Networking,* ed. Carol Gould, 57–70. Boulder, CO: Westview.

———. 1990. The Ethics of Privacy Protection. *Library Trends* 39 (1, 2: Summer-Fall): 69–82.

NOU (Norges Offentlige Utredninger). 1993. *Pseudonyme Helseregistre.* (22) Oslo: Statens Forvaltningstjeneste.

Rachels, James. 1984. Why Privacy Is Important. In *Philosophical Dimensions of Privacy,* ed. F. D. Schoeman, 290–99. Cambridge: Cambridge University Press.

Rawls, John. 1982. The Basic Liberties and Their Priority. In *The Tanner Lectures on Human Values,* 3: 3–87. Cambridge: Cambridge University Press.

————. 1993. *Political Liberalism.* New York: Columbia University Press.

Raz, Joseph. 1979. The Rule of Law and Its Virtue. In *The Authority of Law.* Oxford: Clarendon Press.

Schoeman, Ferdinand D. 1992. *Privacy and Social Freedom.* Cambridge: Cambridge University Press.

Selmer, Knut. 1987. Innledning [Introduction], *Personregisterloven* [The Personal Register Act]. Oslo: Universitetsforlaget.

————. 1990. Data Protection Policy. In *From Data Protection to Knowledge Machines,* ed. P. Seipel, 11–28. Deventer: Kluwer.

Shrader-Frechette, Kristin. 1991. *Risk and Rationality.* Berkeley: University California Press.

Wallace, R. Jay, Jr. 1982. Privacy and the Use of Data in Epidemiology. In *Ethical Issues in Social Science Research,* ed. T. L. Beauchamp et al., 274–90. Baltimore: Johns Hopkins University Press.

Westin, Alan F. 1967. *Privacy and Freedom.* New York: Atheneum.

4

Pseudonyms, MailBots, and Virtual Letterheads: The Evolution of Computer-Mediated Ethics

PETER DANIELSON[1]

Introduction[2]

Open computer networks support a remarkable new form of evolution.[3] Whole new institutions—bulletin-board systems (BBSs), Internet Relay Chat, and e-mail lists—are encapsulated in software, spread at the speed of an ftp/install cycle, and mutate when people modify them. This evolutionary process is crucial to the Net's incredible growth, bootstrapped with the devices needed to provide and access services. While rapid, technologically driven social change is generally problematic, upsetting our expectations and challenging our norms, in this case the problems run deeper. Open computer networks are a commons; far-flung, informal, computer-mediated communities such as Usenet lack many organized defenses against abuse. So the pace of technologically mediated social evolution threatens to leave behind the ethical resources on which community depends.

The problem of technology driving social change beyond existing ethical resources in computer-mediated communication (CMC) may find a solution in my theory of Artificial Morality. I will argue here that Artificial Morality provides some new ways to turn social evolution in beneficial directions.

Starting from the pragmatic observation that (some) moral virtues make agents better cooperative partners in unstable social situations, I try to isolate distinctly moral mechanisms for testing and improvement. So far, I have worked in drastically simplified artificial toy domains, designing and evolving small software robots to play games like Prisoner's Dilemma and Chicken. In crucial tests, distinctly moral robots, who can commit themselves to mutually beneficial cooperation, do better than amoral maximizers. Unfortunately, it is not easy to apply Artificial Morality to people. So my strategy in this paper will be to shift domains, focusing on something intermediate between complex people and simple robot players: computational agents—the person-machine ensembles that feature in networked interaction—and show how my theory can influence their design for the better. Roughly, in networks we interact via our robots, whose rapid evolution is so problematic. If I can show how these robots can be made to evolve in morally better directions, I can turn the problem around.

This paper has five sections. The first reviews the relevant technical and social aspects of the Net and sketches Artificial Morality. The next three sections develop my approach by considering three current practical problems for open networks. Trashing of e-mail servers illustrates how open networks are a commons. The ambiguity of e-mail causes surprising problems, which can be solved by breeding some new conventions. Anonymous and pseudonymous e-mail pose a deeper threat, but they may also be amenable to the techniques of evolutionary computer-mediated ethics. I close by reflecting on why the Net is a good culture medium for ethical evolution and cyberspace a good place for moral experimentation.

The Technical and Ethical Bases of the Net

Networks of Computational Agents

Talk of cyberspace naturally leads to a conservative reaction. As Phil Agre (1993) reminds us, the Net is just people. But this response overreacts; it is too deflating in two respects. First, there are new things out there. Computer viruses and Telescript agents are extreme examples of what I have in mind (Markoff 1994). Second, these agents—short for computational agents or computationally active rules or principles[4]—relate people in new ways. Together, we and our new devices create new ethical problems.

Agents are the essence of CMC—they do the mediating for us. I e-mail through a mailer and go Net surfing via gopher. Admittedly, these are pretty boring and stupid programs, but they do act in all sorts of ways for us, and so warrant attention as our agents. (Telescript programs and viruses introduce *independent* or *autonomous* agents into the network ecology.) Even boring agents have a pair of properties that make them extremely potent. First, they can propagate with great speed through networks of people and computers. Gopher took over a major portion of my university's communication in the last year, for example. Second, they act for us in all sorts of ways we need neither understand nor micromanage. My mailer lets me leave junk messages unread; but it also lets me send out inappropriate messages all too hastily. The second property makes agents as attractive and dangerous as genies; the first lets anyone have such a genie who wishes to have one!

It is important to see how these computational agents contribute to the Internet's runaway success. Without free supporting software, there would be no Net as we know it (Rheingold 1993, 102). On the supply side, most independent information providers use free software for their mailing lists, ftp repositories, gopher sites, and so on. On the user's side, the very construction of central Net institutions is mediated by (usually free) software. Usenet's thousands of discussion groups are a good example. Within a particular group —say, ubc.general—a newsreader like Tin literally sorts out the different threads of discussion from the Subject headers of individual messages. This device turns a nearly incomprehensible hodgepodge of topics, ranging from the sighting of a three-legged dog through the Karen Homolka censorship controversy, into an ordered set of discussions. Second, the flood of information would be overwhelming were it not for the filtering devices built into the software. One need not even see the headers of most Usenet postings; one can exclude them wholesale by not subscribing to their newsgroup or by avoiding a particular thread. Kill files (bozo filters) and the ROT-13 cipher add further selectivity; the former filter out messages by subject or source and the latter allows one to protect material, such as an off-color joke or spoiler in a film review, from unintended reading. Without this discriminating software to construct Usenet, connecting to the Net would be like wiring an all-band antenna to one's brain.

Cheap, Fast, and Out of Control

But the easy and rapid propagation of agents is worrisome, subjecting the Net community, remarkably civilized as it is, to strong destabilizing pressures. For example, a few people pressing for anonymous communication means that the Net is stuck with anonymity for anyone and any purpose and remailing agents that let anyone duplicate and customize this service. As Karl Kleinpaste complained, "nobody asked the greater Usenet" whether the proliferation of anonymous mail was a good idea (Detweiler 1993, sect. 2.3). This is not an oversight. Cypherpunks are quite reflective about the fact that they need no social permission: "We don't much care if you don't approve of the software we write. We know that software can't be destroyed and that a widely dispersed system can't be shut down" (Hughes 1993).[5]

A pair of contrasts are instructive. First, note the opposite default conventions on the Net and the telephone. E-mail defaults to what the telephone companies are trying to introduce as caller ID; telephones at present default to anonymity. Now consider the enormous ballasting effect of regulatory and popular resistance to the telephone companies' efforts to shift from anonymity to caller ID. In contrast, a few people shifted the Net in a few months. The anon.penet remailer is responsible for 5 percent of all postings, or 3,000 messages a day, by one count (Detweiler 1993, sec. 2.3). Second, contrast the speed of the spread of gopher with how long it might take the Russians to learn how to do (white) markets or (democratic) parliaments. One recalls Michael Oakeshott's conservative warnings that one can't expect to export parliamentary institutions to newly decolonized societies (1962, 122). But you can export BBSs and FidoNet intact anywhere with phone lines.[6]

It is important to see that what is ethically significant about CMC is not the technological change but the *social* changes it enables. It really doesn't matter much if my neighbors switch to faster modems, PowerPCs, or electronic fuel injection. But e-mail lists, BBSs, and PGP[7] change the way people interact; they generate whole new functioning institutions. Like the market or democracy, these innovations have a life—a social evolutionary dynamic—of their own. Extraordinarily useful, they find wide acceptance, and their new medium lets them propagate and change with remarkable speed.[8] Switching to an historical analogy, where Luther wrote up his ninety-nine theses and then waited for printing to spread their impact, a hacker Reformer could spawn *almost immediately* new working protestant churches, each with the (modifiable) recipe for creating more of the same and—more importantly from the evolutionary point of view—more of the different, too. As it was, the Reformation was a technologically driven social change of unprecedented speed and magnitude. In contrast, we face an even wilder ride, because the CMC generator has greater range (anything programmable) and fewer constraints, since any nerd can change crucial technological institutions, by himself, without a supportive congregation or friendly prince.

We are becoming aware of the enormous potential of computer mediation to change communication. I am suggesting we attend to the analogous potential for computer technology to alter the evolution of institutions. A new type of social evolution—computer-mediated social evolution—is upon us.

The Networked Commons

The Internet is a great and growing commons: Its resources are generally available to whoever has access.[9] Since costs to users do not reflect impacts on the system, there is a tendency to overuse resources. Here is the link between resource commons and social dilemmas. Each does better to use more resources; we all do worse when they are overexploited.[10] Therefore, the science of social dilemmas and the management of commons promises to aid in understanding and improving the virtual network community.

A few caveats are in order. First, one leading branch of this science, economics, is committed to a model of motivation that may be too meagre to explain the observed phenomena, namely, widespread cooperative use of the network commons. The striking success of this global nonmarket anarchy is a challenge to the prevailing conception of economic man (i.e., the perfectly self-interested, always competitive individual). Indeed, an economist-colleague once suggested to me that Richard Stallman's GNU (GNU's Not Unix) project, which aims to give away for free (a reverse engineered copy of) what is arguably the world's most valuable piece of intellectual property, was motivationally impossible! Not all social scientists are so doctrinaire; for example, Elinor Ostrom (1991) makes progress toward a positive theory of commons cooperation, and Peter Kollock and Marc Smith (in press) apply this theory to the network commons.

A second caveat: The standard phrase for the commons problem—"free riding" referring to the choice of some to exploit, or ride on, the resources of the commons without contributing their own—tempts us prematurely to moralize and to see such behaviour as exploitative, intentional abuse. I think this is a mistake. Hobbes's stress on the amoral innocence of preconventional behaviour is a welcome corrective. Note that the standard examples of free riding include things that many of us do quite innocently: contributing to traffic jams, air pollution, global warming, and overpopulation (Danielson 1993b). In the areas of network abuse, many of the "offenses" are merely failures to take greater care. For example, just this morning at breakfast (why so early? because my university has distributed "free" access to students, turning our commons—a Unix machine—into a computational desert) I went to ftp the latest version of PGP. There were a few files, distinguished by the suffixes that indicate compression methods. I didn't sort these out sufficiently, and with a slip of the fingers I mistakenly moved a superfluous 600 kilobytes across a few continents (PGP can't be downloaded from the United States). I added to the Internet load in a way I would have likely taken more care to avoid were I paying per packet.

Open computing on networked resources involves sharing a commons without authority. This phenomenon is best exemplified by Usenet's extremely open environment. Usenet is not an organization and has, so far, proved flexible and robust enough to deal with the stresses its anarchy spawns. A positive characterization of its success is more difficult. Cooperation in commons is not well understood. I conjecture that ethical processes—self-constraint, informal sanctioning, and appeal to shared standards for justification—play an important role in sustaining the Net. Are these traditional methods able to deal with the barrage of new problems generated by computer-mediated evolution? Deeper is the worry that the evolutionary process is biased against the trust essential to ethically supported cooperation. For example, computer viruses—easier and "way cooler" to write and spread than to block—undercut free- and shareware, and anonymous messages undercut responsibility generally.

So the computer-mediated evolution, so basic to the Net, threatens its ethical foundations. But this evolutionary process is not something that befalls us, like a fact of nature—quite the contrary, as this process, technologically generated and socially selected, lies at the other pole from natural evolution. While it doesn't follow that because we do this process to ourselves we can shape it, our large input does gives grounds for hope.[11] I propose hacking an evolutionary mechanism to try to strengthen the ethical resources of the Net.[12]

The Visible Hand of Artificial Morality

I take evolution and the social instability of traditional sources of ethical constraint very seriously. Seriousness requires that we learn the lessons of elementary game theory and economics, which prompt us to ask not only the utopian question, What if everyone does (the right thing)? but also, What happens when, predictably, some do not? The worry is that even the most meagre moral goal—cooperation where every participant does better than the noncooperative alternative—is often unstable and therefore practically unattainable. (I focus on the minimal moral goal of cooperation not to recommend it as morally sufficient but as morally necessary. If we cannot build a rational, pragmatic case for cooperation, *a fortiori* we are unlikely to build one for higher moral goals.) Similarly, I focus on unstable semiethical worlds —that is, situations where not everyone can be counted on to join in morally preferable cooperation—as the hard cases for an ethics that wishes to be pragmatically attractive. Evolutionary theory supports the reasonableness of this basic model. Given individual (rather than species or group) selection, were there only ethically constrained agents, we would expect them to be invaded by less ethical predators, who would prosper differentially by the ethical population's beneficence or justice. Thus, evolution reinforces the pessimistic conclusions of the sciences of rational choice concerning the prospects for ethics in these difficult situations.

Nonetheless, I remain optimistic, because I can show that some ethical strategies are evolutionary successes. In my book *Artificial Morality,* I argue that social evolution can be trusted to solve some difficult social dilemmas if some participants can constrain themselves, identify others' cooperative dispositions, and use them to discriminate whose behavior they accept.[13] These conditional strategies are effective because if you know that I won't cooperate unless you do, you have a new reason to cooperate.

As a simplifying tactic, I worked out this theory for simple transparent robots, computer programs that played artificial games modeling social dilemmas. For example, sharing of common computing resources can be modeled as a Prisoner's Dilemma, where two of us each has two alternative actions: to use less or more network resources:

FIGURE 1

The Network Dilemma

I use-------------------	--------------------
less less good for both	more best for me, worst for you
You use------------- more best for you worst for you	less bad for both

Situations like this are called dilemmas because they bring out the tension between two ways of choosing. First, and most obviously, we can look at the outcomes from a collective or social point of view. Were we to choose together, we would likely agree both to use fewer resources, since neither has a reason to allow the other to exploit him, and both do better with using fewer than with using more. Second, consider the problem as one calling for individual choice. Notice that regardless of what you do, I do better to use more network resources. Best is better than good, and bad is better than worst. The same holds for you, so you move down (regardless of what I do) and I move right (regardless of what you do), and we end up in the lower right corner of the matrix. The first line of reasoning shows why the good outcome is the moral choice, but the second line shows why it is unstable.

We should be a bit more specific about the conditions under which cooperation poses a difficult problem. As is well known, if we can identify each other and expect to interact repeatedly, we can coordinate on cooperative outcomes by means of strategies like Tit for Tat, where we signal willingness to cooperate by doing so at first and then refusing to tolerate noncooperation (Axelrod 1984). But where we expect to interact but once or cannot repeatedly identify cooperative partners, say, because our interaction is so entangled in a wider social context—consider atmospheric pollution (Danielson 1993b)—this strategy breaks down.

I have shown elsewhere how to extend something like Tit for Tat to these more difficult unstable situations. I construct various responsive agents, who condition their cooperation on the other agents' actions or principles. Some of these agents can achieve optimal (fewer, fewer) outcomes in difficult situations. One surprising result is that the conditional cooperator favored by David Gauthier (1986) is not successful; a more cynical reciprocal cooperator, which exploits naive unconditional cooperators, does consistently better. In general, we should expect mixed populations of more and less moral agents. More recently, I have shown how to *evolve* several kinds of successful moral agents using even weaker assumptions (Danielson 1993a).

Unfortunately, Artificial Morality doesn't readily apply directly to people, except in small, face-to-face groups, since it is difficult for us to discern the dispositions of strangers and to make our own principles transparent.[14] But this problem is less fatal when our subject shifts from human face-to-face (or F2F) interaction to interaction in computer networks. The computer-mediated basis of networking means that our subject is never straightforward human interaction—each is working through a (at least one) computational agent.

Let me sketch very schematically how my pragmatic ethical theory can be applied to improve interaction on computer networks. Let's assume that senders can act in two alternative ways: A annoys recipients and B benefits them. A might consist of flaming e-mail, questions already answered in the FAQ (documents containing answers to frequently asked questions, as defined by the interests and scope of a given list or group), or administrative messages misdirected to an entire list; B would be courteous, informed, and well-directed mail. If the better B messages are reliably marked by some discernible feature, recipients will tend to (acquire technology to) discriminate in favor of B. This gives senders reason to (acquire technology to) make plain their messages' B features. Any B features that agents can help generate will spread, as will technology to generate and discriminate for B. Things should get B-better.

Case 1: Pseudonymity

Having stated my discriminating approach abstractly, let's turn to some concrete cases to see how it might actually apply to some practical network problems. I begin with an application of my theory to the problem of anonymous mail. Anonymous messages are especially disruptive of social cooperation. They undercut the recognition of participants that is the basis of reciprocity and discrimination. When we communicate by normal name-revealing messages, we can establish reputations and open the prospect of future interaction. The shadow of the former and the promise of the latter both encourage cooperation. This much is clear without the special tricks introduced in Artificial Morality.

ANON.PENET

Here is the sort of thing that can land in your e-mail box:

> Message 1/13 From an43489@anon.penet.fiOct 20 '93 at 10:45 am utc
> X-Anonymously-To: ethick@unixg.ubc.ca
> Organization: Anonymous contact service
> Reply-To: an43489@anon.penet.fi
> Subject: TA Unqualified [Subject and body changed by PAD]
>   Prof, the TA hasn't read Dawkins.
>
> To find out more about the anon service, send mail to help@anon.penet.
> fi. Due to the double-blind, any mail replies to this message will be
> anonymized, and an anonymous id will be allocated automatically. You
> have been warned. Please report any problems, inappropriate use etc. to
> admin@anon.penet.fi.

Evidently one of my students has chosen to blow the whistle on the teaching assistant in my course on Evolutionary Ethics. Or maybe not; maybe someone is just playing a trick.

It is difficult to tell, since the student has protected him or herself by routing the message through an anonymous remailer. Messages like this raise all sorts of pragmatic and ethical issues about the credibility of anonymous messages and the rights of the accused to meet this challenge to his competence, which I won't discuss here; Detweiler (1993) contains some useful examples and references. I want to move us in a less standard ethical direction. Notice that this isn't a message from NOBODY@NOWHERE; my (fictitious) correspondent has used a server that, while hiding the author's true identity, gives me a way to reply. (In contrast, the basic cypherpunk remailers do not provide reply paths; cf. Finney 1993). Strictly speaking, this is pseudonymous, not anonymous, mail. I can reply to and thus carry on a conversation with the continuing persona addressed by an43489.[15] I am not arguing (yet) that this feature makes the message acceptable, but it *is* an ethically relevant feature. For example, it means that I can contact the sender and ask for further information that might help me authenticate the complaint. In particular, I want to focus on how the features of this remailer fit my scheme of Artificial Morality. For example, the message clearly identifies itself as special—anonymous and then pseudonymous—by its From header. This feature makes the message readily identifiable and thus easier for us to decide—automatically, if we like—whether to accept or reject it.

Applying Artificial Morality in this case is straightforward. One might simply reject anonymous or pseudonymous messages. But it might be even more effective to return the messages, unread, with a note explaining your reaction. You might say that you do not accept anonymous mail, or only pseudonymous mail, or whatever. I have tried this and it works. Actually the test was too easy; the message I received was unintentionally anonymous![16] But the response was encouraging; the sender was happy to correct his virtual faux pas. So I suspect that if receivers were to return unacceptable mail with plainly stated reasons, things would get better in this respect (*B*-better), as predicted by my theory.

Ethical Content

This is progress, but is it *ethical* progress? The scheme is compatible with demanding correspondents to use JIVE or PC filters (parody programs that turn English into street jive or politically correct speech, respectively)! *B*-better just means more acceptable to me—not (so far) ethically better. This is true but exaggerated. The values furthered by this process are minimal, but they are real: Someone prefers them. This puts an ethical spin on the entire evolutionary process: Selection is not determined by mere (amoral) success but success at giving users what they want. We have a model of a mutually beneficial informal exchange process.[17]

Second, filtering becomes a distinctively ethical process as it moves along this continuum: Minimally it shows a willingness to evaluate behavior and to act on one's evaluations. To filter is to commend some and to sanction other behaviors, to discriminate and thus to begin to stake ethical claims. This process will be more ethical if discrimination is principled, and more ethical still if filter users are willing to discuss and justify their action by appeal to shared or (even better) impartial standards. Anon@penet moves somewhat in this direction; its signature offers a pointer to a responsible owner: Johan Helsingius. So I can reject this class of message easily, I can query the sender, and I can ask the owner to justify his policies.[18] An ethical filterer will also be concerned about the consequences of her policy for the network system. For example, sending rejected messages back to their senders (this is called "bouncing") increases the amount of bounce-mail, a category of message notorious for destabilizing mailing systems. (What if the sender bounces rejections?)

Finally, when I use a pseudonymous server in my graduate (virtual) seminar Ethics and Policy of Information Technology, I will further select and add features. For example, the remailer might only post to our class conference system and our campus ethics newsgroup.[19] Social evolution adds a third ethical dimension because we are the selectors and mutators, and our values (and discussions of them) influence our designs.

Ethical Servers

But notice that were you to judge pseudonymous messages unacceptable for some purpose—e-mail or your mailing list—it might not be easy to do anything automatically about it. The filter system for my mailer (Elm) was never installed at my site, and our primitive mailing list software doesn't allow any filtering. Here is a chance to work rapid computer-mediated evolution on the right side of ethics: Write and make (and customize and defend) attractive, easy-to-use ethical filters. They might filter negatively (against anonymous e-mail) or positively (for messages from trusted sources). The positive side indicates how the scheme of computer-mediated ethical evolution might be elaborated. My filter could require that you use a (remote) ethical server that checks for or against valued properties (true name, anonymity, drivel, spleen) suggesting a proliferation of ethical "laundry" services. Each filter changes the rewards to various behaviors. (Those who think ethics must go deeper than behaviour, indeed, mere communicative behaviour, may denigrate these devices as "lip servers.")

Ethically preferable filters should not only separate the better from the worse but also return what they reject with a helpful message, explaining to whom they belong and what they stand for. Most important, they should be local services, filtering the mail or postings of their clients, not attempts at global "reform," like Depew's ill-fated reaction to the anon.penet server (Wilson 1993; Detweiler 1993). On this last point ethics and evolution evidently work together: No one has the right to act for the whole Net and evolution can't select on global processes. (See "Ethical Experimentation," below.)

My conjecture is that they can work together in more ways. I am optimistic, but there is nothing necessary about this happy outcome. For example, if cypherpunks take our filtering as a reason to hide anonymity behind false identities and addresses, my ethical approach will fail. The cooperative game of ethical discrimination will change into a nastier arms race, for which legal and technical solutions may be more appropriate. But we should not rush to legislate: Accepting pseudonymity (while rejecting anonymity) should provide incentives supporting the cooperative ethical approach.

Case 2: Mailing Lists

E-mail lists are a surprisingly vital new phenomenon. They allow many imaginative kinds of self-publishing with a wide range of results.

Pathologies

E-mail lists are susceptible to their own specific technosocial pathologies. The most common is well described by Phil Agre:

[Consider] the following irritating dynamic:

- Someone wishes to subscribe to a given discussion list, so they send a request directly to the list rather than to the list maintainer (probably because nobody ever told them how).
- The request goes out to several hundred readers, a few of whom mistakenly reply to it, and these replies also go out to the whole list.
- Whereupon several more readers send notes to the whole list complaining about the previous messages.
- Whereupon several people wish to remove themselves from the discussion list, but they don't know how, so they send messages to the whole list.
- Whereupon several more readers send out-and-out flames demanding that everyone else stop sending the meaningless messages. (1994, 1–2)

This is a standard user-interface problem. The mailing list software needs more controlling inputs than the interface—e-mail—makes readily available. So, like the costly little buttons on our VCRs, the available channels get overused and we get confused, sending control messages to the list when they should have gone to the special request address. Noisy lists are the CMC analogue of unprogrammed VCRs' flashing clocks!

Solutions

Agre continues:

What can we do about these problems? One common response is to promulgate rules or etiquette guidelines or "principles of user responsibility" and so forth. In each case, the image is one of restraining unfortunate behavior through written instructions, which does not work very well.

But more effective responses exist. One of them, crucially different from the rules and guidelines, is to write instructions for the most effective ways of using the net to get things done, including clear explanations of *why* these methods work best. . . . Here's the wonderful thing. Given how the net works, it happens that the most effective ways of networking, getting help, finding information, gathering people together, making friends, and so forth are also the most socially responsible ways of doing these things. Why is this? It's because of the network's tremendous capacity for cultural self-regulation. (1994, 2)

I agree with Agre's assessment about what works and what does not. Nonetheless, I suspect that we can both firm up his notion of cultural self-regulation and help the process along as well. The firming comes from our results in case 1: One of the reasons responsibility works is that others are willing to discriminate in its favor. Otherwise, were experienced users, for example, to go out of their way to answer only misplaced questions by the unread, incentives to responsibility would be weakened. We can help responsibility along by noticing that there are ways list owners can improve the service they provide.[20] Agre's own Red Rock Eater service is fully moderated. As a send-only list (where the owner selects and sends out items) it is free of this pathology and offers a correspondingly higher signal-to-noise ratio. But this is a drastic solution—from many-many to one-many narrowcasting—because it requires more human intervention and because it dampens many-many interaction. An intermediate step is taken by Peter Neumann, who moderates the contributions to the Usenet discussion group <comp.risks>, again resulting in a high-quality service, now many-many. Both procedures can be labor intensive; most many-many mailing list networks cannot afford this (or do not want this degree of management). A third alternative is to redirect replies to the sender instead of to the list. This feature is available in LISTSERV software, lamentably evidently going extinct with the IBM mainframes on which it originally ran. It was designed into the Listserv list PHILOSOP@VM1. yorku.ca by my co-owner Nollaig MacKenzie. It means that you, the sender, and not everyone on the list, gets the feedback from your contributions. Netiquette suggests that you summarize and report results back to the list if appropriate.[21]

While this feature cannot block "unsubscribe" messages appearing on the list, I believe that it has saved PHILOSOP from the secondary and tertiary waves of response sketched by Agre.

MailBots

But we can go even further. Successors to LISTSERV could provide filters for these known pathogens. The offending messages are often syntactically stylized for the sake of automatic response; one need only filter out messages containing the words "subscribe" and "unsubscribe" to reduce greatly the problem. Better, filter these messages out of the distribution stream into the administrative stream. Better yet, tell all on the list that now "subscribe" and "unsubscribe" are reserved words, subject to automatic filtering out of all messages.[22] Perhaps this will lead to awareness of the possibility of increasing the set of banned (filtered) terms to include whatever the list users (or list owners) can agree to declare as unusable words. (This digression raises some interesting ethical issues. For example, should all such filtering mechanisms be transparent, so that one knows what words are filtered off a list? See "A Right to Context," below.) Better yet, the list should notify the filterees of what was done to their messages, to encourage them to learn from their mistakes (which have been made less embarrassing by the filter).

It is utopian to rely on getting all the right features into some server (because there is no such ideal mix or because it won't run on some provider's Osbourne or . . .). So we should also find less technologically dependent ways for list owners to do these jobs themselves. For example, we might support them with a series of EmilyPost-Its—prewritten corrective missives, perhaps light or humorous but at least polite and clear ways to point out problems to list users.[23] I have tried this out lately on PHILOSOP with some success.

Separate Lines

Finally, we should remember that one person's noise is another's signal and that some mailing list "problems" may amount to differences in taste. For example, I've noticed that during conference season, professional and technical lists often break into chatting about the weather in city X or the party after session Y. This leads some subscribers to moralize about what the list is "really for" and others to tell them to lighten up, and so on. Perhaps the chatterers simply need a separate chat channel; the e-mail list medium suffers from low bandwidth. A low-tech solution is to create a virtual side-channel with the convention of adding a prominent "CHAT" to the subject line to allow more serious folk to filter away the chaff.

Summing up, those who run e-mail list services need handy kits of tools that allow users to derive mutual benefit by using the lists in cooperative ways.

Case 3: E-mail as Tabula Rasa

It is important not to overstress the negative side of filtering.[24] It may be more effective—and certainly more respectful of the humane basis of the Net—to thank people who get these things right than to sanction those who get them wrong, even in the case of firmly established conventions. But where conventions don't yet exist, premature sanctioning is clearly misplaced. Let's turn, then, to a case where conventions are unclear, to see how my theory might guide us in less well charted domains.

Try this experiment. Look through the paper mail you received today, noting the types of messages and how the classifications are signaled. I got a few official letters, on university and business letterhead, a few memos on forms from various parts of my university's bureaucracy, some of which are addressed to multiple recipients, message and action slips from my secretary, several flyers announcing talks, and an informal note from my research assistant. Now turn to your day's e-mail. Mine is remarkably unvaried; almost twenty undifferentiated messages.

The informality of e-mail is widely noted and often celebrated. It likely comes in part from the speed of the medium. But part may also be due to a lack of structuring conventions. When I reach for paper, I must choose: letterhead, memo pad, plain white stationery, action slips, or frilly stuff with little flowers all about. In contrast, my mailer puts up a plain page, or quotes your message back. So what, you might say. Should we lament the formality of paper mail, mourn the passing of the engraved note? Generally not, perhaps. But there are costs to an undifferentiated message stream. Most obviously, one needs to read more of each e-mail message to classify it. (In my paper mail today were several easily recognized, and thus easily dismissed, formal letters acknowledging letters of recommendation.) More serious is the confusion of message types. Is this chatty note rejecting my conference submission or what? Even more serious is a problem I owe to Virginia Rezmierski:

> How do the laws that deal with records (FOIA [Freedom of Information Act], FERPA [Family Educational Rights and Privacy Act]), interact with those that deal with privacy expectations and rights (ECPA [Electronic Communications], Privacy Act)? . . . [H]ow shall we distinguish between the official decisions of the institution and the informal communication that is also important for the community, ensuring that the decisions that are increasingly being communicated via the electronic systems are preserved? (1993, 15, 17)

I do not claim that differentiating e-mail conventions will solve this legal problem.[25] But they may help us avoid some confusions and intrusive regulations. The case helps us understand conventions a bit better. My using differentiated e-mail doesn't solve the problem, because by itself it cannot create a convention. Others need to respond appropriately to what I do. But we can push the adoption of beneficial conventions in two ways. Negatively, we can sanction people who fail to use conventions—in this case, by simply returning their undifferentiated e-mail and asking for clarification (classification, really). (We might [help people to] do this semi-automatically or automatically.) But, of course, it is odd (and unfair) to expect people to use and respect unknown conventions, so it is probably better to start with the positive, constructive side: Use differentiated message forms and help others to do so as well.

Virtual Letterhead

Here is an example:

Date: Mon, 7 Mar 94 20:06:55–0800
From: pad@ethics.ubc.ca
To: pad@robo.ethics.ubc.ca
X-message-type: letterhead
Subject: DEMO of Convention Mail

THE UNIVERSITY OF BRITISH COLUMBIA

```
Centre for  _/     _/   _/_/_/      _/_/_/  227-6354 Agricultural Rd
Applied    _/     _/   _/      _/   _/      Vancouver, B.C.
Ethics     _/     _/   _/_/_/      _/       Canada V6T 1Z2
           _/     _/   _/      _/   _/      (604) 822-5139
           _/  _/ _/   _/      _/   _/      FAX 822-8627
           _/_/_/  _/_/_/      _/_/_/
```

7 March 1994

Prof. Someone
Particular University
Cowtown, USA

Dear Prof. Someone,

<Message>

Sincerely yours,

Peter Danielson
Associate Professor, Philosophy
Senior Research Fellow
NOTE: This message is an attempt to introduce structuring conventions
to e-mail. For more information, please see http://www.ethics.ubc.ca/
~pad.

   This example indicates some of the general features of conventions.
First, it is handy to work with familiar conventions, so we begin with ordinary
paper mail. But we cannot simply *move* our existing conventional solutions.
E-mail is a new medium; one can't literally use existing letterhead.[26] Second,
conventions work by providing a framework; they must be relatively stable.
So letterhead replacement should be salient: recognizable as letterhead, attractive, and easy for people to use. I suspect that meeting these conditions will
take some artistic flair, to which I make no claims: so my letterhead example
is only an illustrative first attempt. I tried replacing the impressive feudal crest

my university uses with a virtual emblem, thinking that this suits the medium. But I may have departed too much from the university's stodgy design. (Is it appropriate to refuse an application or article submission on virtual letterhead that looks like something from a B-grade sci-fi flick?)

The example also allows us to develop our general proposal further. Some of my proposed techniques make one's messages and responses salient to *people* (as with the design of the virtual "look" of letterhead). Others make them salient to computerized *agents*. Notice the new header line, "X-message-type: letterhead," I inserted in the sample message that would allow a mailer or other server to differentiate it as letterhead. I think *both* are important. The latter is important if we are to automate our awareness of and responsiveness to conventions. The former will let us debug the latter and reminds us that e-mail finds its way onto paper.

A Right to Context

We can see my proposed e-mail convention in a broader perspective. Rick Crawford proposes new rights to balance the power imbalances introduced by CMC technologies:

> A corollary to this right of reply is, itself, a central requirement of a *right to know* how one has been targeted. That is, at a minimum, one should know what characteristics of one's digital persona met the selection criteria that retrieved the original target audience. With this information (and the economic wherewithal to pay for distribution of one's targeted reply), receivers of targeted communications would be empowered to a significant degree. They would know, to some degree, *why* they were selected, and could communicate with other members of this virtual class. This would go a long way toward counteracting the imbalance of communicative power between individuals and institutions. (1993, 53)

In this context, we can see featureless communication as disadvantaging the recipient, who is left to wonder, Why am I receiving this message? In what role am I supposed to receive it? What role is the sender adopting? More context—say, by means of conventionalized forms and wrappers—empowers the recipient. This more general description also suggests further development of the idea. Another convention might be to identify mailings by the size of the automated mailing list base:

X-automatically-sent-to: 465

might appear in the header. One would be able automatically to reject junk mail so marked (and any mail not marked appropriately, to tie this example back in with the section on pseudonymity). At a more abstract level, we can see how moral principles, such as Crawford's rights, function as higher-level conventions, drawing our attention to salient features of lower-level conventions that we might wish to support, oppose, develop, retard, etc. For example, were users of CMC to adopt this standard of transparency, maybe people would start treating fake "personalized" paper mailings differently. Higher-level principles also draw our attention to conflicts. As Crawford points out, there is a conflict between my right to know context, which includes something about the target audience of which I am a part, and your right to privacy, which blocks my knowing that you are in that audience.

Snailed Mail

A third e-mail pathology may also be amenable to new conventions. One often sends off e-mail messages too rashly. It is easy to reply (readdressing and quoting are automatic) and some pay for connect time. But once one has hit SEND, the message is irrevocably committed. Contrast paper mail (often called "snail mail"), where I can reconsider before I print the letter or before I print the envelope, before I seal the letter or stamp it or take it to the postbox or, finally, drop it in. I suggest that it would be beneficial to reconstruct some of these decision points for e-mail. The Mac's trashcan halfway file delete provides an analogy here. One could have a postbox or outbasket that swelled until emptied or that sent things off after a preset delay. The device would act as an editable queue. (Indeed, such devices save me wasted faxes and paper on my NeXT and Mac.) So far this will help one to be personally more prudent, but it won't lead to a convention of greater prudence, because no one will notice the absence of my ill-considered messages when I slow down my act. To make the change more public and hence more effective, I suggest that such an enhanced mailer might add a line like

X-mail-delay: 1440 <minutes>

so that others might filter and otherwise discriminate my mail accordingly. Some might not accept (what we might come to call) rash-mail; others might simply sometimes chide in the spirit of Pascal: Had you delayed more you might have made this message better; please increase your mail delay time.

Summary

I am proposing an approach to cultivating ethics on the Net, which can be summarized by considering the three cases in reverse order. First, we need better conventions. They should mark the right distinctions and be easy to perceive and use. To take Thomas Schelling's well-known example, cities often have obvious meeting places (1960). But in a new artificial medium, these bright lines need to be constructed. Designing good ones will take skill; we need

CMC architects. But I suspect that evolution will always improve on design, and evolving better conventions also takes skill. We need open programs and a cooperative democratic spirit. Second, we need to educate ourselves. I suggest ways to make it easier for e-mail list providers to show users that skillful use of the conventions is good for them. Third, this process will work only if it *is* more useful to comply with our conventions. To make it so, we need to discriminate on the basis of respect for the conventions. I put the sanctioning step last because, although it is crucial to the whole structure, we naturally place too much emphasis on it. But if we *start* with sanctions, we are likely to fall into value-destructive flame wars instead of mutually beneficial cooperation.

Ethics, Cooperation, and Experimentation: The Net as an Ethical Culture

In this section I will reflect on how my proposals relate to my theory of Artificial Morality and point out some of the argument's assumptions and limitations.

Beyond Artificial Morality

First, our results go beyond and specify the argument in *Artificial Morality*. There I focused largely on simple games where the cooperative outcome was obvious. But CMC greatly increases our possible actions, with an exponential increase in possible outcomes for interaction. It is not clear how existing conventions apply (witness our confusion about software "piracy") or which conventions to extend or how to extend them. So the first extension is to find cooperative outcomes that might be stable in an environment where some, but evidently not all, are willing to seek cooperative outcomes. As in the case of e-mail letterhead, we need to devise conventions to make (some) mutually preferred outcomes the focus of attention. Second, in my simple models, communication between agents was easy. But in the real—oops, virtual— world we need to find creative ways to lower transaction and communication costs, to alert others to the possibility of mutually beneficial cooperation and the salience of the conventions as a means thereto. Third, games oversimplify the options for discrimination. We need to distinguish among various forms of discrimination, pro and con desired behaviour, and approach carefully the use of sanctions. (In contrast, there are no sanctions, strictly speaking, in the Prisoners' Dilemma game; see Danielson 1992a, sect. 9.1.1). Finally, we need to devise easily propagated and improvable software to carry these ideas into practice on the Net. (There may be difficult trade-offs here. Perhaps software can be *too* protean to fix particular conventions.)

Too Easy?

I have tried to apply my theory of Artificial Morality to the problem of strengthening the ethical resources of the Net. By now it should be obvious that my success was, in a sense, preordained. CMC is close to the ideal domain for my approach. Two features stand out. First, the Net is artificial. On the negative side, it carries with it little of the natural motivational baggage that might compete with the artifice that I propose. (In contrast, Artificial Morality would make a poor theory of groups such as the family rich in natural motivation and, hopefully, F2F interaction.) This is not to say that my solution is not based on natural motivations—clearly the Net is driven by our very human need to communicate and associate—but only to point out the limits of natural moral motivation in a medium that blocks off so much of the human face. On the positive side, an artificial realm is malleable, so it can be turned to purposes of ethical construction. Raw human F2F is more constraining.

Second, the Net is rich in cooperative opportunities. Indeed, the communication at the center of Network interaction is itself cooperative. I have no reason to send anyone a message who does not cooperate, minimally, by reading it. And, of course, cooperation on the Net extends much further, to legions of helpful and skillful people providing a vast array of services to the Net community.

Limits

The cooperative core of the Net illuminates where it fails as well, as in the cases of cracking and viruses. This brings us to the limits of my argument. When I break into your system or infect it with a computer virus, I do not need your cooperation. (A finer point: What if I seek recognition? True, I need you to recognize me, but the Hegelian interaction of master and slave, like any protection racket, is not a cooperative game, since the victim in each case is better off without the interaction.) Where this is the case—where we are in strict competition or, worse, you malevolently desire me to fail—my techniques for promoting cooperation simply get no grip.

Viruses point to a second limitation on my approach. I have assumed that we can experiment rather freely with a variety of kinds of interaction and responses to it. But this free experimentation is morally permissible only in special circumstances, namely, where the harms from interaction are limited in certain ways. We would not allow free experimentation with various forms of thermonuclear "self-defense" (as least not in Canada :-)). What allows so much room in the case of the Net? The answer turns on the extent and kind of harms one can cause via CMC. One can't get shot, or mugged, or run over in cyberspace. This feature may be trivially obvious, but it is ethically crucial. It means that cybernauts can't harm each other in Mill's narrow, direct sense. It follows, on Mill's utilitarian and other grounds, that there are good reasons to leave people to interact as they have chosen in this realm. It is a harmless playground for grownups.[27]

While I can't directly harm you—in Mill's narrow sense—via e-mail or newsgroup communication, this does not mean that no one will be harmed. For example, the women seduced by Alex's deceptive female persona, Joan, were clearly harmed by this deception (Van Gelder 1991). Of course you can come to harm by reading, but, again leaning on the liberal tradition, this takes another act on your part: You need to read or otherwise act on the message in order to be harmed (or benefited). This is not the place to define or defend a liberal principle. I simply want to note that some such principle must be called on to allow the free experimentation that I propose, and I want to suggest that the Net provides such a large arena for this experimentation because it vastly increases the realm of communication in contrast to other forms of interaction.

Computer viruses show the limits of this arena, to the extent that they cause harm without (voluntary) user interaction. (This is not to take a position on those whose computers get infected as the result of software piracy.) But viruses are an extreme case; other forms of enriched communications are problematic in this way as well. For example, my NeXT workstation is Postscript® based. Since Postscript® is itself a computer language, enhanced NeXTMail® originally could set loose a rogue program by the mere act of opening a mail message. More subtly, the enhancement of Net traffic with sounds, pictures, and movies also moves us from more central to less clear ground for the liberal defense of harmless communication. This may be a reason for those of us who value the Net as a moral and sociological experimental lab to be less enthusiastic about the tendency to ''enhance'' its services. (This is a special concern, over and above the obvious problem of increased bandwidth use as exacerbating the commons problem.)

Ethical Experimentation

The Net is very new and impresses us with how little we understand its ethical basis. (Its founding fathers are still with us and modestly don't pretend to oracular moral, political, and social wisdom.) It is hard not to be modest in the face of this remarkable phenomenon of world-spanning, informal, anarchistic cooperation. A priori and intuitionistic approaches to ethics are no match for the Net's evident capacity for rapid growth and innovation. So it is hard to see any but an experimental method as adequate to its ethical challenges.

However, the *global* nature of the Net also interferes with my preferred experimental approach. Experiments can be interpreted only against a relatively fixed background. Releasing new and untested devices to the Net is exciting but it is difficult to control in either of two relevant senses: to limit (when something goes wrong) and to evaluate (to know if it is going right or wrong). So I recommend more studiously local experiments. We should restrain our rush to share and also resist the Net ethos of openness (and against ''censorship'') in this respect: We should try out limited servers and report, discuss, and debate their effects in local (virtual) communities first.

Finally, none of this is neutral. Were I a Christian fundamentalist, a Muslim revivalist, or a Moorean Intuitionist, I can imagine finding the development of Net culture a deep threat. Clearly the Net has a bias (toward openness, liberty, and democracy) and an attitude (of brash impatience with the less wired world's tired ways). By now it should be obvious that I share these values and welcome this vibrant extension of the liberal and democratic movements that have revolutionized some societies. I have suggested that ethics can also be improved in this way; it need not be seen as a conservative constraint on this evolutionary process but as a way of facilitating its cooperative basis.

Conclusion

I have indicated how one problematic feature of open networks, the rapid evolution of computer-mediated institutions, can be used in new ethical ways. I have suggested that we focus on the cooperative aspect of Net interaction and the support that ethics can provide for this form of behaviour. In particular, we should creatively try to develop and spread beneficial conventions, ways to inform providers and users of these conventions, and filtering techniques to aid and humanize discrimination based on these conventions.

The conference invitation that led to this essay asked participants to consider ways "in which law, ethics, and technology can contribute to influencing the bounds of acceptable behavior in a shared computing environment." Of course, if we legally forbid or technically block a behavior, it is no longer an option for the play of informal ethical choice, commendation, sanction, or discussion. But law and technology can support as well as bound ethics. I have argued that technical innovation can support ethical innovation, so we should be careful to forbid only what we must and allow fruitful if unruly ethical evolution to take its experimental course. I conjecture that the Net will turn out to be a good culture medium for evolving better ethics.

Notes

1. Author's address: Centre for Applied Ethics, 227–6354 Agricultural Rd., Vancouver, B.C., Canada V6T 1Z2. Email: pad@robo.ethics.ubc.ca. URL:http://www.ethics.ubc.ca/~pad.

2. Thanks to Charles Ess for motivating this paper and for his insightful editing, Michael McDonald and Leslie Burkholder for helpful comments on a draft, Colin Macleod and Richard Rorty for stimulating conversations, and the Centre for Applied Ethics for a superb research environment. I learned much from presenting an

earlier version to the American Association for the Advancement of Science-American Bar Association National Conference of Lawyers and Scientists Invitational Workshop on Legal, Ethical and Technological Aspects of Computer and Network Use and Abuse, 17–19 December 1993, Irvine, California. This research was supported by a grant for the Social Sciences and Humanities Research Council of Canada.

3. My colleague Leslie Burkholder reminds me of the need for historical perspective here. For example, Steven Levy describes the evolution of early software projects at Project Mac (1985).

4. The digital Webster's gives a chain of definitions that makes "agents" peculiarly appropriate: agent takes us to "a chemically, physically, or biologically active principle." We extend this to include computationally active, and pun on principle (meaning ingredient) to include "a rule or code of conduct."

5. For example, my section heading was applied to research in artificial life by Kelly (1990) and Kelly (1994, 36–37, 479) notes the original use of the phrase by Rodney Brooks and Anita Flynn to describe their bold proposal for "a robot invasion of the solar system."

6. Indeed, much of what I say probably reflects my narrow experience with virtual communities of the academic flavor and exclusively on the Internet. For a broader point of view, starting from the communitarian WELL and reaching out to independent BBSs and FidoNet, see Howard Rheingold 1993, chap. 4.

7. PGP stands for Pretty Good Privacy: Public Key Encryption for the Masses, by Phil's Pretty Good Software, likely the most political piece of software in the world.

8. A fuller discussion would relate computer-mediated evolution to the evolution of ideas. Two stimulating introductions to cultural evolution are Richard Dawkins (1989, chap. 10) and Robert Boyd and Peter Richardson (1985).

9. Issues of ownership may be too prominent in the commons literature. Phil Agre offers this corrective: "The Internet is—a commons. What does that mean? Well, we're not talking about common ownership, since the Internet is owned by all sorts of organizations. Rather, we're talking about a certain social system within the Internet, which includes, for example, the convention that discussion lists are open to all" (1994, 3). On the other hand, I will suggest (under solutions to "Case 2: Mailing Lists," below) that list ownership is part of the solution.

10. I elaborate on the Hacker's Dilemma and problems for virtual communities in Danielson 1992a, sect. 1.2.3.

11. It doesn't follow because this argument commits the fallacy of composition: The "we" that cause the changes (at the limit, individually) are not the same "we" that might shape it (collectively). This is just to restate the so-called tragedy of the commons: that what each finds in her interest may not be in the common interest. Cf. Hardin 1968.

12. In Danielson 1992a, sect. 3.3.1, I called some of my proposals "moral engineering"; here I use "hack" to signal how far I deviate from professional engineering practice. However, there is a place for hacking as well as engineering. Perhaps no professional software engineer could let PGP loose, but wilder practice can be justifiable, especially if we work out mechanisms of responsibility and accountability.

13. Danielson 1992a builds on the computer simulations in Axelrod 1984 and the moral theory in Gauthier 1986. The section subtitle stresses the need to make these moral techniques into cues agents can discriminate upon. Cf. Danielson 1988.

14. See "Beyond Artificial Morality," below, for other limitations. Frank 1988 is more optimistic about human perceptual support for cooperative discrimination.

15. We shouldn't overlook that this is a remarkable new form of communication. See Danielson 1992b and Stodolsky 1989. Notice that anon.penet will automatically establish a pseudonym for me should I choose to reply to an43489. Notice as well the crucial role of the software agent—the remailer constitutes these two double-blinded personae by quite complex mediation.

16. This was a possibility I had never considered; the cryptic userids of some systems (which may also lack finger-like identifying utilities) amount to crude, de facto pseudonymity; a font substitution added mystery. There is a lesson here: Better a reasoned note than a moralistic reaction in case the perceived offense is rather a misunderstanding.

17. I spell this out explicitly to forestall the mistake of truncating it to: market. On the Net it is especially important not to assimilate all reciprocity and exchange to markets.

18. Indeed, the anon.penet server evolved to have these features because of an intense debate on Usenet. See Detweiler 1993 for an account.

19. For the latest version of this design, contact info@robo.ethics.ubc.ca.

20. I follow the LISTSERV convention which designates list moderators as "owners." We need not, of course, own the equipment on which our lists run.

21. The Usenet newsgroup <news.announce.newusers> periodically reposts summaries of the netiquette conventions. Brad Templeton provides a straight account (1994), and Horton and Spafford (1993) offer a sarcastic variation.

22. Brent Chapman's Majordomo Mail-list program offers some filtering. Philosophers will be aware of the need to complicate these schemes a bit, to allow quoted instances to be mentioned to the list, especially if this very filtering policy is to be discussed there, as it probably should, in the spirit of my general proposal.

23. The name is inspired by Emily Post in David Brin's novel, which takes the idea in the other direction: invasive sanctions for miscreants (1990, 325). Thus, Brin's idea is closer to Depew's (discussed above and in Wilson 1993 and Detweiler 1993) than to what I recommend.

24. Thanks to Rob Kling for noting my overemphasis on sanctioning in the conference version of this paper.

25. I am no jurist and, more cynically, I doubt that legal conflicts have evolved to be resolved this easily. As for the acronym soup, as a Canadian resident, I see this as an Americanism that I hope does not spread north too fast.

26. Actually, *I* can, as I have a Postscript® version of real UBC letterhead which I can send in NeXTMail®, but the profusion of trademarks should make the point: this doesn't do much good unless you have Postscript® and NeXTMail®, which you likely don't, given the (commendably) open system of e-mail. Perhaps there is a point here about metasolutions to convention problems: General and high standards might let us port existing conventional solutions with less reworking. Think how much easier fax machines are than e-mail in this regard; one simply uses existing letterhead, forms, and the like. Similarly, high-bandwith client interfaces, such as Mosiac, allow one easily to control sophisticated servers using familiar graphical user-interface tools.

27. The classic source for Mill's utilitarian defense of unrestricted harmless action is Mill 1861. I begin an application of these liberal arguments in Danielson 1992c.

References

A note on electronic texts. I have provided access information for all texts I obtained electronically. When quoting electronic documents, I have restored the emphasis, changing from *text* to *text* where appropriate. In citing unpaginated electronic texts, I have used the page numbers produced by the Unix pr command's default, thus extending a paper convention in the way suggested under "Case 3: E-mail as Tabula Rasa," above.

Agre, Phil. 1994. *The Network Observer,* Number 1:3. [Electronic document distributed through the Red Rock Eater NewsService. For back issues, send a message to the RRE server, rre-request@weber.ucsd.edu, with the subject line "archive send index".]

———. 1993. Networking on the Network. [Electronic document; to fetch the current version, send a message to rre-request@weber.ucsd.edu with the subject line "archive send network".]

Axelrod, Robert. 1984. *The Evolution of Cooperation.* New York: Basic Books.

Boyd, Robert, and Peter Richardson. 1985. *Culture and the Evolutionary Process.* Chicago: University of Chicago Press.

Brin, David. 1990. *Earth.* New York: Bantam Books.

Crawford, Rick. 1993. Computer-Assisted Crises. In *Invisible Crises,* ed. George Gerbner, Hamid Mowlana, and Herb Schiller. Boulder, CO: Westview Press.

[Electronic document available via ftp from Phil-Preprints.L.Chiba-U.ac.jp, under the filename /pub/preprints/Political_Phil/Crawford.Computer-assisted_Crises.]

Danielson, Peter. 1993a. How to Evolve Amoral Players: Artificial Morality and Genetic Programming. Research Report #1, Computer Modeling and Communication Group, Centre for Applied Ethics, University of British Columbia, Vancouver.

———. 1993b. Personal Responsibility. In *The Ethics of Atmospheric Change*, ed. Thomas Hurka and Harold Coward. London, Ontario: Wilfred Laurier Press.

———. 1992a. *Artificial Morality.* London: Routledge & Chapman Hall.

———. 1992b. Computer Ethics through Thick and Thin. In *Computer Ethics: Issues in Academic Computing; Proceedings of the First National Conference on Computing and Values.* New Haven: Research Center on Computing and Society.

———. 1992c. Ethics and the Internet. [Electronic document available via ftp from ucs.ubc.ca, under the filename /pub/docs/appropriate_use.]

———. 1988. The Visible Hand of Morality. *Canadian Journal of Philosophy* 18: 357–84.

Dawkins, Richard. 1989. *The Selfish Gene.* New ed. Oxford: Oxford University Press.

Detweiler, L. 1993. The Anonymity FAQ. [Electronic document available via ftp from rtfm.mit.edu, under the filename /pub/usenet/news.answers/netanonymity.]

Finney, Hal. 1993. How to Use the Cypherpunk Re-mailers. [Electronic document available via ftp from ftp://ftp.csua.soda.edu, under the filename /pub/ cypherpunks/re-mailer/hal's.instructions.gz.]

Frank, Robert. 1988. *Passions within Reason.* New York: Basic Books.

Gauthier, David. 1986. *Morals by Agreement.* Oxford: Oxford University Press.

Hardin, Garrett. 1968. The Tragedy of the Commons. *Science* 162: 1243–48.

Horton, Mark, and Gene Spafford. 1993. Rules for Posting to Usenet. [Posted periodically to the Usenet newsgroup <news.announce.newusers>]

Hughes, Eric. 1993. A Cypherpunk's Manifesto. Paper presented to the Computers, Freedom and Privacy Conference, 1993. [Electronic document available via ftp from ftp://ftp.csua.soda.edu, under the filename /pub/cypherpunks/rants/ A_Cypherpunk's_Manifesto.gz.]

Kelly, Kevin. 1994. *Out of Control.* Reading, MA.: Addison Wesley.

———. 1990. Perpetual Novelty: Selected Notes from the Second Artificial Life Conference. *Whole Earth Review* 67: 20–29.

Kollock, Peter, and Marc Smith. In press. Managing the Commons: Cooperation and Conflict in Computer Communities. In *Computer Mediated Communication,* ed. Susan Herring. Amsterdam: John Benjamins.

Levy, Steven. 1985. *Hackers: Heroes of the Computer Revolutions.* New York: Doubleday.

Markoff, John. 1994. Hopes and Fears on New Computer Organisms. *New York Times,* 6 January 1994, C1, C4.

Mill, John Stuart. 1861. *On Liberty.* In *The Philosophy of John Stuart Mill,* ed. Marshall Cohen. New York: Modern Library.

Oakeshott, Michael. 1962. *Rationalism in Politics and Other Essays.* London: Methuen.

Ostrom, Elinor. 1991. *Governing the Commons: The Evolution of Institutions for Collective Action.* Cambridge: Cambridge University Press.

Rezmierski, Virginia. 1993. Electronic Communications: Vapor or Paper? Balancing the Individual's Right to Privacy with the Public's Right to Know in the New Electronic Environment. Paper presented to American Association for the Advancement of Science-American Bar Association National Conference of Lawyers and Scientists Invitational Workshop on Legal, Ethical and Technological Aspects of Computer and Network Use and Abuse, 17–19 December, Irvine, California.

Rheingold, Harold. 1993. *The Virtual Community: Homesteading on the Electronic Frontier.* Reading, MA: Addison-Wesley.

Schelling, Thomas. 1960. *The Strategy of Conflict.* Cambridge: Harvard University Press.

Stodolsky, David. 1989. Protecting Expression in Teleconferencing: Pseudonym-based Peer Review Journals. *Canadian Journal of Educational Communication,* 18 (May). [Electronic document available in Communication Research and Theory Network (CRTNET), No. 175, from comserve@cios.llc.rpi.edu.]

Templeton, Brad. 1994. Emily Postnews Answers Your Questions on Netiquette. [Posted periodically to the Usenet newsgroup <news.announce.newusers>.]

Van Gelder, Leslie. 1991. The Strange Case of the Electronic Lover. In *Computerization and Controversy,* ed. C. Dunlop and R. Kling, 364–75. New York: Academic Press.

Webster's Ninth New Collegiate Dictionary. 1st digital ed. S.v. "agent."

Wilson, David. 1993. A Computer Program that Can Censor Electronic Messages Sets off a Furor. *Chronicle of Higher Education,* 12 May, A21, A25.

5

Intellectual Property Futures: The Paper Club and the Digital Commons

JOHN LAWRENCE

By intellectual property I mean the inventions of the mind—original ideas, expressions, and their "ownership." "Ownership of ideas" is both a morally and a legally recognized identification with the creation of a distinctive set of ideas and its attendant privileges—the right to derive prestige, the esteem of peers and subordinates, the appointments to positions that depend upon creativity, and income from such ownership. The most readily grasped examples of intellectual property and its privileges come from the commercial realm: the hula hoop, the frisbee, the recent novel *The Bridges of Madison County.* Each brought to its respective owner personal fame, patents or copyrights, and instant material rewards in the millions of dollars.

The dividends of intellectual property in the academy are more discretely veiled, less material—but real. We know well the story of happy fortune associated with having "good ideas" and expressing them nicely. Good ideas are published in the best journals; they become books at the best academic presses. Successful dissemination of good ideas confers rewards such as appointments at the best academic institutions, promotions and higher salaries, illustrious lectureships, Guggenheim or MacArthur fellowships, invitations to stay at the Villa Serboni, and reduced teaching loads meant to foster the production of more good ideas.

Unfortunately for the multitude of aspirants, all such rewards are scarce. Eminence is inherently hierarchical. Accordingly, the most impressive expressions of "good ideas" are carefully limited. Only a small fleet of university presses and journals—the so-called flagships—can hoist these best good ideas. And their embodiments are relatively expensive—nicely bound and jacketed, impeccably edited and designed, beautifully printed on quality paper and handsomely advertised. The "package" for the paper journal or book offers its own aesthetic frame, which—in addition to its informational content

—confers a bonus experience of connoisseurship upon the person who holds and looks at it. One sees nicely formed letters, specialized typographical effects such as italics, diacritical marks, and em-dashes, all elegantly reinforcing the ideational content of written expression.

And the sparse sources of the best good ideas have their own rigorous and well-vetted gatekeepers—editors, referees who credibly certify the pinnacle-of-the-hierarchy stature of the intellectual property conveyed to their audience. Their credentials as guardians must at least partially match or exceed those of the aspirants for performance within their paper frames.

I call this system the world of the paper club—"club" because of the emphasis on qualifications for membership and a resulting exclusion of the less talented. And it is "paper" because printed books and journals have for so long been the marks of membership in the elite group of the well-published.

The tone of my description may suggest my skepticism about the paper club's elite character. Although ambivalent about its snobbish tendencies, I hardly reject invitations to join. After all, my authorship of this essay proves that I wish to reaffirm my membership. I have always admired and consumed presentations of the club and have only regretted that I could not be a more exemplary member. Rather than denigrating the paper club, I hope here to describe its values and rules accurately so that we understand what it would mean to move beyond it.

The questions I raise are the following. What potential does digital communication have for challenging and changing the paper-based intellectual system of property and prestige that has reigned for so long in the universities? In what ways might electronic dissemination of ideas democratize the status system based on scholarly publishing? What kinds and levels of maturity must cyberdiscourse attain before it can take the central place now occupied by the paper club? And which publication forms are most likely to supersede paper? These questions are important because it is a commonplace that digital discourse will eventually displace paper as the medium of exchange. But given the entrenched privileges at the club, can we really believe that we are on the threshold of a new system of academic status? Can reading a scholar's words on a screen ever fully supplant reading them in a bound paper format?

I begin with some illustrative stories that suggest merits and hazards in all existing forms of scholarly communication—and some related possibilities for change. The examples will range from the rather formal world of paper publishing to the very informal, often raucous, disorienting world of list-based chatting. Don't be surprised if the answer lies somewhere between the extremes.

Snail-Paced Publishing at the Paper Club

In early 1987 I served as guest speaker in a lecture series aimed at publication. I came with a well-prepared text discussing the popular appeal of the Rambo films (of which there were two at that time). I edited intensively with a colleague who shared the platform and felt ready to publish within a few weeks after the lectures. We submitted text and illustrations to the university press in the spring of 1987.

Two and a half years passed. Then I received a letter indicating a delay of indefinite length while the university sought special financing for the book. I was invited to make any corrections or additions to the text. With a fresh eye on a thoroughly cooled-off text, I submitted one more lightly edited version.

Years passed and I heard nothing more. There could have been many causes of delay—financial concerns, procrastination by other contributors, postponement of the editor's work. My career did not depend on this publication, so I didn't ask and nobody explained. I eventually assumed that the book had died or that our contribution had been abandoned because an embarrassed editor felt it had become too outdated in the interval. Or perhaps referees had become involved who rejected our essay.

Then in December of 1993—without warning—a handsomely done book arrived (Metzger 1993). The Rambo piece was there. The pictures submitted as illustrations had disappeared—no doubt because of the cost of plates for the book. The six and a half years of production finally seemed well spent. But I felt a little embarrassed to tell my friends that my aging essay had just appeared! Sylvester Stallone's last Rambo film had appeared in 1988. By the early 1990s it seemed clear that he had retired both the Rocky and the Rambo characters. So much for engaged, timely commentary, I thought to myself. Despite the beauty of the volume as a whole and the elements in our essay that transcended the merely timely, the piece just seemed far too long delayed in its appearance.

This episode reminded me of the afflictions of young professors in publish-or-perish situations. How many times had I heard them complain about their uncertainty over the fate of a manuscript submitted to a university press or journal? I recalled the humiliating, deferential, and devious means through which they had sought information from those they suspected of acquaintance with referees for the journals, and then, following rejections phrased in vague formulas to the effect of ''Your work does not quite fit our publishing program at this time,'' repeated submissions of those same manuscripts to other journals and presses. Much bitterness and sense of hopelessness in academe comes from such experiences of ambivalence and unpredictability. When one's path to tenure depends on timely publication in a notable journal, the whole process will be seen with ambivalence and frustration.

Another example of paper publishing involved a much shorter but also frustrating delay. As everyone knows, the Gulf War occasioned by Iraq's invasion of Kuwait focused world attention intensely between late July 1990 and March 1991. In the United States, we saw relatively unlimited media coverage and strong efforts to mobilize citizen support for service personnel with yellow ribbons, flags, rallies, and parades. Patriotic merchandising of t-shirts, mugs, and trading cards was evident in many communities.

I am a member of groups—the Popular Culture Association and the American Culture Association—that frequently direct their scholarly attention to contemporary social behavior. For their national meetings in the spring of 1992, it was possible to have thematic presentations related to the Gulf War. I attended all the panels on the topic and had the immediate inspiration to pull together several pieces into a theme edition of the *Journal of American Culture* (1994) that would carry the title "Desert Storm: The Public Spectacle." I had been impressed with how quickly and intelligently my contributors had taken to the streets and done their "flash scholarship" during the Gulf Crisis —in several cases taking important documentary photographs that were later printed in the journal. The editor of the journal agreed and the project began.

Given the short span of the war itself and given the alertness required to do "field work" associated with the project, I felt it appropriate to publish the special issue of the journal as close to the events as possible. The value of the discussions to our readers would depend in part on evoking memories of experiences they had during the brief period of the war. Too long a delay could lead to the extinction of those recollections. My contributors shared this common feeling of urgency about getting to print, and all managed to meet their manuscript deadlines by August 1992, at which time the manuscripts went to press. And moving faster than is usual for an academic journal, the special issue appeared in April 1994. It had moved from raw convention presentation to publication in less than two years. Yet I still had the feeling that we lacked the desired "timeliness" and that academic print publication was a significant obstacle to scholarship on contemporary events. I did not want to equate scholarship with journalism, because the latter lacks depth in theory and citations of literature related to the subjects of discussion. Subsequent experiences in the world of electronic publication strengthened my belief in the validity of timely scholarly commentary.

Electronic Publishing in the Digital Commons

In the month following my long-delayed Rambo publication, I became a co-moderator with Peter Rollins for a listserv-based forum of the Popular

Culture and American Culture Associations. A "moderated list" is a group of electronically linked subscriber-contributors who communicate with one another about topics of common interest. Any acceptable message "posted to the list" will eventually appear in the e-mailbox of every subscriber. Some of the contemporary academic lists have more than a thousand subscribers.

Moderators for a list can communicate without delay to these large audiences. They sometimes feel like disk jockeys. They don't want air silence for too long a period. Otherwise, subscribers might complain that "nothing ever happens" at their list and sign themselves off. Occasionally, I decided that our list was too quiet and needed some stimulus to discussion. If I wanted to write a short "starter essay" on a subject—for example, the gendered character of computer use, the alleged existence of Generation X—I could sit at my computer, compose a call for a discussion thread, compile a brief bibliography, and transmit it immediately to the list. These messages could flow at any time of the day or night, workdays or weekends. I knew from the review of my subscribers that messages were flying to Kazakhstan, England, Finland, and Italy, as well as the North American continent. I worked with a sense of immediacy and reach that I had never felt with the mail or the telephone.

The subscribers of the list had the same freedom to frame a response or to loft a proposed discussion topic of their own. The only rules for publication to the list were ones of self-identification (no anonymous postings), civility toward other members of the list, and focus on the topics germane to our associations. Participants in the list ranged from freshly launched graduate students to professors at lesser-known colleges and universities to well-seasoned, widely published professors at major universities.

As moderator, I noticed that thoughtful multiparagraph responses to postings often came back to the list within a few hours, and these messages came from—and went to—everywhere: a miniessay from a subscriber-contributor in Delaware; a few hours later, a reply from a scholar in Mexico; three hours more and an enthusiastic observation from someone in California; then a contradiction from Vermont. Anyone who has participated in a scholarly list will recognize these as technologically remarkable but familiar experiences. For such reasons, electronic communication has rightly been celebrated as a radical new form of professional discourse and personal development.

The list-based publication also fulfilled my ideal for "flash scholarship." As an example, it was quite apparent in the week of 12–19 June 1994 that the murder of Nicole Brown Simpson and arrest of O. J. Simpson would provide a mirror of contemporary American values in conflict. After O. J. Simpson's televised flight in the white Bronco—as some of his fans stood at the roadside and cheered for him—the subject seemed imperative in a forum committed to the analysis of contemporary cultural values and conflicts. My co-moderator and I issued a call for discussion on Saturday evening, 18 June (H-PCAACA 1994). By Sunday morning, several substantial, literately worded, thought-provoking comments had already arrived for immediate posting to the list. Suitable messages about attitudes, laws, and social statistics continued to arrive for more than a week. Because remarks were concurrent with developing events, each person who read the postings in the list could immediately apply freshly stated insights to the additional evidence that continued to stream past in the popular media and behavior. "Flash scholarship" had finally found its proper medium!

A few decades ago, A. J. Liebling made a cynical remark to the effect that "freedom of the press is guaranteed for the person who can buy one." Reflecting on these adventures in scholarly CMC, I felt that we list members all owned our press. We had a freedom to publish that is quite foreign to the world of waiting for the printed-paper manuscript to appear. We were part of a digital commons where the exclusions of the paper club seldom intruded. It fulfilled the ideal of democratic discourse where the status of the speaker has no effect on her ability to speak to a scholarly audience.

The reason was that my co-moderator and I made few decisions about the quality of the remarks we published. Our publication space was abundant and friendly. So long as remarks could be understood and were basically literate, we published. Occasionally we posted items with spelling errors, which we accepted as part of the conventions of our fast-paced, conversational medium. After all, our contributors were not professional secretaries, and many did not have the means to run spelling checkers on the files they transmitted to us. And as volunteers working without release time for our editorial tasks, my co-moderator and I chose not to process them through our computers for thorough error correction. We understood the mandate of our forum as the expression of ideas rather than the perfection of form.

The List That Suddenly Disappeared

The list I moderated was not the only one I knew. The list-curious can get lists of lists by topic and even lists of new lists (*Internet Unleashed* 1994). I could sign up for an additional list at any time, usually without even identifying myself beyond stating my name. I only had to reckon with the consequence to my e-mailbox. Once subscribed to a list, I could say anything in response to virtually any topic. The digital commons is friendly to most every voice that expresses itself with decency and pertinence.

Some experiences with another, short-lived list compelled me to think about the deep, long-standing attributes of the paper club. The list was associated with the American Society for Aesthetics and called itself ASA-L (1994). I had the misfortune of joining ASA-L within three weeks of its death—or "cryogenic suspension" might be more accurate: Its opening banner to members had announced that it was "experimental," so perhaps its history is not yet concluded.

The very first idea I heard expressed on the list was a call for a bad-writing contest; substantial new books were offered as prizes. A single horrible sentence from a contemporary work in philosophy or cultural commentary would suffice to bring home the booty. As Dennis Dutton put it, "Our challenge is to come up with the ugliest, most stylistically awful single sentence —or two, or at most three sentences—out of an academic book or article." He quoted favorably from one source he admired and then contrasted it with a text by John Spanos that he characterized as "a turgid, unrelenting diatribe against liberal, Enlightenment values in education." He compared his reading experience of the book to "swimming through porridge" (Dutton 1994). He wrote:

> Consider, as a typical instance of what follows it, Spanos's very first sentence: "This book was instigated by the publication of the Harvard Core Curriculum Report in 1978 and was intended to respond to what I took to be an ominous educational reform initiative that, without naming it, would delegitimate the decisive, if spontaneous, disclosure of the complicity of liberal American institutions of higher learning with the state's brutal conduct of the war in Vietnam and the consequent call for opening the university to meet the demands by hitherto marginalized constituencies of American society for enfranchisement." (Spanos 1992, xi)

It became clear in Professor Dutton's commentary that more than literary style was the issue here. A way of thinking and its vocabulary were targets of his scorn, particularly when he examined a sentence from the chapter titled "The Violence of Disinterestedness." Spanos had called the advocacy of impartiality (by Arnold, Babbitt, and I. A. Richards) "a recurrent call for the recuperation of a logocentric pedagogy in the face of historical ruptures that betrayed the complicity of humanistic discourse with an essentially reactionary bourgeois ideology and its discreetly repressive capitalist state apparatuses, which have dominated the vision and practices of liberal Western industrial societies, especially in North America" (Spanos 1992, 118–19). Dutton ridiculed the idea of calling liberal discourse values "violent" while leaving no point on the scale for the tanks of Tienanmen Square, the military regime of Haiti, and the like. Having morally critiqued the outlook of Spanos, he invited the entire list to find a single horrible sentence in any contemporary text and to claim the book prizes. (He later clarified that citations from the

Spanos text were not candidates in the proposed contest, but only examples of the horrors to be found in contemporary cultural criticism.)

Thereafter, a boisterous, fascinating discussion ensued. One angry list member called the whole idea of such a contest "puerile" and announced his intention to unsubscribe himself from the list. In mockery of this rejection, the thread of discussion was christened by some as "Puerile Puerilities," and more "wonderfully bad" examples came in. A subscriber dropped off the list. Speculation developed within the list as to whether this person was quietly disgusted with the "puerile" thread. The report later came back that he had merely unsubscribed his mailbox for a vacation period.

Then a marvelous thrust came in defense of stimulating obscurity. Participant G. V. Wilkes introduced a text by Guy DeBord, *Society as Spectacle,* acknowledging that its thoughts were rendered "in only the most high density and obscure, Hegelian 'epigrammatic style.' " Continuing in his praise of the obscure, Wilkes (1994) elaborated:

> Like a modernist poem . . . DeBord's little book fiercely resists a facile reading, and demands the active engagement of the reader. It was almost, though not quite, as difficult as my struggle to master Deconstruction. This is the essence of writing as a critical practice as it is found in some quarters (especially within the ranks of the political/cultural left). It is writing that is deliberately self-conscious, that deliberately calls attention to itself rather than making itself unfelt and invisible, gesturing away from itself as prose of the "transparent," Official Style asks us to do.

Then came a civil, but pointedly critical reply from Don Keefer (1994):

> A desire to leave Hegel at his word, to experience the poetry of Hegel, it seems to me is either to dwell in the mystery of incomprehension or to endeavor to keep it all to oneself. Hegel could barely speak, so accounts of his lecturing report. Should we stammer and stutter in our lectures the way current descendants of his bad writing, such as DeBord, stammer and trip over their words?

As this lively conversation flowed back and forth a few more people dropped off, some sending inarticulate cries to the list—"I want off!" and "How do I get off!" (They had apparently erased the "Info Refcards" that came with their subscriptions and were unaware of how to sign off from a list.) Some didn't even sign their complaints, so that a reader had to study the headers for the identity of authors.

Just when I was becoming interested enough to start saving every fragment of this lively discussion, the list disappeared. A Senior Systems Programmer at the college hosting ASA-L had been delegated the task of announcing its suspension. In his words:

> I have been requested by the ASA-L list maintainer to shut down the ASA-L list. Effective immediately, the ASA-L list is no longer in operation. It is the hope of the list maintainer that ASA-L will revive in the future, perhaps under different circumstances. (Sturm 1994)

I was curious and wanted to know about the circumstances of the shutdown. Had the list maintainer been spammed (that is, e-bombed) into withdrawal by the proponents of postmodernist critique? Or was the disappearance merely a technical or logistical problem related to the list maintainer's access to the Internet? And could I manage to retrieve the interesting thread about obscurity and lucidity in contemporary philosophical style? I wanted to use them in a contemporary philosophy course to illustrate the vigor of debate about fundamental values.

I sent a message to the system administrator who had announced the death of the list. I requested answers to some of my questions. He merely promised to forward my message to the list maintainer.

Then I attempted to retrieve the log files for the transactions to the list. The mailserver that hosted the list apparently contained none. I then tried to find the name of the list in one of the lists of lists provided on the Internet. I hoped that I could find the name of an editor or organization that might have saved the log files for the discussions in ASA-L. No success. (I found a list with an identical name, but it turned out to be the African American Students Association.) From some of the members of the list whose contributions I had saved I was able to retrieve via Internet some interesting fragments. But the entire thread of discussion was inaccessible to me. I later obtained the name and e-mail address of the list maintainer, but was unable to elicit response to my queries.

This incident taught me in a concrete way about the ephemeral, inaccessible character of casually organized ''listcourse'' used principally as a conversational medium. Regardless of the intrinsic merit of the ideas expressed, their documentation and retrieval required diligence and luck that lay beyond me. But my futile search for the discussion thread led me to think more analytically and appreciatively about the virtues of the paper club.

By contrast to the most free-flowing, semiorganized listcourse, the paper-centered universe affords powerful, redundant indexing and stable accessibility of its contents. Checking a couple of flagships in the paper flotilla, I determined that *Ethics: An International Journal of Social, Political and Legal Philosophy,* published by the University of Chicago Press, had been issued continuously since 1890. Its contents were indexed in some nineteen sources, including, of course, *The Philosophers Index*. It was available in microform and offered a reprint service. *Mind,* published by Oxford University Press, had been published since 1876. Twelve indexes—available in paper, microform, and reprint formats—tracked its contents. Both journals also received full entries in *Ulrich's Guide to Periodicals*. By comparison, the ASA-L was like a conversation overheard in a subway.

I don't mean to offer the career of the ASA-L that I knew as a limiting model for electronic discourse. (Many lists, for example, have made a commitment to maintain permanent, indexed electronic archives of their transactions.) But ASA-L helps us to understand what the mature integration of scholarly e-communication will eventually demand of us.

The Values of the Paper Club: Requirements for a Cybercentric Prestige

The centrality of the paper club to academic esteem rests significantly on the indexing of texts, understandable methods of access to those texts, and the stability of sources for those texts. The underlying premise for these values is related to the understanding of what critical scholarship requires: whatever claims excellence must readily present itself for inspection and evaluation; and scholarship as collective enterprise demands that the building blocks be available for new constructions. We can measure with real exactness the values of availability, access, and stability in the paper world. We can also make a necessarily rougher estimate of the contemporary achievements for scholarly cybertexts.

Index: We Must Know What Texts Are Available

The paper world sets a high standard for any rival to match. The previously mentioned *Ulrich's Guide* is a world-encompassing annual publication whose thirty-second edition lists more than 140,000 periodical titles categorized according to 966 subject headings. The conceptual reach of these headings is extended by a "Cross Index to Subjects." *Ulrich's Guide* provides editorial and subscription information plus obituaries (9,176), birth announcements (11,000+), and title changes.

Books receive indexed coverage in Bowker's annual *Books in Print,* which in paper form provides listings in separate volumes by subject, by author name, and by title. The 1993–1994 edition provided information for 1,153,000 books from more than 41,000 American publishers. In its electronic form, available through numerous online vendors (such as DIALOG), it provides all this information simultaneously, with strong retrospective information on books no longer available. The power of the indexing in *Books in Print* is amplified by the *Library of Congress Subject Guide,* which provides a thesaurus of descriptor terms that can be applied within the subject guides. Library of Congress classifications are provided by professional indexers who typically specialize in the subject fields they index.

Next comes the question that bears on the electronic displacement of paper. What kind of indexing is provided for the electronic world? Here one should not mistake the momentary state, which is rapidly changing, with the possible. But, as of this writing, the search for scholarly texts in the electronic world frustrates even the most technically proficient searcher. The problem is less one of disorder than lack of order.

Just compare the travel based on paper tracks to a trip through a typical gopher space. If one wants to know, for example, what printed books have been written on the Gulf War of 1990–1991, one can apply typical Library of Congress descriptor terms such as "Persian Gulf Conflict, 1990–91" or "Persian Gulf War." A single search in the electronic *Books in Print* yields more than 120 titles. If one wants to know what commentary on the Gulf War exists in periodical literature, one can use guides such as *Magazine Index, Historical Abstracts, U.S. History and Life,* or CARL's *Uncover/Reveal* to quickly identify thousands of printed commentaries. With the exception of *Uncover,* the periodical citation databases exist in both paper and electronic formats.

But suppose we want to search this same topic in gopher space. We hop onto the Internet at our local university and typically confront options to use Lynx or World Wide Web (WWW), gophers of particular universities, or a sweeping invitation to use "all the gopher servers in the world." At some point within the maze of possibilities, we receive a prompt inviting us to type in the subject of our gopher search. We insert "Gulf War" and then see the message "Searching. . . ."; we might wait for ten minutes, leave for lunch, come back, and the gopher is still searching. At this point, we attempt various keystroke combinations to unlock ourselves from a search that has no apparent terminus.

Or perhaps we have been told something more helpful—that a particular gopher, say, the Supreme Court server at Cornell University Law School (FATTY.LAW.CORNELL), carries the text of all Supreme Court decisions since 1990. You search for the one you want—say, *Feist v. Rural Telephone* —and find that it isn't there. You back out to a higher vantage point on gopher space and begin making your way through the tunnels of Project Hermes, a group of servers organized to disseminate legal documents and information. The Case Western Reserve legal gopher looks promising. You attempt to go via gopher commands and your connection is denied. But you are stubborn and resourceful. You wait for a while and telnet to the Case Western Reserve host computer and actually reach a directory that contains the sought-for decision. You attempt to retrieve it but the file transfer aborts because of a line condition or some peculiarity of your own institution's host system. You retreat after trying this a couple of times and decide to send an e-mail message to Case requesting the decision. It turns out that you must know the precise document number because you are making the request from an automated listserver. You didn't write down the number when you were in the directory at CWRC. So you telnet back to look into the directory again. But this time, too many users are aboard and your access to the host system is denied. You resolve to deal with the problem just before you go to bed, hoping that you will get access at an off-peak time. This time you get the document number and send a listserver request by e-mail. Bingo! The next morning you have your document—another electronic miracle on the Internet. But the aftertaste of the incident is a wish for a better navigational map.

I have not mentioned a single issue here that has not been widely discussed. Gopher administrators around the world are working on the problems of naming files, indexing them, and coordinating selective efforts to develop electronic documents for the world community. And some gopher servers are beautifully organized to give you immediate, intuitive access to documents and send them to your e-mailbox immediately (e.g., gopher.nwu.edu). But the current reality is that gopher's original or early states feel amateurish from a paper-centered indexical standpoint. This is not a criticism of the efforts that have gone into gopher development, but simply a recognition of early immaturity. But without central responsibility and conceptual categories for indexing, we are unlikely to move very far beyond the serendipities of gopher discovery (Plotkin 1993).

Similar observations can be made about the development of electronic journals. Electronic publishers are certainly aware of the difference between casual "listcourse" and refereed journals for which the gatekeepers make qualitative judgments about the value of what they deliver to their readers. Many electronic journals are, in fact, duplicating the efforts at quality control in the paper world and attempting to deliver formal scholarly commentary that matches paper counterparts. They are doing so at speeds and prices that argue for their inevitable triumph, a point to which we will return later.

Access: There Must Be Standardized, Reliable Ways to Gain
the Texts We Want

In illustrating the navigational issue, I have also indicated some of the access problems. The experiences described are those typically encountered by persons who are relatively proficient, fearless, and stubborn in using their computers. Many scholars, to the extent that they use computers, are uncomfortable with any task beyond word processing. They can never be frustrated in the ways just described because they are unlikely, unless prompted or coerced, to begin internavigating for their primary or commentary texts. By mid-1994, there were several hundred books dealing with how to use the Internet. To read the books titles is to recognize the widespread frustration among users, the desire for a magic talisman that will open the right doors: *Internet for the Mac for Dummies, The Internet Troubleshooter: Help for the Logged-On and Lost, Internet Slick Tricks, Internet Express Lane* (with disk), *The PC Internet Tour Guide: Cruising the Internet the Easy Way* (with disk). (The latter two remind me of the several books about the Internet that have arrived with shareware disks. I could not make any of the "simplifying" interfaces work.) A market has also developed for books that popularize the Unix operating system that one often directly confronts in Internet. Que's *I Hate Unix* frankly acknowledges that the Unix prompt is mystifying for many Net users.

Suppose, happily, that a scholar solves the navigational and access issues; there remain accuracy and formatting issues in the texts they receive. Transmissions are seldom perfect, frequently dropping lines, words, or letters. An often-heard guideline is that 95 percent accuracy is normal. Pretending that one could have a text printed with a uniform pagination that permits one to make page references, how should one cope with the missing 3 to 5 percent? Criticize the author for omissions? Clip out the apparently damaged portion and send it to the author and ask what's missing? Post on a scholarly list and invite others to send a more authoritative portion of that text? These are irritations that scholarship will find it difficult to accept.

Stability of the Source: Texts Referred to Must Remain Available

Print technology has existed for centuries. Many of the individual texts from the birth of printing still exist in legible form. But computer file formats change often. Many scholars have owned evolutionary versions of the same word processor in which the file formats change every two or three years. Files become retrospectively compatible, that is, a later version of the program can read files from the previous version or two. Some of the gopher/ftp-accessible documents are stored in contemporary file formats such as Word-Perfect 5.1, Word, Postscript, or Macintosh. (They sometimes cause system crashes when loaded into the appropriate word processor.) But what about twenty to thirty years from now? We already know that some electronically stored texts have already been lost. Assorted technical and administrative initiatives aim to prevent this happening again (*Accuracy and Accountability in Scholarly Information* 1994), but will they succeed?

The Future of Electronic Discourse

In 1983, Ithiel de Solla Pool wrote that "increasingly the most economical way of moving, storing, and displaying words is electronically. The use of paper is becoming a luxury" (190). This understanding, first articulated in the

1960s (Bagdikian 1971), has been qualified since de Solla Pool reiterated the idea. We probably use *more* paper today in printing the information that computers bring to us. And because digital text can be manipulated so easily, we are printing versions of our text more often than we could in the typewriter era. But despite the new outpourings of paper, *relative* cost is a powerful ally in the shift from paper to e-text in the context of formal publication. The cost, for example, of electronically transmitting and laser printing a Supreme Court decision is virtually negligible when compared to the cost of traveling to a law library and making photocopies. A reliable electronic method of locating and transmitting documents will provide a powerful economic incentive for users to abandon paper sources. But the same inducements for users will raise the threshold of fear among producers of information who have traditionally disseminated through the paper media (Plotkin 1993).

But where will the economic appeals of e-discourse make the most decisive thrusts at the paper club's current monopoly on status? I suggest two areas that may provide the most leverage—CD-ROM publishing and electronically delivered book reviews. These two ventures alone, however, will be insufficient to move the current center of gravity unless the world of electronically distributed scholarship can improve its indexing and remote-access problems.

Publishing on CD-ROM

To this moment in the history of scholarship, CD-ROM has been a parasitic publication form. It has specialized in republishing materials that first saw the light of day in the paper world. As the republication of historical source materials becomes prohibitive in paper formats, CD-ROM can provide low-cost, high-density text packages. With storage capacities at 550 mega-bytes, it is actually difficult to find coherent bodies of material to fill a single disk. The InteLex Corporation, in its Past Masters series, has exploited this enormous capacity with its "custom burn" service, in which the customer can specify that a number of different textbases be placed on a single CD-ROM (InteLex 1994). For example, if one wants an English philosophy collection, one can take on a single disk the collected works of Hobbes, the works of Locke, Berkeley, and Hume, and the complete works of the Utilitarians from Jeremy Bentham through Henry Sidgwick. Since the Folio Views program, which provides the user with text-search and -retrieve capabilities, also compresses the texts placed on CD-ROM, the entire line of texts—from Plato and Aristotle through Wittgenstein—occupies only 30 megabytes on a single disk.

Not only are the works themselves drawn from the recognized critical editions; they are further accompanied by powerful, swift search engines that compensate for weak text indexing in the original sources. They also permit the building of personal concordances. In conjunction with the fact that some important works have become unavailable in paper form, these CD-ROM editions become the only thinkable alternative for the scholar who aspires to a complete collection in the field of study. (Some of the Wittgenstein corpus, for example, is otherwise available only in bound volumes of association proceedings that do not circulate.) There are also signs that CD-ROM will become the medium of first publication for creating new corpi of major figures (InteLex 1994).

As further argument for the ability of CD-ROM texts to occupy a respected place in the world of scholarship, I note that they are being favorably reviewed in mainstream paper journals. Leading universities are purchasing them for their collections and, in some instances, placing them on local area or client server networks. The beautiful book is thus displaced by a disk that cannot even be seen when it is doing its work of yielding text to its reader.

But if CD-ROMs qualify as digital discourse, we must remember how long they have been sitting as beggars outside the doors of the paper club, merely reproducing what had already received its imprimatur in the traditional form. Given the peculiar packages of information that are well suited to its formats, we cannot expect it to quickly move the center away from paper.

There are other reasons, however, to think that e-space might become a primary publication, the location of choice for at-the-pinnacle intellectual discourse.

Timely Book Reviews and Critical Exchanges

One reason that the paper club has so tenaciously retained its position of supremacy is that timeliness often does not matter. What significant difference does it make to the world of ideas whether Elaine Pagels's *The Gnostic Gospels* is published in 1979 or 1980? Or Robert Nozick's *Anarchy, State and Utopia* is published in 1974 or 1977? Where the subject of a book is esoteric or antiquarian, timeliness hardly matters at all.

Book reviews are another matter. Psychologically, the best time for a review comes at the moment of its publication. The advertising staff is best prepared to publicize the work. The author's identification with the text is probably strongest—she has pushed to get the text done, peaked in her mastery of material. With passing time, an author becomes more distanced from her own material, perhaps a little forgetful about what she said or precisely why; less agile, energetic, precise about elaborating, defending the text. The feelings of ''Did I say that? Really? I wonder why?'' may set in. The world of ideas may thus lose the best ''performance'' of those ideas in terms of the author becoming engaged in discussions.

A more commercial consideration is that some books will actually be out of print before they are reviewed. Examine a flagship journal and check the year of publication for the books reviewed. It is rare to see a book title that is less than two years behind the publication date of the journal and common to see books that are three or four years old (*Ethics* 1994; *American Society of Church History* 1994). Yet, in the world of trade publishing, which yields many titles of interest to scholarship (for example, the memoirs of retired public figures or timely books on contemporary social problems such as abortion, gun control, and so on), the time between release and remainder sales and out-of-print status can be less than two years. Some books are actually being reviewed after they have gone out of print! This means that someone influenced by a review to read the book would have to borrow the book or have the luck to buy it from a remainder outlet! This kind of delay subverts the recommending purpose of a review.

The review situation is even worse when we look at the college textbook scene. Publishers maintain short edition lives in order to outwit the used-book markets. Many suppliers will not even list price or edition information in *Books in Print* because such information would so often be out of date. Some textbooks are distributed only in a single printing before they are revised, requiring the professor and student to buy a new edition so that the publisher can make a new "first sale" to the market. Even though textbooks are enormously important to instruction, scholarly publishing's paper world moves too slowly to consistently review books that actually remain in print at the time a review appears.

These problems of delay are easily overcome in the electronic journal or list. A writer can publish a review almost at the moment of completion, even in a refereed electronic journal. Books are typically assigned to scholars of known capability. When their reviews come in, lengthy editorial consulting about whether to publish is not required. In any case, an electronically submitted review can be quickly shared within an electronic network and published within mere months, if not weeks, of the book's initial appearance.

To illustrate, consider *The Law and Politics Book Review* that is electronically published to free subscriptions by the Law and Courts Section of the American Political Science Association. For nonsubscribers, the reviews can be selected through a "push button gopher" that will mail selected reviews to the tunneler's address. In its reviews published during April and May 1994, the oldest book was published in 1992. Most books reviewed had been published in 1993 and some in 1994. Consider what you would like as a reader—reviews of books from the past two years, weighted toward those published within the last six to twelve months and delivered cost free, or reviews of books published in the last two to four years, delivered in expensive bound volumes that will increasingly occupy your limited shelf space or that of your library? Once the logic of electronic book reviews becomes widely understood, it is easy to imagine that they will become the norm.

We can also anticipate lively new discussion formats associated with book reviews. Why not have, for example, authors of books responding to their reviews in the same issue of the e-journal that publishes the review? They might even speak to a panel of reviewers (Jensen 1994). Richard Jensen of H-Net has called the rhythm of contemporary debate in print a "slow-motion, intellectual ping pong." To illustrate the attention-span problems in an overtly journalistic medium that aims at timely exchanges, consider the *New York Review of Books* discussions of Jason Epstein's 21 April 1994 review of the film *Schindler's List.* The 9 June 1994 issue contained extended comments from Marion Doenhoff, editor of *Die Zeit* in Hamburg, and London playwright Harold Pinter. Many readers would find it difficult to follow such detailed discussions without picking up Epstein's review again. In the same issue, two other letters of criticism from less well known persons were directed to Joyce Carol Oates for an article that she wrote on 24 March. And these will occasion additional letters weeks or months later. Who can remember long enough fully to appreciate such comments?

In a parallel example from a more professionally focused publication, the *Proceedings and Addresses of the American Philosophical Association* (1992) have carried an extended, acrimonious debate between Christina Sommers, who offended many feminists by her allegations that they are intolerant, and numerous feminist detractors, who insist that they have been maligned. The letters go on for pages in numerous issues of the *Proceedings.* But the intervals for the publications mean that much of the context for the critical ripostes has been forgotten. Some of the letters that came in were directed at letters published not in the previous issue but in earlier issues. The issue of September 1993, for example, contains letters referencing the discussions of January and June 1992. A debate of this kind could move far more swiftly in electronic formats. The dialectics would be more instructive to more people, because they could retain in memory more of what they need to know to understand the critical differences in the discussions. Again, as with the book review, the logic of electronic discourse becomes difficult to resist.

The Coming Shift?

Making predictions about the adoption or rejection of a technology can make one a comic figure in hindsight. The *New York Times* of 1947 buried its announcement regarding the creation of the transistor in "News of the Radio" —where the principal application forecast was "to develop better hearing aids for the deaf." In 1949 IBM foresaw a world computer market for ten to fifteen units. The VCR's anticipated uses were restricted to television stations (*Stanford Observer* 1994). What is common to these errors is that they fail to envision new possibilities. More generous, imaginative forecasts would have fit the future better.

I have tried to show here that electronics can play a valuable role in the evolution of our scholarship and publication. I would rather err on the side of generosity, given the remarkable achievements in communication that have emerged in the past decade. I can comfortably envision that electronic publication will rapidly and rightfully claim a much more important position in the world of intellectual property and academic prestige. We are doubtless decades away from a thorough shift toward electronic discourse. In the meantime, there will be many slow logons, failed gopher connections, files mutilated in ftp transmission, and countless other irritations. The electronic future is not filled with unremitting happiness.

But as we experience these frustrations, let us not forget that we order beautiful, precious books for our libraries and they don't come for months. We go to the world's greatest libraries to experience their riches and discover that the book we want is checked out—perhaps to a professor who has no obligation to return it. Or maybe we walk the stacks and see that many books have been heaped on the floor rather than being shelved. Perhaps the student worker had a final exam and didn't show up. Or maybe the state legislature is in the second year of its fiscal crisis and has denied the library sufficient funding for staff to keep the books shelved during the academic year. The assets at the paper club cannot be brought to bear upon these ills. The time has come for the club, if not to yield its supremacy as the location for the most important ideas, at least to share it with a technology that can compensate for its sluggish, traditional ways of delivering the word to a world that craves to read.

Annotated References

Accuracy and Accountability in Scholarly Information: A Symposium—The Quality of Information in the Electronic Age. 1994. Prospectus for a conference at McGill University, Montreal, Quebec, 12–13 August 1994. The program included sessions such as "Dealing with Delusion and Duplicity," a discussion of electronic peer reviewing; "Quality and Electronic Publishing: An Oxymoron?"; "Is Quality an Outmoded Concept in the Electronic Age?" These are typical subjects at contemporary forums on scholarly publishing.

American Society of Church History. 1994. 63.1. This publication, which has a license to express more antiquarian tastes, has three reviewed books that were published in 1988. The largest cluster of books reviewed was in 1991. The freshest books (three of them) had been published in 1993.

ASA-L@MAILSERV.MTROYAL.AB.CA. 1994. This was a list for a group called the American Society for Aesthetics. Stan Godlovitch was identified as the list maintainer at the time of the incidents described. The host computer was at Mount Royal College in Canada.

Bagdikian, Ben. 1971. *The Information Machines: Their Impact on Men and the Media.* New York: Harper. Badgdikian presents survey information about beliefs of personnel in the news media. Though there were many disbelievers, it was widely believed that electronic data transmission systems would replace paper.

de Solla Poole, Ithiel. 1983. *Technologies of Freedom.* Cambridge: Harvard University Press.

Dutton, Dennis. 1994. Bad Writing Contest. Electronic posting to ASA-L, 25 May.

Ethics 104 (3 April 1994). Books selected for reviews were published from 1991 to 1992. The "freshest" book reviewed thus had a lag time of about two years.

InteLex Corporation. 1994. Past Masters Winter Catalogue. InteLex Corp., P.O. Box 1827, Clayton, GA 30525–1827. E-mail address: 70671.1673@compuserve.com. Bradley Lambert of InteLex provided some information on the series in a telephone conversation with the author. InteLex is planning to put out a new critical edition of works by and on Henry Sidgwick.

The Internet Unleashed. 1994. Indianapolis: Sams. This large resource book contains information on lists and how to maintain currency in the knowledge of lists. It also contains a disk that generates a list of Listserv groups.

H-PCAACA@MSU.EDU. This is the list of the American Culture and Popular Culture Associations that forms a part of H-Net, hosted by the University of Illinois at Chicago. Archival files available from the author: send e-mail request to js1001@ chief. morningside. edu.

Jensen, Richard. 1994. Conversations with the author. Jensen, Executive Director of H-Net (a group of history-related lists with thousands of subscribers), has proposed that interactive reviewer-author formats become the norm for book reviews at H-Net.

Journal of American Culture 17.1. 1994. See "Desert Storm: The Public Spectacle," 1–58.

Keefer, Don. 1994. Reply to G.V. Wilkes, posted to ASA-L@MAILSERV. MOUNTROYAL.AB.CA on June 1.

The Law and Politics Book Review (ISSN 1062–7421). Electronic journal: to subscribe, send e-mail "SUBSCRIBE LPBR-L your name" to: LISTSERV@LISTSERV. ACNS.NWU.EDU.

Metzger, Robert, ed. 1993. *Transforming Texts: Classical Images in New Contexts.* Lewisburg, PA: Bucknell University Press. See Robert Jewett and John Lawrence, "Rambo and the Myth of Redemption," 63–83.

Plotkin, Wendy. 1993. Electronic Texts in the Historical Profession: Perspectives of Historians, Governments, Libraries, Academic Computing Centers. Unpublished, comprehensive version of 23 August 1993. This is a wide-ranging, detailed survey that describes numerous technical initiatives aimed at giving electronic texts either parity with paper sources or superiority over them. This theme, however, is not central to her treatment. She also condenses much of the economic argument over electronic distribution that has occurred among publishers. Among her listed sources is the journal *Scholarly Publishing* from the University of Toronto, which has been discussing the quality, delivery, and economic issues in e-publication for more than a decade. See, for example, Daniel Eisenberg, "The Electronic Journal," 20.2 (October 1988), 49–58; and idem, "Problems of the Paperless Book," 21.1 (October, 1989), 11–26. An e-publication that deals with a range of such issues is *EJournal*—"an Electronic Journal concerned with the implications of electronic networks and texts." Subscriptions available at LISTSERV@ALBANY.BITNET.

Proceedings and Addresses of the American Philosophical Association. In connection with the Christina Sommers controversy, see the "Letters to the Editor" sections for the following issues: in 1992, 65.5, 65.7; in 1993, 66.5; in 1994, 67.4. The exchange reflected in *Proceedings* now spans almost two years.

Spanos, William V. 1992. *The End of Education: Toward Posthumanism.* Minneapolis: University of Minnesota Press.

Stanford Observer. 1994. The future was "obviously not obvious." May-June, 13. A summary of studies by Professor Nathan Rosenberg on the adoption of new technologies.

Sturm, Warren. 1994. Shutdown of ASA-L. Electronic posting to the list ASA-L, dated 8 June.

Wilkes, G. V. 1994. Puerile puerilities; a few notes against lucidity. Electronic posting to the list ASA-L, 1 June.

6

Posting in a Different Voice: Gender and Ethics in Computer-Mediated Communication

Susan Herring

Introduction[1]

Much of the discussion of ethical issues associated with computer-mediated communication (CMC) has been concerned with the use (or abuse) of CMC in the service of other, essentially CMC-external goals—for example, using computer networks to advertise one's commercial services or products, striking up electronic contact with women (and, in some cases, children) for the purpose of establishing sexual liaisons, or making improper use of computer-mediated information by violating copyright or the privacy of the sender (Dunlop and Kling 1991; Johnson and Snapper 1985; Shea 1994). As yet, however, little work has addressed the ethics of computer-mediated interaction itself, by which I mean the conflicts of interest and potential harm to others which can result from the manner and the extent to which computer-mediated messages are posted in public places. Although posting behavior falls partially under the rubric of netiquette (as network etiquette is called), more than manners is involved. Netiquette norms have both a moral and a political dimension, in that they are founded on systems of values and judgments which may vary according to different groups of users. Yet it is typically the most powerful or dominant group whose values take on a normative status.

Such is the case with regard to gender and computer-mediated communication. In this essay, I claim that women and men appeal to different—and partially incompatible—systems of values both as the rational foundation of their posting behavior and in interpreting and evaluating the behavior of others online. These values correspond to differences in posting style, and are evident as well in official netiquette guidelines, where the general bias in favor of values preferred by men has practical consequences for how comfortable women feel in mainstream electronic forums.

These claims run counter to two popular beliefs, one about gender and the other about CMC. First, any claim that women and men are different in other than a relatively trivial physiological sense is considered politically incorrect by many feminists, regardless of its intent. Consider, for example, the response generated by the work of psychologist Carol Gilligan.[2] Gilligan (1977, 1982; Gilligan and Attanucci 1988) interviewed adolescents and adults about their responses to moral dilemmas and observed that her female subjects regularly evoked different ethical priorities than did male subjects. Gilligan's concern was that women's "different voice" is traditionally assessed as deviant or defective relative to a male norm; she presents evidence instead for a mature and internally coherent female moral orientation which she terms an "ethic of care," as compared with the "ethic of justice" preferentially evoked by men. Feminist critics such as Martha Mednick (1989), Katha Pollitt (1992), and Linda Steiner (1989), however, consider such claims dangerous, in that they resemble traditional stereotypes and thus are all too readily embraced by conservative and antifeminist elements as proof that gender inequality— especially the division of labor between highly rewarded male activity in the public domain and devalued female domestic activity—is part of the preordained natural order and should not be changed.[3] Indeed, it is wrong, according to some critics, even to *describe* the differences: "Descriptions/prescriptions of a female ethic wrongly imply that women are locked into a female experience which is self-authenticating and self-validating" (Grimshaw 1986, 17, cited in Steiner 1989, 161).

The claim that there are gender differences in CMC is also problematic from the perspective of the dominant discourse about computer-mediated communications technology. Part of the idealism surrounding the technology in the early decades of its development, and which still persists in many circles, was the belief that computer networks would neutralize gender and other status-related differences and empower traditionally underrepresented groups (Hiltz and Turoff 1993; Kiesler, Siegal, and McGuire 1984; Graddol and Swann 1989; Rheingold 1993). The reasoning was deductive: Because of the "mediated" nature of the medium, messages posted to others are decontextualized and potentially anonymous, free from physical cues to the sender's sex, age, race, able-bodiedness, attractiveness, and so forth. Never mind that users overwhelmingly choose to forgo the anonymity option by signing their messages. Never mind that similar claims could be made about letter writing, which is hardly gender-neutral. People wanted to believe in the potential of the new technology for equalizing social relations, and thus the assumption of gender neutrality initially was not questioned.

In principle, however, the accuracy of claims of gender differences—in CMC or elsewhere—is independent of their "naturalness," their political consequences, or the idealism that accompanies the introduction of a new technology. Moreover, describing gender differences need not be incompatible with feminist or egalitarian ideals. Quite to the contrary, differences that reproduce patterns of dominance must be named and understood, lest inequality be perpetuated and recreated through the uncritical acting out of familiar scripts. It is in this spirit that the present essay was written—with the goal of revealing gender differences (and gender inequalities) in cyberspace that some readers may well find disconcerting, but hopefully will no longer be able to ignore.

The Investigation

The claims advanced in this paper are based on an empirical investigation of gender, ethics, and etiquette on the Internet carried out (with the exception of the first part) during the spring of 1994. The investigation is comprised of three parts:

Behavior: I conducted ethnographic observation ranging from periods of two weeks to three years of daily exchanges in nine computer-mediated discussion lists with varying concentrations of female subscribers (from 11% to 88%),[4] and analyzed the discourse of selected discussions from the lists in terms of amount and style of participation, controlling for gender.

Values: I prepared an anonymous survey that was distributed on eight computer-mediated discussion lists;[5] the survey included three open-ended questions about what Net users most appreciate, dislike, and would like to change about the behavior of others online. I also analyzed the content of metadiscourse about what constitutes appropriate and inappropriate behavior in the nine lists from the "behavior" part of the investigation.

Netiquette guidelines: A content analysis was performed of explicit netiquette statements from the introductory messages sent out to new subscribers on seven discussion lists and from two general collections of recommended network etiquette.[6] The content of the netiquette guidelines was then compared with the behaviors and values identified in the first two parts of the investigation.

The results of the investigation reveal that not only do many women and men use recognizably gendered posting styles, but they also appeal to different systems of values in rationalizing their posting behavior and in interpreting and judging the behavior of others. Women preferentially evoke an ethic of politeness and consideration for the wants of others, especially their desire to be ratified and liked, while men evoke an ethic of agonistic debate and freedom from rules or imposition. The male ethic predominates in official netiquette guidelines and in discourse about the Internet in general, with the result that women with a politeness ethic must create and defend women-centered spaces online in order to carry out the kind of discourse they value. Although the observed differences do not describe all male and female net users, they are important in that they affect norms of interpretation and evaluation in cyberspace more generally.

The Evidence for Difference

Contrary to the claim that CMC neutralizes gender distinctions, recent empirical studies of computer-mediated interaction suggest that gender differences online reproduce and even exaggerate gender differences found in face-to-face interaction (Hall, forthcoming; Herring 1992, 1993a; Herring, Johnson, and DiBenedetto 1992; Herring and Lombard 1995; Kramarae and Taylor 1993; Selfe and Meyer 1991; Sutton 1994). In what ways do men and women differ in their computer-mediated communication?

In this section, I discuss differences in two domains: public posting to Internet discussion groups and values associated with posting behavior. Since I have already presented considerable evidence for the former in other publications (see especially Herring 1993a), after summarizing this evidence, I will devote most of my attention to making a case for the latter. The third part of this section presents evidence for gender bias in netiquette guidelines.

Different Posting Styles

There is a recognizable style of posting found in most, if not all, public forums on the Internet which, in its most extreme form, manifests itself as "flaming," or personal put-downs, and which is generally characterized by a challenging, adversarial, or superior stance vis à vis the intended addressee(s). This style is often, although not always, accompanied by a tendency to post lengthy and/ or frequent messages and to participate disproportionately more than others in a given discussion. In forum after electronic forum, the overwhelming majority of participants exhibiting this style are male. Examples of the Adversarial style are given below.[7]

1) [PHILOSOP] While I do not especially care how this gets settled, I am surprised by the continuing absurdity of the discussion. [distancing stance, presupposed put-down ('this discussion is absurd')]

2) [LINGUIST] [Jean Linguiste's] proposals towards a more transparent morphology in French are exactly what he calls them: a farce. Nobody could ever take them seriously—unless we want to look as well at pairs such as *père-mère*, *coq-poule* and defigure the French language in the process. [strong assertions, put-down ('JL's proposals are a farce'; implied: 'JL wants to defigure the French language')]

3) [POLITICS] In article <[message number]> [address (Ed [Lastname])
    writes:
    >No, but I shall emphasize that should the news admins take it upon
    >themselves to decide the truth of your claim—a remote possibility
    >indeed—we surely would not weight most highly your word on the

Who the hell are 'we,' 'edo boy'. I was unaware that a net-clown was required
to agree on the US Constitution. Well anyway, enough entertainment for
a self-exposed 'wieneramus'. The criminal acts of the x-Soviet Armenian
Government come directly under the scope of the Convention on Genocide
adopted by the General Assembly of the United Nations on December 8,
1948, containing the following provisions: [continues another 8 screens]
[name-calling ('edo boy,' 'net-clown,' 'wieneramus'), profanity ('who the
hell')]

There exists an equally distinct style, although less widespread in its
distribution, that is characterized by expressions of support and appreciation,
and in which views are presented in a hedged fashion, often with appeals for
ratification from the group. This style is exhibited almost exclusively by
women and is the discursive norm in many women-only and women-centered
lists. The following examples illustrate the Supportive/Attenuated style.

4) [WOMEN]
    >Aileen,
    >I just wanted to let you know that I have really enjoyed all your posts
    about
    >Women's herstory. They have been extremely informative and I've
    learned alot
    >about the women's movement. Thank you!
    >-Erika

    DITTO!!!! They are wonderful! Did anyone else catch the first part of a
    Century of Women? I really enjoyed it. Of course, I didn't agree with
    everything they said. . . . but it was really informative. Roberta~~~~~~~
    [appreciates, thanks, agrees, appeals to group]
5) [WMST] Well, enough of my ranting. I am very interested in this subject.
    My area is experimental social psychology. I am also very excited about
    the book you mentioned. It is a very worthwhile project. If I can help in
    any way, typing, whatever, I would love to help. Please let me know if
    there is anything I can do. [apologizes, appreciates, offers help]
6) [TESL] [. . .] I hope this makes sense. This is kind of what I had in mind
    when I realized I couldn't give a real definitive answer. Of course, maybe
    I'm just getting into the nuances of the language when it would be easier

to just give the simple answer. Any response? [hedges, expresses doubt
(supplies counterargument to own position), appeals to group]

In what sense can these two styles be generalized to represent gender
differences in posting behavior? Certainly, not all men who post on the Internet are adversarial; indeed, discourse in mixed-sex lists is typically dominated by a small male minority which posts a lot (Selfe and Meyer 1991;
Herring 1993a) and accounts for the majority of adversarial behaviors (Herring 1993a, 1993b), while many men are relatively neutral and informative
and others are supportive or attenuated in their posting style, especially on
women-centered lists. Similarly, not all women are supportive and attenuated;
many also adopt a neutral, informative style, and some can be adversarial,
especially on male-dominated lists where adversariality is the discursive norm.
Nevertheless, the two styles are gendered in that the extremes of each are
manifested almost exclusively by one gender and not the other. Moreover,
men tend toward adversariality and women toward support/attenuation even
in the area of overlap between the two extremes. The distribution of the styles
in relation to gender can be represented schematically as two bell-shaped
curves that overlap but are out of phase, as shown in figure 1.

FIGURE 1

Distribution of adversarial and attenuated/supportive posting styles by gender

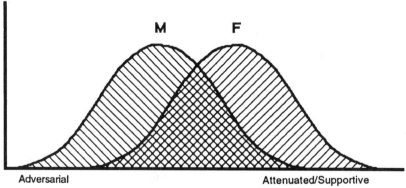

Adversarial   Attenuated/Supportive

Figure 1 illustrates two points. First, male and female behaviors are not dis-
junctive; that is, men and women online are not separate species (cf. Holmstrom 1982). Many posts fall into a middle category that includes mixing
male-and female-gendered features or the absence of either.[8] Second, despite
the large area of overlap, two distinct populations are involved—in other
words, behaviors at the extremes are not randomly distributed between males

and females, but are virtually male exclusive (for extreme forms of adversariality) and female exclusive (for extreme forms of appreciation and support). It is this distribution that I seek to explain.

Why focus on the extremes, rather than on the area of overlap where women and men exhibit similar kinds of variation? The existence of gendered styles must be explicitly demonstrated in order to put to rest the myth that gender is invisible on computer networks. This myth not only misrepresents the reality of gender on-line, but further perpetuates the uncritical tolerance of practices (such as flaming) which discourage women from using computer networks (Herring 1992, 1993a). Such practices affect large numbers of users even when only a minority of men are responsible, and thus it behooves those concerned with gender equality in cyberspace to understand them well.

Further, there is evidence that the extreme gendered posting styles illustrated above are psychologically and socially real for net users; that is, they have a *symbolic* status over and above their actual distribution. Thus participants in electronic discussions regularly infer the gender of message posters on the basis of the presence of features of one or the other of these styles. Cases where the self-identified gender of the poster is in question are especially revealing in this regard. Consider the following situations, the first involving a male posing as a female, and the second, a (suspected) female posing as a male.

(i)   A male subscriber on SWIP-L posted a message disagreeing with the general consensus that discourse on SWIP should be nonagonistic, commenting, ''There's nothing like a healthy denunciation by one's colleagues every once in a while to get one's blood flowing, and spur one to greater subtlety and exactness of thought.'' He signed his message with a female pseudonym, however, causing another (female) subscriber to comment later, ''I must confess to looking for the name of the male who wrote the posting that [Suzi] sent originally and was surprised to find a female name at the end of it.'' The female subscriber had (accurately) inferred that anyone actively advocating ''denunciation by one's colleagues'' was probably male.

(ii)   At a time when another male subscriber had been posting frequent messages to the WOMEN list, a subscriber professing to be a man posted a message inquiring what the list's policy was toward men participating on the list, admitting, ''I sometimes feel guilty for taking up bandwidth.'' The message, in addition to showing consideration for the concerns of others on the list, was very attenuated in style and explicitly appreciative of the list: ''I really enjoy this list (actually, it's the best one I'm on).'' This prompted another (female) subscriber to respond, "now that you've posed the question . . . how's one to know you're not a woman posing this question as a man?" Her suspicion indicates that on some level she recognized that anyone posting a message expressing appreciation and consideration for the desires of others was likely to be female.

The existence of gendered prototypes is also supported by cases where males and females are miscast as members of the opposite gender because they do not conform to the expected gender pattern. Hall (forthcoming) cites a case on a women-only list of a poster, "J.," suspected of being male on the basis of "her" offensive, adversarial postings. Discussion ensued on the list of how to handle the case, until someone reported they had met "J." in real life in Southern California: "While they had found her offensive too, they had met her and she was a woman" (155). This shows how probabilistic inferences (based on the empirical tendency for men to be more adversarial than women online) can take on symbolic and even political signification: In order not to be suspected of being male, women must express themselves on this women-only list in an appropriately "female" style.[9]

These styles and their association with gender are of both practical and theoretical significance. They are of practical significance in that they determine how successfully one is able to "pass" as a member of a different gender on the Net. They are of theoretical significance in that the existence of different styles and the forms they take are facts requiring further explanation.

Different Values

Why do many Net users post in ways that signal their gender? Why, specifically, do men specialize in flaming and women in supporting others? Flaming is generally considered hostile and rude. Yet the phenomenon is too widespread to be explained away as the crank behavior of a few sociopathic individuals. Indeed, many male-predominant groups, including stuffy academic ones, are adversarial in tone to a degree that, in my female-biased perception, borders on the uncivil. Could it be that men and women have different assessments of what is "polite" and "rude" in online communication?

In order to test this hypothesis, I prepared and disseminated an anonymous electronic questionnaire on netiquette. In addition to background questions about respondents' sex, age, ethnicity, professional status, and years of networking, the questionnaire included three open-ended questions asking respondents what online behaviors bother them most, what they most appreciate, and what changes they would like to see in Net interaction in an ideal world.

The questionnaire generated considerable interest: I received nearly 300 usable responses, 60% from men and 40% from women. Immediately I noticed a pattern relating to gender in the responses: Male respondents were more likely than female respondents to "flame" me about the questionnaire itself.[10] Compare, for example, the following complaints about the length of the questionnaire sent to me by two individuals who elected not to answer it, the first female, the second male.[11]

[F:]   I hope this doesn't sound terribly rude, but a survey is one of the last things I want to see in my mailbox. And I suspect I'm not alone. This is not to say that you shouldn't have posted it. Rather, please treat your results with caution. They likely will not be representative.

[M:]   What bothers me most are abuses of networking such as yours: unsolicited, lengthy and intrusive postings designed to further others' research by wasting my time.

The female frames her complaint about the survey as a concern for the validity of the investigator's results, while the male expresses concern about the way the survey imposes on him. The female message contains numerous attenuation features, including hedges ("not terribly," "I suspect," "likely"), an apology, and the use of the politeness marker "please." The male message contains no attenuation or politeness features but instead insults the sender of the survey by characterizing the survey in negatively loaded terms such as "abuse" and "intrusive" and by intimating that the motives for sending it were selfish and exploitative. While both messages are complaints and thus inherently face-threatening, their style is very different: The first attenuates the threat to the addressee's face, while the second emphasizes it.

Fortunately, many more individuals responded supportively than critically to the survey. However, there were gender differences in the expressions of support as well, as illustrated by the following two comments preceding the completed survey:

[F:]   What an interesting survey! It looks like you've already done at least some informal research into people's "net peeves"! I'd be very interested to receive a copy of your results at my email address: [address]. Thanks!

[M:]   Here is the response to your survey. Under most circumstances, I would discard the survey due to its length. Kindly, I am replying. I wish you the best of luck in your research!

The female comment compliments the survey (it is interesting) and the sender of the survey (you have done your research), and demonstrates the sincerity of her interest by asking for a copy of the results; the message concludes with an expression of appreciation ("Thanks!"). The male comment criticizes the survey (it is too long) and compliments himself (I am kind for replying);[12] the expression of support comes in the last sentence when he wishes the investigator luck. Both of these messages are friendly and the respondents cooperative, but the first explicitly seeks to make the addressee feel positively valued, while the latter does not.

I reproduce these extraneous comments because they are consistent with the stylistic differences described in the previous section (although the context in which they were produced is quite different) and because they reveal much about the politeness norms of the individuals who wrote them. Politeness can be conceptualized as behavior that addresses two kinds of "face": positive face, or a person's desire to be ratified and liked, and negative face, or the desire not to be constrained or imposed upon (Brown and Levinson 1987). The comments of the female questionnaire respondents are polite in that they attend to both kinds of face wants in the addressee. The first woman takes pains to lessen the imposition ("I hope this doesn't sound terribly rude") and the potential threat to the addressee's positive face ("This is not to say that you shouldn't have posted it") caused by her complaint, and the second woman actively bolsters the addressee's positive face in her appreciative message. In contrast, the men make virtually no concessions to the addressee's positive face (indeed the first man threatens it directly), but do display a concern with their own negative face wants, namely, the desire not to be imposed upon by long surveys. In addition to the apparent contrast between the other-and self-orientation of these concerns, the most striking difference is that only the women appear to be concerned with positive politeness.

Hypothesizing that the difference between the two types of politeness might therefore be significant, I coded each response to the three open-ended questions on the questionnaire in terms of positive and negative politeness. Some examples of common Net behaviors cited in response that illustrate observances (+) and violations (−) of positive (P) and negative (N) politeness are as follows:

Messages support or thank others	(+ P; makes others feel valued)
Participants "flame" or insult others	(− P; makes others feel bad)
Participants post concise messages	(+ N; saves others' time)
Messages quote all of the message being responded to	(− N; wastes others' time)

The results of the analysis indicate that women supply politeness-related responses more often than men: 87% of female responses relate to some kind of politeness, as compared with 73% for men. Of politeness-related answers given, women supplied 53% of those related to negative politeness and 61%

TABLE 1

Distribution of responses to open-ended questions by gender and politeness type

	\multicolumn{2}{c}{Bothers}	\multicolumn{2}{c}{Like}	\multicolumn{2}{c}{Change}	\multicolumn{2}{c}{Combined}
	−N	−P	+N	+P	+N	+P	+/−N	+/−P
M	39	21	16	16	9	2	64	39
	49%	42%	47%	39%	39%	20%	47%	39%
F	40	29	18	25	14	8	72	62
	51%	58%	53%	61%	61%	80%	53%	61%
Total	79	50	34	41	23	10	136	101
	100%	100%	100%	100%	100%	100%	100%	100%

of those related to positive politeness. A pattern is also evident whereby women evoked *observances* of positive politeness (in response to the questions of what they most like and what changes they would like to see) more often than *violations* (in response to the question of what bothers them most), while for men this pattern is reversed. The distribution of politeness-related responses by gender is summarized for each question and for all questions combined in table 1.[13]

Some examples of responses relating to politeness are as follows. When asked what behaviors they most appreciate on the Net, female respondents cited "thoughtfulness," "politeness," "short, to the point messages," "supportive behaviors," and "helpful advice," and indicated they would like to see "more please and thank yous," "more consideration of others," and more "conciseness" in Net interaction. Women report being most bothered by "overlong, longwinded messages," "rude insensitive remarks," "unnecessary nastiness," and "angry responses or responses designed to provoke." As one female respondent elaborated:

The thing that absolutely bothers me the most is when people (in my experience it has always been men) disrupt the list by making provocative and inflammatory remarks designed simply to distress. This only happens on unmoderated lists—but it can be very upsetting.

Rude, nasty, and inflammatory remarks are violations of positive politeness in that they may be taken by the addressee as insulting, and thus threaten her positive face.

Men, in contrast, preferentially mention politeness behaviors associated with the avoidance of imposition. Thus, male respondents complain about "test messages," "cross-posting of messages," "advertising," "low content and off-topic posts," "sending listserv commands to the discussion group," "requests by others to do things for them," "idiocy and repetitions," and "stupid questions," all of which impose on the receiver's time and resources and threaten negative face. Such abuses are commonly attributed to a lack of knowledge:

> I'd like to see more knowledge out there. Like any public activity, people go on and screw around when they have no idea what they are doing, which wastes a lot of time and energy. People should learn what the net is and how to use it before flooding sixteen groups with the umpteenth repetition [*sic*] of very simple questions.

While these results would appear to support my initial observations concerning different kinds of politeness, they still leave a basic question unanswered: Why do men violate positive politeness, for example, by engaging in bald criticism, to say nothing of flaming? There is nothing inherent in a desire for freedom from imposition that leads inevitably to an adversarial interactional style. Moreover, despite male concern with freedom from imposition, men are responsible for the majority of violations of negative politeness (my questionnaire notwithstanding) as well: It is men, not women, who post the longest messages, do the most cross-posting, copy the most text from previous messages (and respond, point by point), have the longest signature files, and generally take up the most bandwidth on the net. How can these behaviors be explained?

The questionnaire responses provide the key to this question. Three themes occur repeatedly in male responses to the open-ended questions—themes that are missing almost entirely from female responses. These themes are *freedom from censorship, candor,* and *debate.* Taken together, they make up a coherent and rationally motivated system of values that is separate from and, in some cases, in conflict with politeness values. This system of values, which I call the "anarchic/agonistic system," can even be evoked to justify flaming.

Consider, for example, the value accorded *freedom from censorship.* According to this view, the Internet and cyberspace in general is a glorious anarchy, one of the few places in the world in which absolute freedom of speech is possible. Censorship in this view is equated with rules and any form of imposed regulation, with the ultimate threat being take-over and control of the Net by government and/or large corporations. Rather than having imposed rules on the Internet, individual users should self-regulate their behavior to show consideration (i.e., in terms of negative politeness) for others. One male respondent comments as follows in response to the question, In an ideal world, what changes would you like to see in the way people interact on the Net?

None. Seriously. The net is monitored enough as it is (maybe too much). It should be a forum for free speech and should not be policed by anything but common sense. Though this may seem inconsistent with my answer to (1) above [where he said he was bothered by receiving posts totally unrelated to the topic of a list], just because something bothers me doesn't mean I believe it should be eliminated. In an ideal world people should exercise their rationality more.

Since we do not live in an ideal world, of course, behavior problems on the Net inevitably arise. In keeping with the value placed on individual autonomy, proponents of free speech may advocate harassing offenders until they desist rather than cutting off their access (considered to be ''heavy-handed censorship''). Hauben (1993), writing about the Usenet, expresses this in positive terms as follows:

When people feel someone is abusing the nature of Usenet News, they let the offender know through e-mail. In this manner . . . people fight to keep it a resource that is helpful to society as a whole.

The ideal of ''fight[ing] to keep [the Net] a resource that is helpful to society as a whole'' often translates into action as flaming. One man wrote the following in response to the question, What behaviors bother you most on the Net?

As much as I am irritated by [incompetent posters], I don't want imposed rules. I would prefer to ''out'' such a person and let some public minded citizen fire bomb his house to imposing rules on the net. Letter bombing a [sic] annoying individual's feed is usually preferable to building a formal heirarchy [sic] of net cops.

Underlying the violent imagery of ''bombing'' is the ideal of the ''public minded citizen'' who dispenses a rough and ready form of justice in a free and individualistic Net society. A similar ideal underlies the response to the same question by another ''Net vigilante'':

I'd have to say commercial shit. Whenever someone advertises some damn get-rich-quick scheme and plasters it all over the net by crossposting it to every newsgroup, I reach for my ''gatling gun mailer crasher'' and fire away at the source address.

Thus an anarchistic value system is constructed: Within this system, by evoking freedom from censorship, flaming and other aggressive behaviors can be interpreted in a prosocial light, as a form of corrective justice. This is not to say that all or even most men who flame have the good of Net society at heart, but rather that the behavior is in principle justifiable for men (and hence tolerable) in ways that it is not for most women.

The second theme evoked by male respondents is *candor.* In this view, honest and frank expression of one's opinions is a desirable attribute in Net interaction: Everything is out in the open, and others know exactly where one stands. One man gave the following response to the question, What Net behaviors do you most appreciate when you encounter them?

> The willingness to respond to just about anything with candor and honesty. There are no positions to hide behind or from on a list.

For many men, candor takes precedence over the positive face wants of the addressee. An extreme expression of this is the response of an African American male citing "honest bigotry" as what he most appreciates about Net interaction. Expressions of bigotry (e.g., in the form of racial hatred) presumably directly threaten this man's desire to feel ratified and liked, yet for him the advantages of honesty outweigh the threat: "I'm glad to talk to those who are truly hateful on the net so that I'm prepared for them when I meet them in real life."

If one disagrees with someone, one should say so directly. It follows from this that failure to disagree openly may be perceived by adherents of this ethic as hypocritical or insincere. Thus a male participant on the SWIP list recently accused feminist philosophers of "feign[ing] agreement where none exists" when they write "I wish to *expand* upon so-and-so's thinking,"

> when what's really at issue is the complete rejection of so-and-so. Tamsin Lorraine suggests this is the positive feature of the "cooperative spirit" of feminist philosophy. But I disagree. I think it's better, when one rejects another feminist's thinking on a matter, simply to say "I reject so-and-so's approach." . . . I frankly think [it is] exactly this kind of automatic non-criticism which is partially responsible for feminist philosophy not being taken as seriously as it should by non-feminist philosophers.

Both the poster's critical views (that feminist philosophers "feign agreement"; that feminist philosophy is not "taken seriously") and his directly confrontational tone ("But I disagree"; "I frankly think") are consistent with the value accorded candor by male survey respondents.

More is expressed in this last post than a value on honesty, however; disagreement is also implicitly valued. This leads to the third theme mentioned preferentially by male survey respondents: *debate*. According to this value, confrontational exchanges should be encouraged as a means of arriving at deeper understandings of issues and sharpening one's intellectual skills. As the male participant on the SWIP list (quoted previously) put it, "There's nothing like a healthy denunciation by one's colleagues every once in a while to get one's blood flowing, and spur one to greater subtlety and exactness of thought." He goes on, however, to add an important caveat: "At least if it's constructive denunciation, rather than the mere expression of hostility or misunderstanding." The distinction between "constructive denunciation" and "hostility," or some version of this distinction, is crucial to many men: Male survey respondents regularly cite "flaming" as behavior that bothers them online, but exclude from the definition of flaming critical exchanges that are calm and rationally argued, which they characterize instead as "good debate," "balanced argument," or "noncombative disagreement." In other words, there is good adversariality (i.e., agonistic debate) and bad adversariality (i.e., flaming).

In contrast, many—if not most—female Net users do not distinguish between hostile, angry adversariality and calm, rational adversariality, but rather interpret adversariality of any kind (which may include any politeness-threatening act) as unconstructive and hostile in intent. Thus, unlike men, female survey respondents tend to group together all forms of adversariality as "flaming," "rudeness," or "provocation," all "designed simply to distress." Further, female participants in online discussions are more likely than men to characterize exchanges as "flaming" any time baldly face-threatening acts are committed (disagreement, rejection, protest, etc.). This tendency led a male participant in one such discussion to complain recently that "some members of [this list] perceive aggression where none was intended."

The problem is not simply one of individual misunderstanding; rather, different sets of values are involved. The strength of the clash in values is evident in the strongly emotive language women use to describe their aversion to adversariality online and off. The following quote was posted by the listowner of the SWIP list to explain why the list follows a nonagonistic practice:

At the first APA (SWIP) meeting, we discovered we were all offended and disabled by the hierarchies in the profession, by the star system, by the old boy networks. We talked together and shared our feelings about the adversarial method of combat and attack of commentator against presenter, by audience against presenter. We found it ugly, harmful, and counterproductive.[14]

Or, as a female respondent commented about an adversarial discussion in which participants baldly criticized one another's views on the LINGUIST list,[15]

> That is precisely the kind of human interaction I committedly avoid. . . .
> I am dismayed that human beings treat each other this way. It makes the world a dangerous place to be.

The choice of evaluative terms such as "ugly," "harmful," and "dangerous" to characterize agonistic behaviors and "offended," "disabled," and "dismayed" to characterize the women's response reveals the extent to which some women are alienated by behaviors that are positively valued by men.

The set of values cited preferentially by female survey respondents I will call henceforth the "positive politeness ethic," in that it is concerned with attending to and protecting participants' positive face or desire to be accepted, supported, and liked. The set of values referred to almost exclusively by male survey respondents I will refer to as the "anarchic/agonistic ethic," in that it is concerned with promoting freedom of expression and vigorous exchange of conflicting views. According to the positive politeness ethic, right interaction involves supporting, helping, and generally being considerate of others. As a woman on the WOMEN list posted recently:

> If we take responsibility for developing our own sensitivities to others and controlling our actions to minimize damage—we will each be doing [good deeds] for the whole world constantly.

In contrast, right interaction according to the anarchic/agonistic ethic, is that which permits the development of the individual, in service of which it is desirable to be maximally free to speak and act in the pursuit of one's self-interest. The connection between free speech and self-interest is made explicit by a male survey respondent who quoted American Revolutionary author Thomas Paine:[16]

> He that would make his own liberty secure must guard even his enemy from oppression; for if he violates this duty he establishes a precedent that will reach to himself.

Thus, self-interest leads one to extend concern to others in a principled way.

As with gendered discursive styles, the generalizations I have made here

FIGURE 2

Distribution of politeness-based and anarchic/agonistic values by gender

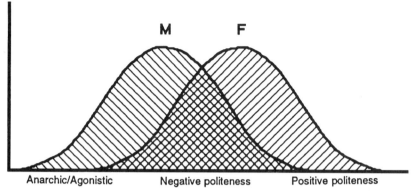

regarding gendered values do not apply universally. The distribution of male and female responses to the combined open-ended questions in terms of the values described above are represented schematically in figure 2.

Figure 2 shows that there is a considerable overlap in male and female assessments regarding appropriate behavior on the Net. This area corresponds primarily with dislike of violations of negative politeness. Thus, respondents of both genders cited negative politeness violations such as uninformative subject headers, quoting text, misdirected/inappropriate messages, messages with little content, and long messages as behaviors that bother them in Net interaction. There was also some agreement on dislike of violations of positive politeness—especially of flaming and egotism, although more women than men said they disliked these behaviors (in the case of flaming, twice as many women as men). Men and women agreed much less about what they like and would like to see more of, however, with women preferentially citing helpful and supportive (positive politeness) behaviors and men citing anarchic and agonistic behaviors. Note, however, that there is a fundamental tension between the values represented by these gendered extremes: Uncensored agonistic expression threatens positive face, and protecting positive face at any cost (e.g., by prohibiting adversariality) threatens freedom of expression.

These results show that when male and female Net users are asked open-ended questions about what they like and dislike, they provide qualitatively different answers. Moreover, the answers cluster and pattern in ways that reflect patterns in posting styles: Expressions of support and appreciation are natural manifestations of positive politeness, and attenuation follows from negative politeness, while adversariality and even flaming can be seen to derive from (and be rationally justified by) anarchic and agonistic ideals.

Netiquette Guidelines

Having established distributional tendencies for different male and female value systems that correspond to different posting styles, we turn now to netiquette guidelines—publicly available statements of recommended posting and Net use practices. Whose values inform the content of netiquette guidelines? In particular, how do netiquette guidelines resolve the tension inherent between positive politeness values on the one hand and anarchic/agonistic values on the other?

For this part of the study, I analyzed the content of nine sets of netiquette statements: seven from introductory messages to discussion lists and two global sets of guidelines (one for Usenet and the other for electronic mail in general).[17] The data include two women-centered lists, WMST and SWIP, and one list, TESL, which has a slight majority of female subscribers and represents a feminized field; all three have female listowners. It was hypothesized that netiquette statements for these lists would incorporate positive politeness values. In contrast, while no lists in the data self-identify as "male-centered," POLITICS and the Computer Underground Digest (CuD) represent masculinized areas of interest, and PHILOSOP is 90% male; these lists are also owned by men. I hypothesized, therefore, that netiquette statements for these lists would incorporate anarchic/agonistic values. Finally, the global Usenet and e-mail netiquette guidelines are intended to apply to users of either sex, and thus in principle should reflect the values of each (or neither) group.

Each normative statement found in the documents was categorized in terms of positive and negative politeness, if applicable. These statements are of two types: avoid violating N/P (abbreviated Avoid $-N/-P$), and observe N/P (abbreviated $+N/+P$). An example of each type of statement is given below.

Avoid $-N$: Avoid irrelevancies. Given the limited phosphor window we have onto this electronic universe, succinctness and relevance become prized attributes. The message that makes its point and fits on one screen does its job best, and you will be well regarded. (Shapiro and Anderson 1985)

$+N$: Please include a meaningful subject header, so that people will know whether your message deals with a topic of interest to them. (WMST)

Avoid $-P$: There may be no flames of a personal nature on this list. (POLITICS)

$+P$: We are strongly committed to maintaining an uncensored list; but to do this, it is important that members respect in their postings the attitudes and sensibilities of all other members. (TESL)

In addition, statements communicating agonistic and anarchic values (abbreviated A/A) were coded. An example of this type is the following:

> *A/A*
> *those who have never tried electronic communication may not be aware of what a "social skill" really is. One social skill that must be learned, is that other people have points of view that are not only different, but *threatening*, to your own. In turn, your opinions may be threatening to others. There is nothing wrong with this* [emphasis added—SH]. Your beliefs need not be hidden behind a facade, as happens with face-to-face conversation. Not everybody in the world is a bosom buddy, but you can still have a meaningful conversation with them. The person who cannot do this lacks in social skills. (Nick Szabo, quoted in Salzenberg and Spafford 1993)

The distribution of statements of each type by source is summarized in table 2. (An asterisk after list name indicates that messages sent to that list are screened by the listowner(s) before being posted; i.e., the list is moderated).

Table 2 shows that the guidelines for all of the electronic forums include prescriptive statements about negative politeness. Three, in fact, mention *only* negative politeness; I will call this the "conservative type." This type is conservative in that it does not address potentially controversial behaviors such as flaming or supporting others, but, rather, is concerned solely with the avoidance of imposition, a concern that male and female users share. It is noteworthy that the three lists whose guidelines illustrate this pattern—LINGUIST, PHILOSOP, and WMST—are all academic lists that restrict their

TABLE 2

Distribution of netiquette statements by source and type

	Gender of listowner	Percentage of female subscribers[18]	A/A	Avoid −N	+N	Avoid −P	−P
CuD*	M	5	x	x	x	(x)	
PHILOSOP	M	11		x	x		
POLITICS	M	17	x	x	x	(x)	
LINGUIST*	M & F	36		x	x		
TESL	F	56		x	x	x	x
SWIP*	F	80		x		x	x
WMST	F	88		x	x		
Usenet	n.a.	?	x	x	x		
e-mail	n.a.	?	x	x	x	(x)	

focus to exchange of information and discussion of academic issues. Possibly, the listowners who prepared these netiquette guidelines consider the sorts of behaviors that lead to strong disagreement or supportive interaction as outside the scope of the lists, and thus did not think it necessary to provide for such eventualities. In any event, the academic nature of these lists appears to take precedence over gender make-up, as there is no correlation between the conservative pattern and gender of subscribers or listowner.

Beyond this, however, the distribution of values across lists supports the hypotheses advanced above with regard to gender. Male-centered lists are more likely than female-centered lists to evoke agonistic/anarchic values; of the three male-centered lists—CuD, PHILOSOP, and POLITICS—two contain statements of this type, as compared with none of the female-centered lists. Conversely, female-centered lists are more likely to recommend observations of positive politeness (+ P); of the three female-centered lists—SWIP, TESL, and WMST—two contain statements of this type, as compared with none of the male-centered lists. It is possible to observe in this distribution a pattern of partial overlap similar to that found in posting styles and posting ethics, with A/A values on the 'male' end, $+/-$ N values in the area of overlap in the middle, and $+$ P values on the 'female' end. Thus, it is not only individuals who are gendered in their evaluation of Net behaviors but electronic forums as well.

Further support for this conclusion is found in the various lists' recommendations involving avoiding violations of positive politeness (Avoid $-$ P). A different attitude is evident toward adversariality and flaming in the guidelines for the female-and the male-centered lists. SWIP and TESL make it clear that such behavior is not welcome on the lists in any form; SWIP makes it a matter of policy to "be respectful and constructive rather than agonistic in our discussions," and the TESL guidelines state: "If you find something posted on the net objectionable, you have every right to voice your objections . . . but not in public." In contrast, POLITICS, CuD, and the e-mail guidelines all proscribe flaming in ways that explicitly or implicitly authorize public disagreement. Thus POLITICS prohibits "flames of a personal nature," but presumably allows for flames of a nonpersonal nature (e.g., of another participant's views), and explicitly advocates "argument." Similarly, Shapiro and Anderson's e-mail guidelines decry "insult[ing] or criticiz[ing] third parties without giving them a chance to respond," although if one gives them a chance to respond—which in most electronic forums is automatic if the criticized party reads the forum—insults and criticism are presumably acceptable(!). Finally, CuD discourages "ad hominem attacks or personal squabbles," but describes itself as "a forum for opposing points of view" and stresses "reasoned debate." These distinctions are consistent with the distinction made by male survey respondents between "hostile" adversariality and "rational" adversariality: The former is to be avoided, while the latter is held up as the ideal for Net interaction.

What, then, of the global guidelines, those that supposedly apply to all three million users and four thousand-plus newsgroups of the Usenet, and those that apply to sending electronic mail in general? The Usenet guidelines (Horton and Spafford 1993; Salzenberg and Spafford 1993) are compatible with a male rather than a female or conservative interactional ethic: They value anarchy as desirable and conflict as inevitable, as can be seen in the statement about "social skill" given as an example of A/A norms above. They also include, under the heading "Words to live by," the following statement:

> Anarchy means having to put up with things that really piss you off. (Salzenberg and Spafford 1993)

The interactional norm assumed in these statements is one of threat, conflict, and control of one's hostile or violent reactions (defined as "social skill"). While this may represent the reality of online interaction for many men, it is not a comfortable scenario for those whose value system emphasizes harmonious and supportive interaction, and no doubt accounts for why participation on Usenet is overwhelmingly male.[19]

Finally, as if this were not potentially alienating enough to female users, the Usenet guidelines also actively discourage appreciative and supportive postings in the name of reducing message volume:

> In aggregate, small savings in disk or CPU add up to a great deal. For instance, messages offering thanks, jibes, or congratulations will only need to be seen by the interested parties—send these by mail rather than posting them. The same goes for simple questions, and especially for any form of "me too" posting. (Horton and Spafford 1993)

It is not hard to imagine that users with a supportive interactional style could feel uncomfortable participating in forums where exclusively supportive posts are not only not valued but are defined as violations of netiquette.

Shapiro and Anderson's print pamphlet, *Toward an Ethics and Etiquette for Electronic Mail* (1985), also gives an androcentric view. In addition to authorizing insults and criticisms (provided one gives the other party a chance to respond), the guidelines stress the undesirability of emotion in responding to e-mail ("avoid responding while emotional"; "if a message generates emotion, look again"), advocating instead "self-control." Consistent with other sets of guidelines with a male bias, there is no mention of appreciative, supportive, or relationship-building behaviors. It is important to recall that what I have characterized (for the sake of balancing my corpus) as "male-centered" lists are ostensibly ungendered and open to all.[20] When we add to this the masculine orientation of global Net guidelines, the picture that emerges is one in which masculine norms of interaction constitute the default, the exception being in a few women-centered groups. These results not only support the claim that there are different value systems preferentially associated with male and female users, but further reveal gender bias in netiquette guidelines.

This bias is not limited to the particular sets of guidelines included in the present analysis, but can be found in the "etiquette" section of almost any popular guide to using the Internet. Moreover, it is well on its way to becoming the unquestioned norm for cyberspace as a whole. Thus, a brand-new, attractively packaged paperback volume on netiquette (Shea 1994) advertises itself as "the first and only book to offer the guidance that all users need to be perfectly polite online." It has the following to say about flaming:

Does Netiquette forbid flaming? Not at all. Flaming is a longstanding network tradition (and Netiquette never messes with tradition). Flames can be lots of fun, both to write and to read. And the recipients of flames sometimes deserve the heat. . . . Netiquette doesn't require you to stand idly by while other people spout offensive nonsense. (43, 78)

What Netiquette does forbid, according to Shea, is extended flame wars, which are "an unfair monopolization of bandwidth." In other words, agonism is more highly valued than positive face (it's fun; other people deserve it) and only becomes a problem if extended to the point that it violates negative face (monopolizes bandwidth). But what if the person flamed did not "deserve" it? What if they merely expressed a view that someone else did not like, a feminist view, for example, in response to which they were treated to offensive sexist remarks? And what if, further, that person happens to operate from within an ethical system in which flaming is the ultimate online insult? In that case, according to the new guidelines, "if you're a sensitive person, it may be best to avoid the many hang-outs of the politically incorrect" (78). Avoidance is, of course, one solution, but as one of the sources quoted in the book itself observes, "*Every* discussion list of which I have been a part—no matter what its subject—has fallen victim to such ills—a few have gone down in e-flames. The pattern is absolutely consistent" (73). Should people with a positive politeness-based communication ethic avoid all discussion lists then? When we consider that the positive politeness ethic is associated predominantly with women, the adverse implications for women's use of the Net become uncomfortably clear: As one contributor to CuD put it, "if you can't stand the heat, ladies, then get out of the kitchen" (quoted in Taylor and Kramarae, forthcoming, 4). In effect, a proflaming netiquette implicitly sanctions the domination of Net discourse by a minority of men.

Discussion

In this paper, I have argued that, contrary to the assumption that CMC neutralizes indications of gender, there are gender differences in public discourse on the Internet. Moreover, these differences are not randomly distributed across individuals, but rather display a systematic pattern of distribution with male users as a group tending toward more adversarial behavior and female users as a group tending toward more attenuated and supportive behaviors. I further submit that these systematic behaviors correspond to two distinctive systems of values each of which can be characterized in positive terms: One considers individual freedom to be the highest good, and the other idealizes harmonious interpersonal interaction.

As with all ideologies, however, these value systems also serve to rationalize less noble behaviors. Thus, adversarial participants justify intimidation of others and excessive use of bandwidth with rhetoric about freedom, openness, and intellectual vigor, and attenuated participants justify flattery, indirectness, and deference to others (and perhaps silence) in terms of ideals of care and consideration. Given that members of the former population are mostly men and members of the latter population mostly women (and, in some cases, male students), the value systems can be seen to reproduce male dominance and female (and other less powerful individuals') submission. They provide a mechanism by which these behaviors can be understood in a favorable, face-saving light by those who engage in them, and thereby facilitate their unquestioned continuation. This arrangement, in which both genders are complicit, is in one sense highly adaptive: It allows people to continue to operate within an oppressive power arrangement that might otherwise make them feel intolerably guilty or angry, depending on the role they play. But from a standpoint that affirms gender equality, a standpoint implicit in proponents' original claim that computer networks would neutralize gender differences, dominance and submission patterns on the Net are disadvantageous to women (as well as to nonadversarial men), and therefore it is important that they be recognized and questioned.

Gendered arrangements of values perpetuate dominance even in cases where no intimidation is intended. The same behavior—for example, directly criticizing another participant—is susceptible to different interpretations under an anarchic/agonistic system, as opposed to a politeness system. As a consequence, cyberspace may be perceived as more hostile and less hospitable by women than by men, thus discouraging female participation. There is no simple solution to this problem, since to require women to understand adversariality differently is to place all the burden for change on the less powerful group, and to prohibit direct criticism, or to require that criticism be attenuated, is to impose what would be seen from the anarchic perspective as unreasonable restrictions on freedom of speech. Nevertheless, this is an issue that must be addressed if the dominant adversarial culture in cyberspace is not to marginalize women by rendering them largely silent in mixed-sex forums or by limiting their active participation to women-centered groups, as is currently the case.

Even women-centered groups are not free from adversarial incursion. Some men are resentful of the existence of women-only groups and attempt to infiltrate their ranks by presenting themselves as women. One male contributor to CuD offers the following tips to "she-males," men who impersonate women to gain access to women-only forums:

> The lesbian channels are hilarious, where the women ask you questions that the men 'couldn't possibly' know the answers to, like the small print on a packet of tampons. Also you have to string off a list of very right-on lesbian-friendly music that you're supposed to like . . . They seem to think this will keep the she-males out. Bwahahaha!

Even when gender imposters are exposed, however, it is difficult to exclude them, since they can always present themselves again from a different account under a different name. Partly for this reason, women-centered lists such as WOMEN and SWIP do not restrict membership on the basis of gender but rather allow men to participate who are friendly to the purposes of the list. Inevitably, however, there arise incidents of adversariality involving men, some of whom are perhaps initially well-intentioned, while others clearly aim to be disruptive. Thus, within the past several months, SWIP adopted a moderated format and TESL is contemplating switching to a moderated format because of repeated contentious posts from a few men and the effects these had on the overall quality of the discourse.[21] Similarly, the GENDER hotline on COMSERVE was shut down in 1992 and reopened as a moderated forum after being taken over by several men who bombarded the list with misogynistic messages, until only a few hardcore subscribers remained. In each case, the female listowner who made the decision to restrict access became the target of angry messages from the offending men accusing her of "heavy-handed tactics," "censorship," and "authoritarian expressions of power." These cases illustrate that freedom of speech when combined with adversariality may effectively translate into freedom of speech only for the adversarial; some restrictions on free speech were necessary in these cases in order to preserve the common good.

In contrast, the anarchic solution of harassing (or ignoring) the offender until he desists requires a tolerance for adversariality—perhaps even extreme forms of adversariality—that may be anathema to participants who are offended by adversariality in the first place. This solution has also been spectacularly unsuccessful in two of the worst cases of recent abuse in cyberspace: the repeated, lengthy, cross-posted flames by several individuals on Turkish-Armenian hostilities, and the repeated ''spamming'' of the Usenet with advertisements from a small law firm in Phoenix. The individuals responsible for these behaviors have been warned, flamed, and, by feats of technological adversariality, had their messages zapped by ''kill files'' and intercepted by electronic ''patriot missiles'' before reaching their destination (Elmer-Dewitt 1994; Lewis 1994). Yet still they persist (fueled, no doubt, to new heights of determination by the challenge of holding out against their multiple adversaries). These are cases of anarchy taken to the extreme, anarchy that cannot be stopped by anarchic means. It is interesting in this regard to note that while male Usenet administrators continue to propose ever more violent forms of harassment in the law firm case, a female administrator, less encumbered by anarchic scruples, recently proposed partitioning the net in such a way that incidents of this sort would be impossible.[22] Whether or not such a solution is feasible is irrelevant here; the point is that it is a different kind of solution, one in the spirit of the actions of the women-centered list owners who limited the speech of a troublemaking minority in order to insure that the majority would still have a place to speak.

Conclusion

We have seen that the existence of gender differences in cyberspace has implications for the norms, demographics, and distribution of power on the Internet. I hope to have demonstrated that it is in the interests of those concerned with actualizing egalitarian ideals of CMC to recognize these differences—and their practical implications—for what they are. In particular, I hope to have pointed out that there are problems with an uncritical acceptance of the dominant anarchic/agonistic model as the ideal for CMC: Not only does it incorporate a male bias that marginalizes women, but it authorizes abuse that more generally threatens the common good.

That said, the description of gender differences presented here should not be taken as a prescription for difference, or a glorification of female ways of communicating and valuing to the exclusion of those of men. Both of the gendered extremes described here are just that: extremes. Ideally, citizens of cyberspace would cooperate in minimizing intimidation and abuses of others' resources; failing self-enforcement of this ideal, limits on extreme abuses would be imposed to preserve the "virtual commons" as a resource for all (Kollock and Smith, forthcoming). Most interaction would fall ideally into a vast middle ground of self-regulated behavior, where free speech would be tempered by consideration for others and where politeness would not preclude the honest exchange of differing views. Ritual adversariality and ritual agreement would be replaced by mature, respectful, and dynamic joint exploration of ideas, leading to the creation of a Net society greater and wiser than the sum of its parts.

Whether such a Net society can in fact be achieved depends in part on our ability to set aside narrow self-interest in the pursuit of shared goals. It also depends on educating a critical mass of the Net population to recognize limiting gender stereotypes in all their manifestations; the present work is intended as a contribution toward this end. Finally, it requires exposing systems of rationalization that mask dominance and opportunistic abuse. At a minimum, freedom from blatant intimidation must be ensured if the majority of users are to have meaningful access to the communicative potential of the Internet, irrespective of gender.

Notes

1. The research reported here was partially supported by National Endowment for the Humanities grant no. FT-40112. The author wishes to thank Charles Ess and Robin Lakoff for writing letters of support for the grant application. Thanks also to Robin Lombard and Jim Thomas for commenting on an earlier version of this paper and to Brett Benham for assistance in producing the bell curves.

2. The work of other "difference feminists" (Pollitt 1992) has provoked similar popular response and similar criticism; notable in this category are Chodorow 1978; Ruddick 1989; and Tannen 1990 (criticized by Troemel-Ploetz 1991).

3. In the case of CMC, the danger is presumably that gender differences could be cited to justify excluding women from influential computer-mediated forums or from policy decisions regarding CMC.

4. The nine lists are, in order of increasing percentage of female subscribers: PHILOSOP (11%), POLITICS (17%), PAGLIA (discussion of the writings of antifeminist feminist Camille Paglia; 34%), LINGUIST (36%), MBU (discussion of computers and writing; 42%), TESL (Teaching English as a Second Language; 56%), SWIP (Society for Women in Philosophy; 80%), WMSPRT (Women's Spirituality and Femi-

nist-Oriented Religions; 81%), and WMST (Women's Studies; 88%). At the time they were sampled, all were active lists generating 20–100 messages per week.

5. The eight lists surveyed are CuD (Computer Underground Digest, a weekly electronic newsletter whose readership includes many computing professionals), PHILCOMM (Philosophy of Communication), PHILOSOP, LINGUIST, SWIP, TESL, WMSPRT, and WMST.

6. Netiquette statements were analyzed from the intoductory messages of CuD, PHILOSOP, POLITICS, LINGUIST, SWIP, TESL, WMST; the general collections analyzed are "Rules for Posting to Usenet" (Horton and Spafford 1993), "What is Usenet?" (Salzenberg and Spafford 1993), and *Toward an Ethics and Etiquette for Electronic Mail* (Shapiro and Anderson 1985).

7. All examples given in this section are from messages posted to public-accessible discussion groups on the Internet. To protect the anonymity of individual participants, names and electronic addresses that appear in the messages have been changed.

8. This distributional model generalizes across variation based on local list-serve norms and topics of discussion. All other things being equal, normative posting style for both genders tends to shift in the adversarial direction in male-predominant lists such as PAGLIA and LINGUIST and in the attenuated/supportive direction in female-predominant lists such as WMST and TESL, although differences in degree still characterize prototypical 'male' and 'female' contributions. The effect of dominant list usage on gender style is documented in Herring (forthcoming) and Herring and Lombard (1995).

9. Interestingly, even gay and lesbian lists are not free of traditionally gendered styles. Hall (forthcoming) reports that men on GAYNET often display an adversarial style, driving some women off the list, while women on SAPPHO display a supportive and attenuated style.

10. Two aspects of the survey generated criticism: its length (about two and a half printed pages), and the fact that respondents were asked to indicate their ethnicity.

11. In keeping with my promise to respondents, all comments quoted in response to the questionnaire are anonymous. For a more detailed description of the survey, see Herring 1994.

12. I assume this was intended ironically, as an attempt at humor.

13. These calculations are based on a subset of survey respondents derived by sampling responses received over time: the first 23 received, then 100–110, 200–210 and all 23 received by nonelectronic means. This produced a sample of 68 respondents, 34 male and 34 female.

14. From a panel presentation given by Kathy Pyne Addelson at the Eastern Division American Philosophical Association meeting, Atlanta, 30 December 1993. The title of the panel was "Feminist Philosophy after Twenty Years."

15. See Herring 1992 for a more extensive analysis of the gender dynamics in this discussion.

16. I note, in passing, that Paine is an excellent role model for the CMC anarchic/agonistic ethical standard: He advocated "the omnipotence of reason when there is freedom to debate all questions," and claimed he sought to write "simply, candidly, and clearly; to be bold and forthright in order to shock readers into attention, partly by sharp contrasts; [and] to use wit and satire in order to bring opposing ideas into ridicule" (Encyclopedia Britannica 1971, 17:65).

17. See note 6.

18. These percentages are rough estimates calculated from counting unambiguously female and male names on publicly available lists of subscribers to each discussion list. Gender-ambiguous names, organizations, and distribution lists (which typically comprise 10–15% of subscribers to any given list) are then excluded, and the percentages of women and men calculated out of 100%. Thus, if a list has 17% female subscribers, 83% of the subscribers are male. Since subscription is not necessary to read Usenet newsgroups or to send e-mail, comparable figures are not available for the two sets of global guidelines.

19. For a telling example of male domination even in a female-centered newsgroup, see Sutton 1994. According to one estimate, 95% of postings to the Net overall are from men (Sproull, cited in Ebben and Kramarae 1993); this percentage may be higher on the Usenet.

20. We do not have, for example, a list for the Society for Men in Philosophy (SMIP) corrresponding to the SWIP list; the men's list is simply called PHILOSOP (Philosophy).

21. As of this writing, the TESL list is attempting to avoid shifting to a moderated format, but has instigated several new guidelines. Notable among these are limits on frequency of posting ("no more than 2 postings per day, 10 per week, per netter") and a proscription against "baiting, goading, demeaning messages" and "complaints about postings, the net, the way the net is run, etc." As the listowner, Anthea Tillyer, explained in a recent post to the list (13 July 1994):

> No one is suggesting or advocating a humorlessly rigid and doctrinaire application of inflexible rules; the goal is to keep TESL-L on focus and to return it to its previous state of pleasant and co-operative collegiality. There will always be netters who enjoy a more abrasive and wide-ranging set of debates than we wish to see on TESL-L; and for those netters, we will continue to post news of other lists and netnews groups that suit other kinds of discourse. We hope that in this way we can serve all our members and at the same time keep TESL-L

true to its stated focus and to the pleasant atmosphere that has characterized the list for most of its existence.

22. I am indebted to Arthur Hyun (personal communication) for this information, which is based on recent discussions on the Usenet group <news.admin.misc>.

References

Brown, Penelope, and Stephen C. Levinson. 1987. *Politeness: Some Universals in Language Usage.* Cambridge: Cambridge University Press.

Chodorow, Nancy. 1978. *The Reproduction of Mothering: Psychoanalysis and the Sociology of Gender.* Berkeley: University of California Press.

Dunlop, Charles, and Rob Kling, eds. 1991. *Computerization and Controversy.* New York: Academic Press.

Ebben, Maureen, and Cheris Kramarae. 1993. Women and Information Technologies: Creating a Cyberspace of Our Own. In *Women, Information Technology, and Scholarship,* ed. H. Jeannie Taylor, Cheris Kramarae, and Maureen Ebben, 15–27. Urbana, IL: Center for Advanced Study.

Elmer-Dewitt, Philip. 1994. Battle for the Soul of the Internet. *Time,* 25 July, 50–56.

Gilligan, Carol. 1977. Concepts of the Self and of Morality. *Harvard Educational Review* 47(4): 481–517.

———. 1982. *In a Different Voice.* Cambridge: Harvard University Press.

Gilligan, Carol, and Jane Attanucci. 1988. Two Moral Orientations. In *Mapping the Moral Domain,* ed. Carol Gilligan, Janie Victoria Ward, and Jill McLean Taylor, 73–86. Cambridge: Harvard University Press.

Graddol, David, and Joan Swann. 1989. *Gender Voices.* London: Blackwell.

Grimshaw, Jean. 1986. *Feminist Philosophers.* Sussex: Wheatsheaf Books.

Hall, Kira. Forthcoming. Cyberfeminism. In *Computer Mediated Communication,* ed. Susan Herring. Amsterdam: John Benjamins.

Hauben, Michael. 1993. The Social Forces behind the Development of Usenet News. [Electronic document, available by ftp from weber.ucsd.edu, directory /pub/usenet.hist.]

Herring, Susan. 1992. Gender and Participation in Computer-Mediated Linguistic Discourse. ERIC document (ED345552).

———. 1993a. Gender and Democracy in Computer-Mediated Communication. *Electronic Journal of Communication* 3(2), special issue on Computer-Mediated

Communication, ed. T. Benson. Reprinted in *Computerization and Controversy,* 2nd edition, ed. Rob Kling. New York: Academic Press, forthcoming.

————. 1993b. Men's Language: A Study of the Discourse of the LINGUIST List. In *Les langues menacées: actes du XVe congrès international des linguistes, Vol. 3,* ed. André Crochetière, Jean-Claude Boulanger, and Conrad Ouellon, 347–50. Sainte-Foy, Québec: Les Presses de l'Université Laval.

————. 1994. Politeness in Computer Culture: Why Women Thank and Men Flame. In *Communicating in, through, and across Cultures: Proceedings of the Third Berkeley Women and Language Conference,* ed. Mary Bucholtz, Anita Liang, and Laurel Sutton. Berkeley, CA: Berkeley Women and Language Group.

————. Forthcoming. Two Variants of an Electronic Message Schema. In *Computer Mediated Communication,* ed. Susan Herring. Amsterdam: John Benjamins.

Herring, Susan, Deborah Johnson, and Tamra DiBenedetto. 1992. Participation in Electronic Discourse in a "Feminist" Field. In *Locating Power: Proceedings of the Second Berkeley Women and Language Conference,* ed. Mary Bucholtz, Kira Hall, and Birch Moonwomon, 250–62. Berkeley, CA: Berkeley Women and Language Group.

Herring, Susan and Robin Lombard. 1995. Negotiating Gendered Faces: Requests and Disagreements Among Computer Professionals on the Internet. Paper presented at the Georgetown University Round Table on Languages and Linguistics presession on Computer-Mediated Discourse Analysis. Georgetown University, March 8, 1995.

Hiltz, Starr Roxanne, and Murray Turoff. 1993. *The Network Nation: Human Communication via Computer,* 2d ed. Cambridge: MIT Press. [1st ed., 1978, Addison-Wesley.]

Holmstrom, Nancy. 1982. Do Women Have a Distinctive Nature? *Philosophical Forum* 14(1): 22–42.

Horton, Mark, and Gene Spafford. 1993. Rules for posting to Usenet. [Electronic document available by ftp from: rtfm.mit.edu, directory /pub/usenet/news.announce.newusers.]

Johnson, Deborah G., and John W. Snapper, eds. 1985. *Ethical Issues in the Use of Computers.* Belmont, CA: Wadsworth.

Kiesler, Sara, Jane Siegel, and Timothy W. McGuire. 1984. Social Psychological Aspects of Computer-Mediated Communication. *American Psychologist* 39: 1123–34.

Kollock, Peter, and Marc Smith. Forthcoming. Managing the Virtual Commons: Cooperation and Conflict in Computer Communities. In *Computer-Mediated Communication,* ed. Susan Herring. Amsterdam: John Benjamins.

Kramarae, Cheris, and H. Jeannie Taylor. 1993. Women and Men on Electronic Networks: A Conversation or a Monologue? In *Women, Information Technology, and Scholarship,* ed. H. Jeannie Taylor, Cheris Kramarae, and Maureen Ebben, 52–61. Urbana, IL: Center for Advanced Study.

Lewis, Peter H. 1994. Censorship Growing on Networks of Cyberspace. *Dallas Morning News,* 29 June, 2D.

Mednick, Martha T. 1989. On the Politics of Psychological Constructs: Stop the Bandwagon, I Want to Get Off. *American Psychologist* 44(8): 1118–23.

Pollitt, Katha. 1992. Are Women Morally Superior to Men? *The Nation,* 28 December, 799–807.

Rheingold, Howard. 1993. *The Virtual Community: Homesteading on the Electronic Frontier.* Reading, MA: Addison-Wesley.

Ruddick, Sara. 1989. *Maternal Thinking: Toward a Politics of Peace.* Boston: Beacon Press.

Salzenberg, Chip, and Gene Spafford. 1993. What Is Usenet? [Electronic document available by ftp from: rtfm.mit.edu, directory /pub/usenet/news.announce.newusers.]

Selfe, Cynthia L., and Paul R. Meyer. 1991. Testing Claims for On-line Conferences. *Written Communication* 8(2): 163–92.

Shapiro, Norman Z., and Robert H. Anderson. 1985. *Toward an Ethics and Etiquette for Electronic Mail.* The Rand Corporation.

Shea, Virginia. 1994. *Netiquette.* San Francisco: Albion Books.

Steiner, Linda. 1989. Feminist Theorizing and Communication Ethics. *Communication* 12: 157–173.

Sutton, Laurel. 1994. Gender, Power, and Silencing in Electronic Discourse on USENET. *Proceedings of the 20th Berkeley Linguistics Society.* University of California, Berkeley.

Tannen, Deborah. 1990. *You Just Don't Understand.* New York: Ballantine.

Taylor, Jeannie H., and Cheris Kramarae. Forthcoming. Creating Cybertrust in the Margins. In *The Cultures of Computing,* ed. Susan Leigh Star. Oxford: Basil Blackwell.

Troemel-Ploetz, Senta. 1991. Selling the Apolitical: Review of Deborah Tannen's *You Just Don't Understand. Discourse and Society* 2(4): 489–502.

7

"This Is Not Our Fathers' Pornography:" Sex, Lies, and Computers

CAROL J. ADAMS

"We're rapidly approaching the point where's there a physical world and an electronic world. And they're doing exactly the same things," [Al] Olsen said, "One of those things is sex."

—Quoted in Associated Press article 3/7/94 (read online)

All women live in sexual objectification the way fish live in water.

—Catharine MacKinnon (1989, 149)

"This is not our fathers' pornography." So averred Larry Miller, one of the founders of Intererotica, an "erotic" software company (quoted in Robinson and Tamosaitis 1993, 20). Does one note a degree of anxiety, of protesting too much, in this assertion? What if computer-related software, and all of its relatives, especially online bulletin boards and other forms of sexualized computer-mediated communication, actually *were* their father's pornography? Indeed, what if cyberspace, and the opportunities it affords pornography, offers the best confirmation of the feminist analysis of pornography?

The feminist antipornography analysis does not focus on issues of morality and the effect on the consumer (the sort of arguments that arise from the religious right). It focuses on the dimension of the political, the harm in the making of pornography (see Lovelace 1980), and the collective harm pornography has on women (see Dworkin 1981, 1985; Lederer 1980; MacKinnon 1991, 1992; Kappeler 1986). Pornography invokes and affirms "heteropatriarchy"—a term which refers to a male-dominant world that presumes and reinforces male-dominant heterosexuality. Pornography is seen as the core constitutive practice of gender inequality. Gender, according to Catharine

MacKinnon, is "a material division of power" (1989, 58). Gender is a hierarchy, a matter of domination and subordination: "As sexual inequality is gendered as man and women, gender inequality is sexualized as dominance and subordination" (MacKinnon 1989, 241). In other words, gender is a systematic inequality of power: "Gender is sexual. Pornography constitutes the meaning of that sexuality." (MacKinnon 1989, 197).

Has cyberspace become yet another pornographic place in a heteropatriarchal world? Or is it so vast that it cannot be so delimited? On the other hand, does the pervasiveness of cyberpornography (and the male dominance that it constitutes), reveal that cyberspace cannot shed the social realities of the so-called real world? Can any other theory account so completely for the sexualized dynamics on the Internet, examined in this essay, as does the feminist theory of pornography?

To answer these questions, I begin by examining the sexualized world of computers, including the various forms of sex-related communication which take place on bulletin boards and the Internet. I argue that multiple examples—including overt computer-based pornography and a careful analysis of male privilege in cyberspace—powerfully confirm feminist analyses of society and pornography. Indeed, it appears that certain features of cyberspace can accelerate and expand the male dominance and exploitation of women already familiar to us "in real life" (IRL). In the face of this ramification of sexism in cyberspace, I take up the question of how women and men genuinely interested in equality can counter such exploitation and thereby redeem the promise of democratization and equality of access often made for communication via computers—in the face of typical free-speech arguments against the regulation of discourse in cyberspace.

Prolog: The Male Culture of the Computer

You know those little bumps on the "f" and "j" keys to keep our fingers appropriately placed when typing? Well, hackers have given them a name: tits on a keyboard (Raymond 1993, 415). Given this, you probably can imagine what those labels are called that are designed to be placed on top of certain keys to announce a function: pasties (Raymond 1993, 320). These are not examples, as some might think, of hackers confusing their sex drive and their hard drive, or at least their hardware. (Though the emphasis on *hard* is telling.) This is an example of the way computers themselves are sexualized in a male sexual-dominant world. It is a point of departure for examining the male-dominant sexualizing of the Internet. The male environment from which much of our computer culture arises becomes evident in a variety of ways.

First, the *hardware* is sexualized. Thus we can learn about female connectors and male connectors. How does one distinguish between them? Well, not surprisingly, the female connector is receptive, that is, it is a receptacle for the prongs, pins, or "other protruding part that is designed to fit into a female counterpart." Don't fear confusion, however: "When you see the connector on the end of a cable, it is not very difficult to guess which plug is the male connector and what is the female" (Williams and Cummings 1993, 328; see also 207). The pornographic message of women's continual receptivity is captured in this description. When we enter the computer culture— whether it is the images that are dancing along from modem to modem in the evening or the language used to describe hardware or computer processes— we encounter heteropatriarchal presumptions. For instance, what happens when the connectors are mismatched? A *gender mender* is required: "A cable connector shell with either 2 male or 2 female connectors on it, used to connect . . . mismatches. . . . Also called gender bender, gender blender, sex changer, and even homosexual adapter; however there appears to be some confusion as to whether a *male homosexual adapter* has pins on both sides (is doubly male) or sockets on both sides (connects two males)" (Raymond 1993, 200). Imposing gender on connectors obviously leads to confusion. Heteropatriarchal assumptions grant no legitimate conceptual space to other relationships that do not adhere to gender assumptions about female receptivity. Thus, we encounter a debate about what exactly a male homosexual adapter would consist of. That the debate moves in the direction of whether it consists of pins or sockets rather than in the direction of questioning the gender labels that have caused such confusion reveals a strong allegiance to the instantiation (and the inequality) of gender.

Second, computer *processes* have been sexualized according to heteropatriarchal sexuality. Thus, we learn about gang banging and rapes:

> *gang bang:* The use of a large numbers of loosely coupled programmers in an attempt to wedge a great many features into a product in a short time. (Raymond 1993, 198)

> *rape:* 1. To *screw* someone or something, violently; in particular, to destroy a program or information irrecoverably. Often used in describing file-system damage. 2. To strip a piece of hardware for parts. . . . 3. . . . To mass-copy files from an anonymous ftp site. (Raymond 1993, 347)

One could easily observe that the male environment of computer creation generated such appropriation of sexist language.[1] But how does it function, the computer with its titties and its pasties, another controllable object? One finds a multiplicity of sexualized roles/images assigned to the computer: It can be used to attack and rape others' files when it is "up." In its active role it may be referred to as male, but in its passive role, when it is down (as in the missionary position) it is female, rapeable, controllable, a sexual possession.

Elizabeth Dodson Gray offers one explanation for this language:

> It is clear that males and females experience a life journey from within bodies which differ physically. Men have long been clear how women's experience was shaped and limited by having a vagina and uterus. We are only beginning to perceive how men's experience is shaped and limited by having a penis and testicles. The male life-experience has saturated the intellectual and technological spaces of our culture and has been the assumed norm and referent. But it is the feminists in academia, for example, who have noted the omnipresence of phrases about "the thrust of his argument" or about someone's "penetrating statement." One also notes with humor that when a computer is working it is "up" and when it is unable to compute it is "down." Yet the pervasiveness of this male physical "viewing point" not only in our language but in our ways of thinking and in our artifacts has been scarcely noted, let alone its limitations radically assessed. Perhaps the reason is that males by themselves have been unable to do this.[2]

To add to Dodson Gray's examples: Software telling the computer what to do has been compared to sperm carrying its own DNA message with "the computer's operating system at one receiving end, and a woman's egg at the other"! (Robinson and Tamosaitis 1993, 19). While the mixed gender assignments one perceives here might suggest simple playfulness, notice that in each case the male role is the dominant role, as when in *Demon Seed* a computer sexually assaults the character played by Julie Christie (Jaffe 1977).

Given this environment, the heteropatriarchal worldview will inevitably be revealed and enacted not only in the ways the computer is talked about and perceived but also through what the computer enabled by a modem does, namely, provide for rapid exchange of information, including images of women—images which are further malleable thanks to additional computer software. Interestingly, the words that have been coined to describe the kind of sexual information being exchanged are often gender neutral, so that one thinks we are talking about something that has been experienced in the same way by both men and women: *binary erotica, compusex, electronic sex, hot chat, intererotica, netsex, online sex,* and *teledildonics.*[3]

On the Internet, there has been *cyberlove* as well as *cybersex* (though some think the coined word is an oxymoron) and now cyberweddings. We are told that computer sex is supposedly safe sex, since neither AIDS nor insemination can be transferred over the phone lines. But what happens when they meet f2f [face-to-face], when wetware meets wetmare?[4]

Love at First Byte: Rush Limbaugh has found love. Marta Fitzgerald, twice-married mother of two from Florida who used to be an aerobics instructor. Moved into a Big Apple condo together. She's seriously decorating it and herself. Said a source: "She's having her teeth done. She's buying clothes. She's changing her hair. And she's looking into plastic surgery. It's a Pygmalion transformation." The pro talker met her on a bulletin board on CompuServe, an on-line computer service. ("People," *Dallas Morning News,* April 1994)

Does one need to call attention to the fact that dear old Rush is doing nothing to change his appearance? If two puns are instrinsic to the coinage of the phrase *baudy language* (i.e., not only *body* but also *bawdy* [words about prostitutes]), this phrase begins to alert us to the heteropatriarchal environment of all this hot chat in which *cyberbabes* are sought and discussed and *giffy girls* are sought and exchanged.

The Case of Men with }:) Seeking :)8
Adult Bulletin Boards—When Computers Become "Whorehouses"

The symbol }:) means horny smile. It clearly tells us whose horniness is presupposed in cybersex. ("*Horny: Vulgar slang.* a. Desirous of sexual activity. b. sexually aroused. [Sense 4 from HORN, an erection.]" [*American Heritage Dictionary*]). The symbol :)8 means "big breasted lady" (Robinson and Tamosaitis 1993, 130). A film maker-friend of mine reported that the first question asked of her when she logged on was "How big are your breasts?" [5]

Just as }:) establishes the male perspective as normative, so pornographic images of women dominate the heteropatriarchal world of cybersex. "Don't laugh," we are told in one book on computer jargon, "computers all over the world become *whorehouses* at night" (Williams and Cummings 1993, 377). Again, such a statement presupposes that the reader and the computer user is a heterosexual man. Of course, the presumption is correct: The majority of computers have been purchased by men (Kantrowitz 1994b), though we do not know their sexual orientation. We are informed of the "overwhelmingly male demographics of the net" (Katz 1994, 39). "According to *Boardwatch Magazine,* only 10% of bulletin board callers are female" (Robinson and Tamosaitis 1993, 86). Consider this:

"The Hot Tub Club." (BBS) Log on to the following: "Better hurry up and get your clothes off! The Hot Tub is cumming!" Run by Meat Eater and Lusty Linda, the board caters to singles and couples—with a waiting list for single men—and has strict policies regarding the treatment of women. Other than that, anything goes'' (Rutten et al. 1994, 232).

Two revealing statements in this description confirm the heteropatriarchal context: The existence of strict policies regarding the treatment of women informs us that strict policies were necessary; and the one group that obviously oversubscribes to this are single men. This latter demographic may be why *Playboy* is planning to introduce its own adult bulletin board. Or perhaps Nick, founder of NixPix, says it better: ''I think the majority of BBS users are sex-crazed, male computer geeks'' (Robinson and Tamosaitis 1993, 177).

If single men aren't excluded through the establishment of a waiting list, another attempt to achieve some form of sexual parity is by giving women free access, as does Compu-Erotica (BBS): ''If you love your chat hot, you'll love CEBBS!'' (Rutten, 236). Apparently women don't love hot chat to the degree that men do, since they are offered free access to this BBS. As Nancy Tamosaitis observes, ''The global digital village I entered is overwhelmingly and disproportionately male-dominated. Women are such a rare commodity on adult boards'' (Robinson and Tamosaitis 1993, 85).

Robinson and Tamosaitis, who have established themselves as the guides to *The Joy of Cybersex,* inform us that ''some men latch onto the adult bulletin boards looking for a free ticket into sexy phone chat heaven'' (Robinson and Tamosaitis 1993, 86). As a result, some men ''beg for a woman's phone number'' (Robinson and Tamosaitis 1993, 85). The fact is, in a heteropatriarchal world, words about sex have different meanings and purposes depending on whether one is a man or a woman. What constitutes ''sexy phone chat heaven'' may actually be more complex and extensive than has been considered. For instance, when women discuss their experience of sex, and, specifically, their experience of sexual victimization, even this can be experienced as ''sexy phone chat heaven.'' Catharine MacKinnon offers an insight into this process: Women are ''heard only when mouthing a sexual script'' (1989, 196). When women's words about sex and sexual violence circulate, they do so in contaminated, patriarchal space. When victims of sexually violent men and sexually harassing men report their experiences, it becomes pornography. In other words, accounts of sexual violation for women are a form of sex for men. The woman who speaks about sexual harassment is experienced as part of a pornographic narrative. Describing the Clarence Thomas hearings, MacKinnon said:

The more silent he is, the more powerful and credible. But the moment she opens her mouth, her credibility founders. Senators said they were offended by her; President Bush said he felt unclean. The dirt and uncleanliness stuck to her. When she spoke truth to power, she was treated like a pig in a parlor. He said these things, but she was blamed.

Once you are used for sex, you lose your human status. Your own testimony becomes live oral porn in a drama starring you. (MacKinnon, quoted in Landsberg 1992, 3)

Perhaps men respond sexually when women give an account of sexual violation because sexual words are a sexual reality, in the same way that men respond to pornography, which is (among other things) an account of the sexual violation of a woman. Seen in this way, much therapy as well as court testimony in sexual abuse cases is live oral pornography. (MacKinnon 1989, 152)

And, I would argue, hot chat is chat pornography.

But words aren't the only form of communication on bulletin boards—images can be exchanged as well. Because of widely available and commonly used graphics file formats such as the graphics interchange format (GIF), graphic pornography can now be downloaded and uploaded all over the net. Scanners allow individuals to choose their own favorite pictures, scan them, view them on screen, manipulate them, and send them to a bulletin board. With an image-processing program, one can enlarge any part of a figure's anatomy as desired, or remove one person and add another. Pin-ups, or GIFs, as they are called (hence giffy girls), are available on the Net: "Amateur, professional, and stolen, depicting everyone from the couple next door to the new model on the block to this month's centerfold, the world's largest collection of erotic photographs reposes in Cyberspace." And, predictably, while "there is a small (less than 5%) contingency of female GIF collectors, the predominate collector is male" (Robinson and Tamosaitis 1993, 79).

If *Hustler* magazine initiated the idea that every man could become a pornographer by sending in shots of his female partner's genital area (for the page in the magazine entitled "Beaver Shots"), cyberspace has multiplied the opportunities for coercive sex with and coercive pornography of one's partner. Men have a new arena for being pornographers of their partners; after all, despite the reference to "couples," in the description of an adult bulletin board, there is never a gender-neutral couple in a gender-specific world. One file called "My wife's thighs" had 1,200 downloads (Harmon 1993). This example demonstrates who is the object of the pornographic gaze (the wife) and who controls the image (the husband and the users with whom he chooses to share the image).

The authors of *The Joy of Cybersex* argue that, for men who collect images of women, the computer provides a private, personal way to live out fantasies. Perhaps, they tell us, their wives do not let them have *Penthouse* or

Playboy in the house, or perhaps men are living in remote/conservative areas of the country, or they are too ashamed to buy magazines, but they can download "adult images" anytime they want. What about this explanation: Pornography is a vehicle for the construction of men's subjectivity. Or, more directly, this is the way some men have sex.

The Case of the Killer App: "High-Tech Peep Shows" on Seedy-ROMs[6]

The term "killer app" (truly a term indebted to male domination) is applied to that function of a new technology "that makes a gadget appealing" (Tierney 1994, 1). Pornographers have been some of the pioneers in using new technologies, recognizing long before anyone else the benefits of videotape: "In 1978 and 1979, when fewer than 1 percent of American homes had VCR's and the major movie studios were reluctant to try the new technology, more than 75 percent of the videocassettes sold were pornographic" (Tierney 1994, 18). Likewise, the killer app for CD-ROM is pornography. CD-ROM technology is "interactive" in a phenomenologically consistent way, reinforcing a heteropatriarchal worldview (subject + object = sex) and enhancing the male privilege of the BBS. Demographically, "Men are the chief consumers of pornography, and men are also the main enthusiasts for new communications gadgets. This means, for instance, that the markets for the first home-movie projectors or CD-ROM drives have conveniently overlapped with the market for pornography" (Tierney 1994, 18). As one of the founders for Interotica observed: "Regardless of the content, it's men who buy it" (Robinson and Tamosaitis 1993, 31). One company, in fact, advertises "wife-proof" labels—a reminder, as if we needed it, that pornography users are heterosexual men: "Nearly all the cybersex software on the market is intended for straight men" (Robinson and Tamosaitis 1993, 48). While sexually explicit material might be constructed for consumers of either sex, "the brave new interactive world is still a club for white male members" (Robinson and Tamosaitis 1993, 31). In other words, the material speaks to the standard male, pornographic gaze. Laura Mulvey described the male gaze in an important 1975 article, "Visual Pleasure and Narrative Cinema":

> In a world ordered by sexual imbalance, pleasure in looking has been split between active/male and passive/female. The determining male gaze projects its phantasy onto the female figure which is styled accordingly. In their traditional exhibitionist role women are simultaneously looked at and displayed, with their appearance coded for strong visual and erotic impact so that they can be said to connote *to-be-looked-at-ness*. (Mulvey 1975, 11)

Given this analysis of the male gaze, consider the cover of *The Joy of Cybersex:* a headless woman with red finger nails holding a 3.5″ blue disk. Her black dress, unzipped so that one senses inviting breasts, melds into the black background of the book cover, as though the woman's body is the book's text. Indeed, it is.

The Phenomenology of the Computer Reifying Pornography

If early modern pornography is notable for its bookishness, for "sly allusions to Ovid's *Metamorphoses* and other classical works" (Findlen 1993, 77), cyberpornography is noted for its *lookishness.* Computer pornography mirrors back the patriarchal culture mirroring itself. One soon discovers an intensely circular, self-referential feeling to computer pornography. It isn't only reinforced through discussion groups like <alt.sex.movies> ("Enjoy X-rated movies? Post about porn queens, describe your favorite scenes, and review the latest in triple X" [Rutten 1994, 234]) or the sharing of photographs and discussion of supermodels ("their careers, ages, measurements. Announcements of where the models are appearing both in person and in print are posted" [Rutten 1994, 236]). It is that the pornography itself reifies the act of the male gaze by representing the male gaze in action. In other words, we watch someone watching women. For instance, the plot of "The Interactive Adventures of Seymour Butts" is that a man takes his video camera where he goes, knowing that women will flock to him, and then he has the opportunity to score [*sic*] "until you lose count" (Robinson and Tamosaitis 1993, 37). Or there is "Nightwatch," in which you are invited by a female security guard to check out the tapes taken by a security camera at a waterside apartment complex. Part of the plot, therefore, involves us watching what is ostensibly on a videotape. Part of the action in this pornography involves controlling how quickly the woman strips. Or consider "Penthouse Interactive," perhaps the epitome of such circular self-referentiality. The person at the computer takes on the persona of a photographer of models for *Penthouse* and can command each figure to take her top off or to strip naked. One can take shots of the models along the way (and printout the favorite ones), and when one is finished, Bob Guccione comments on one's skills in choosing the shots. Then there is "Centerfolds on Disk": "No matter how revealing their costumes, the ladies are ready to pull them aside and show you more. . . . Many of the photos seem to imply that some of these women are prepared to do more than just model" (Robinson and Tamosaitis 1993, 45).

One of the aspects of pornography is conveying precisely this message: Women want it, and they want it more and more. Compuporn is no different. Bulletin boards proclaim this, such as NixPix Denver (BBS) which is "Home to many hot-blooded yummy Nixxies who love to share their slithering, lurching sexualities with you!'' (Rutten 1994, 233). From the first pornographic computer game, Chuck Benton's 1980 ''Softporn Adventure,'' the message to the male gaze is that this is what women want; in this case, the scenario was attempting to ''score three times'' in a night. ''Virtual Valerie,'' released in a CD-ROM format, requires one to ''say the right things and Valerie will let you undress her. And more'' (Robinson and Tamosaitis 1993, 29).

The Phenomenology of Computer-Controlled Pornography

So-called interactive CD-ROMs and computer videos allow for the computer/ pornography user to control the action: Do you want the woman to strip? She will. Do you want to ''interactively stimulate'' a woman ''with the devices of your choice''? Then consider ''MacFoxes,'' in which one can pick ''a vibrator, a cucumber, an inanimate object, which the program calls a 'dick,' a telescoping dildo . . .'' and, using one's mouse, stimulate ''Misty'' (Robinson and Tamosaitis 1993, 60).[7] Or with the new computer technology you can manipulate your favorite scene from an X-rated movie to do what you wish it to do.

What's the problem? As Linda Jacobson, editor of *CyberArts* observes, ''These products show men that they can have control over women. You can force them to do your bidding and they do it willingly'' (quoted in Stefanac 1993, 41). Literally, what is done to women and what is done to the machine is exactly the same thing: moving the mouse, stimulating the woman. Metaphysically, the user controls the machine, and the user controls the sex, and this is called ''interactive.''

More than ten years ago, Sherry Turkle remarked, ''For adults as well as children, computers, reactive and interactive, offer companionship without the mutuality and complexity of a human relationship. They seduce because they provide a chance to be in complete control, but they can trap people into an infatuation with control, with building one's own private world'' (1984, 19). Deborah Tannen extends that observation, commenting that ''Boys are typically motivated by a social structure that says if you don't dominate you will be dominated. Computers, by their nature, balk: you type a perfectly appropriate command and it refuses to do what it should. Many boys and men are incited by this defiance: 'I'm going to whip this into line and teach it who's boss! I'll get it to do what I say!' (and if they work hard enough, they always can)'' (1994, 53). Computer pornography mirrors the same message as the computer itself—it's just a matter of finding the proper way to stimulate the woman, who actually does want it: ''I'm going to whip her into line and teach her who's boss! I'll get her to do what I say!'' Male dominion over the computer and over the female image are established in the same act: Both the equipment and the woman are submissive to the person at the keyboard. The standard male project of recreating and controlling the female has found a new ratification.

The Case of Privilege: Male Entitlement in Cyberspace

> From the male perspective, all space, public and private, including the women in it, appears to belong to and be owned by man.
>
> —Ellyn Kaschak, *Engendered Lives* (132)

Before we can discuss male entitlement *on* the Internet, we have to remind ourselves of male entitlement *to* the Internet. The question my feminist friends have asked me as we discuss the discoveries I have been making about pornographic values and computers is, Who has the time for all of this? Recalling standard information on economics, we might acknowledge that women, on the average, have less expendable income than men. Moreover, women, on the average, have less expendable time than men. Should it surprise us that "an estimated 85 to 90 percent of the users [of the Internet] are male"? (Kramarae and Kramer 1995, 33). Women who work outside the home are more likely to be performing work as the second shift at home. The computer is his recreation; it is more likely to be her maintenance. Men's material and sexual entitlements interact: material entitlement *to* computers, sexual entitlement *with* computers.

Psychotherapist Ellyn Kaschak's *Engendered Lives: A New Psychology of Women's Experience* argues that men in patriarchal society feel "a sense of entitlement to women" (1992, 62). Male entitlement in cyberspace, like male entitlement everywhere else, is evidenced by certain key behaviors. Masculine psychology in a patriarchal system "is characterized by extensive boundaries that subsume others, particularly females, who are considered to contain the feelings, conflicts, and meanings that men attribute to them" (Kaschak 1992, 62). Women who log onto the Internet thinking they are escaping the heteropatriarchal system that surrounds us like water to a fish discover instead the near impossibility of such an escape. This is not because we, like fish, cannot live without water but because heteropatriarchy floods every space in which we seek or presume equality. *Our* boundaries are contained and redefined and invaded by *their* boundaries. Kashak identifies several aspects of masculine psychology in a patriarchal culture: experiences self as superior to females; voyeuristic; has a sense of entitlement; experiences sex as power, which can manifest itself as sadism, violence, or domination;

projection of adult male sexuality onto women and children (1992, 72–73). What she identifies is the basic pornographic script. Let us consider how it is manifested in cyberspace.

Experiences Self as Superior to Females

A man who considers himself superior to females can manifest this behavior in several ways in cyberspace: flaming, acting hostile when it is discovered a woman has "passed" as a man, attacking intellectual claims made by a woman, invading feminist/women's discussion groups, ignoring women's posts, responding to men's posts, male dominance of discussion groups (see, for example, Selfe and Meyer 1991), threatening to quit a group if women post more messages (for examples and statistics see discussion by Ebben and Kramarae 1993, 17), and sexual harassment:

> "When a man disagrees with another man on a bulletin board, he's likely to go for a point by point argument and pretty much stay on topic," Moore says. "With a female, he's likely to call her a bull-dyke bitch and leave it at that." (Wiener 1994, 828)

Voyeuristic

To ground the above discussion of pornographic material, consider a statistic from *one* school: "Using computers on the Carnegie Mellon campus, Rimm [a university research associate] was able to collect 917,410 sexually-oriented pictures. . . . He was able to determine that the pictures had been downloaded by others more than 6.4 million times." (Buscaglia 1995, 6)

Sense of Entitlement

Cyberspace ostensibly is public space. But, as analyses of sexual harassment indicate, public space has always been a space for sexually harassing women, treating women as sexually accessible, and stalking women. Male entitlement in cyberspace might be more noticeable because the come-ons and harassment are not oral but written. Many men greet women by begging for their phone numbers, hitting up any woman who logs onto a bulletin board. There are men who deluge women with questions about their appearance and invitations to sex. On college campuses, as soon as women students log on, they are bombarded by references to sex (Tannen 1994, 53).

> Cindy Tittle Moore, a moderator on Usenet's soc.feminism, says, "It should be mandatory for every male on the Net to seriously pretend being female for two weeks to see the difference." They will get sexually explicit invitations from other men, she says, "some polite, some gross." (Wiener 1994, 828)

Consider, for instance the use of "yo," a high-priority message, in the Echo service by men. Ms. Horn of Echo explains:

"There's a whole etiquette of when to yo, when not to yo," she said. "A man new to Echo gets on and yos all the women. That's considered impolite. A frequent thing that men do is, 'Yo, Horn, what are you wearing?' or 'Yo, Horn, do you come here often?' I don't know what possesses these guys. I don't know why they think stupid, banal lines are more effective on line than off. Women do not yo strangers." (Barron 1995, B4)

Nancy Tamosaitis describes the most common type of personality she found in her exploration of the global digital village, "the thruster": "a distinctly male, heterosexual on-line personality who simply never takes no for an answer. . . . Thruster repeatedly pages any new female on-line with requests for personal one-on-one chats." (Robinson and Tamosaitis 1993, 88)

We know this about street harassment:

Central to the freedom to be at ease in public spaces is the capacity to pass through them while retaining a certain zone of privacy and autonomy—a zone of interpersonal distance that is crossed only by mutual consent. If, by contrast, women are subject to violation of that zone of personal privacy when they enter public areas, that very invasion of privacy effectively drives women back into the private sphere, where they may avoid such violations. Thus, by turning women into objects of public attention when they are in public, harassers drive home the message that women belong only in the world of the private (Bowman 1993, 526–27).

So, too, the effects of cybersexual harassment: It silences women, threatens women, promotes male monologues in place of dialogues.

Experiences Self as Extensive, Engulfing, Subsuming Others, Especially Females, Who Are Extensions of Himself

The engulfing male will not respect women's space for discussion. Ellen Broidy, history bibliographer at the University of California, Irvine, library, described what happened in feminist discussion groups: "Two or three men will get on and dominate the conversation—either by being provocative, or by flooding the system with comments on everything. It's like talk radio, only worse" (Wiener 1994, 828). When a researcher checked out the Women On-Line forum, "the posts were overwhelmingly from males (85% or more while she was looking)" (cited in Kramarae 1995, 54, no. 6.) The engulfing, controlling male will not respect women's refusal to continue a relationship. Stalking will occur on the Net, just as it does off; at least one case resulted in charges against an alleged stalker (see Steinert-Threlkeld 1994).

Experiences Sex as Power

Various sources describe rapes in cyberspace, particularly in MUDs (or multi-user dungeon) and their offspring, MOOs (multi-user dungeon-object oriented), including classic rape scenarios in which the woman, during the description of an acknowledged painful violation, is said to want more (for one example, see Bennahum 1994, 35, and Dibell 1993 for one example and its consequences), and discussion groups where stories graphically describe violence against women (for instance, <alt.sex.bondage> and <alt.sex.stories>).

Projection of Adult Male Sexuality onto Women and Children

Besides the come-ons, the ''yos,'' and other harassing behavior, men may use the computer to gain sexual access to younger women and girls and to find affirmation for their attraction to younger women (see <alt.sex.integen>).[8]

"Worried and Waiting for Guidance" wrote to Ann Landers (16 March 1994):

> I am in my late teens and very much concerned about my 12-year-old sister. I was looking for something in her desk and found a bunch of pornographic letters written to 'Margie' from some man across the country on the on-line computer interactive network that my parents subscribe to. These letters are not merely suggestive. They are sexually explicit. This man is in college, and I'm sure he has no idea that my sister is 12 years old. [Or maybe he does.]

And there are cases that go beyond letter writing:

> A Seattle man has been charged with endangering the welfare of a 14-year-old Westchester girl in a case involving the exchange of sexually explicit electronic mail. . . . In one case last year, a suspect in Warwick Township, Pa., was charged with raping a victim he had met through a computer bulletin board (Hevesi 1994, 13)

The advantage to men of computer seduction is the opportunity to assume a variety of characteristics to lower the inhibitions of their targets. By listening to their targets and what they have to say, they begin a grooming process by which they can eventually send pornography. (Pornography is used to break down inhibitions and to show prospective victims that others have done these sexual acts.) Women and children meanwhile may have lowered their defenses because they assume they have the protection of a computer (thinking this cannot really happen because the only access is through the computer), or they may be deliberately taking risks because the computer gives them a sense of security.

Cyber-SexChanges

The net is heavily male and women who want to play with the big boys either have to be ultra tough-talking—one of the boys—or else play off as coy, charming, "little-ol-ME?"-feminine. (Even geeks have fantasy lives, I suppose.) Or use a male/neutral alias with no one the wiser. (Seabrook 1994, 76)

Catharine MacKinnon comments that in a society of sex inequality, "sex is what women *have* to sell, sex is what we are, sex is what we are valued for, we are born sex, we die sex" (1990, 10), and (I would add) online we are sex. How then to escape? If we live in sexual objectification the way fish live in water, and we have not been able to change the water, then the only thing for us is to stop being fish. While this is difficult to accomplish in real life (IRL), all that is required online is changing one's name from Carol to Carl. The way to enter the cyberworld and be unassaulted is by what literary critics Sandra Gilbert and Susan Gubar (1989) call "sexchanges."

The Internet offers the possibility of escaping the pornographic system precisely because, ostensibly, on it everyone is disembodied from the physical markers that generally constitute who we are. In fact, the Internet confirms Ellyn Kaschak's claim that "gender is achieved.... It is something that one *does* repeatedly, probably thousands of times a day. It is a higher-order abstraction whose actual content or referent is, in principle, irrelevant but, in practice, crucial" (1992, 43). This is why successful gender crossing can occur on the Net.

Some women choose this strategy of hiding their gender to protect themselves from male entitlement and the sexual harassment that is expressed. When women pose as men on the Internet, they may experience an "unprecedented sense of entitlement." (Katz 1994, 39) But gaining such privilege is not without repercussions:

When women like LJ manage to pass as male, it makes some men on the net uneasy. Women who wear their new gender as a protective cloak against harassment play a perilous game: if their shroud is suddenly torn away, they find themselves far more besieged than they ever were be-

fore. One Philadelphia woman who was recently caught cross-dressing
on the Internet was threatened with rape—"real" rape—by an enraged
man who reportedly stalked her, having figured out her whereabouts
with the help of her e-mail address. (Katz 1994, 39)

It is not simply that you (female) suddenly benefit from male entitlement: as
well, when gender is a hierarchy, there will be hostility toward those who try
to escape their subordinate status—if you (female) are unlocatable in terms of
gender, you are unavailable as sex.

Perhaps nothing more strongly confirms the feminist analysis of pornography than this: We escape sexual objectification by passing as men. In cyberspace, anyone can experience sexual harassment (simply use a feminine
name), and anyone can achieve male entitlement (use a male name). Though
individually it may free us from its cyber-consequences, sadly, such cyber-
sexchanges do not undermine the pornographic construction of sex at all.

What Can Be Done?

We have long encountered the deceptive presumption that technological
breakthroughs necessarily transform the way culture is ordered. *Who Framed
Roger Rabbit?* was considered a breakthrough in movie making because a
" 'toon" and a living human being seamlessly interact (Watts and Marshall
1988). But the story line could not have been more traditional in asserting the
male gaze, revolving as it did around the to-be-looked-at-ness of a buxom
female. I propose a formula for understanding the current problem:

the killer app + overwhelming male use of computer = spread of
pornographic worldview.

Given this formula, I wish not to argue that computers must be abandoned
(though the disparately negative effect that computer technology has on
women around the world must be addressed[9]) but to establish that any social
problems in real life (IRL) will also be social problems in cyberspace. We fish
are still swimming in the same water. Indeed, perhaps we see the water more
clearly since ostensibly cyberspace is unlocatable. How is it that women are
so locatable in this space that is unlocatable? Cyberspace cannot escape the
social construction of gender because it was constructed by gendered individuals, and because gendered individuals access it, in ways that reinforce the
subjugation of women. Despite hopes that the computer is a democratizing
force in our culture, as long as the culture is suffused with dominance/subordi-
nation along the lines of sex, then the computer environment will participate
in, ratify, and extend this. Moreover, because cyberspace lessens some of the

structures of accountability that "real life" offers, cyberspace may actually accelerate the process of sexual objectification. IRL accountability is provided through the fact that one's actions seldom can be anonymous; in cyberspace, anonymity can be achieved easily. Thus, beside the "killer app" formulation, a second phenomenon occurs in cyberspace that intensifies women's experience of objectification:

> male entitlement + absence of accountability = abusive treatment of women in cyberspace.

Many ways exist to institute accountability in cyberspace. It requires recognizing the harm that is done and creating mechanisms for establishing accountability for the harmful behavior and eliminating it. But recognizing that behavior arising from male entitlement causes harm is not simple. "Pornography is a harm of male supremacy made difficult to see because of its pervasiveness, potency, and principally, because of its success in making the world a pornographic place" (MacKinnon 1992, 463; see also Kappeler 1986). By its rapid transmission of words and images, cyberspace accelerates the making of the world a pornographic place. MacKinnon explains further, "Pornography is not an idea any more than segregation is an idea, although both institutionalize the idea of the inferiority of one group to another. . . . So the issue is not whether pornography is harmful, but how the harm of pornography is to become visible. As compared with what? To the extent pornography succeeds in constructing social reality, it becomes *invisible as harm*" (1987, 154–55). Yet, perhaps cyberspace confirms the radical feminist analysis; because all other markers that locate us are shed, we are faced, inevitably, with the force of gender construction in explaining what happens on the Net. Moreover, cyberspace provides a record: Though e-mail may have a feel of evanescence to it, it, like all other cybertransmissions, may be saved on a disk.

Cyberspace proves radical feminism's claim about the inseparability of speech from act. Consider Julian Dibell's description of the aftermath of a rape in cyberspace:

> Sometimes, for instance, it was hard for me to understand why RL society classifies RL rape alongside crimes against person or property. Since rape can occur without any physical pain or damage [debatable], I found myself reasoning, then it must be classed as a crime against the mind—more intimately and deeply hurtful, to be sure, than cross burnings, wolf whistles, and virtual rape, but undeniably located on the same conceptual continuum. I did not, however, conclude as a result that rapists were protected in any fashion by the First Amendment. Quite the opposite, in fact: the more seriously I took the notion of virtual rape, the

less seriously I was able to take the notion of freedom of speech, with its tidy division of the world into the symbolic and the real. . . . [Here we find] the conflation of speech and act that's inevitable in any computer-mediated world. . . . I can no longer convince myself that our wishful insulation of language from the realm of action has ever been anything but a valuable kludge. (Dibell 1993, 42)

"Laws govern people, not places," we are told in an article called "Computer Network Abuse" (Dierks 1993, 307). So, ostensibly, laws can govern people's actions, people's speech acts, in cyberspace. If free-speech issues had been balanced by concern for equality IRL, then the problems in cyberspace would be easier to confront, since on the one hand cybercommunication seems to be pure speech. But laws have recognized that speech does cause harm: most of sexual harassment, yelling "fire" in a crowded movie theater, libel, invasion of privacy, blackmail, bribery, conspiracy (see MacKinnon 1987, 156). Some speech is regulated and rightly so, and arguments that equality interests must balance any free-speech claims could make inroads against pornography as protected speech. Even antihunting activists' speech has been curbed to protect hunters' interests (see Comninou 1995). Clearly, some people's interests can be protected from speech acts. But which people's?

In fact, another thing being made perfectly clear in cyberspace is that women are being denied free speech. Who has access to making speech and whose speech is being silenced? Cheris Kramarae indicates the irony here:

The journal *NewMedia* states the problem on one cover as "Digital Sex, Technology, Law & Censorship" with a photo of a nude woman covered only by the words. (If we want to begin to understand the problem, we can wonder why not a photo of a nude man with genitalia hanging out? Would that sell as many copies or mean the same?) The argument is basically the same as those we've heard so many times: The First Amendment guarantees each of us free speech. Why, then, isn't there concern about those who don't have access to free speech and those whose free speech is impeded by the "Virtual Valerie" programs? (1995, 48).

If equality interests did balance free-speech claims, cyberspace could become a less hostile space. Cheris Kramarae and H. Jeannie Taylor suggest some valuable responses that universities could—at the minimum—take: women-only forums for speech; training for moderators around issues of racism and sexism and who would have the right to censor material; a grievance procedure for complaints of sexual harassment on the nets (which "should be part of the sexual harassment policy of any institution that sponsors [or allows] electronic network communication'') with "periodic reports, to a central body, on the number and types of complaints and action taken" (1993, 57–59).

Universities have excluded sexually explicit material as well as sexual and racial jokes. For instance, Carnegie Mellon University decided to exclude sexually explicit material on the Internet from the campus computer system. They did so fearing that the school could be subject to prosecution under state obscenity and pornography laws. Similarly, "Stanford University officials decided that since one of the goals of the university was to provide an educational atmosphere free of racism, bigotry and other forms of prejudice, computer resources should not be used to exploit them." They authored a message for those attempting to call up racial and sexual jokes:

> Jokes based on . . . stereotypes perpetuate racism, sexism and intolerance. . . . This bulletin board does not serve a university education purpose; its content is offensive; it does not . . . provide a forum for the examination and discussion of intolerance, an exchange of views of the members of the University community. (cited in Kramarae and Kramer 1995, 33)

Moreover, sexual harassment and stalking through use of e-mail is actionable. One aspect of the sexual harassment case settled by Chevron in 1995 included "offensive jokes, E-mail messages and comments about their clothes and body parts, and, in one case, sadistic pornography sent through the company mail. . . . Women would boot their computers and find a graphic of a man masturbating, or E-mail lists of reasons why beer is better than women" (Lewin 1995, A10). The court found that this created a sexually hostile environment. Finally, in one case, a man has been charged with the federal crime of "transporting threatening material across state lines" for writing a sexually explicit story of rape, bondage, sadism, and murder that used the actual name of a student at his university (Lewis 1995).

Until pornography is seen as an issue of equality for women more than as a free-speech issue for men, one further alternative exists for creating a less hostile environment for women: It is for men to call other men to accountability for their speech acts and their use of pornography.

We are told by historians of pornography that "To evoke 'reading with one hand' is usually to evoke a founding image in the history of pornography at the same time" (DeJean 1993, 110). Interestingly, this founding image is expressly evoked when the subject is compusex: Compusex leads to "one-handed typing" (Robinson and Tamosaitis 1993, 154). Catharine MacKinnon reminds us that "what pornography does, it does in the real world, not only in the mind" (1993, 15), which is why, after all, one-handed typing is needed.

What this tells us, in essence, is that this is no brave new world of erotica: Actually it is still their father's pornography, it's just not their father's technology. And we fish are still living in it.

Notes

Thanks to Charles Ess, Marie Fortune, Cheris Kramarae, Jayne Loader, and Heidi Thompson-Pena, for their assistance with citations, reflections, and cyberspace anecdotes.

1. "There are few women hackers. This is a male world. Though hackers would deny that theirs is a macho culture, the preoccupation with winning and of subjecting oneself to increasingly violent tests (or stress?) makes their world peculiarly male in spirit, peculiarly unfriendly to women. There is, too, a flight from relationship with people to relationship with the machine—a defensive maneuver more common to men than to women. The computer that is the partner in this relationship offers a particularly seductive refuge to someone who is having trouble dealing with people. It is active, reactive, it talks back" (Turkle 1984, 210–11).

2. Elizabeth Dodson Gray 1981, 110. Thanks to Charles Ess for calling my attention to this discussion.

3. Even a word such as *algolagnia* (sexual gratification derived from inflicting or experiencing pain) takes on computer nuances, because of ALGOL (ALGebraic Oriented Language).

4. Wetware: "a hard-wired cyberspace cowpokes' euphemism for flesh and blood people" (Robinson and Tamosaitis 1993, 31).

5. Barringer reports a similar experience: after Angel introduces herself as a stripper, "the next person to join the conversion—his sign-on was Kurt—asked Angel her chest measurement" (Barringer 1994, B7).

6. "High-tech peep shows: interactive videos on CD-ROM featuring naked Penthouse models and hard-core porn actresses who respond to commands from a keyboard" (Tierny 1994, 1).

7. Whether one inserts these objects or imagines inserting them is not explicitly told in this description. The issue of rape with any of these objects is unspoken, but it needs to be raised.

8. I am not here addressing the issue of pedophilia itself and the way pedophiles use computer bulletin boards. It is almost inevitable that the least-protected speech would gravitate to the Internet with its disembodied culture of anonymity. With the Internet, the computer is not only tool for the pedophile's compulsive record-keeping but also resource and, for some, contact point with future victims. On the Net, pedophiles can find other pedophiles (through <alt.sex.pedophile> and other bulletin boards known only to them) and affirm their interests as acceptable. Pedophiles have a need

to discuss their experiences, their plans, or share victims (though, admittedly, on the Net they may also overstate their own experiences). They may not have many close adult friends since "they cannot share the most important part of their life (their sexual interest in children) with most adults" (Lanning 1992, 18), but through the Net they discover people with similar compulsions. This subject, raised as early as 1988 (Crewsdon), has recently gained a great deal of attention (see Lanning 1992; Bates 1994; Kantrowitz 1994a).

9. Feminists have examined these negative effects and pointed out that women are the laborers producing the chips, women become the "wordprocessors" whose work is now fragmented, and women experience diffential access to cyberspace (see for instance, Barker and Downing 1985).

References

The American Heritage Dictionary of the English Language. 3d ed. S.v. "horny."

Barker, Jane, and Hazel Downing. 1985. Word Processing and the Transformation of Patriarchal Relations of Control in the Office. In *The Social Shaping of Technology: How the Refrigerator Got Its Hum,* ed. Donald MacKenzie and Judy Wajcman, 147–64. Philadelphia: Open University Press.

Barringer, Felicity. 1994. Exploring Cyberspace, Talking to Strangers. *New York Times,* 30 June, B7.

Barron, James. 1995. Internet Etiquette: Mind Your E-Manners. *New York Times,* January 11, B1, B4.

Bates, Stephen. 1994. The First Amendment in Cyberspace. *Wall Street Journal,* 1 June, A19.

Bennahum, David. 1994. Fly Me to the MOO: Adventures in Textual Reality. *Lingua Franca,* June, 1, 22–36.

Bowman, Cynthia Grant. 1993. Street Harassment and the Informal Ghettoization of Women. *Harvard Law Review* 106, no. 3 (January): 517–80.

Buscaglia, Marco. 1995. Carnegie Mellon University Decision Could Set Internet Censorship Precedent. *The Mirror,* 10 February, 6.

Comninou, Maria. 1995. Speech, Pornography, and Hunting. In *Animals and Women: Feminist Theoretical Explorations,* ed. Carol J. Adams and Josephine Donovan. Durham, NC: Duke University Press.

Crewdson, John. 1988. *By Silence Betrayed: Sexual Abuse of Children in America.* New York: Harper and Row.

DeJean, Joan. 1993. The Politics of Pornography: L'Ecole des Filles. In *The Invention of Pornography: Obscenity and the Origins of Modernity, 1500–1800,* ed. Lynn Hunt. New York: Zone Books.

Dibell, Julian. 1993. A Rape in Cyberspace. *Village Voice,* 21 December, 36–42.

Dierks, Michael P. 1993. Computer Network Abuse. *Harvard Journal of Law and Technology* 6 (Spring): 307–42.

Dworkin, Andrea. 1981. *Pornography: Men Possessing Women.* New York: Perigee.

———. 1985. Against the Male Flood: Censorship, Pornography, and Equality. *Harvard Women's Law Journal* 8: 1–29.

Ebben, Maureen, and Cheris Kramarae. 1993. Women and Information Technologies: Creating a Cyberspace of Our Own. *In Women, Information, Technology, and Scholarship,* ed. H. Jeannie Taylor, Cheris Kramarae, and Maureen Ebben, 15–27. Urbana, IL: Center for Advanced Study.

Findlen, Paula. 1993. Humanism, Politics and Pornography in Renaissance Italy. In *The Invention of Pornography: Obscenity and the Origins of Modernity, 1500–1800,* ed. Lynn Hunt. New York: Zone Books.

Gilbert, Sandra M., and Susan Gubar. 1989. *No Man's Land: The Place of the Woman Writer in the Twentieth Century.* Vol. 2, *Sexchanges.* New Haven: Yale University Press.

Gray, Elizabeth Dodson. 1981. *Green Paradise Lost.* Wellesley, MA: Roundtable Press.

Harmon, Amy. 1993. Computers Are Newest Market for Pornography. *Los Angeles Times,* 30 November.

Hevesi, Dennis. 1994. Man Charged in E-Mail Sex Talk. *New York Times,* 26 June, 13.

Jaffe, Herb, producer. 1977. *Demon Seed.* Los Angeles: MGM.

Kantrowitz, Barbara. 1994a. Child Abuse in Cyberspace. *Newsweek,* 18 April, 40.

———. 1994b. Men, Women, Computers. *Newsweek,* 16 May, 48–55.

Kappeler, Susanne. 1986. *The Pornography of Representation.* Minneapolis: University of Minnesota Press.

Kaschak, Ellyn. 1992. *Engendered Lives: A New Psychology of Women's Experiences.* New York: Basic Books.

Katz, Alyssa. 1994. Modem Butterfly: The Politics of Online Gender Bending. *Village Voice,* 15 March, 39–40.

Kramarae, Cheris. 1995. A Backstage Critique of Virtual Reality. In *Cybersociety: Computer-Mediated Communication and Community,* ed. Steven G. Jones, 36–56. Thousand Oaks, CA: Sage Publications.

Kramarae, Cheris, and Jane Kramer. 1995. Net Gains, Net Losses. *Women's Review of Books* 12, no. 5 (February): 33–35.

Kramarae, Cheris, and H. Jeanne Taylor. 1993. Women and Men on Electronic Networks: A Conversation or a Monologue? In *Women, Information, Technology, and Scholarship,* ed. H. Jeannie Taylor, Cheris Kramarae, and Maureen Ebben, 52–61. Urbana, IL: Center for Advanced Study.

Landsberg, Michelle. 1992. Demand Power and Parity: Feminists Vow to Take Back Politics. *New Directions for Women,* July-August, 3.

Lanning, Kenneth V. 1992. *Child Molesters: A Behavioral Analysis.* Arlington, VA: National Center for Missing and Exploited Children.

Lederer, Laura, ed. 1980. *Take Back the Night: Women on Pornography.* New York: William Morrow.

Lewin, Tamar. 1995. Chevron Agrees to Pay $2.2 Million in Settlement of Sexual Harassment Case. *New York Times,* 22 February, A10.

Lewis, Peter H. 1995. An Internet Author of Sexually Violent Fiction Faces Charges. *New York Times,* 11 February, 7.

"Lovelace, Linda," with Mike McGrady. 1980. *Ordeal.* New York: Citadel.

MacKinnon, Catharine. 1987. *Feminism Unmodified.* Cambridge: Harvard University Press.

———. 1989. *Toward a Feminist Theory of State.* Cambridge: Harvard University Press.

———. 1990. Liberalism and the Death of Feminism. In *The Sexual Liberals and the Attack on Feminism,* ed. Dorchen Leidholdt and Janice G. Raymond, 3–13. Elmsford, NY: Pergamon Press.

———. 1991. Pornography as Defamation and Discrimination. *Boston University Law Review* 71: 793–815.

———. 1992. Pornography, Civil Rights and Speech. In *Pornography: Women, Violence and Civil Liberties. A Radical New View,* ed. Catherine Itzin, 456–511. New York: Oxford University Press.

———. 1993. *Only Words.* Cambridge: Harvard University Press.

Mulvey, Laura. 1975. Visual Pleasure and Narrative Cinema. *Screen* 16(3): 11.

Raymond, Eric S. 1993. *The New Hacker's Dictionary.* 2d ed. Cambridge: MIT Press.

Robinson, Phillip, and Nancy Tamosaitis. 1993. *The Joy of Cybersex: An Underground Guide to Electronic Erotica.* New York: Brady.

Rutten, Peter, et al. 1994. *Netguide.*™ *Your Map to the Services, Information, and Entertainment on the Electronic Highway.* New York: Random House.

Seabrook, John. 1994. My First Flame. *New Yorker,* 6 June, 70–79.

Selfe, Cynthia L., and Paul R. Meyer. 1991. Testing Claims for On-Line Conferences. *Written Communication* 8, no. 2 (April): 163–92.

Stefanac, Suzanne. 1993. Sex and the New Media. *Newmedia,* April, 38–45.

Steinert-Threlkeld, Tom. 1994. North Texas Free Net, and Other Wandering. *Dallas Morning News,* 28 May, 2F.

Tannen, Deborah. 1994. Gender Gap in Cyberspace. *Newsweek,* 16 May, 52–53.

Tierney, John. 1994. Porn, the Low-Slung Engine of Progress. *New York Times,* 9 January, Section 2, 1, 18.

Turkle, Sherry. 1984. *The Second Self: Computers and the Human Spirit.* New York: Simon and Schuster.

Watts, Robert, and Frank Marshall, producers. 1988. *Who Framed Roger Rabbit?* Los Angeles: Warner/Touchstone/Amblin.

Wiener, Jon. 1994. Free Speech on the Internet. *The Nation,* 13 June, 825–28.

Williams, Robin, and Steve Cummings. 1993. *Jargon: An Informal Dictionary of Computer Terms.* Berkeley, CA: Peachpit Press.

8

Power Online: A Poststructuralist Perspective on Computer-Mediated Communication

SUNH-HEE YOON

Introduction

South Korea (hereafter, Korea) is one of many countries that have developed computerization to promote productivity and public welfare. It has become a fad to spread the notion of "the computer mind" in Korea. "The computer mind" is a governmentally constructed phrase, now part of a larger discourse, that connotes that public and private institutions, as well as individual users, should adopt and learn about computers in order to take advantage of convenient services and to modernize their life styles. The government has disseminated this notion to develop computerization on a national scale. Although in governmental policy analysis, technology refers simply to a neutral tool that will promote economic productivity and convenience for the public, I will argue that the discourse of the computer mind reveals technology's involvement in shaping the mind of an individual.

I begin by developing a new methodology for examining the complex process of technological deployment and its relationship to human life. In an initial discussion of such conventional theories as liberalism-positivism and Marxism-structuralism, I argue that these theories do not adequately explicate the complex phenomena of technological power. Liberalism-positivism usually emphasizes the positive side of technology and sees communication technology as a developmental impetus. Marxism-structuralism emphasizes the power dimension of technology and considers communication technology as an instrument of social inequality. Rejecting the epistemological grounds of both views, I formulate an alternative methodology, one that relies primarily on Michel Foucault's analysis of power. Using this methodology to analyze the Korean discourse of the computer mind, I then develop an alternative

theory of technology which can more fully explain the complexity of technological power in modern society.

The claim that technology is a neutral tool rests on the assumption that
technologies are somehow distinct from the human self and human existence.
By examining the discourse of the computer mind, however, we will see that
technological knowledge is involved in fashioning the human mind and body.
In particular, technological power is sustained by human engagement in practice: Human beings are not separated from technological power but, in fact,
engage in it. This analysis shows that technologies are not separate from the
self, but affect the conditions of human existence. This does not mean that
technology as a material form determines the course of human life and the
path of social evolution. Nevertheless, technology as a knowledge form is
deeply involved in human life at the microlevel—in everyday life rather than
in an institutionalized social power.

Liberalist Views of Technology

Conventional liberal theories tend to assume that technology provides an
impetus for social development and the promotion of human welfare. For the
sake of convenience, I will call these theories "developmentalist." They have
the idealistic notion that technology will create a new world that will relieve
humans of their material needs and dispense with physical limitations such as
depleting natural resources. Developmentalists believe that modern technology contributes to economic prosperity as well as political and cultural mod-
ernization. They anticipate positive changes in the world through new
technologies, particularly communication technology such as computer networks, satellites, value-added networks (VAN) and integrated-services digital
networks (ISDN). They believe these new technologies will provide a solution
for economic and social problems in the world by organizing society in a
progressive way. First, developmentalists appreciate the economic value of
communication technology. They believe that it provides a means of prosperity by creating value-added resources (Rogers 1986). Moreover, communication technology best fits into the corporate structure in the contemporary
world. When business is computerized, it boosts the economy by lowering
costs and accelerating communication within and between companies (Harrington 1991). For example, in the contemporary world, because business
organizations are becoming more and more multinationalized and internation-
alized, reducing transaction costs for transborder communications is profitable
for multinational corporations.

Second, communication technology is considered to be a promising
solution for conservation of natural resources. People all over the world now
face environmental problems and the fear of depletion because they have

used up natural resources in the process of industrialization. Struggle for environmental conservation is an inevitable consequence. Some people believe communication technology will forestall environmental disaster because it promotes "deindustrialization" (Agger 1985). Deindustrialization refers to an alternative production system through high-tech industries as opposed to the production system of heavy resource consumption in industrialization. If the work process is computerized, it augments productivity while consuming fewer natural resources and creating fewer environmental side effects. Communication technology is considered to contribute to the conservation of nature as well as to produce high economic values.

Third, developmentalists argue that communication technology will relieve workers from sweat and toil, or "dirty work," because the production process will be totally automated (Bell 1973). The economy will be transformed from a manufacturing center in the industrial society to a service center in the information society. According to Daniel Bell, "in a postindustrial society . . . [w]hat counts is not raw muscle power, or energy, but information" (1973, 127). In the postindustrial society, the professional and technical (white collar) class becomes the dominant workforce as compared to semiskilled (blue collar) workers in the industrial society.

Fourth, according to the developmentalist perspective, communication technology promotes decentralization of the society. People can do their work through computers without commuting to the office every day. People do not have to make long trips, but can have meetings through teleconferences, and shop and bank at home through the two-way communication system and so forth. Alvin Toffler (1980) argues that communication technology contributes to the decentralization of society by creating a new civilization, or what he calls the "third wave." According to him, information technology disorganizes the mass society which has been created in the process of industrialization, or the "second wave." The third wave creates a new way of life in the production process and in the family structure. Toffler believes that technological development brings about diversified and decentralized life styles in the public and private sectors. As technology develops, society becomes demassified by flexible work hours, spread-out workplaces, and diverse mechanisms of communication (Toffler 1980, 171–83, 210–23). In the demassified society, people can enjoy their diverse life styles and communal lives by belonging to regional and social subcultures. Toffler also believes that information technology provides a tool for constructing democracy through the decentralization of society and two-way communication channels.

Fifth, developmentalists argue that communication technology brings about changes in organizations or in social relations. Bell argues that the most significant aspect of postindustrial society is increasing bureaucratization. Despite the differences in social systems such as capitalist and socialist systems, technology reorganizes all of society into a similar form based on bureaucratization through science and technology. As an economy is changed into a service economy, the market does not adequately meet people's needs, so that bureaucracy increasingly plays the important role of guiding the economy and organizing social welfare (Bell 1973, 128). Bell believes that conflicts between ideologies will end as capitalist and socialist societies converge into a bureaucratic and technocratic social system (Bell 1960). He predicts that technocrats will rule the postindustrial society by controlling information and using communication technology in contrast with previous societies where politicians ruled through ideology.

Marxist Views of Technology

Unlike developmentalists, many Marxists do not believe that communication technology benefits the people in general. The general public experiences the disadvantages of communication technology because the development of technology leads to commercialization of information. Due to commercialization, people sometimes have to pay for information that they used to get free of charge, for example, through public libraries and public information systems (Schiller 1989). Also unlike developmentalists, Marxist political economists argue that the economic value of communication technology will never trickle down to the bottom. Instead, communication technology deepens social inequality because it favors business interests and people in power. As opposed to the developmentalist view of technology, Marxism emphasizes the power dimension in technology. Marxism investigates the social relations of technology by characterizing human history according to modes of production. Although technology, defined as the means of production, is an important part of Marxist historical materialism, Marxism does not view technology in its material form only. Marxists seek to uncover the political economy of technology, or the power dimension of technology.

In Marx's historical materialism, technology does not unilaterally determine social relations, nor do social relations deliberately manipulate history. Nevertheless, technology represents a significant part of historical development because people, particularly the labor class, engage in class conflicts in their interaction with technology in everyday life, even if unconsciously. The labor class does not always confront the capitalist class, nor does the labor class instantly head toward revolution. Instead, the labor class is involved in class conflicts by consistently confronting machines and the production process until the structure is mature enough to be exploded.

For Marx, technology cannot be a neutral tool or simply a set of objects. It is involved in class conflicts because it creates conditions that alienate people from human nature and work processes from human creativity (Fromm

1961). For Marxists, the history of technological development is the history of implanting social inequality. In the Marxist framework, technological development deepens social inequality and ignites class conflicts. In the precapitalist society, class relations were less conflictive because the forces of production were slowly developed and the upper class had a very limited means of production: land. Marx argues that in the process of industrialization and commercialization in capitalism, a majority of the people lost all their means of production, except labor power (Hindess and Hirst 1975).

Marxist political economists provide insightful criticism of communication technology in general and computerization in particular. Applying Marxism, political economists in communication, such as Mosco (1989) and Robins and Webster (1984), demonstrate the role of computerization for class dominance. Theories of political economy bring up a number of points that demonstrate the impacts of technology on social relations. In the production process, labor power becomes degraded according to the technological development of capital-intensive industries. In traditional society and the early capitalist society, according to Marx, exploitation of labor is the most important source of economic value. In late capitalism, by contrast, technology replaces the major production process with machines, so that labor appears to be auxiliary in the production process. Accordingly, computerization frequently brings about an increase in the unemployment rate. Mosco demonstrates the decline of employment rate in the telecommunication industry in the United States due to automation.

Moreover, technological development obscures class conflicts by reorganizing labor power. In late capitalism, the labor class is often segregated from the direct production process. Society is reorganized, as white-collar workers increase and blue-collar workers decrease. The existence of a large white-collar class, or middle class, disguises class conflicts between capitalists and the labor class. According to Marxists, middle-class people lose their identity as the labor class while consuming bourgeois culture, particularly through mass communication. Thus, in late capitalism, class relations are amalgamated with cultural and political matters. The development of communication technology leads to isolation of the labor class as a group. Computerization and automation of factory and office increasingly eliminate the common space for the labor class. In technologically developed societies, as compared to early capitalism, the working class has less chance to gather together and complain about their working conditions. In early capitalism, working conditions were certainly unpleasant and harmful for workers' health and welfare. Paradoxically, in the early industrial society, the compact space and unpleasant working conditions provided a common space for the labor class where they organized collective actions and shared working-class culture. On the contrary, in late capitalism, technology loosens the spatial confinement of the workplace; computerization and automation of factories and offices allow dispersed spaces. Due to geographical dispersion, the labor class has less human interaction in the working process. As technology develops, workers are more frequently interfaced with computers and automated machines, and less frequently meet with other workers. As workers lose a common place to confer about collective bargainings, labor becomes deunionized. Due to the development of communication technology, the labor class is deunionized and loses bargaining power. This is detrimental to the labor class, not only with regard to specific labor groups (e.g., those in computer and telecommunication industries) but also with regard to the labor class as a whole, both nationally and internationally. Labor value is determined not by the individual firm but by the society as a whole.

A Poststructuralist View of Technological Power

Marxist political economy provides a valuable framework in which to critique the idealized vision of developmentalism. However, Marxism is limited in its ability to explain the complex and diverse social phenomena of the contemporary world. While addressing the power dimension of technology, Marxist political economy offers only a limited understanding of the complex power relations involved in technological deployment. It characterizes technological power only in the context of class conflict. It assumes that class relations dominate every aspect of human life. Marxist political economy only explicates the intervention of repressive power involved in technological employment. It assumes that humans and technology are separate entities in confrontation. Based on this assumption, Marxist political economists tend to demonstrate simply the negative effects of technological development by demonstrating how benefits to the power center in society work against the interests of the majority of the population.

However, such negative effects are only a portion of all the power relations involved in technological deployment. By concentrating on class dominance, Marxist political economy oversimplifies diverse aspects of human engagement in technological deployment. Contrary to the Marxist assumption, people integrate technology into their lives more often through voluntary adoption than through the dictates of a power center. Technology is normalized in everyday life, including the workplace, home and public places, to the extent that it has become a part of one's life style and thinking process. But as part of life style and thought, technology thus shapes what counts as "knowledge" in a society. In turn, this "knowledge" plays an important role in consolidating power in the contemporary technological society. Thus, knowledge and power are so closely connected to one another that these two cannot be discussed separately.

To portray the complexity of human engagement in technology, this study refines a methodology drawn from Michel Foucault. Foucault provides an insightful conceptual framework for examining the complex interrelationship between human life and technology. Using Foucault's concept of power, one can detect the presence of technological power even when people voluntarily use and enjoy the benefits of technology. Technology exercises what Foucault calls positive power as well as repressive power.[1] From the Foucauldian perspective, power is too pervasive to situate it only in the centers. It is dispersed and discursively practiced by people in diverse social settings. The dispersion of power is channeled through discourse in everyday life. Discourse reveals the process by which technology is materialized through human practice. Technology has no objective nature, but it is constantly formed through discursive practice. The Foucauldian approach transforms the focus of research from an analysis of structural power to a description of power in practice. In contrast with Habermas, Foucault does not seek to create a grand theory and a universal model of technology and democracy.[2]

Although Foucault does not intend to totally deconstruct rationality itself, he withdraws himself from constructing any alternative vision of universal rationality because it has exercised power in history, particularly in the Western Enlightenment tradition. A theory of dialectical Enlightenment dominates discourse by identifying a subject as a rational being and excluding disqualified discourses from its rational discourse.[3] What is missing in dialectical Enlightenment theory, according to Foucault, is the fact that theorists also situate themselves in a specific historical and structural momentum and engage in one form of discourse which is genealogically constructed not by autonomous and rational subjects but by power (Foucault 1972). Thus, universal validity claims in dialectical Enlightenment are at most valid only at the local level.

A Foucauldian Concept of Technology

In Foucault's view, modern technology is empirically used as a tool for imprisoning and surveilling individuals. Unlike other critical scholars such as Habermas, Foucault would not argue that the suppressive tool of modern technology may lead to emancipation of individuals and the social system at the end of the dialectic process. What he clearly perceives in the genealogy of technology is that modern technology provides a docile means of controlling people and training them, as if people were in a prison of global scale (Foucault 1979, 135).

Foucault elaborates a theory of technology in his genealogical analysis of criminality. Foucault (1979) observes that the mechanism of punishment has been changed from torture to scientific application. According to the development of techno-politics of punishment, or "humanization of the penalties," punishment is no longer directed to the body but to the soul, and not only to the soul of a criminal but also to the souls of all people outside the prison (Foucault 1979, 101). Punishment is no longer a theatrical event separating a criminal from individuals outside the prison. Foucault states that

> a whole corpus of individualizing knowledge was being organized that took as its field of reference not so much the crime committed (at least in isolation), but the potentiality of danger that lies hidden in an individual and which is manifested in his observed everyday conduct. The prison functions in this as an apparatus of knowledge. (126)

According to Foucault, punishment in the modern period works as a criterion of creating "legitimate" knowledge rather than as a means of reforming criminals. Foucault goes on to say that the technology of punishment and discipline creates "docile bodies" so that individuals are "voluntarily" confined in the prison. No third party such as a repressive monarch or cruel executioner is needed to imprison individuals, but individuals discipline themselves according to scientific criteria and the technique of subjection. Through this technique of subjection, a new self, a "docile body," is formed (Foucault 1979, 135–69). Foucault identifies prison as the disciplinary model of factories, schools, and hospitals in the contemporary society. Thus, for Foucault (1988), there is no essential nature of self, but a subject, his/her body and soul, is constructed by power/knowledge.

Foucault visualizes the prison as a disciplinary mechanism in modern society, a vision he constructs by borrowing Bentham's architectural figure of the Panopticon. Foucault describes Panopticism as follows:

> This enclosed, segmented space, observed at every point, in which the individuals are inserted in a fixed place, in which the slightest movements are supervised, in which all events are recorded, in which an uninterrupted work of writing links the center and periphery, in which power is exercised without division, according to a continuous hierarchical figure, in which each individual is constantly located, examined and distributed among the living beings, the sick and the dead—all this constitutes a compact model of the disciplinary mechanism. (1979, 197)

One could imagine that the technology of microelectronics serves as a means of recording and surveillance in the Panopticon (Provenzo 1992). Foucault clearly criticizes Panoptic technology as he states that "he [each individual] is seen, but he does not see; he is the object of information, never a subject in communication" (1979, 200).

However, Foucault demonstrates an ambivalent position about Panopticism. He does not totally dismiss modern technology because of the disciplinary power he observes through his theoretical interrogation of the Panopticon. At times, he also acknowledges the positive functions of the Panopticon. According to Foucault, Panopticism is "a functional mechanism that improves the exercise of power by making it lighter, more rapid, more effective, a design of subtle coercion for a society to come" (1979, 209). Furthermore, he does go beyond simply assessing the efficiency of disciplinary power of Panopticism. Foucault argues that the disciplinary power of Panopticism is not a tyrannical, repressive power. He states, "There is no risk, therefore, that the increase of power created by the Panoptic machine may degenerate into tyranny; the disciplinary mechanism will be democratically controlled" (209). Foucault affirms that Panopticism is more democratic than tyrannical. Obviously, Foucault would not identify the surveillance system of Panopticism with democracy if one defines democracy as a Habermasian notion. Foucault, however, does not construct any democratic project as Habermas and other Enlightenment theorists do. Here, Foucault does not presume democracy as an emancipatory process, nor as an accomplishment of a true communitarian society. For Foucault, human beings have no essential characteristics, but subjects are constructed in relation to power/knowledge. The Panopticon is the most efficient power mechanism that creates the body and mind of a subject. Foucault conceives the voluntary disciplinary process of Panopticism as democracy. Thus, for Foucault, democracy is only one form of rule in which power/knowledge is embedded.

From the Foucauldian perspective, the development of technology does not change the power structure, nor does it promote communication among individuals. It only peripheralizes individuals, as in the Panopticon. Computerization only advances visibility and recordability of the supervisor at the top of the tower while segregating and confining the people at peripheral cells in the Panopticon. Computerization provides a tool for efficient surveillance in the Panopticon. Computers store massive data about individuals, a process never done in the past. Computers collect detailed information as well as information that is private. Oscar Gandy demonstrates that "technological developments are making the invasion of privacy less difficult and competitive markets are making such information more valuable" (Gandy and Simmons 1986, 163). As technology develops, information is delivered through more diversified and privatized channels such as computer networks. Meanwhile, individuals become more transparent due to the development of computerization. Through computer networks private information is easily accessible. However, individuals rarely have private information under their control. Gandy (1993) argues that privatization of information is produced in the process of losing the public sphere. Individuals become data sources without having control over the data themselves. This computer network constitutes Panoptic architecture where individuals are instantly seen but they cannot see.

Foucault provides valuable insight by turning attention from the structure to the empirical process and from the negative concept of power to positive power. Moreover, Foucault attempts to deconstruct any scientific method and universal principle which has had a dogmatic power in academic discourse. In the Foucauldian framework, no society is prejudged by theoretical assumptions and methodological procedures until discourse is stated by voices of local people and defined by a concrete political economic context and a local cultural term.

Foucauldian Methodology

Foucault develops discourse analysis with his unique methodology, and thereby attempts to break up the tradition of structuralism in Western thought. He is critical of Marxism as well as positivism, as both pursue rationality beyond human practice. Foucault wants to get down to the ground by looking at the discourse that ordinary people use in their everyday life. For Foucault, there is no power behind discourse which manipulates human life. Discourse channels power in its apparent form as it is heard and read (Foucault 1972, 48, 55). In discourse analysis, researchers do not situate themselves to judge truth beyond the empirical process, nor do they interpret discourse in people's everyday lives from a transcendent position. Discourse reveals itself as power and reality without being mediated by transcendental rationality. Thus, discourse analysis has to start with the concrete, empirical process.

Discourse analysis is one way of assessing the discursive practice of human life. Through discourse analysis, linguists attempt to understand social contexts by looking at the thematic structure or cognitive interpretation of the text and speech (Dijk 1985). Foucault initiates a new methodology of discourse analysis by going beyond the linguistic system. Foucault tries to discern how discourse becomes a common vehicle for people to produce and reproduce power. According to Foucault, discourses are not groups of signs but "practices that systematically form the objects of which they speak" (1972, 49). The main point in his argument on discourse is that language does not represent objects, but objects are formed by the practice of speaking, that is, discourse.

Despite Foucault's epistemological contributions, the concept of discourse is not crystal clear in his theory. He admits that he has abused and overexpanded the term "discourse." According to Foucault's definition, "the term discourse can be defined as the group of statements that belong to a single system of [discursive] formation" (1972, 107). In this definition, statements and discourses are events in human practices rather than a representation of objective relations between objects and language. Statements are not randomly uttered, but they repetitively appear in certain patterns, or what Foucault called "discursive formation." Hence, discursive formations impose certain forms in discourse. For Foucault, there is no objective relation between language and objects, nor is there any true essence behind discourse. Thus, discourse is only temporal and historical, and exists only within a certain historical time and space. Discourse is defined in a given time and in a given social, economic, geographic, and linguistic area. Discourse is defined in a given time and in a given social, economic, geographic, and linguistic area.

Foucault elaborates a methodological guideline for discourse analysis by looking at the formation of objects through discourse. In order to detect the relation between discourse and objects, a researcher must first describe the discourse of objects on a surface level. Then she has to identify the authority of creating a certain discourse while limiting others (Foucault 1972, 41). For Foucault, discourse is not necessarily related to objects but is formed by suppressing other forms of discourse. At the last level, one analyzes the specific process in order to demonstrate how different kinds of discourse are related and divided as objects (Foucault 1972, 42). In the Foucauldian framework, power/knowledge is involved in discourse. For Foucault, power is visible not only in a form of institutionalized and repressive power. Foucault discerns power in a broader realm of human life by including positive power in everyday life. Even when people communicate with each other and reach a consensus, power may still exist in an invisible form.

Poststructuralist Analysis of Korean Computerization

The Foucauldian approach is useful in scrutinizing the concrete process of technological deployment, particularly in non-Western societies, such as Korea, where social formations are different from the Western mode. Foucault tries to deconstruct the universal model of development by bringing up epistemological criticism of grand theories, including liberalism-positivism and structuralism-Marxism. He challenges the assumption that human history is determined by the universal principle or the structure as a hidden force behind everyday practice. By criticizing the concept of historical totality and continuity as dogmatic, Foucault seeks the fragmented, sporadic, and discontinuous events and discourses that represent human practice in history. Adopting Foucault's insight, this section describes the political economic and cultural context of Korean computerization in critical comparison with the universal models of liberalism and Marxism that have represented Western societies.

In Korea, social relations have been formed through a process different from that of Western societies. As compared to Western societies, the social formation of Korea cannot be discussed without considering international factors. Because Korea is one of the industrializing countries, international factors significantly influence governmental policies, domestic economy, and business practices. Although Neo-Marxian theories explain situations in the Third World, they cannot adequately explicate Korean development in general and computerization in particular. Unlike the dependency model, for instance, Korea not only is passively exploited by international power, but also simultaneously experiences a contradictory process of international interactions including development and dependency. Through this process, Korea has passed from underdevelopment to the status of a newly industrializing country. Korea's economic development, nonetheless, does not prove the triumph of the neoclassical economic theory, because Korea remains fundamentally affected by the political economy of industrialized countries. Thus, one needs to account for a number of complex factors in order adequately to examine social relations of technological development and computerization in Korea.

Moreover, neither liberal nor Marxist theories sufficiently explain the role of the state in technological development in the non-Western context. Liberal theories do not take account of the strong state phenomena in economic and technological development in Korea. Marxist political economy, on the other hand, does not sufficiently explain the fact that the Korean government has kept strong autonomous power over the capitalist class, not vice versa. The state not only has relative autonomy from the capitalist class, but also creates the capitalist class itself and its interests. Through planning economic development, the state has established the Korean economic and big business conglomerates (*chaebols*) in the process of industrialization. Accordingly, the capitalist class is usually subordinated to the state. The state plays a strong role in controlling the entire social system.

Computerization is one of the examples in which the state plays an important role in initiating technological development. The process of computerization is assessed by different criteria than the liberal and Marxist measurements. The Korean government has dominated the planning and implementation process of computerization. Since the early 1980s, the Korean government has developed communication technology. It has not evolved based simply on a technical process and the market principle. The process of technological development reflects the particular political economy of Korean society. It is not a coincidence that the Korean government plays the most important role in directing technological adoption.

In Korea, computers were first introduced in 1967 during the Park period. Although the introduction of computers was a historical event, the Park administration did not pay much attention to the development of computer technology, concentrating instead on manufacturing industries such as light and heavy chemical industries. In the 1980s, the Chun administration switched economic development strategies from heavy chemical industries to the high-tech information industry because the people heavily criticized the former president's development plans. For political reasons, Chun integrated those criticisms into his development plans. Information technology was Chun's strategic industry for promoting economic development as well as for avoiding political criticisms, including labor disputes. Communication technology has provided a number of advantages to reduce economic and political crisis. It has mitigated labor disputes by segregating the labor force. The information industry is a less labor-intensive industry as compared to heavy, chemical industries and light manufacturing industries. Through automation of factory and office, laborers are separated from each other. Communication technology also needs less muscular labor power than other industries. It changes the employment structure and working conditions by multiplying white-collar and service workers.

In Korea, until the 1980s, the information industry was not well-developed. The basic telecommunication systems had been monopolized by the government. Due to the small market of the information industry, the government played an active role in creating supply and demand in the information industry using the political mechanism. In the early 1980s, in order to accelerate the development of telecommunications, the Chun government established various new agencies, including the KTA (Korea Telecommunication Authority), Dacom (Data Communication Corp.) and ETRI (Electronic and Telecommunications Research Institute). During the Chun period, from 1980 through 1987, the supply of telephones per one hundred people increased from ten to thirty (Korea Telecomm 1991). Moreover, Korea started to invest in advanced telecommunication technology including computerization, CATV, and satellite.

Computerization is one of the most ambitious government projects for domestically developing the information industry and establishing national technological self-determinism in the face of international forces. The Korean government deliberately developed a domestic computer system through its computerization plan. Even though the domestic computer system is more costly and less efficient than foreign systems, the Korean government endeavors to localize computer technology for the purpose of establishing international competitiveness and technological self-determination. In 1984, the Chun government began actively to promote national computerization based on government authority by establishing the National Computerization Coordination Committee (CCC)(KISDI 1990; CCC 1992). Within two years, the government set up a legal system for national computerization and a specific plan for the public administration network. During the Chun regime, the CCC had strong authority under the power of the Blue House. (The Blue House is the Korean equivalent of the American White House.) The role of the CCC is to coordinate conflicting interests of each bureaucratic organization. The President's strong commitment also contributed to consolidating the authority of the CCC. In 1987, Chun directly led the extended meeting on national computerization. Relying on the strong authority of the CCC, computerization advanced quickly during the Chun administration. The Korean government is establishing five networks based on the national computerization plan, consisting of public administration, banks, education and research, military, and police networks.

The objectives of computerization are to systematize information management and to provide convenient services for the public. The government claims that computerization can contribute to enhancing efficiency in production systems and democratization in political institutions. The Korean government has attempted to localize computer technology by manufacturing Korea's own computer system. As a part of the computerization plan, the government has invested a large amount of its budget in developing mainframe computers. The government-invested Electronics and Telecommunications Research Institute (ETRI) has led the public project of developing mainframe computers in cooperation with other research institutes, universities, Dacom, and four private firms (CCC 1992, 32). In 1987, ETRI created the first generation Mainframe Computer Model I in Korea. It was produced as a result of technological transfer from a United States computer system, Tolerant. During 1987–1991, by investing $41.8 million, the Korean government created the second generation mainframe computer, Ticom (KISDI 1991, 102). From 1991, the Korean government began to develop the third-generation mainframe computer (CCC 1992, 32). Mainframe Model III is a high-speed mid-range computer. Through the development of Mainframe III, the Korean government is attempting to gain international competitiveness in the global computer market.

Since the Korean government rapidly advances the computerization plan using the strong state power, the total process of computerization has been politicized. There have been constant political debates on the computerization plan. As an illustration, I will analyze the political discourse on computerization in the National Assembly, Korea's legislative body. The public discussion in the National Assembly has brought up political criticism of mainframe computers. In a political debate, Legislator Kim Jung-Kil pointed out the frequent mechanical problems with Korean mainframe computers:

> In 1987, the CCC made a contract with Tolerant, an American company.... but due to frequent breakdowns of the system, it just wasted the governmental budget.... [A]ccording to an ETRI report, because Tolerant does not keep up with multiple managements in connecting the center with peripheries of the computer and translating the computer language into the Korean code, it is not useful as a main system, nor has it a high market value. Then, why do you adopt the

Tolerant system? . . . Moreover, since the Tolerant headquarters is about to go bankrupt, we cannot expect a success. . . . In conclusion, the failure of the mainframe adoption is derived from the fact that the Prime Secretary of the President who is not an expert in computers was the chairman of the CCC.[4]

The underlying logic of Kim's criticism is not a mechanical one but political criticism. He challenged the political power of the government executive branch by illustrating the problem of political power embedded in the computer system. In the political debate in the National Assembly, Legislator Kim participated in the formation of power/knowledge in computerization. His statement above demonstrates the power dimension of computerization: not only repressive power but also positive power. Interestingly enough, while the legislator indicated the negative power of bureaucracy, conversely, he participated in creating a positive power. In other words, by criticizing his political counterpart, Kim used the language that was created by technological experts in government agencies like ETRI. By doing so, he participated in legitimating the dominant discourse of computerization.

Regarding the question of legislators, in the same National Assembly committee meeting, the bureaucracy justified the government's position in selecting Tolerant. Lee Woo-Jae, the previous Minister of Communication, answered legislators' questions using technical terms, and this prevented him from being involved in political controversy:

The Korean brand of Tolerant products has stabilized, and we are in the process of negotiating with Australia and Taiwan to export these products. Since the US Tolerant company stopped producing hardware and now makes only software, we have a promising future for exporting Tolerants to North America and European countries. Because the administrative network is the backbone of our country, if we are dependent on a mainframe produced by other countries, we may have not only technological dependency, but also a problem with national security. Therefore, we should develop autonomous equipment and management skill.[5]

In this debate, Minister Lee demonstrated the market value of the Korean brand of the Tolerant and announced that Korea is going to export a Korean brand of Tolerant to other countries. The Minister also attempted to demonstrate the market value of Tolerant by making a reverse interpretation of Kim Jung-Kil's critical statement. Legislator Kim has argued that Tolerant was a poor choice for the system of national computerization partly because of the bankruptcy of the Tolerant company. Conversely, Minister Lee made an alternative interpretation that the Tolerant computer system has a high market value. Because the Tolerant headquarters no longer produces its own hardware, Korea can export a Korean brand of Tolerant computers to supply the original demand for Tolerant computers.

When two statements compete with each other for legitimate interpretation of the same phenomena or two interpretations competitively represent themselves as the truth claim, the credibility goes to the one who holds the source of knowledge. From the Foucauldian perspective, there is no true knowledge as such. Knowledge is constructed from the amalgamation of power with knowledge. Tangible objects and facts cannot be absolutely true since objects and facts are formed by discourse (Foucault 1972). No power center unilaterally creates power/knowledge. Nevertheless, society is organized in such a way that some segments of society have more of an eminent privilege of reproducing the dominant discourse than others.

In the political debate on national computerization, Korean legislators resist the process of infusing power in technology by bringing up questions and criticism of governmental executives. However, the resistance process is highly ritualistic while legislators compete with bureaucracy for power. The imminent interest of public discussion initiated by members of the National Assembly lies in power competition rather than in providing an alternative framework. Legislators are not much interested in formulating an alternative framework to the technological discourse. Consequently, the public discussion in the National Assembly is limited to a superficial level of political attacks. In this ritual, the bureaucracy does not appear to compete with legislators. The bureaucracy gathers information through a standardized knowledge form and presents it as the truth and the objective fact. Political rituals by legislators are often defeated by the scientific presentation of bureaucracy. In public discussion, strong arguments for democracy are often undermined by technological rationality because legislators are not outside the technological discourse. They rely heavily on information produced by technocratic organizations.

Democratic Claims and Computerization

The government emphasizes the public interest of computerization. It claims that computerization will promote convenient and diverse public services and establish a more democratic, decentralized government. In the bureaucratic state of mind, democracy is assessed in terms of technocratic values: productivity and efficiency. For democratic purposes, the government designs the plan for establishing a small government through computerization, increasing the efficiency of bureaucracy and reducing its size. The Korean government defines democracy as an extension of instrumental rationality as understood (and subsequently critiqued) by Habermas (1971, 1975). By designing the computerization plan, bureaucracy simply applies economic principles to claims of democracy. In practice, computerization does not appear to promote the decentralization of power and the public communication which are necessary, if not sufficient, conditions of democracy. The government does not take advantage of computerization as a means of communication, but relies solely on instrumental values such as efficiency and productivity. Decentralization is also limited only to technical matters without reforming the persistent power structure of the Korean political economy. Moreover, computerization does not accomplish efficiency and productivity as planned. Unlike its political proposals, the government has delayed providing diverse public services using the computerized public administration network because of power conflicts between bureaucracies.

For the decentralization plan, the government has proceeded with the localization of information through the public administration network, the distribution of computers to local schools, and computer education in local areas. Localization is a necessary condition for developing a democratic information system. For democratic use, computerization has to be integrated into people's everyday life in order to foster public communication. The Ministry of Communication (MOC) is realizing national computerization by providing equal distribution of computers as well as basic telecommunication services to local areas (KISDI, 1991). The government also has established local information centers in each province to spread the "information culture" to local areas.

The Korean government justifies the need to develop computerization as a means to foster a more even development of the national economy in contrast to the earlier development strategy, which was uneven, urban-centered development. In public reports, the government frequently states that communication technology will promote equal development by referring to the theory of "the information society." The argument is that development of the information industry will geographically and socially decentralize economic and political power. The Korean government argues that the information industry will evenly develop the rural as well as the urban areas and the small and medium-sized as well as the big businesses.

Although Korea emphasizes the development of information technology, the preexisting industrial structure remains intact. Business practices in the information industry and related public projects, such as the computerization plan, are conducted in the same manner as those that have been implemented in manufacturing industries. The *chaebols* (big conglomerates) monopolize the market as well as research and development (R & D) of computer networks and hardware, whereas small companies work under the direction of big companies by obtaining a small segment of profit determined by the big company's decision.

The government has not actually supported small and medium-sized businesses in the process of developing computerization. A manager at Dacom stated in an interview that the Ministry of Communication selected companies who manufactured the computer system and personal computers (PC) that provided hardware for the computerization of public administration. Most of these companies were *chaebols*. On the other hand, Dacom competitively selected software companies and telecommunication equipment companies through newspaper announcements. These companies included medium-sized and small companies.[6]

Although computerization is a public project, the government favors *chaebols* for developing computer networks and hardware instead of equally distributing business opportunities to small and medium-sized companies. Because the government does not support innovative small and medium-sized companies and the mass production system still remains as the model for the information industry, Korean computer software is not internationally competitive. The software industry reflects the highest import rate in Korea's information industry. In 1987, the software industry contributed $7.2 million to exports while importing $29 million worth of goods. In 1990, the Korean software industry was even further dependent on imports by spending six times more on imports than it received for its exports (Telecommunications Yearbook 1992). The Korean industrial structure has not adjusted to the need for innovative development that characterizes the software industry.

One of the reasons that the government fails to support small businesses is derived from bureaucratic inertia which has practiced by what Foucault calls normalization. Institutions as well as people consciously or unconsciously follow the normalized practice because it exercises positive power in everyday life. During the industrialization process, the Korean government has created and supported big conglomerates in accordance with the assumptions of the economic theory of uneven development: namely, that wealth will eventually trickle down to the entire society. It has served the powerful at the expense of the powerless. The rich have become richer, but wealth has not trickled down over the thirty-year history of uneven development. Nevertheless, this observation does not simply suggest a negative power by which the power center consciously suppresses the powerless. Even when the power center concedes to serve the general interests by making democratic claims through computerization, it still follows old normalized practices which have been fossilized by positive power. In the Korean government, bureaucracy promotes the information industry based on normalized procedures that were employed to support manufacturing industries. Also, the business sectors, particularly *chaebols*, manage the information industry by using the old modes of production without changing the industrial structure.

Not only in the business area but also in the public administration,

Korean computerization does not fulfill its claims for democracy and public services. The Korean government computerizes the public administration network in order to establish a democratic or small government, which means reducing its size and power and increasing the efficiency and services of the government. However, an officer at the Ministry of Communication gave a contradictory response to my interview question about sharing information among different bureaucratic organizations. Contrary to the blueprint for "the one-stop services," he stated that "we are developing computer networking within an organization, but it is not possible to share information between different ministries due to the problems of responsibility, information control, and security."[7] An engineer at Dacom also pointed out that "two-way communication is technically possible but politically problematic."[8] Unlike the claims of the government, in reality, national computerization does not seem to promote either decentralization of power or horizontal two-way communication, the two basic conditions for democracy.

Localization of information has not yet been integrated into the everyday life of people in local areas. Without having much knowledge of the computer network, local administrators who are daily users of the network conduct their daily routine as the central government directs. Due to the centralized power system, local administrators do not have opportunities to represent the interests of the local public with whom they interact daily, nor do they participate in creating communication through the computer network. The task of local administrators is limited to mechanical operations of computer data which may further contribute to the central control over the population. Meanwhile, local administrators whom I interviewed agree that the computerization of public administration may contribute to centralized control.[9] Computerized information on residents is more easily accessible than written documents. According to a local administrator, police and tax offices make the most frequent request for information about residents. Thus, computerization is centrally controlled. Localization of information is peripheral to the existing power structure. By means of computerization, individuals are easily seen, but do not see, as in the Panopticon (Yoon 1993).

Through the plan for localization of information, the Korean government is spreading the information culture to the public. Government agencies have established local public-relations centers to provide information technology facilities to the public. The government agency Information Culture Center (ICC) manages local computer classes for agricultural and fishing areas. Local computer classes provide computer training free of charge for the public in rural areas. In 1991, the government established one computer class in each province (MOC, 1991). In 1992, it doubled their number except in Cheju province.

I interviewed a teacher at the local computer class. The computer class for agricultural and fishing areas is open to the public and provides free computer lessons. In his class, most students are company employees, civil servants, and housewives. There are no farmers or fishermen in the computer class. According to Kim, "There were several farmers, but most farmers and fishermen were not interested in computer education, nor did they have time to learn about computers." [10] Although the computer class was established for the purpose of localization of information, it does not seem to encourage local development. First, at the economic level the computer class does not provide a business opportunity for local people. The computer class does not promote local business or local communication channels. There is no localized database that farmers and fishermen can use for their businesses. Dacom set up an information database about agricultural and fishing production through Chunrian II, but, according to my interviewee, "farmers and fishermen are not inclined to invest in computers because they do not find the information useful." Apparently, the computer class does not introduce any local information network for the local population.

At the local level, computerization has not successfully provided any channel of public participation. The computer class does not promote communication through a network, and its education is limited to technical training. Most people in the rural areas are not likely to be interested in computerization unless it provides useful information for the rural population regarding local business and local political life. Computerization has not yet been integrated into people's everyday life in the local areas because computer networks have not established any usable communication channels. Localization of information is constructed in a one-way communication system that integrates local residents into one systematic database, but it is not open to the polyphony, or diverse voices, of the public in the local areas. Public communication is largely excluded from the education process and the public administration network. In fact, the public exists only in the form of written data, or as consumers of computer information. In this way, they are seen, but do not see.

Conclusion

This study has adopted the Foucauldian perspective in order to scrutinize the human practice involved in computerization. Foucault turns the focus of academic discourse from scientific principles and structural power to practice in everyday life. He rejects the assumption that such transcendent forces control human practice behind the empirical process. From the Foucauldian perspective, human agents do not follow the rational logic of structural power. Nor do institutions and other power centers exercise rational and coherent control over the people. In everyday practice, humans discursively participate in constructing reality and creating power as individuals or through institutions. In discursive practice, the empirical process does not concur with rationality at the macrolevel. Although the power center creates and disseminates structural force in physical or ideological forms, at the local level, power is not reproduced as it is encoded by the center. It is discursively practiced in everyday life and leads to a new form of power. Moreover, the power center is not a rational and coherent entity. In everyday practice, the center discontinuously designs and exercises power by being constrained by a larger framework of power/knowledge.

Power/knowledge is not simply manipulated by the structural power centers but is discursively practiced by human engagement in institutions and other forms of social forces. This study has presented the concrete process of technological deployment at the local level. It portrays human engagement in everyday life inside political and technocratic organizations. It highlights the microphysics of power by analyzing the penetration of political and international power into the process of Korean computerization. Although the process of Korean computerization illustrates that power is strongly involved in technological deployment, technology is not identified solely with repressive force. Foucault expands the concept of power beyond the use of repressive force to apprehending power in voluntary subjugation and meaning creation. He looks into the complex aspects of reality using the concept of positive power. As compared to other critical theorists, including Marx and Habermas, Foucault conceptualizes a more sophisticated definition of power by grasping the existence of power in communication and people's everyday life. For Foucault, power is exercised not only when two or more parties confront each other but also when people agree with each other, having the same cultural framework, compatible interests, and mutual understanding.

The Foucauldian concept of power is valuable for analyzing the deployment of Korean computerization. Power intervenes in the process of Korean computerization, but it is not simply repressive power. No physical or ideological power forces the Korean people to develop computerization. The Korean government has voluntarily set up the plan and implemented it. The general public also is willing to adopt computers in the workplace, schools, and home by taking advantage of government support. Does this voluntary adoption of computer technology mean that there is no power involved? The Foucauldian framework provides a useful reference to detect, deep inside technological knowledge and mutual communication, power that has no characteristics of repressive force. The power intervention in Korean computerization is not only negative but also positive. Politicians and technicians who lead computerization pursue not only their own personal interests but also those interests defined by power/knowledge which is created and reproduced through human engagement in everyday practice. In various social organizations, people practice power/knowledge by creating their own procedures of normalization. Power is not practiced as it is rationally designed by the centers. Instead, power is reproduced only through local people's engagement in their political, economic, and cultural contexts.

Notes

1. Foucault believes that we should change our view of power from a negative to a positive conception, and he argues as follows: "We must cease once and for all to describe the effects of power in negative terms: it 'excludes,' it 'represses,' it 'censors,' it 'abstracts,' it 'masks,' it 'conceals.' In fact, power produces; it produces reality; it produces domains of objects and rituals of truth. The individual and the knowledge that may be gained of him belong to this production" (1979, 194).

2. For Habermas, knowledge necessarily has a transcendental and constituting role beyond the power framework. Of course, Habermas does not innocently claim that knowledge has no power basis. Rather, for Habermas (1987), knowledge or truth is in a dialectical contradiction. Even if truth is masked by power and distorted communication, according to Habermas (1971), the universal validity of knowledge and truth potentially exists in human interactions and interests of the subject in emancipation.

3. Foucault's discourse analysis demonstrates a good contrast with Habermas's communicative action. Habermas, for instance, illustrates psychoanalysis as a tangible example of emancipatory communication. Habermas (1971) believes that the communication between the doctor and the patient is a self-reflective and emancipatory process because the doctor's empirical and scientific diagnosis is meaningless until the patient agrees to accept the diagnosis by reconstructing his/her history through self-reflection and intersubjectivity. Therefore, according to Habermas (1984), the emancipatory project is possible only in its participatory process. Foucault, on the contrary, addresses power in the discourse of mental illness and psychiatry in his genealogical study of madness. According to Foucault (1965), the symptoms of mental illness have been created and defined by power/knowledge and there is no objective rationality of diagnosis. A doctor's diagnosis is not grounded in universal truth, or rationality, but is created by power/knowledge (Foucault 1980). No matter how much patients participate in the process, psychoanalytic discourse does not lead to human emancipation because it is constructed by power. Thus, according to Foucault, psychoanalysis is not an emancipatory process but a process of patient subjugation to dominant discourse. Intersubjectivity between the doctor and the patient is created in relation to power/knowledge, and they reach some kind of consensus by subjugating the powerless to the power framework (Foucault 1965).

4. Kim Jung-Kil, 147th National Assembly, Eighth Transportation and Telecommunication Meeting (Seoul: National Assembly), 3.

5. Lee Woo-Jae, 147th National Assembly, Eighth Transportation and Telecommunication Meeting (Seoul: National Assembly), 15.

6. J. Y. Hyun, a manager of the Business Administration Section, Computerization of Public Administration at Dacom, interview with the author (20 July 1992, Seoul).

7. Y. S. Yeom, an official working for the Department of Computerization at the MOC, interview with the author (22 July 1992, Seoul).

8. J. Y. Hyun (see note 6)

9. Kim, a local administrator at Seo Kim Nyoung Ri branch office of Ku Jwa Eup district administration office in Cheju Province, interview with the author (3 August 1992, Cheju Province). Lee, a local administrator at Jung Ang Dong district administrator office in Seo Gui Po city in Cheju Province, interview with the author (31 July 1992, Cheju Province).

10. H. Y. Kim, interview with the author (31 July 1992, Seo Gui Po, Cheju Province).

References

Agger, B. 1985. The Dialectic of Deindustrialization: An Essay on Advanced Capitalism. In *Critical Theory and Public Life,* ed. John Forester, 3–21. Cambridge: MIT Press.

Amsden, A. 1989. *The Asia's Next Giant.* Oxford: Oxford University Press.

Bell, D. 1960. *The End of Ideology.* Glencoe, IL: Free Press.

———. 1973. *The Coming Post-Industrial Society.* New York: Basic Books.

Burchell, G., C. Gordon, and P. Miller, eds. 1991. *The Foucault Effect: Studies in Governmentality.* Chicago: University of Chicago Press.

Dijk, V. T., ed. 1985. *Handbook of Discourse Analysis.* Vol. 4. London: Academic Press.

Evans, P. 1979. *Dependent Development.* Princeton, NJ: Princeton University Press.

Foucault, M. 1965. *Madness and Civilization: A History of Insanity in the Age of Reason.* Trans. R. Howard. New York: Vintage Books.

———. 1970. *The Order of Things.* London: Tavistock.

———. 1972. *The Archaeology of Knowledge.* Trans. A. S. Smith. New York: Pantheon Books.

———. 1978. *The History of Sexuality,* vol. 1. Trans. R. Hurley. New York: Vintage Books.

———. 1979. *Discipline and Punish: Birth of the Prison.* Trans. A. Sheridan. New York: Vintage Books.

———. 1980. *Power/Knowledge: Selected Interviews and Other Writings 1972–1977.* Ed. and trans. C. Gordon. New York: Pantheon Books.

Fromm, E. 1961. *Marx's Concept of Man.* New York: Frederick Ungar.

Gandy, O. 1988. The Political Economy of Communications Competence. In *The Political Economy of Information,* ed. V. Mosco and J. Wasco, 108–24. Madison, WI: University of Wisconsin Press.

———. 1993. Toward a Political Economy of Personal Information. *Critical Studies in Mass Communication* 10(1): 70–97.

Gandy, O., and C. Simmons. 1986. Technology, Privacy and the Democratic Process. *Critical Studies in Mass Communication* 3(2): 155–168.

Habermas, J. 1970. *Toward a Rational Society.* Boston: Beacon Press.

———. 1971. *Knowledge and Human Interests.* Trans. J. Shapiro. Boston: Beacon Press.

———. 1975. *Legitimation Crisis.* Boston: Beacon Press.

———. 1979. *Communication and the Evolution of Society.* Trans. T. McCarthy. Boston: Beacon Press.

———. 1984. *The Theory of Communicative Action,* vols. 1 & 2. Trans. T. McCarthy. Boston: Beacon Press.

———. 1987. *The Philosophical Discourse of Modernity.* Cambridge: MIT Press.

———. 1991. *The Structural Transformation of the Public Sphere.* Trans. T. Burger. Cambridge: MIT Press.

Harrington, J. 1991. *Organizational Structure and Information Technology.* New York: Prentice Hall.

Hindess, B., and P. Hirst. 1975. *Pre-Capitalist Modes of Production.* London: Routledge and Kegan Paul.

Luke, T., and S. White. 1987. Critical Theory, the Information Revolution, and an Ecological Path to Modernity. In *Critical Theory and Public Life,* ed. J. Forester, 22–56. Cambridge: MIT Press.

Marcuse, H. 1964. *One-Dimensional Man: Studies in the Ideology of Advanced Industrial Society.* Boston: Beacon Press.

Martin, L., H. Gutman, and P. Hutton, eds. 1988. *Technologies of the Self: A Seminar with Michel Foucault.* Amherst: University of Massachusetts Press.

Marx, K. 1967. *Capital,* vols. 1 & 3. New York: International Publishers.

———. 1970. *German Ideology.* New York: Greshau Press.

Mosco, V. 1989. *Pay-per Society.* Norwood, NJ: Ablex.

Pool, I. S. 1990. *Technologies without Boundaries.* Cambridge: Harvard University Press.

Poster, M. 1984. *Foucault, Marxism and History: Mode of Production vs. Mode of Information.* Cambridge: Polity Press.

Poulantzas, N. 1973. *Political Power and Social Class.* London: New Left Books.

Provenzo, E. 1992. The Electronic Panopticon: Censorship, Control, and Indoctrination in a Post-Typographic Culture. In *Literacy Online: The Promise (and Peril) of Reading and Writing with Computers,* ed. Myron C. Tuman, 167–88. Pittsburgh: University of Pittsburgh Press.

Robins, K., and F. Webster. 1988. Cybernetic Capitalism: Information, Technology, Everyday Life. In *The Political Economy of Information,* ed. V. Mosco and J. Wasko. Madison, WI: University of Wisconsin Press.

Rogers, E. 1986. *Communication Technology: the New Media in Society.* New York: Free Press.

Schiller, H. 1989. *Culture, INC.: the Corporate Takeover of Public Expression.* New York: Oxford University Press.

Slack, J. 1984. *Communication Technologies and Society.* Norwood, NJ: Ablex.

Tehranian, M. 1990. *Technologies of Power: Information Machines and Democratic Prospects.* Norwood, NJ: Ablex.

Toffler, A. 1980. *The Third Wave.* New York: Bantam Books.

Yoon, Sunh-Hee. 1993. Power and Communication Online: Toward a Discursive Study of Computerization in South Korea. Ph.D. diss., University of Oregon.

Korean Language

Computerization Coordination Commission (CCC). 1992. Basic Planning of National Computerization. Seoul: CCC

Electronics and Telecommunications Research Institute (ETRI). 1992. ETRI Annual Report. Daeduck: ETRI.

Korean Information Society Development Institute (KISDI). 1991. Analysis of Social Effects of National Computerization. Seoul: KISDI.

———. 1990. Toward an Efficient Management of National Computerization. Seoul: KISDI.

————. 1989. Research on the Development of the Information Industry and Advancement of the Industry Structure. Seoul: KISDI.

————. 1988. The Information Society and Advancement of Democracy. Seoul: KISDI.

Korea Telecomm. 1991. Statistics of Telecommunications. Seoul: Korea Telecomm.

Ministry of Communication (MOC). 1986–1991. Annual Reports. Seoul: MOC.

————. 1992. Telecommunication Yearbook. Seoul: MOC.

Telecommunications Issues Research Institute. 1992. Opening the Telecommunication Market and the Information Society. Seoul: Pulbit.

9

The Political Computer: Democracy, CMC, and Habermas

CHARLES ESS

Introduction[1]

A puzzling theoretical topography emerges in the literature on computer-mediated communications (CMC).[2] Proponents of CMC often make the claim of democratization, meaning that the implementation of CMC technologies will result in greater democracy within organizations, within local and national government, and in the world at large. But if we examine representative examples of these claims, several theoretical deficits emerge. In general, there is no consistent understanding of what democracy means: Various writers use the term in diverse and sometimes contradictory fashion. More fundamentally, critics charge that electronic democracy is impractical and utopian or that the preference for democracy rests on nothing more compelling than personal or corporate ideological preferences. Hence, the democratization claim can be easily dismissed by those who do not share the preference for democratic polity, and so it loses much of its justificatory power.

In light of these problems, I turn to Jürgen Habermas's critical theory of democratic polity—first as it seeks to overcome the criticisms of utopianism and ideology launched against modern democracy as such. As well, Habermas's effort to defend modernity and modern technologies, including the computer technologies underlying CMC, against critiques by both other members of the Frankfurt School and by the postmodernist Jean-François Lyotard, adds to the theory's ability to support the democratization claim in CMC. And, by examining Habermas's theory of communicative action and his discourse ethic in greater detail, I show how this theory articulates important connections between communication and democratic polity, so as to provide still stronger theoretical justification for the democratization claim. Finally, I examine how CMC systems would function if they were to fulfill the conditions articulated by Habermas for achieving democratic discourse. Such a Habermasian system turns out to be consistent with many current claims, observations, and, most importantly, *practices* of democratization in electronic forums. At the same time, however, the Habermasian framework sharply distinguishes itself from a prevailing conception of democracy (as plebiscite) and theory (postmodernism), as these apparently fail to justify precisely those current practices which intend to preserve open and equal communication. Most pointedly, by incorporating Habermas's discourse ethic, as this ethic refines both the understanding of democracy and the technological and social conditions necessary for it to emerge, CMC systems may distinguish themselves from systems open to misuse and subversion for authoritarian purposes. In these ways, Habermas's theory of communicative action provides a powerful theoretical framework in support of the democratization claim against its various critiques. At the same time, his discourse ethic offers important guidelines especially regarding the ethical and political practices required for those who wish to redeem the promise of democratization in CMC.

Computers and Democracy: Theory and Practice

In the extensive, if ambiguous, literature on the social and political effects of informatics, the notion of democratization via CMC appears frequently.[3] Sproull and Kiesler (1991b), for example, observe that

> In some companies that use computer networking, communication is strikingly open as employees cross barriers of space, time, and social category to share expertise, opinions, and ideas. In a democracy, people believe that everyone should be included on equal terms in communication; no one should be excluded from the free exchange of information. Independent decision makers expressing themselves lead to more minds contributing to problem solving and innovation. New communication technology is surprisingly consistent with Western images of democracy. (13; cf. Sproull and Kiesler 1991a, 116, 119)

Similarly, Dertouzos (1991) understands democratic communications to prevail when "nearly everyone would be able to put his or her ideas, concerns and demands before all others" (69). This appears to say that democracy has something to do with the free exchange of information ostensibly facilitated by CMC. But this only reiterates the claim that CMC facilitates democracy; it does not tell us what democracy *means*. At the same time, such a conception of democracy is open to the critique that such democracy translates into a glut of information qua garbage (Postman 1993). As Romiszowski (1990, 330) observes regarding Vannevar Bush and Ted Nelson's vision of nearly universal access to a global network of electronic libraries, how is such democracy to be distinguished from an information flood, in which millions drown? In fact, Sproull and Kiesler go on to note that while some organizations will embrace what they characterize as their "vision of the networked organization," they further acknowledge that "not everyone will think these possibilities are positive" (1991b, 14). That is, it appears that the choice for democracy is simply a matter of *preference:* Nothing forces us to prefer democracy over other forms of social organization.

Hiltz and Turoff (1993) come closer to defining democracy as associated with CMC. To begin with, they see computerized conferencing systems as facilitating a direct or participatory democracy, understood as the direct participation and voting of citizens on important state or national issues (195).[4] Hiltz and Turoff further seek to connect grassroots networking with the electronic town hall promised by Ross Perot in 1992 (480). They provide two examples of democracy via CMC: the use of the Internet by Chinese students in the United States to discuss political events (481–84; see also Li 1992) and the PEN (Public Electronic Network) established in Santa Monica (484). PEN can, indeed, be cited as providing an example of how CMC expands access to governmental bodies—at least in the case of several homeless men who had access to the system by way of public terminals (484).

If PEN stands as an example of participatory democracy, however, there is no agreement in the literature that such participatory or direct democracy exhaustively and exclusively defines the sort of political organization to be facilitated by CMC. Howard Rheingold (1993), for example, discusses what he characterizes as "the utopian vision of an electronic agora, an 'Athens without slaves' made possible by telecommunications and cheap computers and implemented through decentralized networks like Usenet and FidoNet" (279). In fact, Rheingold takes up Habermas's early discussion of the public sphere as articulating the "hopes of online advocates who see CMC as a way of revitalizing the open and widespread discussions among citizens that feed the roots of democratic societies" (Rheingold 1993, 279f.; see Habermas 1989b; cf. Benhabib 1992, 11–14).

Rheingold affirms Habermas's account of "the several requirements for authenticity that people who live in democratic societies would recognize: open access, voluntary participation, participation outside institutional roles, the generation of public opinion through assemblies of citizens who engage in rational argument, the freedom to express opinions, and the freedom to discuss matters of the state and criticize the way state power is organized" (Rheingold 1993, 284).

But Rheingold goes on to warn, following James Carey (1989), against too easily falling for a "utopian" rhetoric of democratization which ascribes to technology the power to enhance democracy. In particular, Carey observes that "contemporary advocates of technological liberation regularly describe a new postmodern age of instantaneous daily plebiscitory democracy through a computerized system of electronic voting and opinion polling" (Carey, quoted in Rheingold 1993, 287). In fact, such electronic plebiscites have a dark side. Jean Bethke Elshtain (1982), for example, criticizes experiments with television voting in the early 1980s. She observes that such voting has us confuse "simply performing as the responding 'end' of a prefabricated system of external stimuli" with democratic participation. As well, such plebiscites can allow the majority to overwhelm and tyrannize the minority. Indeed, "plebiscitism is compatible with authoritarian politics carried out under the guise of, or with the connivance of, majority views. That opinion can be registered by easily manipulated, ritualistic plebiscites, so there is no need for debate on substantive questions" (Elshtain, quoted in Rheingold 1993, 287).

In this light, it would appear that most of the authors we have examined —most explicitly, Hiltz and Turoff—understand the democracy they hope to enhance via CMC to mean plebiscite democracy. By contrast, while also a self-described cheerleader for the democratic utopia made possible by CMC, Rheingold notes the clearly *anti*democratic potential of such plebiscites. Clearly, greater definitional precision and clarity is needed regarding what CMC advocates *mean* by democracy.

And, as the opening example from Sproull and Kiesler suggests, the literature further discloses the second major problem facing the democratization claim—namely, whether democracy, however understood, is necessarily *preferred* by CMC users. For example, proponents of democratization can point to the French student strike in the spring of 1992, which exploited the use of the Minitel system to organize demonstrations and so forth. If this is democracy, then it serves as an example of computer communications contributing to democracy. But not all French government administrators greeted the student's use of Minitel as democraticizing communications ("The Machine that Changed the World," pt. 5, 1992). Similarly, the PEN system fails to fulfill the definition of participatory democracy provided by Hiltz and Turoff (1993). They note, to begin with, that the "relatively egalitarian meeting ground where citizens debate issues with one another and talk to public officials" is also the cyberspace in which women participants are harassed and conferences are dominated by a small number of participants. As well, "Most of the politicians do not participate directly," so that on balance, "It is not clear in the Santa Monica effort that the technology has had any fundamental impact on the local political establishment or process" (Hiltz and Turoff 1993, 484; cf. "Electronic Democracy: The PEN Is Mighty"). Others have likewise noted that some managers and administrators believe that such democracy threatens the traditional hierarchy of modern organizations—a belief that has led to the suspension and removal of e-mail systems (Singer 1991; Zachary 1994).[5]

The literature of CMC hence discloses significant problems regarding the democratization claim. The first consists of inadequate and inconsistent definitions of democracy. In addition, the claim of democratization is open to charges of utopianism—meaning, simply, that the goals and values justifying these societies cannot be realized in the real world. The claim of democratization can further be criticized as resting on nothing more than ideological preferences. That is, the choice of either democracy or hierarchy simply reflects personal or socially conditioned preferences, preferences or values that are only relatively valid or ideological because no stronger reason or set of claims support them.

If the democratization claim cannot be defended against these charges, then the claim loses its justificatory force. In particular, if the preference for democratic polity is simply ideological, then the dispute is irresoluble: Some of us prefer democratization and some of us do not, and nothing more can or need be said. Accepting this charge therefore reduces a central justification of CMC to mere ideological preference or, more brutally, to simply a question of the preferences of those who have power.

Redeeming the Democratization Claim

To sustain the claim that CMC democratizes social groups thus requires a theoretical framework that establishes a clear definition of democracy and defends such democracy against the charges of utopianism and ideology.

We can begin to build such a framework by noting the definitions of democracy offered by Abramson, Arterton, and Orren (1988) in their analysis of the democratization potential of mass media (TV, cable, radio, etc.). They distinguish between three forms of democracy they find characteristic of American history and culture. The first is the plebiscite, which emphasizes individual autonomy and thus stresses ''the freedom it [democracy] gives as many persons as possible to participate as directly as possible in the affairs of government'' (19). Plebiscitary democracy thus assumes that political decisions are best made via a direct vote in which all participate, a version of democracy currently most familiar in the form of polls and public opinion surveys, as these influence government policy (20). Echoing Elshtain's objections to TV voting, Abramson, Aterton, and Orren point out that plebiscites threaten to become majoritarian systems in which individual and minority rights may be crushed by majority rule (23f.).

Their second form of democracy is communitarian. This form stresses service to the common good, in contrast with the emphasis on individual autonomy and simply private ends and interests assumed as primary in plebiscitary democracy (22f.). Moreover, communitarian democracy emphasizes ''participation in public space—in the meetings and assemblies, the deliberations and persuasion that distinguish the democractic process and make participation in it a transformative lesson in the common good'' (23). While Abramson and colleagues prefer communitarian over plebiscitary democracy, they also recognize that the communitarian stress also runs a characteristic danger—namely, of becoming an essentially *anti*democratic emphasis on the values and mores of one community, to the exclusion of other communities, for example, in defending segregation as an essential feature of Southern life (25f.).

To meet this danger while preserving the virtues of communitarian democracy, Abramson and colleagues argue for conjoining communitarian democracy with a third type—pluralist democracy. Pluralism in this context is a principle of free competition between groups representing specific interests. Pluralism of this sort should avoid the tyranny of the majority threatened by plebiscitary democracy, as pluralism provides minority groups the chance to organize coalitions with other minority groups to oppose unacceptable policies and practices (28). At the same time, however, this pluralism suggests that democratic politics is nothing more than a ''market game'' of power, with winners and losers (29). Abramson and colleagues argue that conjoining pluralist with communitary democracy will offset the primary deficits of both: Communitarian democracy emphasizes the moral value of the common good (over against the essentially amoral power game suggested by pluralism), while pluralism should work to ensure the participation of many communities in the democratic process (over against the danger in communitarian democracy of one community achieving hegemony over all others).

In light of these three distinct meanings of democracy in American political history, the confusion we have seen in the literature on CMC regarding the meaning of democracy may in part reflect the larger cultural and political debate (if not confusion) over these notions of democracy. In addition, these distinctions reiterate the point that most of the writers we have examined on CMC assume a plebiscitary form of democracy—by no means the most theoretically powerful of democratic forms. Finally, these distinctions sharpen the theoretical problem: What kind(s) of democracy will CMC facilitate—and, again, can these forms of democracy be defended against the charges of ideology and utopianism?

Critical Theory and a Turn to the Frankfurt School

Within CMC literature, the democratization claim—referring especially to plebiscite democracy—seems most fully supported by appeals to poststructuralist and postmodern theory (e.g., Lanham 1993; Chesebro and Bonsall 1989). In addition to insights offered by these frameworks, I propose to examine another form of critical theory, namely, that of the Frankfurt School. Frankfurt School critical theory—specifically, the communication action theory and discourse ethics of Jürgen Habermas—offers a theoretical framework that addresses the deficits we have seen in the claims that CMC may contribute to democratization.[6] First of all, Habermas's theory provides a more complete definition of democratic polity and this in a framework which issues from the explicit effort to defend democratic polity precisely against the charges of utopianism and ideology. Moreover, Habermas's theory makes explicit the connection between democratic polity and the sorts of open communication facilitated by CMC technologies, thus providing clearer justification for how such technologies may result in democratization. In doing so, Habermas's theory endorses a democratic polity that avoids the problems of plebiscite conceptions. Finally, Habermas's theory offers two advantages over postmodern approaches.

First, early Frankfurt School theorists developed an extensive critique of modern technology, including the technologies underlying CMC, as manifestations of a modern, especially Cartesian, rationality seen to work in both the domination of nature and the domination of humanity in totalitarian systems.[7] These critiques, in fact, anticipate postmodern attacks such as Lyotard's on Enlightenment rationalism as authoritarian (Ingram 1990, 198–202). But we will see that Lyotard's postmodernism is hence ambivalent regarding CMC technologies, wanting both to celebrate their ostensibly liberating potential while yet attacking them as expressions of the totalitarianism of modern reason. By contrast, later critical theory addresses these critiques, so as to articulate ways in which such technologies may avoid antidemocratic implementations.

Second, Habermas and other critical theorists see internal contradictions in such postmodernism. Because of its strong tendency toward ethical relativism and the denial of moral universals, postmodernism cannot consistently endorse democratic polity over other forms of social organization. By contrast, precisely because Habermas's theory seeks to defend democratic theory against the charges of relativism, his theory can more consistently endorse democratic polity than can a postmodernism such as Lyotard's.

The Frankfurt School and the Problem of Democracy

Democracy, Relativism, and the Relationship between Theory and Practice

Frankfurt School critical theory began in Germany in response to the great political crises in the 1920s and 1930s—the emergence of fascism in the West (including, of course, Nazism in Germany itself) and the rise of Stalinism in the East.[8] The failures to achieve Enlightenment conceptions of democracy represented by these crises force several questions best stated in terms of the problem of relativism and the relationship between theory and practice.

To begin with, the failure of Enlightenment democracy may argue for ethical relativism, or the claim that no universally valid beliefs or values exist. If such is the case, then the failure of Enlightenment democracy in some parts of the world simply reflects diverse cultural values: Although Enlightenment theorists may have believed that the worth of the individual, freedom, and democratic polity stood as universal values for all human beings, the failure of Enlightenment democracy suggests instead that these values are simply culturally determined.

In the face of such relativism, ethical and political philosophy have historically attempted to establish moral norms valid not simply within a given culture but within all. But the effort to establish universally valid norms issues in a central problem regarding the relationship between theory and practice: Any putatively universal claim runs the danger of excessive transcendence, in which the universal claim fails to represent or reflect precisely the individual and particular dimensions of specific people living in specific times and cultures. The effort to counter ethical relativism, in short, runs the risk of establishing universal norms that at the same time become too transcendent and too utopian to be realized in human praxis. The recognition of these allied problems of relativism and the theory-praxis relationship is at least as old as Plato and Aristotle, but Frankfurt School critical theory takes up this question especially in light of the work of Kant and Hegel.

Habermas attempts to meet the problems of the theory-praxis relationship in part by what he calls reconstruction of the principal theoretical sources of democratic polity. At the same time, Frankfurt School theory responds to the theory-praxis issue by turning its attention to the nature of theory itself. In their efforts to establish a theory capable of generating universally valid norms (that could thus overcome the problems of relativism and the charge of ideology attaching to the democratic preference), critical theorists, including Habermas, attempt to join more traditional philosophical theories with more recent, empirically oriented psychological and sociological theories, most especially those of Max Weber and Sigmund Freud. In so doing, they hope to bring together the normative or *prescriptive* power of traditional ethics and politics (as these seek universal norms that prescribe what *ought* to be the case) and the *descriptive* accounts of empirical sciences (as these carefully attend to the particularities of human praxis in their descriptions of what *is* the case).

By thus refashioning the philosophical theories that undergird the ethical and political values of Enlightenment democracy, the Frankfurt School seeks to establish what Benhabib (1986) calls "quasi-transcendent" norms. Such norms remain compelling since they may possess universal validity and thus overcome the problems of relativism and ideology. At the same time, they more fully incorporate descriptive accounts of the particularities and realities of human praxis and thus more successfully avoid the charge of utopianism (Benhabib 1986, 263). In these ways, Frankfurt School critical theory offers a theoretical foundation that intends to answer the charges of ideology and utopianism directed against the democratization claim.

Habermas's Theory of Communicative Action

I examine Habermas's theory in four stages, first discussing how he grounds his understanding of communicative reason in what he identifies as the tacit assumptions of discourse. Second, I take up Habermas's effort to defend the universalizability of moral claims in specific kinds of discourse against the relativist position. These two points together provide a defense against the charge of ideology attaching to the preference for democratic politics, especially since they provide a way of countering the relativism underlying this charge. Third, I turn to Habermas's notion of communicative rationality, with a specific focus on Habermas's discourse ethic, especially as it is grounded in carefully defined notions of freedom and community. Fourth, I examine what Habermas identifies as the ideal conditions of discourse—conditions that are at once conditions for democratic polity—and his proposed rules of reason as these structure the context of democratizing discourse. Taken together, these points outline a communicative reason that overcomes criticisms of Cartesian reason and modern technology as intrinsically authoritarian. Furthermore, these points are central to Habermas's effort to establish the quasi-transcendent norms which overcome the opposition between empty (and potentially dogmatic) universals and self-contradictory relativism (cf. Habermas 1991a, 7) and to counter the critiques that democratic polity is utopian or rests solely on merely relative ideology. Finally, these points make clear the theoretical relationships between communication and democratic polity, and distinguish Habermas's conception of pluralistic, democratic polities from plebiscites.

Tacit Assumptions of Discourse

Habermas most extensively developed his theory of communicative action in the two volumes so titled (1984a, 1987b). In addition to especially German philosophical discussion of communicative action, Habermas makes use of the work of Stephen Toulmin (1958, 1972), who examines argument with a view toward the disputes between absolutist positions (that insist with dogmatic certainty on the universal validity of a given set of claims) and relativist claims (Habermas 1984a, 24–28).

Specifically, Habermas draws on Robert Alexy (1978). Alexy articulates as the starting point of a communicative ethic what he identifies as the basic assumption of conversation or discourse:

Whoever expresses a value judgment or an obligational judgment such
as "It is unjust if citizens in a state are discriminated against because of
the color of their skin" or "You should help your friend who has got
into difficulty," raises the claim that it is justifiable and hence correct
or true. (151)

Ingram (1990) summarizes Habermas's version of this crucial starting
point this way:

Discourses typically arise whenever the justice of a norm, the sincerity
of an expressed intention, or the truth of a cognitive belief is disputed.
Claims to justice and truth are of special interest to him [Habermas],
since, whenever we assert that something is true or right, we imply that
all other persons should agree with us. (147)

In this way, consensus emerging from dialogue replaces deductive and inductive validity as "the touchstone for truth and justice" (Ingram 1990, 147).
And, presumably because persons in dialogue bring to their discourse their
individual and particular backgrounds, interests, and so on, along with their
skills in rational analysis, Habermas sees in such consensus a conjunction
between moral claims as ostensibly valid universally (the concern of traditional ethical and political theory) and the instantiation of these claims in ways
that reflect and preserve the individual and particular interests of individuals
in the domain of praxis.[9] In this way, communicative action seeks to avoid a
transcendental set of moral norms so far removed from the particulars of
human praxis that they become utopian in the sense of being unworkable. To
put it another way, if communicative action works by consensus in this way,
it grounds a set of quasi-transcendent, universally valid moral norms that are
neither utopian (because they are too far removed from praxis) nor merely
ideological (because they reflect only particular, culturally relative beliefs).

Relativism and the Universalizability of Moral Claims

What Alexy and Habermas identify as the tacit assumption of discourse—that
our claims are true or valid for others as well as for ourselves—can be restated
as the universal, or potentially universalizable, validity of especially moral
claims (that is, claims surrounding questions of truth and justice). Both Alexy
and Habermas launch their communicative ethic with this claim of universal
validity against the familiar arguments of contemporary naturalism and intu-
itionism that result in ethical relativism—the view that all claims, including
moral ones, are at best valid only for the individual or the individual as
situated in a culture.

In addition to the observation that discourse rests on a tacit assumption of such universally valid claims, Habermas attempts to defend the universal-izability of claims in two ways. First, he offers an analysis of discourse in natural science that relies heavily on Toulmin. Second, he employs the phenomenological notion of the lifeworld as the larger context of discourse. These two points together work, along with his critique of the arguments for relativism, to argue that at least some forms of discourse, primarily in virtue of their *form,* may lead to universally valid claims.

To begin with, Habermas makes use of an analogy with the inductive process that allows scientists to come to agreement on causal relations as factual, necessary, and universal. It is to be emphasized that such agreement on causal relations involves a claim to universal validity; that is, scientists do not assert that their identification of causal relations as factual and necessary is simply a claim valid for individuals or individuals in a given culture. Such an identification of causal relations is not simply the result of personal preference or ideological conditioning.

In particular, according to Habermas, the *conditions* under which the scientists' discourse occurs are necessary (though not necessarily sufficient) conditions for arriving at universal or potentially universal claims. By analogy, and using a model of argument analysis established by Stephen Toulmin, Habermas argues that "under controlled conditions approximating complete impartiality and fairness, the moral principle of universalizability (U) enables us to agree factually on the consequences, favorable or otherwise, of norms, in a manner that is itself normatively binding" (Ingram 1990, 147–48, refer-ring to Habermas 1984b).

More generally, in the first volume of *The Theory of Communicative Action,* Habermas develops a phenomenological notion of a "lifeworld," one "bounded by the totality of interpretations presupposed by the members as background knowledge" (13). Such a lifeworld, with its background of shared assumptions, is then the context for the communicative practice aimed toward "achieving, sustaining, and renewing consensus—and indeed a consensus that rests on the intersubjective recognition of criticizable validity claims" (17). This communicative practice, finally, is bound up with a certain form of rationality, one capable of providing *reasons* in public discourse, over against overt or covert appeals to force: "Thus the rationality proper to the communi-cative practice of everyday life points to the practice of argumentation as a court of appeal that makes it possible to continue communicative action with other means when disagreements can no longer be repaired with everyday routines and yet are not to be settled by the direct or strategic use of force" (17–18).

Moreover, following Toulmin, Habermas emphasizes that rational be-havior includes openness to argument—that is, a willingness to recognize valid reasons, whether in order to accept or criticize these, in contrast with the person "deaf to argument," the person who ignores reasons that run contrary to his views. Rational expressions are thus open to criticism and thus to improvement if mistakes of fact or logic are made. And, as Habermas points out, rationality and argumentation of this sort are further interwoven with "the ability to learn from mistakes, from the refutation of hypotheses and from the failure of interventions" (18).

Finally, given the ability to criticize claims within the context of the lifeworld and thus to identify and correct mistakes,

> forms of argumentation take shape which may be transmitted and developed within a cultural tradition and even embodied in specific cultural institutions. Thus, for instance, the scientific enterprise, the legal system, and the institutions for producing, disseminating, and criticizing art represent enduring possibilities of hypothetically examining the truth of statements, the rightness of actions and norms, or the authenticity of expressions, and of productively assimilating our negative experiences in these dimensions. (McCarthy 1984, xiii)

In short, communicative action, the process of giving and criticizing reasons for holding or rejecting particular claims, is seen to operate in argumentation in the sciences, law, and criticism. Insofar as one grants that such argumentation leads to universally valid claims—an admission one is most likely to make with regard to the sciences—one then concedes Habermas's central point: Communicative action defines a rationality capable, through discourse, of arriving at universal norms.

Of course, Habermas recognizes the facts of cultural relativism, that putatively universal norms agreed upon by all members of a culture are not agreed upon by members of other cultures. Such *cultural* relativism, however, by no means forces us to accept *ethical* relativism, the stronger claim that no universally valid claims or beliefs, especially moral norms, exist. In the first volume of *The Theory of Communicative Action,* Habermas takes up this issue in part as he makes use of Toulmin and others to develop what he calls a "formal-pragmatic" account of communicative action, one fully informed by the recognition of cultural relativism. In addition, he directly faces the arguments for ethical relativism based on cultural relativism by way of reconstructing debates about rationality among English anthropologists and philosophers. Habermas finds that the case for relativism is not conclusive, which means that "while the universalistic claim of formal pragmatics cannot be conclusively redeemed . . . it can be rendered plausible" (138). At the same time, however, in keeping with the thematic interest in Frankfurt School critical theory in avoiding a theory too far removed from the domain of praxis —the claim of universal validity for communicative reason must be tested, and thus verified by praxis. In short, the arguments for ethical relativism are not conclusive, leaving open the possibility of discerning universally valid moral norms—a possibility that, in light of Habermas's communicative theory, is ultimately testable in praxis (McCarthy 1984, xiv).

Freedom and the Ethics of Discourse

In general, Habermas argues that universally valid claims may emerge from discourse, insofar as such discourse meets certain necessary (but not sufficient) conditions, the first of which is freedom and equality for participants. In his essay "Justice and Solidarity," Habermas summarizes what Ingram calls "the basic intuition embodied in a discourse ethic" with the statement that "under the moral point of view, one must be able to test whether a norm or a mode of action could be generally accepted by those affected by it, such that their acceptance would be rationally motivated and hence uncoerced" (Habermas 1989a, 6; see Ingram 1990, 145). In "Discourse Ethics" (1990), Habermas identifies these conditions more precisely in the context of establishing his principle of universalization—a principle that intends to set the conditions for impartial judgment insofar as it "constrains all affected to adopt the perspectives of all others in the balancing of interests" (65). The principle of universalization itself states: "All affected can accept the consequences and the side effects [that] its [a proposed moral norm's] general observance can be anticipated to have for the satisfaction of everyone's interests (and these consequences are preferred to those of known alternative possibilities for regulation)" (65).

In addition, Habermas articulates a second principle that, as he says, "already contains the distinctive idea of an ethics of discourse": "Only those [moral] norms can claim to be valid that meet (or could meet) with the approval of all affected in their capacity as participants in a practical discourse" (66). *In short, the conditions for the practical discourse out of which universally valid norms may emerge include the participation and acceptance of all who are affected by such norms, as such norms meet their interests.*

Finally, Habermas stresses that such discourse requires freedom as a condition. Simply put, we cannot expect the consent of all participants to follow "unless all affected can freely accept the consequences and the side effects that the general observance of a controversial norm can be expected to have for the satisfaction of the interests of each individual" (93). In other words, consent and consensus achieved under constraint are not genuine consent and consensus. Only those norms to which individuals freely assent through such discourse can thus have universal validity.[10]

Justice, Solidarity, and Democratic Polity: The Rules of Reason

To circumscribe such discourse more carefully, Habermas takes up rules first proposed by Robert Alexy as "the Rules of Reason" (1990, 165–67). In Habermas's formulation, these are:

1. Every subject with the competence to speak and act is allowed to take part in a discourse.
2a. Everyone is allowed to question any assertion whatever.
2b. Everyone is allowed to introduce any assertion whatever into the discourse.
2c. Everyone is allowed to express his attitudes, desires, and needs.
3. No speaker may be prevented, by internal or external coercion, from exercising his rights as laid down in (1) and (2). (1990, 86)

As Ingram points out, the ideal speech situation constructed by these rules stresses, first of all, equality and freedom for each participant, but freedom here has a tightly defined meaning. The participants in the ideal speech situation are first free *to* participate in the discourse in critical ways so as to express their attitudes, desires, and needs. In addition, the ideal speech situation must establish a context in which participants are further free *from* coercion of several sorts. Their participation in discourse will be "unobstructed by ideological prejudices, temporal limitations, and external domination—be it cultural, social, political, or economic" (Ingram 1990, 148).

These rules mark out the requirements for a just, if ideal, speech situation. As well, Habermas later argues that the ideal speech situation further requires a sense of *solidarity* between participants. Such solidarity involves concern for the well-being of both one's fellow human beings and of the community at large. As Habermas puts it in "Justice and Solidarity," "Justice concerns the equal freedoms of unique and self-determining individuals, while solidarity concerns the welfare of consociates who are intimately linked in an intersubjectively shared form of life and thus also to the maintenance of the integrity of this form of life itself" (1989a, 47, quoted in Ingram 1990, 149).

The ideal speech situation, especially as it conjoins justice and solidarity, thus means a *procedure* or *form* for discourse. Moreover, this procedure is central to both Habermas's effort to ground democratic polity on quasi-transcendent norms (which strike a middle ground between simple relativism and absolutism) and a concomitant plurality of diverse communities operating according to the discourse ethic. That is, first of all, the ideal speech situation, with its requirements for freedom, equality, and solidarity, also provides a definition of justice "in terms of formal rules of democratic fairplay" (Ingram 1990, 149). This is to say that, for Habermas, the rules and conditions of the ideal speech situation describe the necessary conditions of democratic polity. In fact, the primary arena for the discourse ethic is precisely grassroots democracy. Discourses held under the conditions of the discourse ethic allow people to "define their needs rationally, develop their reflective competencies collectively, regulate their property relations freely, and choose with full consciousness those very specific rights and duties that conform to their sense of justice, given their peculiar historical circumstances" (Ingram 1990, 155). In addition, the requirement for solidarity means that Habermas's theory endorses a *communitarian* conception of democracy (cf. Abramson, Arterton, and Orren 1988, 30).

Furthermore, this thematic effort fully to inform theoretical norms with the particularities of praxis also involves recognizing the legitimacy of a diversity or plurality of norms that reflect a diversity of communities and participants. By circumscribing the *form,* in contrast with the content, of ideal discourse and democratic interchange, Habermas's discourse ethic articulates a standard or criterion that, he claims, is universally valid. That is, the rules and conditions of the ideal speech situation are necessary conditions for achieving legitimate moral norms, norms that legitimately hold for all participants. At the same time, however, the content of this discourse is generated by particular participants at particular times, representing the particular needs and interests of particular communities. In this way, two different communities may hold to the same rules of discourse and so meet the universally valid standard for discourse and democratic interchange. Nonetheless, reflecting precisely the intention of the rules to preserve the free expression of individual interests, two such communities may achieve consensus on quite different moral norms. So Habermas is careful to point out, "The universalist position does not have to deny the pluralism and the incompatibility of historical versions of civilized humanity; but it regards this multiplicity of forms of life as limited to cultural contents, and it asserts that every culture must share certain formal properties of the modern understanding of the world, if it is at all to attain a certain degree of conscious awareness or sublimation" (1984a, 1:180). In this way, Habermas's theory issues in a *pluralistic* conception of democracy, complementing the *communitarian* conception emerging from the requirement for solidarity.

Finally, as the discourse ethic attempts to establish quasi-transcendent norms, in the form of a democratic procedure of discourse, it thereby achieves a crucial middle ground between ethical relativism and moral absolutism. First of all, it avoids the absolute tolerance of a consistent ethical relativism. Whereas an ethical relativist would be forced to accept the legitimacy of moral norms achieved, for example, through the threat of force against a community, the discourse ethic condemns such norms as illegitimate, precisely because they fail to reflect the fundamental norms of freedom, reciprocity, and solidarity required by the discourse ethic. At the same time, however, by articulating a form that may issue in a plurality of norms for a diversity of communities that reflect the particular interests of particular participants, the discourse ethic further avoids the absolute intolerance of dogmatism (1984a, 1:135, 180). The discourse ethic thus articulates the communicative conditions of democratic polity in such a way as to strike a theoretical middle ground that preserves both universally valid forms and a pluralism of diverse communities.

In addition, the discourse ethic represents not only the conditions for legitimating putative moral norms and for democratic polity; it further represents a specific form of rationality. In contrast with the paradigmatic notion of the isolated reason in Descartes, especially the requirement of solidarity means that Habermas's form of communicative rationality or communicative reason *includes* rather than *excludes* the emotive, the expression of individual needs, and so on. Communicative reason is thus distinct from what earlier critical theorists, and later postmodernists, attacked as a Cartesian, instrumental rationality.

Habermas's conception of communicative reason overcomes these critiques in two ways. First, in contrast with the dualistic logic that defines the Cartesian subject solely within a hierarchical relation of domination and subordination, communicative reason begins in relationship with others, thus allowing for the possibility of equality as it simultaneously preserves the intractable difference between free selves. Second, communicative reason does not issue in theoretical norms radically divorced from the particular needs and interests of individuals. Rather, the discourse ethic intends precisely to preserve the particularities of praxis in the universally valid norms that are to emerge from consensus. Accordingly, Habermas's notion of communicative rationality allows for the possibility that modern institutions—notably science, law, and aesthetic criticism—may, in fact, become genuinely democratic insofar as they incorporate communicative reason and the discourse ethic. By implication, modern technologies—specifically, computers and computer communication networks—would appear to avoid critiques such as Marcuse's, insofar as these technologies likewise enable the unconstrained discourse of communicative reason.

Habermas's Critique of Postmodernism

Finally, Habermas's theory supports interests in democratic polity and liberation of the oppressed more consistently than do poststructuralist and postmodernist theories. In particular, Habermas and postmodernists part ways precisely on the question of the viability of democratic politics. Specifically, Habermas argues that the commitment to democratic politics in postmodernist theories threatens to run aground on several internal contradictions between their interest in democratic politics and what Habermas sees as their implicitly *anti*democratic consequences.

To begin with, Habermas charges that both poststructuralists and postmodernists appear to lead in two apolitical, if not antipolitical, directions (Ingram 1990, 197–204). First, Habermas contends that by rejecting Enlightenment notions of freedom, individual autonomy, communal solidarity, and democratic self-determination, poststructuralists and postmodernists undermine the possibility of opposing totalitarianism. This point can then be made in a second way. Poststructuralists and postmodernists reject these modernist notions as they more generally reject the modernist project of attempting to rationally found a universally valid system of beliefs and values. As we have already seen, however, correlative with this rejection is the endorsement of ethical relativism—the position that values and beliefs are valid only within a specific context. But on such a view, the preference for democracy is relative or valid only for those individuals and cultures that affirm such a value: Alternative political forms, such as authoritarianism, must be accepted as equally valid in alternative contexts.

Philosophers commonly note that such relativism tends to undermine itself as it presents an obvious paradox: If there are no universally valid claims, then the relativists' claim that there are no universally valid claims cannot be universally valid. Similarly, Habermas argues that these accounts are internally contradictory and self-defeating. According to Ingram, "The poststructuralist dissolution of the acting subject into a plurality of language games (Lyotard), a forcefield of power relations (Foucault), or an open system of linguistic signifiers (Derrida) relativizes all rational distinctions and identities to the point where political resistance becomes meaningless. Why be political if there is no ideal to be fought over, no subject to be emancipated?" (1990, 205; cf. Bernstein's critique of Derrida in Bernstein 1991, 213f.).[11] In short, if the ethical relativism enjoined by poststructuralists and postmodernists holds, then the preference for democratic polity is, in fact, ideological rather than reflecting a value holding greater validity.

A further contradiction emerges regarding the technologies often celebrated by postmodernists—namely, the technologies of computers and computer-based communications networks. In the context of his critique of modernism, Lyotard (1984) develops an extensive critique of computerized society as inclined toward using computers and computer-based technology in ways that support the power of the state, especially as these technologies function as a "terror" that threatens to silence any dissent. In fact, one of the motives for a shift from modern to postmodern views is precisely the critique launched by Lyotard against modern technology as supporting a form of terror. Lyotard argues specifically that "a generalized computerization of society" (47) by no means serves what he characterizes as the humanistic and idealist narratives of legitimation characteristic of the modern period. These themes, notice, are precisely the modernist themes underlying the commitment to democratic polity—namely, the humanistic, Enlightenment theme of political liberation toward a democratic society by means of scientific advance (31–32, 34) and the subsequent stress in German Idealism on achieving a systematic unity of all knowledge (32–35). Rather, he argues that such technologies serve instead the interests of states and companies in the pursuit of power, not truth, especially as such technologies help define and reinforce what a computerized society accepts as "reality" (46–47). Computers in a computerized society, he concludes, "could then become the 'dream' instrument for controlling and regulating" not simply the market system but the society itself—a use of the computer that would further entail terror (67), defined as "the efficiency gained by eliminating, or threatening to eliminate a participant in the language game of society" (63).

At the same time, however, Lyotard goes on to claim that "justice," as an alternative to terror, would require the public to have "free access to the memory and data banks of computerized society" (67). This, coupled with his analysis of the self as a "nodal point" in the communication circuits that constitute much of social relations (15), implies that he agrees that increased access to information across computer networks is a good thing. Nonetheless, how are we to reconcile Lyotard's critique of technology as "the dream instrument" of totalitarianism with his vision of this same technology as facilitating the free play of language games he calls "paralogy"? Lyotard's critique of computers and computer-based communication networks thus threatens his postmodernism with a crucial contradiction. Simply, this critique directly contradicts his subsequent claim that such systems promise democratization.

Lyotard, in fact, echoes Habermas's turn toward communication as he (Lyotard) bases his notion of paralogy on an analysis of narration as communication (see especially Lyotard 1984, chap. 5). But as Lyotard rejects the Enlightenment narrative of emancipation and democratization—a narrative that would support a democratizing use of technologies over against their totalitarian uses—he thereby falls prey to Habermas's critique that postmodernism undermines the grounds for opposition to totalitarianism. More generally, in light of the relativism associated with postmodernism, it is by no means clear how the justice of paralogy is to be argued for, over against totalitarianism.

By contrast, Habermas's theory of communicative action offers those still drawn by the Enlightenment project of democratization a number of theoretical advantages. These advantages begin with Habermas's showing the democratic preference as grounded in the praxis of everyday discourse. Indeed, the praxis of dialogue and seeking consensus regarding norms, especially in the forms of science, law, and criticism, makes plausible the possibility that the democratic preference and its attendant values (freedom, equality, justice, solidarity) stand as at least quasi-transcendent norms which both provide for a plurality of discourse communities while yet defending the democratic preference against the arguments of ethical relativism. In this way, then, a Habermasian theory undergirding CMC technologies can overcome the critique that democratization via CMC is merely a matter of (relatively valid) preference and ideology.

Second, Habermas makes clear the theoretical connections between communication and democratization. Most simply, the rules and conditions of the ideal speech situation describe the necessary conditions of democratic polity. Insofar as this analysis and definition of democratic polity are sound, CMC theorists who can show that CMC systems facilitate communications which meet these conditions can thereby argue that such systems contribute to democratization. In fact, such systems would serve to test in praxis the validity of Habermas's theory, thus providing an instance of the sort of empirical verification he calls for as part of his effort to resolve the tension between theory and practice. We will see in the next section that current praxis indeed substantiates Habermas's framework.

Third, Habermas's notion of communicative rationality rescues modern technologies, including those underlying CMC systems, from criticisms raised against them as antidemocratic. Again, insofar as CMC theorists can demonstrate that CMC systems facilitate the unconstrained discourse of communicative reason, a discourse that leads to consensus over important norms, such systems would both fulfill the democratization claim and clearly avoid the totalitarian tendency alleged by Marcuse.

Fourth, we have seen that the democratization claim not only can be dismissed as resting on mere ideological preference; it has also been attacked as utopian. But as Habermas takes up the theory-praxis problem thematic of Frankfurt School critical theory, he develops several ways of meeting this criticism as well. As we have seen, Frankfurt School critical theory in general seeks to bridge traditional philosophical theories with such empirically informed theories as sociology, psychology, and so forth. In particular, Habermas's communicative action theory rests in part on empirical analyses of communication. Furthermore, insofar as communicative rationality is to be informed both by the particularities of individual need and desire and by the specific context of given communities, the theoretical norms emerging from this sort of discourse promise to be more closely shaped by the realities of praxis from the outset. Finally, because communicative rationality is always open to further discussion, these norms are always open to revision in light of the failures of such norms to be fully realized in praxis. Communicative rationality thus intends to avoid the critique of utopianism attaching to theoretical norms more at odds with the particularities of praxis. Indeed, if Habermas's analysis of communicative action is correct, the democratic thrust, though not perfectly realizable, is nonetheless already partially realized in everyday discourse. To reject this democratic intention as utopian would succeed only if one chose to ignore this intention in everyday communication.

Finally, Habermas's theory of communicative action avoids the internal inconsistencies threatening the postmodernism often taken up by CMC theorists. Again, Habermas's reconstruction of communicative reason is explicitly intended to counter the authoritarian dimensions of Cartesian rationality and modern technology, including the computer technologies of CMC. In this way, his theory can more consistently endorse democratization via CMC than can Lyotard, for example. Moreover, as Habermas attempts to ground the preference for democratic polity as a universally valid norm, he thus avoids the relativism of a postmodernism that would otherwise only reinforce the ideology critique and the potentially antidemocratic consequences of this relativism.

Discourse Ethics and Electronic Communities:
The Moral Requirements of Democratic Pluralism

We have seen how Habermas's discourse ethic provides a theoretical foundation for redeeming the democratization claim against charges of utopianism and ideology, as it further articulates the connection between critical discourse and democratic communities. As a last point, we can now examine the kind of communication and democratic community entailed by the rules of reason and the requirements of communicative rationality. We will see that the discourse ethic, as it circumscribes the form and character of discourse intended to sustain democratic communities, in fact provides powerful theoretical support for current conceptions of democratizing communication via CMC. In particular, the discourse ethic issues in the call for open and equitable communication and the pluralism of currently existing discourse communities, as it further provides theoretical justification for important elements of current "netiquette" and related efforts at moderating communication in electronic forums which have emerged in response to various abuses. In doing so, however, the discourse ethic distinguishes itself from current, especially plebiscite, conceptions of democracy and communication. Briefly, the plebiscite conception seems to entail a problematic information flood and tolerance for all forms of communicative behavior, and hence cannot justify efforts to curb certain kinds of discourse in the name of democratizing communications. By contrast, the framework of the discourse ethic and its more communitarian and pluralist conception of democracy would moderate the information flood in ways reflecting current practice.

In conversation, Habermas has succinctly described the ideal speech community as follows: "We endeavour to ensure that (a) all voices in any way relevant can get a hearing, and that (b) the best arguments we have in our present state of knowledge are brought to bear, and that (c) disagreement or agreement on the part of the participants follows only from the force of the better argument and no other force" (Nielsen 1990, 104). Beginning with rule 1, the rules of reason work to ensure first of all that all relevant voices participate in a given community. This rule would hence require open and equitable access to the discourse mediated by a computer network.

The remaining rules of reason work to generate a specific *kind* of discourse—namely, a *critical* discourse focused on untrammeled exchange of giving reasons for positions taken. So rules 2a and 2b seek to ensure the ability on the part of all community members to *question* any assertion whatsoever and to introduce any assertion whatever. As well, rules 2c and 3 make the point that discourse cannot be constrained by censorship regarding what texts may be introduced. This would mean, moreover, that discourse within the community must further be free from other forms of social coercion—the subtle but powerful clues of hierarchy, status, gender, and so forth.

Moreover, the discourse of the democratic community would reflect the practices and intentions of what Habermas has circumscribed as communicative rationality. Again, this rationality is marked by the interests of constructing and exchanging the best *arguments* we may have—that is, an interest in providing *reasons* for one's assertions and the concomitant interest in achieving agreement or disagreement based only on the cogency of argument rather than on nonrational elements (such as who is able to dominate discussion because of aggressive rhetorical practice, more time to devote to discussion, and so on). In addition, such rationality incorporates the *emotive* dimension of solidarity with others, a genuine concern for their well-being in the praxis of public discourse that further entails "mutual perspective-taking: everybody is stimulated to adopt the perspective of all others in order that they might examine the acceptability of a solution according to the way every other person understands themselves and the world" (Nielsen 1990, 98; cf. Benhabib 1992, 8–9). These requirements of discourse would allow a community to exclude those who regularly failed to exercise such discourse; such exclusion, notice, does not obviously violate the rules of reason intended to prevent a censorship which would subvert open and critical dialogue. Finally, as circumscribing the *form* or *procedure* of discourse, Habermas's discourse ethics issues in a diversity of communities. Each community of discourse would be marked by equal access, interest in argument, lack of censorship, and solidarity especially in the form of concern for the well-being of community members and the effort to understand others' perspectives. But a wide diversity of such communities can be envisioned, defined by different interests and concerns—analogous to the pluralism of democratic cultures Habermas defends.

At first glance, especially the rules of reason appear to echo notions we have seen of democratizing communication as "open, free-ranging discourse" (Sproull and Kiesler 1991a, 116) that would allow "nearly everyone . . . to put his or her ideas, concerns and demands before all others" (Dertouzos 1991, 69). But we have seen associated with these calls for universal access a number of theoretical problems. In "The Frankfurt School and the Problem of Democracy," above, we have examined how some of these problems (i.e., the problems of definition, utopianism, and ideology) are overcome by Habermas's discourse ethic. We can now note how Habermas's approach counters two additional problems. First, the call for universal access would seem to entail the system envisioned by Nelson of "a hundred million simultaneous users, adding a hundred million documents an hour to the system" (1974, 144). Such a system, however, would seem to result inevitably in the glut of information garbage (Postman 1993), the information flood in which millions drown (Romiszowski 1990). And hence, if we are left to our preferences, we may well prefer to ignore such "communication" entirely (so Baker 1994; McKibben 1993; Postman 1993). Second, these calls are associated with a *plebiscite* vision of the electronic town hall—a vision that is criticized as potentially *anti*democratic, as it allows for individual voices to be overridden by power, whether in the form of aggression by a few or in the form of the "tyranny of the majority." More fundamentally, such plebiscites can be transformed into nondemocratic environments. Indeed, numerous examples demonstrate that electronic plebiscites can be subverted. For instance, theoretically open discourse on Internet lists can be dominated by those with more aggressive communication styles—meaning, in praxis, primarily men (Herring, this volume). More overt examples include the refusal to allow democratizing effects to play themselves out, as top-echelon participants refuse to use e-mail systems (partly just because of the flood of information they entail), and as they remove such systems altogether from their organizations (so Sproull and Kiesler 1991b; Zachary 1994). Consider, finally, the self-proclaimed terrorist attacks on the Post Modern Culture MOO (multi-user dungeon-object oriented) created by John Unsworth, including "virtual rapes" of unsuspecting participants by other users (Bennahum 1994, 34f.). In praxis, then, plebiscites originally intended to be open, egalitarian forums have, in fact, led to undesirable information gluts, as they have also become dominated by a few, to the exclusion of dissenting voices and minorities (most obviously, women).

Of course, in response to these problems, existing discourse communities have attempted to moderate communicative behavior. What is striking is that these efforts appear to be inconsistent with an absolute plebiscite that demands that *all* voices be heard; but such efforts seem to follow from Habermas's discourse ethic. As a first example, Internet lists represent not plebiscites but the plurality of democratic communities which follow from the discourse ethic. That is, such lists are defined by agreed-upon interests and desires. Under a plebiscite call for universal access, anyone would have a right to participate in any list discussion. But in current praxis, in fact, lists routinely deny membership to those whose backgrounds and training make them less competent to engage in a given discussion (e.g., the history of first-century Christianity and Judaism, problems facing editors of electronic journals, etc.). While in conflict with the plebiscite call, such self-definition and exclusion on the part of a discourse community directly follow from the discourse ethic, precisely as it acknowledges the legitimacy of a diversity of communities, each of which is defined by shared interests and norms. Moreover, as lists maintain a finite membership based on interests, they thereby limit the amount of communication members must contend with. At the same time, a great diversity of lists has emerged on the Internet, each defined by different interests and topics, but most sharing a general form that includes exclusion of this sort. This praxis fits closely with Habermas's conception of a diverse plurality of democratic communities—democratic in virtue of the form of discourse they pursue—in contrast with a single community, on a global scale, which follows from the plebiscite vision. In short, over against the plebiscite vision of a hundred million users adding a hundred million documents to the information flood, the finite membership of a plurality of lists defined by agreed-upon interests both instantiates Habermas's conception of a plurality of democratic communities—each marked by voluntary participation and discourse defined by individual needs and interests—and limits the communicative noise participants must contend with.

Moreover, a netiquette has emerged which attempts to insure that discourse fulfills members' interests as fully as possible. Some lists, for example, stress self-censure of discourse that does not directly contribute to discussion; some further rely on a moderator to edit messages before they are broadcast to the list at large. More generally, netiquette almost universally emphasizes the importance of avoiding "flaming." But it is by no means clear how a plebiscite insisting on universal access can consistently endorse these sorts of restrictions. By contrast, as Habermas's discourse ethic, by way of the rules of reason and the solidarity characteristic of communicative rationality, intends a fundamental equality and solidarity, the discourse ethic can justify these restrictions—including the proscription against flaming as destructive of equality and clearly counter to the requirements of solidarity. In particular, the hostility of flaming seems in direct conflict with the requirement to take the perspective of the other as an equal coparticipant in a discourse community.

Similarly, we can consider what are characterized as "democratic" means of controlling characters and discourse which MOOs have developed in response to abuses. For example, admission as a permanent character to the MediaMOO requires a majority vote by an elected committee, chosen in turn from the "citizenry" by secret ballot (Bennahum 1994, 29). We can describe these means of control as democratic, however, only if we abandon the plebiscite insistence on the relevance of all voices—even those voices who use access to acquire power and dominance over others. By contrast, these means of control can be considered democratic insofar as they are more consistent with the requirements of discourse ethics (e.g., the focus on critical exchange of reasons, solidarity, and perspective taking) and thus with the communitarian and pluralist form of democracy associated with discourse ethics.

As these examples make clear, to redeem the promise of democratization via CMC, especially by way of Habermasian guidelines, requires that we attend especially to the social context of the use of CMC systems—in philosophical terms, to the ethical and political dimensions of our use of these technologies. As a first example, if all relevant voices are to be given a hearing, both the overt sexism and the covert privileging of male discourse which currently work to exclude women's voices would require moderation.[12] Somewhat more formally, recent efforts to revise Article 19 of the Universal Declaration of Human Rights might be seen to reflect the Habermasian connection between communication and Habermasian ideals of such communication in both supporting rationales and the formal language of a declaration. The articulated right to communicate, for example, explicitly includes "fair and equitable access to media distribution channels and to adequate resources for the satisfaction of the human need to communicate in the practice of democracy and in the exercise of any other human right and fundamental freedom" (The Bratislava Declaration). But again, such claims may follow from either a plebiscite call for universal access, with all its attendant problems, or a Habermasian discourse ethic. As the crucial distinction between plebiscite and pluralism makes clear, CMC enthusiasts who wish to fulfill the promise of democratization via CMC will have to examine carefully how far the culture of pluralist democracy is understood and practiced by CMC participants, over against the currently more fashionable libertarianism of plebiscite democracy and postmodernism.

The requirements for democratizing discourse in a Habermasian framework are thus rational and moral: The discourse ethic requires the ability to engage in critical discourse and the moral commitment to practicing the ability to take others' perspectives and thus seek solidarity with others in a plurality of democratic discourse communities. Such requirements are neither unusual nor remarkable: On the contrary, they seem to be minimal requirements for citizenship in a democratic society—and, in fact, they appear to be reflected in much current praxis both on and off the Net. More generally, recall the original problem facing Habermas and the Frankfurt School—namely, the problem of how fascism emerges from democratic societies. In the face of this threat, the discourse ethic requires that CMC theorists also be astute political philosophers, well-grounded in and articulate about the political and moral requirements of pluralistic and communitarian democracies. Only then will they be able to defend their discourse communities against the persuasive but sophistical arguments of the would-be tyrants who will otherwise emerge from the fledgling fields of electronic democracies.

Notes

1. This essay, substantially revised, is based on my exploration of democratization with regard to hypertext, titled "The Political Computer: Hypertext, Democracy, and Habermas," in *Hyper/Text/Theory*, edited by George Landow (Baltimore: Johns Hopkins University Press, 1994). Permission to reprint from Johns Hopkins Press is gratefully acknowledged. I would also like to thank Professor George Landow (Brown University), Teresa Harrison (Rensselaer Polytechnic Institute), and Heather Johnson (Drury '94), for their suggestions on how to improve on the original essay. Thanks also to Dr. Barbara Becker (German National Research Centre of Computer Science, St. Augustin) for providing me with recent publications by Habermas.

2. Lee Sproull and Sara Kiesler (1991b) use the phrase "computer-mediated communications" to refer to today's most popular computer-based communication technologies and applications: networks, electronic mail, electronic bulletin boards, and electronic conferencing (10f.). In this essay, I will use CMC in just this sense as well.

3. For a general overview of the technical literatures, see Sproull and Kiesler 1991a, 1991b; and Malone and Rockart 1991. Kahn and Brookshire 1991 provide an overview of pertinent research in education regarding the communications impacts of computer networks.

For representative claims in more popular literature, see Gleick 1994; and Nash 1994 (the latter reports on Vice-President Gore's claim that global communications networks will enhance democracy). For critiques of these claims which suggest the problems of unclear definition of democracy, utopianism, and ideology, see Baker 1994; McKibben 1993; Postman 1993.

4. Over against this claim, however, see McLeod 1992. Her meta-analysis of the literature on electronic group support systems from 1980 through 1990 shows that such technologies increased task focus, increased equality of participation, raised decision quality, lengthened time to decision, lowered consensus, and lowered satisfaction (273). Whether these results bode well or ill for the democratization thesis depends, of course, on what one means by democracy.

Nonetheless, a number of studies support the claim that computer networks indeed facilitate communication and learning. In addition to those cited by Riel 1991–1992 and Kahn and Brookshire 1991, see, for example, Day 1991, Bateson et al. (n.d.), and, with specific reference to scholarly communication, Harrison and Stephen 1992.

For that, earlier research on electronic communications, including the use of communications in an educational setting, reports mixed results regarding the degree to which such communications, in fact, achieve democratization: see Kahn and Brookshire 1991 for a discussion of the pertinent literature. As well, see Riel 1990, 1991–1992 for additional bibliographic sources on networking in education. In the domain of communication theory proper, Walther 1992 summarizes research and theories regarding both negative and positive relational behavior on communications networks.

More generally, see Borgmann 1984, Turkle 1984, especially chap. 6; and Westrum 1991, chap. 14, "The Distancing Effects of Technology," for discussion of how modern technologies—specifically, computers and computer-based communications networks—appear to have disruptive and alienating impacts on users. For additional resources, see Ess 1994.

Finally, for a useful history of the Internet, with a view toward the political and cultural frameworks which shaped its development, see Giese (forthcoming).

5. See as well Kraemer 1991. Kraemer does not use the term *democratization,* but he does refer to a strategic computing thesis which includes the propositions that information technology, including CMC, can change organization structures, especially "by liberating them from past dependency on centralized, hierarchical forms, and that such technology may further open up access between government and citizens" (169). Based on his review of the impacts of these technologies on American public administrartion, however, Kraemer concludes that "the structural impacts of information technology are negligible, and therefore variations in organizational structure are largely irrelevant" (178). Though not quite as negative, Ettema 1989 comes to similar conclusions based on early ventures with videotex: see esp. 121f. Ronfeldt 1992 finds equally ambiguous results in the domain of governmental structures: see esp. 273ff.

6. The literature on Habermas is extensive—a 1990 bibliography lists over 3,000 publications (Rasmussen 1990). Fortunately, several good introductions to Frankfurt School critical theory exist. In addition to the scholars I draw on in this essay, readers seeking more orientation to Habermas can turn to three anthologies of Frankfurt School critical theory: Arato and Gebhardt 1982; Bronner and Kellner 1989; and Ingram and Simon-Ingram 1991. For a close history of the Frankfurt School, see Wiggerhaus 1994. Finally, Ewert 1991 provides a compact introduction to Habermas and his reception in educational theory.

7. Enlightenment theorists, beginning with Descartes, held that modern science and technology contribute to the larger Enlightenment project of greater economic and political freedom in a democratic polity. The paradigm of human rationality is defined for early modernity by Descartes, whose project of seeking absolute certainty by submitting all claims to knowledge to the acid bath of radical doubt resulted in the isolated self, aware only of its own existence, as the sole instance of certain knowledge. As a consequence, however, human reason emerges radically divorced from, and superior to, the senses and nature.

This divorce of human reason from the natural order provides the ideological justification for the human domination of nature by means of technology. Like human masters whose belief in the natural inferiority of the enslaved justifies their domination, radically divorcing human reason from nature allows us to render ourselves, in Descartes's phrase, "masters and possessors of nature" (1972, 119). This domination of nature supposedly brings freedom from labor and disease, which, in turn, makes possible the greater human freedoms of a democratic polity

Drawing upon the sociological insights of Max Weber, the Frankfurt School argued that this dualistic conception of the relationship between self and nature led directly to various problems of modernity and modern technology, including the failure of Enlightenment democracy (see McCarthy 1984, ix; Ingram 1990, 50–54; Benhabib 1986, especially 182–85, 255–60). In particular, the project of modern technology as a primary expression of an isolated Cartesian reason is frequently characterized in the Frankfurt School as a project of domination and oppression of both nature and humanity (e.g., Horkheimer and Adorno 1947; see also Benhabib 1986, 163–171; Ingram 1990, 60–67). Herbert Marcuse (1964), in turn, argues that the totalitarian tendency of modern technology is identical with modern rationality itself (see especially his chap. 6, "Technological Rationality and the Logic of Domination"; see also Ingram 1990, 80).

As Ingram (1990) puts it, the analyses of Adorno (1970, 1973), Adorno et al, (1950), Horkheimer, and Marcuse point to just this dilemma: Either scientific or moral rationality may be realized—but not both (74). Briefly, the pessimism toward the possibility of achieving democratic polity through Enlightenment rationality issues in a turn toward the aesthetic (so Adorno 1970; Marcuse 1955; see Ingram 1990, 74–91, 93–103).

8. Bernstein (1991) emphasizes that this crisis is an intensely personal one for Habermas. Born in 1929, Habermas was confronted with the full horrors of Nazism as he listened to the Nuremberg trials broadcast over the radio when he was fifteen or sixteen (Habermas 1983b, 41, cited in Bernstein 1991, 202). As Bernstein points out, this shock is background to virtually all Habermas has written (202). It further explains Habermas's unrelenting critique of those "young conservatives," including (for him) postmodernists, who, on his view, reopen the door to the terrors of fascism by attacking the foundations of Enlightenment democracy.

9. Habermas takes up these questions of theory, practice, and the legitimation of moral norms very early in his work, most notably in *Theory and Practice* (1973) and in *Knowledge and Human Interests* (1971). For a discussion of these, see McCarthy 1978, 40–60; Ingram 1990, 113–19.

Benhabib (1992), in her effort to refine communicative ethics in light of postmodern, feminist, and communitarian objections, observes that Habermas's use of the term *consensus* can be misleading. On her view, the goal of communication is not complete consensus or unanimity but "anticipated communication with others with whom I know I must finally come to some agreement," requiring "the will and the readiness to reach some reasonable agreement in an open-ended moral conversation" (9). See Ingram 1993 for both a critique and defense of Habermas on this point.

10. In this way, Habermas preserves the central legitimation argument of the Enlightenment philosopher Rousseau, who points out that we do not recognize the legitimacy of agreements made under duress. According to Rousseau (1950), *might* (the ability to coerce agreement through force or intimidation) does not make moral *right* (an agreement legitimate between rational human beings that thus obliges them to observe the conditions of the agreement): see especially Rousseau's argument in the opening book of *The Social Contract,* chaps. 3–6. In this way, Habermas retains

the Enlightenment focus on human freedom and rationality, but he does so by reformu-
lating the notion of freedom as one that is necessarily intertwined with others in the
community of communicative rationalities. Ingram discusses these reformulations in
greater detail (though he omits the reference to Rousseau), especially in relation to
Kant's conception of the human being as a moral autonomy and the correlative ethics
(1990, 145–46).

    11. As Ingram points out, Habermas attacks postmodernists as "young conser-
vatives," thereby associating them with the young conservatives of the 1920s in
Germany who can be seen as precursors to Nazi politics (Ingram 1990, 204; Habermas
1991b, 354f.). On Habermas's view, "both groups seek, by virtue of a shared archaism
and aestheticism, to break free of the normative presuppositions of modernity: the
autonomous conception of the self, liberal-democratic forms of government, and a
rational theory of knowledge" (Wolin 1989, xxx). As the neoconservative turn in
German politics—a turn which, on the view of its critics, attempts to solve the problem
of the Nazi past largely by ignoring it—and the rise of anti-Semitism, hate crimes,
and the like in Germany today make clear, Habermas's concern that postmodern
critiques may contribute to the decay of modern democracy is not an entirely theoretical matter.
    Such a critique is part of Habermas's more general attack on "the varieties of
nihilism, relativism, decisionism, historicism and neo-Aristotelian contextualism" of
the twentieth century (Bernstein 1991, 206). Most broadly, Habermas argues that all
of these positions become self-contradictory. While they offer critique—of modernity,
of instrumental reason, of "totalizing" philosophy in Hegel, and so on—each of these
positions in turn "undermines the possibility of critique that is rationally grounded
and warranted" (Bernstein 1991, 206). Without such rational grounds, Habermas
argues, "If thought can no longer operate in the realms of truth and validity claims,
then analysis and critique lose their meaning." This leaves simply an aestheticism
which "enthrones *taste,* the 'Yes' and 'No' of the palate . . . as the sole organ of
knowledge beyond Truth and Falsity, beyond Good and Evil" (Habermas 1982, 25,
27, in Bernstein 1991, 207). See as well Habermas's critique of Foucault's relativism
as undermining his (Foucault's) own theory (Habermas 1987a, 279f.), and his critique
of Foucault from the standpoint of Habermas's more recent "discourse theory of right
and the democratic constitutional state" (1992, 67, 105).

    12. As an example: Australia has banned Usenet groups devoted to the ex-
change of pornography and discussion of sex, including bestiality and pedophilia.
While this move is decried by free-speech advocates (see Rosenberg 1993), it is a
move that *could* be justified under Habermas's discourse ethic, under two conditions:
(a) The community of discourse participants would have to openly discuss the issue,
and come to consensus on what norms their discourse communities would endorse,
and it may well be that such an open discussion, especially if it included full participation *by all those affected*—specifically, women and children—would result in a consensus to prohibit such discourse and uses of the system; and (b) if it could be
demonstrated that such discourse worked to exclude the voices of all members of a
democratic community—most obviously, the voices of women who are offended,

sometimes into silence and withdrawal, by pornography which degrades them. (On this point, however, feminists are divided: see Rosenberg 1993, 303f.)

References

Abramson, Jeffrey, Christopher Arterton, and Gary Orren. 1988. *The Electronic Commonwealth: The Impact of New Media Technologies on Democratic Politics.* New York: Basic Books.

Adorno, T. W. 1970. *Aesthetische Theorie.* Frankfurt: Suhrkamp. Trans. Christian Lenhardt, under the title *Aesthetic Theory.* London: Routledge and Kegan Paul, 1984.

————. 1973. *Negative Dialectics.* New York: Seabury Press.

Adorno, T. W., and others. 1950. *The Authoritarian Personality.* New York: Harper and Row.

Alexy, Robert. 1990. A Theory of Practical Discourse, Trans. David Frisby. In Benhabib and Dallmayr (1990), 151–190.

Arato, Andrew, and Eike Gebhardt. 1982. *The Essential Frankfurt School Reader.* New York: Continuum.

Baker, Russell. 1994. But Will It Fly? *New York Times,* 4 January, A15.

Bateson, Trent, Joy Peyton, Terence Collins, Michael Spitzer, Christine Neuwirth, and Diane Thompson. N.d. *Final Report: the ENFI Project.* N.p.

Benhabib, Seyla. 1986. *Critique, Norm, and Utopia: A Study of the Foundations of Critical Theory.* New York: Columbia University Press.

————. 1992. *Situating the Self: Gender, Community, and Postmodernism in Contemporary Ethics.* New York: Routledge.

Benhabib, Seyla, and Fred Dallmayr, eds. 1990. *The Communicative Ethics Controversy.* Cambridge: MIT Press.

Bennahum, David. 1994. Fly Me to the MOO: Adventures in Textual Reality. *Lingua Franca* (June): 1, 22–36

Bernstein, Richard J. 1991. *The New Constellation: the Ethical-Political Horizons of Modernity/Postmodernity.* Cambridge: MIT Press.

Borgmann, Albert. 1984. *Technology and the Character of Contemporary Life.* Chicago: University of Chicago Press.

The Bratislava Declaration of the Expert Seminar on ''The Right to Communicate in the Post Cold War Period.'' Bratislava, Slovak Republic, 10–11 June 1993.

Reprinted in IAMCRNET Hotline 22 (26 June-3 Jul 1993). [Electronic document IAMCRNET NB022 available from comserve@cios.llc.rpi.edu.]

Bronner, Stephen Eric, and Douglas MacKay Kellner. 1989. *Critical Theory and Society: A Reader.* New York: Routledge, Chapman and Hall.

Bush, Vannevar. 1945. As We May Think. *Atlantic Monthly* (July), 101–8.

Carey, James. 1989. The Mythos of the Electronic Revolution. In *Communication as Culture: Essays on Media and Society.* Winchester, MA: Unwin Hyman.

Chesebro, James W., and Donald G. Bonsall. 1989. *Computer-Mediated Communication: Human Relationships in a Computerized World.* Tuscaloosa, AL: University of Alabama Press.

Day, Michael. 1991. Networking: The Rhetoric of the New Writing Classroom. Paper presented at EDUCOM conference, 16–19 October, San Diego.

Dertouzos, Michael L. 1991. Communications, Computers and Networks. *Scientific American* 265, no. 3 (September): 62–69.

Descartes, René. 1972. *Discourse on the method of rightly conducting the reason and seeking for truth in the sciences.* Trans. E. S. Haldane and G. R. T. Ross. In *The Philosophical Works of Descartes,* 82–130. Cambridge: Cambridge University Press.

Electronic Democracy: The PEN Is Mighty. 1992. *The Economist,* 1 February, 96.

Elshtain, Jean Bethke. 1982. Interactive TV—Democracy and the QUBE Tube. *The Nation* (7–14 August), 108.

Ess, Charles. 1994. The Political Computer: Hypertext, Democracy, and Habermas In *Hyper/Text/Theory,* ed. George Landow, 225–67. Baltimore: Johns Hopkins Press.

Ettema, James S. 1989. Interactive Electronic Text in the United States: Can Videotex Ever Go Home Again? In *Media Use in the Information Age: Emerging Patterns of Adoption and Consumer Use,* ed. Jerry L. Salvaggio and Jennings Bryant, 105–23. Hillsdale, NJ: Lawrence Erlbaum.

Ewert, Gerry D. 1991. Habermas and Education: A Comprehensive Overview of the Influence of Habermas in Educational Literature. *Review of Educational Research* 61, no. 3 (Fall): 345–78.

Giese, Mark. Forthcoming. Taking the Scenic Route: The Internet as a Precursor to the Information Superhighway. In *Communication and Cyberspace: Social Interaction in an Electronic Environment,* ed. Ron Jacobson, Lance Strate, and Stephanie Gibson. Cresskill, NJ: Hampton Press.

Gleick, James. 1994. The Information Future: Out of Control (And It's a Good Thing, Too). *New York Times Magazine*, 1 May, 54–61.

Habermas, Jürgen. 1970. Technology and Science as Ideology, Trans. Jeremy Shapiro. In *Toward a Rational Society.* Boston: Beacon Press.

———. 1971. *Knowledge and Human Interests,* Trans. Jeremy J. Shapiro. Boston: Beacon Press.

———. 1973. *Theory and Practice,* Trans. John Viertel. Boston: Beacon Press.

———. 1975. *Legitimation Crisis,* Trans. Thomas McCarthy. Boston: Beacon Press.

———. 1982. The Entwinement of Myth and Enlightenment: Re-Reading Dialectic of Enlightenment. *New German Critique* 26: 23, 25, 27.

———. 1983. The German Idealism of the Jewish Philosophers. In *Philosophical-Political Profiles,* Trans. Frederick Lawrence. Cambridge: MIT Press.

———. 1984a. *The Theory of Communicative Action, Vol. 1: Reason and the Rationalization of Society,* Trans. Thomas McCarthy. Boston: Beacon Press.

———. 1984b. Wahrheitstheorien. In *Vorstudien und Ergänzungen zur Theorie des kommunikativen Handelns.* Frankfurt: Suhrkamp.

———. 1987a. *The Philosophical Discourse of Modernity,* Trans. Frederick Lawrence. Cambridge: MIT Press.

———. 1987b. *The Theory of Communicative Action. Volume Two. Lifeworld and System: A Critique of Functionalist Reason,* Trans. Thomas McCarthy. Boston: Beacon Press.

———. 1989a. Justice and Solidarity: On the Discussion Concerning Stage 6. *Philosophical Forum* 21, no. 12 (Fall/Winter): 32–52.

———. 1989b. *The Structural Transformation of the Public Sphere: An Inquiry into a Category of Bourgeois Society,* Trans. Thomas Burger. Cambridge: MIT Press.

———. 1990. Discourse Ethics: Notes on Philosophical Justification. In *Moral Consciousness and Communicative Action,* 43–115. Cambridge: MIT Press, 1990.

———. 1991a. *Erläuterungen zur Diskursethik.* Frankfurt: Suhrkamp.

———. 1991b. Modernity: An Unfinished Project. In *Critical Theory: The Essential Readings,* ed. David Ingram and Julia Simon-Ingram, 342–56. New York: Paragon Press.

———. 1992. *Faktizität und Geltung: Beiträge zur Diskurstheorie des Rechts und des demokratischen Rechtsstaats.* Frankfurt: Suhrkamp.

Harrison, Teresa M., and Timothy Stephen. 1992. On-Line Disciplines: Computer-Mediated Scholarship in the Humanities and Social Sciences. *Computers and the Humanities* 26: 181–193.

Hiltz, Starr Roxanne, and Murray Turoff. 1993. *The Network Nation: Human Communication via Computer.* Rev. ed. Cambridge: MIT Press.

Horkheimer, Max, and Theodor W. Adorno. 1947. *Dialektik der Aufklärung.* Amsterdam. Translated by John Cumming under the title *Dialectic of Enlightenment.* New York: Herder and Herder, 1972.

Ingram, David. 1993. The Limits and Possibilities of Communicative Ethics for Democratic Theory. *Political Theory* 21, no. 2 (May): 294–321.

———. 1990. *Critical Theory and Philosophy.* New York: Paragon House.

———. 1987. *Habermas and the Dialectic of Reason.* New Haven: Yale University Press.

Ingram, David, and Julia Simon-Ingram, eds. 1991. *Critical Theory: The Essential Readings.* New York: Paragon Press.

Jonassen, David H., and Heinz Mandl, eds. 1990. *Designing Hypermedia for Learning* (Proceedings of the NATO Advanced Research Workshop on Designing Hypertext/Hypermedia for Learning, 3–8 July 1989, Rottenburg/Necker, FRG). New York: Springer-Verlag.

Kahn, Arnold S., and Robert G. Brookshire. 1991. Using a Computer Bulletin Board in a Social Psychology Course. *Teaching of Psychology* 18, no. 4 (December): 245–49.

Kraemer, Kenneth L. 1991. Strategic Computing and Administrative Reform. In *Computerization and Controversy: Value Conflicts and Social Choices,* ed. Charles Dunlap and Rob Kling, 167–80. Boston: Academic Press.

Kymlicka, Will. 1990. *Contemporary Political Philosophy: An Introduction.* Oxford: Clarendon Press.

Lanham, Richard. 1993. *The Electronic Word: Democracy, Technology, and the Arts.* Chicago: University of Chicago Press.

Li, Tiger. 1992. Computer-Mediated Communications and the Chinese Students in the U.S. *Information Society* 7: 125–37.

Lyotard, Jean-François. 1984. *The Postmodern Condition: A Report on Knowledge.* Trans. Geoff Bennington and Brian Massumi. Minneapolis: University of Minnesota Press.

McCarthy, Thomas. 1978. *The Critical Theory of Jürgen Habermas.* Cambridge: MIT Press.

———. 1984. Translator's introduction to *The Theory of Communicative Action,* by Jürgen Habermas. Boston: Beacon Press.

McKibben, Bill. 1993. The Data That Are Thrown Away. In We Are the Wired: Some Views on the Fiberoptic Ties that Bind, by George Johnson. *New York Times,* 24 October 1993, sect. 4, 16.

McLeod, Poppy Lauretta. 1992. An Assessment of the Experimental Literature on Electronic Support of Group Work: Results of a Meta-Analysis. *Human-Computer Interaction* 7: 257–80.

The Machine that Changed the World. 1992. Part 5: The World at Your Fingertips. Written, produced, and directed by Robert Hone. Executive producer Jon Palfreman. A WGBH Boston/BBC TV coproduction in association with NDR/Hamburg.

Marcuse, Herbert. 1955. *Eros and Civilization. A Philosophical Inquiry into Freud.* Boston: Beacon Press.

———. 1964. *One-Dimensional Man: Studies in the Ideology of Advanced Industrial Society.* Boston: Beacon Press.

Malone, Thomas W., and John F. Rockart. 1991. Computers, Networks and the Corporation. *Scientific American* 265, no. 3 (September): 128–36.

Nash, Nathaniel C. 1994. Gore Sees Privatization of Global Data Links. *New York Times,* 22 March, D2.

Nelson, Theodor H. 1974. *Dream Machines: New Freedoms through Computer Screens—A Minority Report. Computer-Lib: You Can and Must Understand Computers Now.* Chicago: Hugo's Book Service. Rev. ed. Redmond, WA: Microsoft Press, 1987.

Nielsen, Torben Hviid. 1990. Jürgen Habermas: Morality, Society and Ethics: An Interview with Torben Hviid Nielsen. *Acta Sociologica* 33 (2): 93–114.

Postman, Niel. 1993. Buried in a New Kind of Garbage. In We Are the Wired: Some Views on the Fiberoptic Ties that Bind, by George Johnson. *New York Times,* 24 October, sect. 4, 16.

Rasmussen, David M. 1990. *Reading Habermas.* Cambridge: Basil Blackwell.

Rheingold, Howard. 1993. *The Virtual Community: Homesteading on the Electronic Frontier.* Reading, MA: Addison-Wesley.

Riel, Margaret. 1991–1992. Approaching the Study of Networks. *Computing Teacher* December 1991-January 1992: 5–7, 52.

———. 1990. Computer-Mediated Communication: A Tool for Reconnecting Kids with Society. *Interactive Learning Environments* 1(4): 255–63.

Romiszowski, Alexander J. 1990. The Hypertext/Hypermedia Solution—But What Exactly Is the Problem? In *Designing Hypermedia for Learning,* ed. David Jonassen and Heinz Mandel, 321–53. New York: Springer-Verlag.

Ronfeldt, David. 1992. Cyberocracy Is Coming. *Information Society* 8: 243–96.

Rosenberg, Richard S. 1993. Free Speech, Pornography, Sexual Harassment, and Electronic Networks. *Information Society* 9: 285–331.

Rousseau, Jean Jacques. 1950. *The Social Contract and Discourses.* Trans. G. D. H. Cole. New York: Dutton.

Singer, Benjamin D. 1991. The New Media and Electronic Anomie. In *Communications in Canadian Society,* ed. B. Singer, 424–33. Scarborough, Canada: Nelson Canada.

Sproull, Lee, and Sara Kiesler. 1991a. Computers, Networks, and Work. *Scientific American* 265, no. 3 (September): 116–23.

———. 1991b. *Connections: New Ways of Working in the Networked Organization.* Cambridge: MIT Press.

Toulmin, Stephen. 1972. *Human Understanding.* Princeton: Princeton University Press.

———. 1958. *The Uses of Argument.* Cambridge: Cambridge University Press.

Turkle, Sherry. 1984. *The Second Self: Computers and the Human Spirit.* New York: Simon and Schuster.

Walther, Joseph B. 1992. Interpersonal Effects in Computer-Mediated Interaction: A Relational Perspective. *Communication Research* 19, no. 1 (February): 52–90.

Westrum, Ron. 1991. *Technologies and Society: The Shaping of People and Things.* Belmont, CA: Wadsworth.

Wiggershaus, Rolf. 1994. *The Frankfurt School: Its History, Theories, and Political Significance.* Trans. Michael Robertson. Cambridge: MIT Press.

Wolin, Richard. 1989. Introduction to *The New Conservatism: Cultural Criticism and the Historians' Debate,* by Jürgen Habermas, ed. and trans. Shierry Weber Nicholsen. Cambridge: MIT Press.

Zachary, G. Pascal. 1994. It's a Mail Thing: Electronic Messaging Gets a Rating–Ex: Some Computer Chiefs Dump It as the Masses Invade the I-Way; Bozos Beware. *Wall Street Journal,* 22 June, A1.

III

IMPACTS AND IMPLICATIONS FOR RELIGIOUS AUTHORITY, COMMUNITIES, AND BELIEFS

10

The Unknown God of the Internet: Religious Communication from the Ancient Agora to the Virtual Forum

Stephen D. O'Leary and Brenda E. Brasher

Now while Paul was waiting for them at Athens he was exasperated to see how the city was full of idols. So he argued in the synagogue with the Jews and Gentile worshippers, and also in the city square every day with casual passers-by. And some of the Epicurean and Stoic philosophers joined issue with him. Some said, 'What can this charlatan be trying to say?'; others, 'He would appear to be a propagandist for foreign deities'—this because he was preaching about Jesus and Resurrection. So they took him and brought him before the Court of Areopagus and said, 'May we know what this new doctrine is that you propound? You are introducing ideas that sound strange to us, and we should like to know what they mean.' (Now the Athenians in general and the foreigners there had no time for anything but talking or hearing about the latest novelty.)

Then Paul stood up before the Court of Areopagus and said: 'Men of Athens, I see that in everything that concerns religion you are uncommonly scrupulous. For as I was going around looking at the objects of your worship, I noticed among other things an altar bearing the inscription "To an Unknown God." What you worship but do not know—this is what I now proclaim.' (Acts 17:16–23, New English Bible)

It may seem strange to begin an essay on the religious implications of computer technology with a narrative from the era of Christianity's origin. Yet the story of Paul's advocacy of the Christian religion among the philosophical schools of Athens offers a useful starting point for a discussion of the problems and possibilities of contemporary religious communication. Our thesis is twofold: First, we argue that the modern equivalent of the ancient forum and city square, the place where strangers gather to discuss the latest novelty, is to be found in the rapidly expanding network of electronic communication services. In Usenet newsgroups and LISTSERV discussions on the Internet, in the conversational forums sponsored by commercial services such as Compuserve, Prodigy, and America Online, and on a host of privately operated computer bulletin boards (BBSs), all the traditional discursive forms of religion are flourishing: preaching, witnessing, prayer, ritual, proselytizing, inter- and intrafaith debates. Second, we argue that as traditional religion makes its appearance in the electronic forum, it is undergoing a subtle but profound transformation, one that has parallels in the historical evolution of Christianity as it resisted, adopted, and adapted the concepts and methods of classical rhetoric.

To gain perspective on contemporary uses of computer technology in religious discourse, we first examine the relationship of early Christianity to the theories, forms, and practices of communication that dominated the ancient world. Walter Ong's concept of the evolution of communicative culture, which directs attention to technologies of communication and to the modes of consciousness enabled and promoted by these technologies, is employed to illuminate the religious situations of late antiquity and our own era. We then illustrate the technological transformations of computer-mediated religious practices with a survey of religious discourse currently visible on computer networks and with a speculative meditation on cyborg theology, which focuses on the transformations of religious consciousness accompanying the transition to multiple public squares of cool, electronic discourse.[1] Our purpose is not to provide a detailed map of the spiritual territories now opening up in cyberspace nor to analyze technologized religious texts, but simply to sketch the landscape of a new world of religious communication, to present some of the ways prior forums have significantly altered religious discourse and reorganized concepts of religious believers, and to ponder (rather than answer) the questions: How may *this* new terrain alter those who explore it, and how will traditional faiths be transformed in order to be heard by those who go there?

Christianity and the Tradition of Classical Rhetoric

Whether Paul's address in Acts is fictional or records an actual historical encounter, the speech on the "Unknown God" is an astute adaptation of the Christian message to the understanding of an educated urban audience. The audience in the Athenian forum, and, by extension, those in other urban centers throughout the Roman empire, had very specific expectations and demands. Max Weber characterizes Paul's audiences as a "group of urban proselytes who were accustomed to meditating on the conditions of salvation and who were to some degree conversant with Jewish and Greek casuistry" (1964, 192–93). Early Christian discourses involved far more than the translation of the Christian *kerygma* (literally, proclamation) into philosophic terms; the message itself was transformed by the forum in which it was communicated. Whether as oral preaching or as written text in the form of epistle, gospel, and apology, the success of the Christian message can be traced directly to the efforts of the earliest Christians to find a hearing in the ancient forum by adapting the rhetorical forms and methods that prevailed there, and to transform these forms and methods for their own uses. Yet, from its infancy, Christianity has had a love-hate relationship with rhetoric as an art of communication. In what follows, we shall briefly review the pre-Christian rhetorical tradition to show how it helped shape Christian thought, and sketch some of the tensions and paradoxes that characterized Christian approaches to communication in the classical era.

Rhetoric, conceived as the theory and practice of persuasive oratory, already had a long tradition when Christianity made its appearance on the intellectual and religious scene of the Roman Empire.[2] The pre-Socratic Sophists, the earliest professors of the language arts, sought to train Greek citizens in the varieties of public speech necessary for participation in civic life. They were the first thinkers of ancient Greece to perceive the significance of probabilistic argument in cases where exact knowledge is inaccessible, and the first to make (and exploit) the now-familiar distinction between nature and social convention. For Protagoras, rhetoric became a systematic method for the study and practice of controversy (*dissoi logoi*); in the hands of Gorgias, the stylistic and grammatical resources of language were deployed to form a rhetoric of flamboyant beauty as well as instrumental utility. Isocrates conceived of rhetoric as an essential skill in the practice of statecraft, and helped to shape an ideal conception of the citizen-orator which influenced later generations of Roman rhetoricians; the "Hymn to Speech" in his *Antidosis* is an early statement of a theme that became a staple of Stoic philosophy, the creative and organizing power of the Logos in human affairs. Whatever their emphasis, Sophistic teachers of rhetoric conceived it as a practical art, the cultivation of which could lead human beings toward both power and virtue.

The Sophists' claims for their educational program provoked a profoundly negative response from Plato, whose dialogues repeated the standard popular charges against the Sophists (that they "made the worst case appear the better") and added some new ones. His attack against Sophistic rhetoric (e.g., in the *Gorgias*) claimed that it was not an art, that it was not based on any rational foundation, and that it was unethical. In his dialogue *Phaedrus,* Plato repeated his usual criticisms of Sophistic teaching, but went further, proposing a "true rhetoric" that he opposed to the false art of the Sophists. This was a frankly religious rhetoric grounded in neither probability nor a theory of controversy but in scientific knowledge of the human soul and its influences; its purpose was to find a language that would impel the soul's motion toward God or the realm of divine Forms. Since the exact knowledge of the soul which Plato required as a precondition for his true rhetoric was not available to the many, the rhetoric proposed in the *Phaedrus* represented an elitist alternative to the more populist rhetorics of the Sophists, and was not influential in Plato's lifetime.[3] Its significance for us lies in the fact that, as mediated through the Neoplatonists of the Alexandrian school, Plato's teachings greatly influenced many of the theologians of the early Christian era.

Aristotle responded to Plato's attack by reconstructing the conceptions of art, of knowledge and reason, and of the ethical foundations of rhetoric. His *Techne Rhetorike* rejected the fallacies of Sophistic argument by stressing the link between rhetoric and dialectic, and attempted to reform current communicative practice through a systematic codification of its principles. As the first comprehensive treatment of its subject matter, the strategic construction of discourses, the *Rhetoric* established the theoretical canons that remained in use for centuries: the genres or divisions of oratory (legal, ceremonial, and political), the types of invented proof (reason, emotion, character, or authority), the parts of a discourse (introduction, statement, argument, conclusion). While critics from Plato to the present have vilified rhetoric as (at best) empty technique or (at worst) linguistic flimflammery, Aristotle did not see it in these terms. The placement of rhetoric alongside the Organon of his works, as an art or discipline [*techne*] with substantive and methodological links to politics, ethics, logic, and poetics, indicates the potential for rhetoric to transcend the limitations of mere technique. Others who followed after Aristotle developed this potential with further theoretical contributions, which became commonplaces of Hellenic rhetorical education: the division of rhetoric into the five canons of invention, arrangement, style, memory, and delivery, and the theory of *stasis* or status, which provided a systematic method for analysis of controversies to determine the question at issue.

Limitations of space preclude a more complete discussion of the pre-Christian rhetorical tradition in this essay. However, this brief account of the development of ancient rhetoric provides sufficient context for us to emphasize two themes that will usefully be recalled as we continue our narrative.

First, while a unitary conception of "rhetoric" as a whole may be possible, it is more useful for our purposes to speak of "rhetorics," in the sense of self-conscious theories of discourse. As the differing positions of the various Sophists, Plato, and Aristotle illustrate, such theories are multiple, since they are grounded in the epistemological and ontological assumptions of those who formulate them. If rhetorical theory embraces uncertainty, in the manner of the Sophists, it may provide a foundation for civic discourse and a useful method for the orderly management of controversy; if it devalues contingent knowledge in favor of the Absolute, it may restrict itself to providing a method for presenting truths obtained through science or divine revelation. In either case, the province of rhetoric should not be reduced to the formal techniques by which discourse is organized, presented, and analyzed. Whether conceived in absolute terms or purely strategically, persuasive address to any audience necessitates critical consideration of a whole range of assumptions regarding human psychology, cultural norms, the nature and functions of language, and what passes for reason and knowledge in a given culture. Thus, to theorize the construction, performance, and critique of persuasive discourse requires rhetoricians to assimilate information and insights from related arts and disciplines; and beneath every theory and practice of rhetoric lies a different conception of what counts as reasonable, and therefore of reason itself.

Second, rhetorical theories derive their basic orientation from the modes and technologies of communication that prevail in a given society, and new technologies and communication practices propel the evolution of new forms of consciousness and culture. Here we refer readers to the work of Walter Ong, who, more than any other scholar, has created an intellectual framework for apprehending the significance of evolutionary developments in communication theories and practices while avoiding the pitfalls of technological determinism.[4] Ong identifies the earliest phases in the teaching of public speech as rooted in the Homeric world of oral culture, a stage he defines as one of "primary orality" (1988, 16–77); though rhetoricians sometimes recorded their thoughts or their discourses, rhetorical precepts were derived inductively from discourse practices in the oral tradition, and were in turn orally transmitted to later generations of practitioners. By the time Plato wrote his magisterial and influential attacks on rhetoric, however, the shift from orality to literacy, from a culture that communicated primarily through speech to a culture that communicated primarily through writing, was already well underway. Ong argues that the development of the technological cultures of writing and (eventually) of printing fostered the self-conscious development of rhetorical theory by enabling higher levels of abstraction (1988, 108–16). This thesis is exemplified in the *Phaedrus,* where Plato noted that the introduction of writing enabled authors to address audiences remote in time and space while at the same time diminishing human powers of memory. The paradox of Plato's critique of writing is, of course, that it was a written critique. Ong uses this paradox to comment on the cultural evolution from orality to literacy, claiming that Plato

> lived at the time when the alphabet had first become sufficiently interiorized to affect Greek thought, including his own, the time when patiently analytic, lengthily sequential thought processes were first coming into existence because of the ways in which literacy enabled the mind to process data. . . . Paradoxically, Plato could formulate his phonocentrism, his preference for orality over writing, clearly and effectively only because he could write. (1988, 168)

We are indebted to both Plato and Father Ong for their recognition of the significance of a primary theme of our essay, the relationship between technologies of communication and the modes of consciousness that these technologies enable, require, or allow to atrophy.

If we follow the thread of historical narrative further, the significance of these two themes—rhetorics are multiple, and new technology stimulates theories of discourse and the evolution of new forms of consciousness—will become evident. As Hellenic culture spread throughout the Mediterranean in the wake of the Alexandrian conquest, the Greek rhetorical canons were taken up and elaborated upon by subsequent generations of teachers and philosophers. In the Greek cities of Palestine and Asia Minor, schools were established which fixed rhetorical training into programs for a well-rounded education (*enkyklios paideia*) that ensured the transmission of Greek culture. Under the influence of this curriculum, Roman rhetoricians, such as Cicero and Quintilian, borrowed from the accumulated knowledge of the Greeks regarding the invention of arguments, the construction of discourses, and the stylistic devices available to the rhetor. Inspired by the Isocratean ideal of the citizen-orator, they devised an educational program with rhetoric as its organizing principle. By the time Paul and other early Christian preachers sought their first converts, the classical *paideia* was well established throughout the Hellenized culture of the late Roman Republic and early Empire.

The Greco-Roman educational curriculum is of more than incidental relevance to our story, for, as James Kinneavy notes, the earliest audiences for Christian preaching were largely composed of Hellenized Jews. Many among these audiences were likely to have had training in the *gymnasia* that existed in most large cities of the Empire, an experience that naturally would have exposed them to rhetoric as part of their ordinary instructional curriculum. So pervasive was Hellenic culture throughout the Empire that elements of Greek rhetorical education were adopted in the rabbinic schools of Palestine (Kinneavy 1987, 56–79, 80–91). Even discounting the claims of Kinneavy and other scholars regarding the spread of the rhetorical curriculum, there is no denying that early Christian preachers spoke in Greek to audiences whose primary language was also Greek, and that the conceptual categories available to both preachers and audiences must have been profoundly conditioned by the philosophical and educational history of the terms that they used. In this regard, we have already noted the importance of the philosophic principle of the Logos (variously translated as speech, word, reason, etc.) in the long history of Greek rhetoric and philosophy that predates Christianity. Only with a knowledge of this history can we understand the full import that the opening words of the Fourth Gospel (''In the beginning was the Word [*logos*]'' John 1:1, New Revised Standard Version) would have had for a contemporary Greek-speaking audience. By invoking the Logos and identifying this principle with the Jewish Messiah, the author translates the Christian message into a cultural idiom instantly accessible to those conditioned by rhetorical training and exposure to Greek philosophy to accept the Logos as the generative principle of order in the cosmos. Kinneavy extends the argument for the influence of the rhetorical tradition on Christianity with his analysis of the etymology and history of the Greek term *pistis*. *Pistis*, a term that had been used by rhetoricians since the days of Plato to describe the end or object of rhetorical action, is usually translated as "belief"; but in Christian usage, *pistis* came to signify "faith." If his argument is correct, then the Christian notion of faith as "religious persuasion" can be traced back to a cluster of terms that originated with the Sophists of ancient Greece.

Whereas some early Christian authors stressed commonalities between the classical *paideia* and Christian teaching, others emphasized their conflict. Many of the greatest patristic theologians were either practicing rhetoricians before their conversion or were trained in rhetorical schools, including (to name but a few) Augustine, Basil of Caesarea, Gregory of Nyssa, and Lactantius; yet, for the first four centuries of the Christian era, rhetoric was violently condemned by the fathers of the church. The early Christian rejection of rhetoric must be seen as part of a complex web of historical circumstances. Most scholars agree, for example, that the decay of the Roman Empire was accompanied by a degeneration of rhetorical teaching and practice.[5] During this period, known as the Second Sophistic, rhetoricians attained substantial prestige in Roman society, as evidenced by imperial endowment of professorial chairs in rhetoric at centers of learning throughout the Empire. In spite of this prestige, however, the discourses of late antiquity were frequently given to excesses of style, vanity, and triviality. The vigorous tradition of political eloquence had collapsed with the Roman Republic; as Tacitus notes in his *Dialogue on Oratory*, political rhetoric flourishes best in a relatively free society which allows for a modicum of disorder and which affords its citizens opportunities to deliberate about substantive issues and gain power through effective argument (1946, 127). In a well-ordered imperial state, however, oratory is either rendered superfluous or turned into an instrument for the glorification of imperial rule, while the verbal arts of debate and disputation wither. Hence the paradox: Even as rhetoric occupied a central place in the educational curriculum of the ruling classes, and even as its teachers and practitioners attained wealth and high social status, the declining quality of oratory was noted and lamented by many. The Sophists who competed for the right to wear the royal purple had little of substance on which to speak, and accordingly tended to focus on ornament. As Pierre Duhamel notes, "Preoccupation with form had captured the art of rhetoric and effective expression had become the expression in a well-turned phrase of inconsequential material" (1949, 353).

Another factor to be considered is that classical instruction in rhetoric and poetic relied on examples of pagan literature and the set-pieces of epideictic or ceremonial oratory, which often took the stories of Greek and Roman mythology as their subject matter. Augustine complained that persuading pagans to lead virtuous lives was difficult, when poets and orators sang the praises of adulterous Jupiter and all pagan literature affirmed the drunkenness and licentiousness of the gods; Minucius Felix added, "Such stories are but precedents and sanction for men's vices" (quoted in Murphy 1974, 49–50). If today's producers of cinema and television can be said to occupy a position analogous to that of the ancient poets and Sophists, as the bards, entertainers, and bearers of what passes for myth in mass media culture, a contemporary analogue to the church fathers' complaint can be found in the fundamentalist rejection of the Hollywood cult of celebrity and the mass-media commodification of sex and violence. Our tabloids and talk shows sing of the latest adulteries, intoxications, and indiscretions of the idols currently favored in the celebrity pantheon. While substantial differences exist between the early church fathers and contemporary fundamentalists, so that the comparison cannot reasonably be extended beyond the dynamic of cultural critique, early Christians rejected the popular culture of their day—poetry, drama, and oratory—in much the same terms as conservative Christians today condemn the media culture of Hollywood television and film, assuming a radically oppositional stance against a cultural milieu seen as promoting sexual immorality, idolatry, and materialism.

The patristic attack on rhetoric was thus a condemnation of current rhetorical practice and a challenge to the cultural norms of the late Empire. But there was a deeper philosophical basis for their critique. The fathers of the church condemned the cultivation of eloquence as the quintessential pursuit of worldly wisdom, and at times appeared to reject the stylistic delights and formal elaborations of rhetoric as unnecessary, if not actually sinful. Lactantius condemned pagan literature as "sweets which contain poison" (quoted in Murphy 1974, 49), and claimed that divine truth needed no human embellishment: "God has wished . . . that truth should be more gleaming because it is ornamented enough of itself and would, therefore, be spoiled and corrupted by adornments added externally" (1964, 164). Cyprian, who taught rhetoric at Carthage before his conversion to Christianity, inveighed against his former profession: "In courts of law, in public meetings, in political discussions, a full eloquence may be the pride of vocal ambition, but in speaking of the Lord God, a pure simplicity of expression which is convincing depends on the substance of the argument rather than on the forcefulness of eloquence" (quoted in Murphy 1974, 51). Lactantius and Cyprian echoed the Platonic attack against the Sophists of ancient Athens. For the church fathers, attention to the forms of expression was considered superfluous if one possessed the truth; taking pleasure in the mimetic earthly forms of rhetoric distracted the soul from contemplation of the divine realm of the ultimate Forms, now understood to be given through the Christian revelation.

One of the greatest church fathers, Jerome, perfectly embodies the ambiguous attitude of early Christians toward the communication and culture of Greece and Rome. Rather than trying to match their pagan opponents in learning, he argued, Christians should "lay aside the weapons of the heathens" as they defended themselves from their opponents, for (as James J. Murphy puts it) it was "better to have a just unlearnedness than an evil wisdom" (1974, 51). According to Jerome, divine revelation superseded the knowledge of rhetoric and philosophy: "We do not wish for the field of rhetorical eloquence, nor the snares of dialecticians, nor do we seek the subtleties of Aristotle, but the very words of Scripture must be set down" (quoted in Murphy 1974, 54). However, Jerome was unable to shake his attraction to the literature he had supposedly forsaken. In a famous letter, he recounts a dream in which he felt himself condemned for his preoccupation with pagan eloquence:

> Miserable man that I am! I was fasting and then I began to read Cicero. . . . If by chance, on recollecting my self, I started reading the Prophets, their unadorned style awoke in me feelings of revulsion. My eyes, blinded, no longer saw the light, and it was not on my eyes I laid the blame, it was on heaven. . . . Suddenly I felt myself ravished away in ecstasy and transported before the tribunal of the Judge. Such a dazzling light emanated from those present that, crouched upon the ground, I dared not lift up my eyes. On being asked my profession, I replied, "I am a Christian." Whereupon He who presided, thundered: "Thou dost lie—thou are not a Christian, but a Ciceronian. Where thy treasure is, there is thy heart also." (Quoted in Ellspermann 1949, 159–60)

Jerome then relates that in his dream, he swore an oath to never again be seduced by the pleasures of pagan literature. The implication was clear: One had to choose between classical eloquence and Christianity; one could not pursue both.

In sum, rhetoric as taught and practiced in the waning days of the Roman Empire was intimately linked to a culture that Christians rejected as morally bankrupt, concerned with vanities of style rather than the substance of revealed truth. Tertullian's famous rhetorical question neatly encapsulates the Christian dismissal of the whole of pagan philosophy, including rhetoric: "What indeed has Athens to do with Jerusalem? What concord is there between the Academy and the Church? What between heretics and Christians?"

(1957, 160). Tertullian's question defines the extreme position in the range of attitudes expressed by church fathers toward classical culture; it was a position that no one who hoped to find converts within this culture could hope to sustain. When Christians contended in the forum, they opened themselves to attack from pagan philosophers who were well schooled in rhetoric and dialectic and accustomed to public verbal disputation. Though Christians rejected Roman cultural norms, their doctrines could find adherents only by addressing potential converts within the prevailing structures of plausibility. To engage in debate at all is to lend legitimacy to one's opponents; thus, without some concord between the Academy and the Church, conversion of elites would have been impossible.

Early Christian advocates responded to this situation with contradictory impulses. One tendency was to fall back upon the sufficiency of faith and reject reason itself, as embodied in the classical canons of rhetorical and dialectical argument. The extreme of this impulse may be seen in the defiantly antirhetorical stance adopted by Tertullian, who declared that Christianity was worthy of belief precisely because it was absurd: "The son of God died. This is by all means to be believed because it makes no sense. And he was buried and rose again; this fact is certain, because it is impossible" (1956, 160). Tertullian's solution, however, was not a serious option for those who wished to find converts among the educated upper classes. For this purpose, the ability to make the case for Christianity seem reasonable within the limits of reason as embodied in classical conceptions of argument and proof, as well as a working knowledge of the formal conventions and styles of Greco-Roman rhetoric, was indispensable. Thus, while some Christians rejected rhetoric along with the whole *paideia* of classical antiquity, Justin Martyr, Minucius Felix, Athenagoras, and others in the group known as the Apologists also moved to make Christianity more presentable to those schooled in this *paideia*. To this end, these Christian authors mastered the rhetorical and literary genres of epistle and apologia, produced works that weighed the philosophical claims of Judaism, Christianity, and pagan religion, and strove to defend Christianity as reasonable and worthy of belief. In a representative account that directly parallels Paul's speech on the Unknown God, the apocryphal Acts of the Apostle Philip presents the Apostle as going to Athens in order to present the *"paideia* of Christ" to the philosophers. Werner Jaeger notes that by referring to Christianity as the *paideia* of Christ, the author

> stresses the intention of the apostle to make Christianity appear to be a continuation of the classical Greek *paideia,* which it would be logical for those who possessed the older one to accept. At the same time he implies that the classical *paideia* is being superseded by making Christ the center of a new culture. The ancient *paideia* thereby becomes its instrument. (Jaeger 1961, 12)

Ultimately, the war between the classical *paideia* and the *paideia* of Christ resulted in a truce, as substantial elements of the old were assimilated into the new. As Christianity grew from an outlawed foreign sect to the official state religion of the Roman Empire, it continued to adopt and transform elements of the old culture. Classical theories of communication were severed from many of the philosophical assumptions on which they had been grounded; the rhetorical *paideia* was used in the creation of new forms of discourse, most notably the sermon, which did not fit easily into any of the classical categories of judicial, political, or ceremonial orations. In his land-mark work *De Doctrina Christiana,* Augustine (who, as noted above, had been a teacher of rhetoric before his conversion) applied his knowledge of Cicero's rhetorical theory to the problems of Christian preaching. The result was a treatise that preserved Greek and Roman rhetorical lore in a form useful for Christian homiletics. The need for apologetic disputation diminished as the pagan critics were silenced; hence, Augustine's development of a Christian rhetorical theory abandoned the Sophistic, Aristotelian, and Ciceronian tradi-tions of rhetorical controversy, and adopted a more Platonic stance that re-garded rhetoric as a means of propagating divine truth rather than as a means of adjudicating social disputes.

It is clear, then, that while some fathers of the Church condemned rhetoric along with the whole tradition of pagan philosophy, they had no choice but to embrace its methods and at least some of its philosophical assumptions if they hoped to find converts among the educated classes. How-ever, both Christianity and classical rhetoric were subtly but irreversibly trans-formed by their encounter. The old *paideia* became the instrument of the new; and as Ong and McLuhan have taught us, we are transformed by the tools we use. By presenting the Christian deity as the "unknown God" of the Athenian forum, Paul (or at least the author of Acts) embraced the casuistic conventions of the schools and academies of the philosophers, Sophists, and rhetoricians. The need for persuasive address directed at the educated classes in the terms to which they were accustomed sparked a process in which "religious faith developed into an assertion of intellectual propositions which were products of ratiocination" (Weber 1964, 192–93). The rhetorical encounter with pagan philosophy thus transformed Christianity by forcing its apologists to move beyond the story of Jesus' inauguration of the kingdom of God and of their own encounter with this kingdom, and to articulate an intellectually coherent and persuasive body of philosophical doctrines. Putting this in terms of rhetor-ical form, we may say that, whereas the earliest Christians presented their message as a *narrative* of incarnation, sacrifice, and resurrection, later genera-tions were compelled by their rhetorical situation to restate this message in the form of dialectical *propositions* that could satisfy the philosophical criteria of a rational cosmology.

The transformation from narrative to propositional form reached its peak in the dialectical theology of the medieval Scholastics, of whom Aquinas is the supreme example. Rhetoric survived the encounter with its Christian enemies to find a place in the medieval trivium, the three interrelated verbal arts of grammar, rhetoric, and logic; its longevity through the Renaissance was linked to the rituals of Latin learning practiced by generations of schoolboys, who developed skill in formal prose by studying classical orations and working through the exercises of the ancient *Progymnasmata,* and practiced dialectical disputation as a kind of agonistic ritual. Ong further notes that the use of Learned Latin in the schools of the medieval and Renaissance eras helped to ensure that the rhetorical *paideia* would remain a largely male province: "For well over a thousand years, [Learned Latin] was sex-linked, a language written and spoken only by males, learned outside the home in a tribal setting which was in effect a male puberty rite" (1988, 113). As in ancient times, women were excluded from formal rhetorical training. Denied the education that enabled access to the predominant modes of communication, women as a rule either did not write or cultivated vernacular rhetorics that avoided the formal devices of classical theory in favor of a more intimate, confessional style that found its culmination in the novel.

We close this portion of our own narrative with a final summary of Ong's evolutionary model of rhetorical theories and communication practices and some implications of technological changes for religious consciousness. Taken in their totality, classical rhetorical theories may be seen as comprising a technology of oral communication. The introduction of writing opened up new avenues of consciousness by making the development of self-conscious, abstract communication theories possible; though these theories appeared as written works, they were still rooted in the world of oral culture in that they privileged speech over writing by taking the oration as the model of human communication. As the lore of rhetorical practice grew into an increasingly sophisticated body of expert theory, access to knowledge as well as the ability to communicate in public forums was limited to those whose stature in social hierarchies (law, clergy, and nobility) enabled them to acquire literacy skills. The next major evolutionary shift came with the widespread use of the printing press and the expansion of literacy beyond the upper classes. Print technology loosened hierarchical control of knowledge by offering a cheaper method of reproducing texts and granting access to communication media to nonexperts unschooled in Latin. Thereafter, rhetorical theories increasingly tended to function as technologies of written composition, as distinct from speech.

Ong argues that these technological changes wrought profound changes in human consciousness. Oral communication, according to Ong, is participatory and instantaneous; rooted in the daily life of the tribe or polis, it is dependent on the tribal lifeworld for its images and symbolic inducements, and relies on memory to fix that which is socially useful in the store of human knowledge. By contrast, literate communication is passive, introducing a time delay into the communication process by separating the reception of the message from its construction and delivery; it thus encourages the development of abstract temporal categories, and gives humans a sense of history, newly constituting individuals and cultures as historical entities by fixing social knowledge of the past in a way that is more permanent. The mass production of printed works accelerated the changes wrought by writing, making possible the creation of new publics, constituting social identities in terms of multiple audiences, and favoring visual over auditory and tactile modes of apprehension. Oral communication, as Ong puts it, "unites people in groups," while "writing and reading are solitary activities that throw the psyche back on itself" (1988, 69). Hence, one of the most dramatic effects of the introduction of writing and print was the creation of a new kind of interiority, an awareness of the self that constitutes a new fact in the lifeworld of postliterate humanity. We would add that the interiority, abstraction, and historicity characteristic of literate cultures can create profound alienation in members of these cultures; as this response deepens, alienation itself becomes a motive for renewed attempts to communicate with others.

The alienation induced by print culture is surely a significant aspect of Christian religiosity. The religious aesthetic and sacramental theology of the Roman Catholic Church has always appealed to the aural and tactile imagination as well as the visual; in the Catholic mass, the spoken word retains the magical efficacy of language that Ong finds characteristic of an earlier stage of primary orality, and ritual action directs attention outward toward the exterior manifestation of the Word in the eucharist. By contrast, the liturgical and cultural forms of Protestantism direct attention inward; the preaching of the Word, conceived and embodied textually rather than sacramentally, is meant to induce an interior conviction of sin that is prerequisite to the experience of grace. Believing that the sole legitimate functions of language were education and exhortation, by which members of the congregation were to be taught the message of the gospel and urged to improve their lives, the Protestant reformers set out to strip away the incantatory functions of language in worship. The worship services devised by Calvin, Zwingli, and the more radical reformers enacted a theory of language that differed radically from the Roman Catholic conception of the relationship of Word and sacrament; they reached their climax not in the communion, but in the sermon, a discourse that is delivered orally but that lacks the supernatural efficacy of the Catholic priest's speech over the eucharistic elements.[6] Protestantism may thus be described as rooted in textuality, a "religion of the book" (as attested by the fetishization of biblical inerrancy in modern fundamentalism) which both provokes and is an aftereffect of the crisis of the self that ensues with the advent of print culture.

The evolutionary model of culture that Ong proposes, it should be noted, is not strictly linear. Humans do not suddenly abandon earlier technologies when new ones are discovered or invented; culture grows by accretion, so that speech remains an essential and indispensable means of communication that supplements writing, printing, and electronic media as options for human communication. More than this: Ong tells us that the basic orality of language remains as speech is transcribed, quoted, imitated, and broadcasted, so that even written and electronic text retain residues of speech forms. Most significantly for our purposes, Ong argues that the development of electronic media such as television, video, and computers brings us to a stage of cultural evolution beyond writing and print literacy, a stage he designates as ''secondary orality'' (1988, 135–38). At times, he appears to claim that these changes in human consciousness are driven as much by ontological necessity as by technology:

> The evolution of the media of communication, with the continuous psychological reorganization which this evolution entails, was implied from the very beginning by the very structure of actuality. Because of its impermanence, the spoken word needs supplementing. Writing, particularly the alphabet, supplemented it while at the same time denaturing it. . . . The fragmentation of consciousness initiated by the alphabet has in turn been countered by the electronic media which have made man present to himself [*sic*] across the globe, creating an intensity of self-possession on the part of the human race which is a new, and at times an upsetting, experience. (1988, 136)

Modern electronic media share many characteristics of communication in oral cultures, yet differ in fundamental ways from the old modes. They recapture the instantaneous aspect of oral communication by making it possible for speech to be shared in real time; but they also retain the self-consciousness of print culture, since in most cases the construction of media messages, from political speeches to entertainment, still begins with an act of writing. Ong argues that communication in the phase of secondary orality, particularly television, ''has generated a strong group sense, for listening to spoken words forms hearers into a group, a true audience, just as reading written or printed texts turns individuals in on themselves. But secondary orality generates a sense for groups immeasurably larger than those of the primary oral culture —McLuhan's 'global village' '' (1988, 136). Computer communication expands the global village created by television, constituting vast new publics connected to each other not by geography but by technological links and shared interests; it recaptures and transforms the participatory aspect of oral discourse by forcing its users to interact with keyboards and screens. Aspects of orality and literacy are combined into a new, hybrid form of communication that, as one networker puts it,

> is both talking and writing yet isn't completely either one. It's talking by writing. It's writing because you type it on a keyboard and people read it. But because of the ephemeral nature of luminescent letters on a screen, and because it has such a quick—sometimes instant—turn-around, it's more like talking. (Coate 1992)

In sum: the culture of secondary orality reintroduces the immediacy of oral communication, brings sound and gesture back into the human sensorium, and changes written text from something that is fixed and unchangeable to something malleable, or, as Richard Lanham puts it, "volatile and interactive" (1993, 73). The transformation to secondary orality is no less momentous than the shift from primary orality to literacy, and the full implications of this transformation will take centuries to appreciate.

Whether or not they agree with Ong's theorems, whether they applaud or bemoan modern developments in communication technology, most scholars today recognize that the new forms of communication will have consequences that we can barely imagine, let alone predict. What is certain is that, just as it did after the introduction of the printing press, rhetoric will have to reinvent itself to keep pace with modern technology. It seems reasonable to anticipate that religious rhetoric will be transformed along with other cultural forms as they are taken up in the virtual environment; and it is already possible to watch this process of transformation at work. As we embark on a discussion of contemporary communication technology and religion, we draw the following lessons from our narrative of Christianity's relationship with the rhetorical tradition. First, the forms of persuasive discourse are not neutral carriers of meaning; they are embedded in a web of social and philosophical assumptions, norms, and practices which ensure that diverse voices will be heard only insofar as they adopt the grammatical and rhetorical conventions of those they are trying to persuade, and turn these to their own uses. Second, as Paul and other early Christian apologists had to adapt their discourse to the conceptions of reason that prevailed in the ancient agora, so, too, will modern religion be transformed as it encounters the technical conceptions of reason that predominate in the electronic forum. We should not be surprised if the propositional content and presentational form of religion in the electronic communities of the future differs as greatly from its contemporary incarnations as the teachings of Jesus differ from the dialectical theology of Aquinas or as the eucharistic ceremonies of the earliest Christians differ from the Latin high mass. At the same time, the history of Christian rhetoric shows that innovation is accomplished not only through newly invented forms but by *bricolage,* as fragments of the old *paideia* are incorporated into the new cultural mosaic; thus we can also expect to see elements of familiar forms in the religious discourses of the future, albeit in some surprising and unexpected combinations. Third, conceiving of rhetorics as essentially technologies of communication, or as the rules and norms that socialize individuals into the use and mastery of communication practices (whether oral, written, or electronic), requires sensitivity to the perennial issue of access. Mastery of any technology requires both means and education; as we celebrate the birth of democratic publics in the ancient polis or in the modern global village, we cannot forget those excluded by gender, education, or economic status from access to contemporary communication media.

We turn now to a discussion of the present state and potential future of religious communication in cyberspace, and to a meditation on the spiritual problematics engendered by the technologizing of religious consciousness.

Preaching the Electronic Word: Some Aspects of Computer-Mediated Religion on the Global Network

A thorough exploration of computer-mediated religion will require a book-length study. While our discussion here is not intended to do more than identify certain trends and phenomena that must await a fuller treatment elsewhere, we are willing to risk the claim that religious discourse on the global network shows signs of a new and vital response to the anomic condition that Philip Rieff has characterized as "post-communal culture" (Rieff 1987, 11), in which the breakdown of traditional social and religious institutions results in atomization and alienation of the self. While the traditional forms of religion appear to be flourishing in the new electronic forum, subtle changes are taking place and new genres of religious discourse, such as online prayer and cyber-rituals, are emerging. We will not attempt to catalogue or describe all of these developments, or to perform rhetorical analysis of particular verbal transactions; we limit ourselves to sketching out some broad patterns visible in the electronic public squares and forums, illustrating these patterns with examples that we hope will convey to readers who may be unfamiliar with these networks some sense of the activities to be found on them (see Strangelove 1993). We believe that a review of the types of religious behavior that are currently visible online, and a discussion of their similarities to and differences from more traditional manifestations of religion, will aid in the effort to anticipate the future of religious communication via computer. Accordingly, we present the following observations about current religious activity on computer networks, accompanied by discussion of the tensions and paradoxes that we have observed operating in these discourses.

We have considered a number of topical schemes and categories by which the subject could be approached. One could divide the topic in terms of the way communication is structured: on LISTSERV groups, postings are sent as letters to all members of the group, while Usenet newsgroups resemble bulletin boards, with postings placed in a common electronic space into which readers can enter and choose messages by topic. Many computer networks also feature electronic "rooms" that participants can enter spontaneously or at a prearranged time in order to conduct real-time "conversations." These various mechanisms for structuring the distribution of messages produce very different kinds of discussions. Another division of the topic that would be worth pursuing relates to the economic bases of the various systems providing access to cyberspace: The Internet historically has tended to be populated with academicians, technocrats, and government employees (though this situation is rapidly changing with the growth of commercial providers of Internet access), while Compuserve, Prodigy, and America Online are more somewhat proletarian services, used by millions of ordinary people who are unable to enter cyberspace from the nodes provided to academic knowledge elites.

It is instructive to study the variations in the way religious discourse is organized and presented on the different networks. The categories into which Compuserve's Religion Forum divides its message boards, for example, are limited in ways that reveal something about the public presence of religion. Jews have one message board of their own, as do Muslims, Latter Day Saints, and Baha'i; Catholic and Orthodox Christians are grouped together but are distinct from the board titled Christianity, which mostly features evangelical Protestants. There is a message board titled "Pagan/Occult," and another called New Age, though there is considerable crossover between these two; however, there is no Buddhist message board, only one called "Eastern Religions" that features posts from devotees of Hindu philosophy and a variety of Westernized gurus as well as from Buddhists. There is a lively message board called Interfaith Dialogue, where we recently observed Latter-Day Saints trading information about faith traditions and comparing doctrines with Baha'i. For these services, users pay special fees for connect time in addition to their regular membership charges. On America Online, the Religion/Ethics Forum has message boards devoted to Atheism and Humanism; here both Buddhism and Hinduism are formally represented with boards of their own, while Jews may choose between boards for Orthodox and Reform/Conservative. While forums exist on the Internet for all of these interest groups to meet separately or in common, the range of choices available to the knowledgable navigator of cyberspace is much greater on the Internet than on the commercial services, and (as of this writing) they are provided free of charge—once the user has gained access to the Net. Our point is that commercial networks structure religious dialogue simply by charging money to take part in the conversation, as well as by promoting or assuming certain divisions and conceptual categories that have important consequences for the way users perceive their religious choices in the marketplace of culture.

Perhaps the most useful way to understand the evolving structures of cyber-religion is to conceive of two models for religious communication in cyberspace: the electronic church, temple, or sangha, on the one hand, and the electronic public square, on the other. In electronic churches, people meet to share beliefs and traditions, to pray and to worship, or simply to discuss the latest news from a particular religious perspective. In the electronic public square, they meet to expose their religious and philosophical beliefs to the scrutiny of nonbelievers or exponents of other faiths, and to engage in debate and discussion with others. These models will inevitably break down, due to the fluid nature of communication in this medium; the doors of the electronic churches open onto the public square, so that religious discussions between believers may take place in public forums and occasionally move to other sites, while nonbelievers frequently enter discussions intended for members of a particular religious tradition.[7] Further, we do not claim that they exhaust all possibilities for religious communication via computer. Nevertheless, the analogies of the church and the public square do offer a useful way to think about the purposes and activities of religious communicators. Keeping in mind the permeability of boundaries in cyberspace, we will now selectively describe some of the discourses that can be found in the electronic forums we have explored.

There are a multitude of electronic churches or intrafaith communication systems. Representatives of various religions have uploaded their sacred texts onto electronic networks: At this writing, the Book of Mormon, the Koran, the Tanach (the Hebrew Bible), and some Vedic texts are available for believers or the merely curious to study online, along with multiple translations of the Bible.[8] On a professional practitioner level, there are private services used primarily by church pastors and administrators, including PresbyNet (Presbyterian), FishNet (Catholic), American Baptist Network, and Lutheran Link; many of these are linked to the loosely affiliated network Ecunet, which allows pastors around the country to work together on sermons or on common pastoral problems. Religious discussions and activities appear on a variety of Usenet groups, LISTSERVs, and electronic journals for Episcopalians, Jews, Orthodox Christians, Quakers, Catholics, Buddhists, Neopagans, Satanists, and other communities too numerous to list here. The official certification of the earliest sighting of the new crescent moon that inaugurates Islamic holidays is regularly posted to the Usenet group <soc.religion.islam>. The New Age group on Compuserve's Religion Forum recently featured a complete Wiccan full moon initiation ritual, with a Neopagan priestess ''drawing down the moon'' for those who logged into one of its electronic ''rooms'' at a preordained time. Jews can engage in halakic discussions on Jewishnet; Buddhists can discuss the Four Noble Truths and debate the relative merits of Tibetan wisdom and Zen on GASSHO, which describes itself as "The Electronic Journal of DharmaNet International and the Global Online Sangha"; Episcopalians trade prayer requests on the list ANGLICAN-L. Some electronic forums are devoted to general discussion of issues within a particular faith or denomination; others are organized around a particular interest or topic within a tradition. Monks and contemplatives share insights on the monastic life on MERTON-L; the list ECOTHEOL-L sponsors discussion of ecology and religion, and the relationship of Christianity to the natural world. On APAR-L, a LISTSERV for Catholics interested in apparitions of the Virgin Mary, the latest messages dictated by the Blessed Mother at Medjugorge and lesser-known sites are posted alongside seasonal devotions, conversion narratives, and speculations about the Third Secret of Fatima.

In general, much religious discourse in the "electronic church" category resembles "preaching to the choir." Conversations take place among believers who may differ with each other about details of their faith, or about which elements of their faith should be deemed essential or superfluous, but who share common religious assumptions and (usually) discourse conventions. Nonbelievers and outsiders may "lurk" in these electronic spaces, but rarely post messages unless their purpose is to provoke or taunt. Exceptions to this rule can be found on the religious newsgroups on Usenet, the bulletin board network readily accessible through the Internet's thousands of sites worldwide. Atheists and apologists for other religions regularly post to newsgroups devoted to particular faiths or traditions in order to inquire about doctrinal matters, to argue matters of fact or dogma, or simply to "flame" other readers with invectives that resemble the classical diatribe.

The Usenet is of particular interest for our study of contemporary religious discourse because it is the closest analogue to the ancient forum in which religious and philosophical conceptions were publicly presented and subjected to critical scrutiny. While there are private forums or lists in which dialogues between members of different faiths take place, Usenet communication reaches audiences that, potentially at least, can number in the millions. The sheer volume of traffic makes it highly likely, if not inevitable, that anyone who explores the world of the Usenet will encounter a stranger preaching about foreign deities or challenging one's beliefs. Nowhere else on the interconnected web of networks is there anything that remotely resembles the freewheeling anarchy and brawling vitality of Usenet discussions. These qualities are most clearly evident in the formation of newsgroups, which on Usenet is a democratic process requiring debate and a formal vote in which any of the Usenet's millions of readers are allowed to participate. The procedure for creating a new group mandates a request for discussion, which must last for thirty days, and a formal charter, which specifies the rationale for the group and the discourse conventions that will govern it (such as what topics are welcomed for discussion, or whether the group will be moderated by an editor who has the power to censor postings). After the discussion period, a vote is taken and results are posted to the network: New groups must win by a 2:1 margin. When they are concerned with religion, the denominational and sectarian warfare surrounding the creation and maintenance of these groups can be quite intense. Struggles between the various sects of Islam are visible in the flood of messages that attends the creation of any new group on Muslim topics; and we have recently enjoyed the opportunity to learn more about Unitarian Universalism through reading the recent heated debate in <news.-groups> over the proposed charter for <talk.religion.unitarian-univ>. (Some aggrieved readers opposed the charter's plan for a moderated list by claiming that the proposal violated the spirit of Unitarian Universalism.) Finally, no discussion of religion on the Usenet would be complete without mentioning the existence of numerous groups devoted to conspiracy theories, alien abductions, channeling, and a host of other bizzare manifestations that can only be described as religious but that do not fit into the stream of mainline American denominational life. On <alt.conspiracy>, fundamentalists and survivalists anticipating the advent of the one-world Antichrist government speak among a cacophony of voices purportedly from alien intelligences, channeled spirits from Atlantis or other long-buried civilizations, or psychics predicting cataclysmic geographical upheavals.

The increasing specialization of religion groups on the Internet may be seen as unfortunate by some who see in electronic communication a potential for reversing the centrifugal fragmentation of culture. However, we remind readers that while the new electronic communities do mirror the divisions of the old, based as they often are on narrow doctrinal or traditional affiliation, the boundaries that distinguish these groups are much more permeable and fluid than the old boundaries marked by class, race, geography, and language. In the old world, these barriers are difficult to surmount; in the new electronic world, once the crucial step of access is surmounted they do not disappear, but are subject to ongoing reformulation of a sort that is impossible through the old communication media. In particular, net discourse has the potential to level old hierarchies of authority and status or to allow people to move more freely among them, enabling (for example) people without theological training or status in a church hierarchy to engage in dialogues with clergy or university professors. The mere fact that the various electronic nodes and forums are connected to each other by a vast web of information technology itself marks a breakdown of the old divisions; the technical capacity to move vertically and horizontally with unprecedented ease, both through the hierarchies of one's religious community and beyond one's own communal affiliations to explore other worlds of discourse, invites dialogue that can overcome differences. A concrete illustration of the way computer communication makes this possible can be seen in the difference between computer networks and telephones. If a stranger without institutional authority tries to reach an important person on the telephone—a bishop, say, or an editor of an important journal—they will most likely not get past the secretary whose job it is to screen inquiries. An e-mail message to such a person may result in a speedy and warm personal response.

Countless electronic forums now exist that promote horizontal dialogue between people of different denominations or faith traditions. DIFTX-L is a relatively new LISTSERV that provides a place where "Different Christianities" can meet and discuss their own interpretations and experiences of faith. It has already spawned lively dialogues between Mormons and feminists, fundamentalists and gay Christians, and other dissimilar groups who might not have occasions to meet and engage in the world off-line. This high-traffic list is notable for the civility of its discussions. FEMREL-L is an international list whose regular participants hail from Wales, Australia, Japan, and the United States. While its identified topic is feminism and religion, FEMREL is famous or infamous, depending on your point of view, for its flexible, friendly willingness to pursue topics on and beyond the edge of social acceptance and far outside the framework of anything easily identified as religious. Especially notable is one Welsh participant's contribution of a description of his amphallang operation (the insertion of a decorative steel pin below the head of the penis). At the end of his description, he included a schematic drawing detailing exactly where the pin was placed. At another time, list members spent two weeks playing a "What do you think I look like?" game, where regular participants described the images they had of others based on their list contributions; the game illustrates a significant issue in CMC with potentially profound implications for religion, the virtual construction of identity on computer networks. Unlike many more specialized lists, FEMREL is the site of exchanges between highly diverse religious practitioners. In an extended discussion of abortion, the three primary contributors were an evangelical Christian, a Roman Catholic academic theologian, and a neo-pagan witch. One of us (Brasher) participates in FEMREL from time to time and was surprised to discover the amount of face-to-face community it spawns. Femrellers don't just connect over the computer. They have planned and held regional meetings, retreats and parties, and even have their own FEMREL t-shirts whose design was determined by on-line negotiations among list participants. With its one hundred-plus messages a day and eclectic coterie of contributors, this list is not for the faint of heart or for those unwilling to tolerate a reasonable amount of cognitive dissonance.

One of the most unusual forums for religious discussion in cyberspace is BRIDGE-L, "The Bridge across Consciousness." A founder of this list,

Bruce Schuman, describes the ambitious ultimate goal of the BRIDGE project as a "high-speed high-volume global ecumenical dialogue, conducted by responsible representatives from all the world's major religions . . . [which will employ] Internet technology to build a highly informed consensus that yet preserves the finest and most delicate nuances of cultural difference" (Schuman 1993). BRIDGE participants are not content to use their forum to learn about each other's faiths; they are actively on a spiritual quest for a synthesis of global religions, and see the computer network as an essential tool for the elaboration of a new spirituality appropriate to the electronic age. Whatever one may think of the feasibility of such a project, it is surely significant that it is even being attempted.

Our journey from the agora of ancient Athens to the contemporary electronic forum is now complete. We have shown that in cyberspace, as in the ancient forum, one may encounter and engage in debate with devotees of many gods, old and new, known and unknown. In short, computerized religion is alive and well; and as the encounter with the technology of communication that we call classical rhetoric helped reshape the Christian faith, so modern computer networks may well contribute to an emerging conception of spirituality that is profoundly different from the old. Lest we be accused of an overweening optimism regarding the future of net religion, however, we believe it is necessary, before we conclude, to acknowledge and ponder a few of the cultural nightmares technologized humanity has inspired and projected upon the quasi-fictional creature known as the cyborg.

[What] [Who] Do You Say that I Am? . . . Thoughts on the [Tactical
Description] [Ontological Status] of the Cyborg

Our emphasis on the changing rhetorical strategies and the making and unmaking of religio-spiritual connections in cyberspace directs the reader's gaze outward toward that which is produced and automatically reproduced on the cool grey or pale blue of a terminal screen; however, redirect this gaze from text to human user, and previously unnoted but quite important aspects of cyberspace religious discourse suddenly come into view. Located outside the texts but brought into being by their creation are cyborgs, the simultaneously fictional and real creatures produced by the human/machine semiotic integral to cybernetic signification. Thus, our examination of religion in the technological age shifts its attention from the new religious discourse to the changes wrought in the audiences for this discourse as they participate in it: the self-interpretive transformation of the questing, questioning citizens who frequent cybernetic churches and electronic public squares.

People who engage in computer-supported discourse become cyborgs. To perform the communicative act of cybernetic interconnection they must conform with the computer hardware and technology in a manner that mandates they transform. And the transformation they make is into cyborgs. The steps to becoming a cyborg are simple. To noncyborgs they may appear discrete. A person sits down in front of a computer terminal, turns the unit on, types a few characters and is connected via a modem over telephone lines to the nonexistent, ethereal web of computer nodes that function as the spatial coordinates of cyberspace. There, the operator assumes the role of a symbol manipulator and constructs the dissolvable, endlessly reproducible texts that are the stuff of cybercommunication. The computer contributes protocols that guide the process along. When an embryonic cyborg concludes a text construction project, she strikes three or four keys which codedly convey that terminal input has ceased. The letters on the screen instantly vanish. Eventually, gradually, suddenly but not always, the text reappears in the computer mail boxes of other cyborgs who, when online, can summon them to the terminal screen and read them by typing another coded keystroke pattern. People who undertake these exchanges in cyberspace form an intimate, tactile bond with the computer that eventually recenters their consciousness and alters their ontological status. To phrase this process in the hyperlanguage of computerish parole, cybernetic transactions give birth to cyborgs.

To some, the tight interconnection between human and machine that produces cyborgs is a source of distress, and the very idea of cyborg existence anxiety provoking. To others, the cyborg is a metaphor, a harbinger of the possibility of more sensitive, attuned relationships between humanity and material culture. Regardless, since the human tendency to interlink a determination of what is human with what is humane typically is materially affected by whatever is pertinent in the cultural milieu, the entry of the computer into the fray should not be particularly surprising, although its possible revolutionary impact must not be underestimated (see Ihde 1983, 65–77). For example, Carl Mitcham notes that children who play with computer toys may conceive the human being as a ''feeling machine rather than a thinking animal'' (1986, 176). The religio-ethical ramifications of such a recentered idea of humanity may eventually be as startling and transformative as the recentered Copernican universe. Any anticipation of the future of religious rhetoric in cyberspace would therefore be incomplete without directing some attention to the ontological questions the virtual forum raises about those who participate in it. Thus, we will now briefly examine a few of the moral quandaries cyborgs have inspired in American culture, surfacing most notably in popular literature and film, and offer a preliminary assessment of their import for those attending to the unknown God of the Internet. While we admittedly wade into rather murky existential water by broaching this topic, the question we will address here is not whether human beings become cyborgs through participation in the virtual forum. We accept that they do. What arouses our curiosity and stimulates our terminal-generated musings is the cyborg's ontological status. In the terms of Christian incarnational theology, traditional philosophical conceptions of the embodiment of the Logos in human form are profoundly challenged by the human-machine coupling. If there were such a thing as a cyborg savior who opted to echo Jesus in Matthew 8:29 and query followers regarding their understanding of the nature of her/his/its existence, would the question this cyborg-savior ask be, [Who] or [What] do you say I am?

Given Western society's highly technological environment, it can be argued that all Westerners are cyborgs of some type. No human beings in our culture live independent of machines. In any event, the technological, machine-permeated environment of Western urban life thins the boundaries between humans and machines for everyone. The roles machines play in the countless variations of human/machine cyborgs that exist vary. For medical cyborgs, the machine partner is often what makes survival possible. For both participants, cyborg mergers result in an explosion of the self, an expansion of the human and the machine beyond the precyborg limits of each. There are certain industrial cyborgs, for example, that, due to carefully constructed human/machine couplings, can function in environments lethal to humans alone and accomplish complex tasks that machines by themselves could not manage.

For the human participant, the explosion has been followed at times by implosion, a withdrawal of the self from interactive social endeavors. Television is perhaps the ingredient of technological culture best known for its explosive promise yet implosive effect on human community. In an extended study of computerization of an office setting, Shoshana Zuboff (1988) traced the extent of implosion by asking office workers to draw pictures of themselves at work before and after the introduction of computers. The "before" portraits show people talking together, laughing, and asking each other questions. The "after" pictures show rows of people sitting at individual desks staring at computer screens. Zuboff observed that along with computerization new rules of social control were introduced to channel office workers' intercommunications through their machines. This forced them to switch to the cooler sociability of cyberspace. The bleak, line drawings the change inspired are like memory scars of the pain that can accompany the (in this case, involuntary) birth of a generation of cyborgs.

While Descartes's bedrock existential statement *cogito ergo sum* is ultimately a contestable claim about the determinate factor of what it is to be human, the computer understood as a machine that thinks does appear to chip away at a widely recognized boundary employed to affirm human existence and mark human uniqueness. This is true even though the putative intelligence of the computer owes more to its genesis in the arena of elite sciences than to any innate intellectual property of the machine. Still, it is the computer's aura as a "thinking machine" that provokes human identity issues. One procedure that could help reduce this anxiety is to keep clear borders between humans and thinking machines. A cyborg does the opposite. With its sustained human/machine interactions controlled by the machines' capabilities in terms of hardware or equipment and software or programming, the human/computer cyborg violates the provisions of this putative psychological relief by exulting in the intermesh between the two, and thus creates a more threatening and more obvious cyborg than any other.

Human dreams and nightmares about the comparative value and moral standing of people and machines stirred to life in fiction long before machines had capabilities remotely sufficient to raise the question and before the merging of the two into cyborgs was a viable interpretation of human life. The first generation of fictional creatures that served as outlet for human technological fear were known as robots. These cyborg progenitors were clearly mechanical creations, conspicuously distinct from human beings, and possessed few human characteristics (most commonly motion and speech); they were free-standing, metal machines with limited computational capacities who existed solely to serve human "owners." They might be friendly and addressed via diminutives such as Robbie the Robot in *Forbidden Planet;* but the creation's shape, material, behavioral patterns, and voice set up clear boundaries between it and the human. No one could ever mistake Robbie for a human being. Much later, the sophisticated C3PO of the popular *Star Wars* film trilogy and the less articulate but more "compassionate" R2D2 offered a drama teeming with interactive life stories between humans and machines. Yet within this popular saga, clear, distinct boundaries were drawn between the two. R2D2 and C3PO were machines. In fact, they were good machines, perhaps because they manifested their categorical distinctions so unambiguously. Their clean dualism becomes more obvious when they are contrasted with another character from the film, Darth Vader, the terrifyingly dark creature within whom appropriate human/machine boundaries have not been kept. In Vader, the machine has penetrated the human and, the viewer is carefully instructed, inappropriately taken him over: Vader cannot live without the mask that connects him with his enhanced mechanized abilities. Thus, a message of ambiguity is introduced regarding human/machine relationships. Machines by themselves are good, or at least can be good if they are programmed (by humans) correctly; but get too close to one and watch out!

In *Star Wars,* relations between machines and humans invoke Durkheimian distinctions between the sacred and the profane (Durkheim 1915). Where clear distinctions are kept, both humans and machines can exist within the realm of the sacred, the place of order and recognized limits; but once these distinctions are dissolved, disorder takes over and the profane threatens to absorb everyone. The overt threat portrayed in the blending of human and machine threatens sacred and profane distinctions and makes us question whether there are latent implications within this dualism of the machine as Victorianesque female—that which can be pure on its own but also is easily corrupting and corruptible, and must be handled with care. If so, one underlying message of the dualist worldview of *Star Wars* is that when the universe is deemed male, machines are cast as the threatening female "other" of human/mechanical interactions.

Androids, robots that resemble humans, are the fictional icons where many fears of the cyborg have been played out. The robot-to-android evolution in fiction shows that communicative, mechanical, thinking machines can be beneficial as long as boundaries between humans and machines are carefully maintained. When the boundaries are crossed, monsters are born. The film *Blade Runner*, based on the Philip K. Dick story, *Do Androids Dream of Electric Sheep?* (1982), is one early attempt to chart the increasingly blurry edges between humans and machines and ponder the moral ambiguities that result. The film's androids look, move, and speak so much like human beings that it requires a machine to distinguish an android from a human. Unaided, a human being cannot discern the difference. Director Ridley Scott casts the androids as stronger and, in three cases, more beautiful than the human beings with whom they interact. The film's plot centers on a small group of androids who try to find their human creator, in order to have him remove the termination devices incorporated into their mechanisms. Throughout the film, androids are presented as operating within a wider moral framework than most humans. The film's audience, exposed to what must be read as an android existential crisis and presented with the possibility of human/android love, is lured into questioning the validity of categorical distinctions between human and machine. We are encouraged to raise the question of whether the valuation of human life over android existence is an arbitrary, capricious decision or an unquestionable reflection of an underlying, essential moral order.

Thus, when cyborgs encounter each other in cyberspace and engage in religious discourse, in deliberations over ultimate meanings, critical theological considerations arise. Since it is only through the physical coalescence of humans and machines that cyberspace communication is possible, we may say that these considerations are best conceived not in terms of the old theological anthropology but in terms of theological cyborgology. One early pioneer of the unknown territory where cybernetics impinges upon religion, Norbert Wiener, argues in his prescient work *God and Golem, Inc.* that "it is only when it involves a real risk of heresy that there is any point to [such speculation]" (1964, 6). Drawing courage from Wiener's admonition, we plunge to the heart of our concern. If humans have spent the last two millennia pondering the implications of the Gospel's statement that "the Word became flesh, and dwelt among us" (John 1:14), is it even possible for us to imagine—let alone assimilate—the incarnation of the Logos in an age of technologized humans and humanized machines? Who or what is born in the human-machine meld integral to cybernetic conversation? What creature is it that the cool, abstract discourse of cybernetics summons toward Bethlehem to be born?

The Virtual Body: Computers and Humanity's Relation to the Material

A significant factor in the normative evaluation of the cyborg is the character of embodiment in the human/computer experience. If cyborg experiences widen an individual's gaps in awareness between his cognitive processes and his existence as an embodied human being, this may be reason enough to declare the cyborg an unwelcome development in modern society. Again, fears over this issue first surfaced in the arts. In his science fiction classic *Ender's Game* (1985), Orson Scott Card penned a tale of young children raised on computer games whose strategic skills and reflexes are cultivated and harnessed by others to destroy an entire species of life—an act they were willing to perform because they had been inured to destruction by computer games that diminished their capacity for empathy. In Card's story, children's compassion for others and interest in personal survival is intentionally atrophied to convert them into killing machines. This tale highlights a significant apprehension about cyborgs: that the communicative consciousnesses facilitated by human/mechanical interactions will be prone to engage in destructive acts, and more adept than humans alone in accomplishing such destruction. The fear derives from the innate processes of cyborg experience. For cyborgs, the cool medium of cyberspace disengages much of the human body and encourages the mind and computer to perceive itself as a source of experience separate from both. In the cyborgian link between humans and computers, the computer's function can be viewed as parallel to that of wives and servants for Western elite, propertied males during much of our history, as that which buffers the privileged from full awareness of the conditions of embodied existence.

A related area in need of further analysis is the curious alloy of cybernetics and gender. In her *Manifesto for Cyborgs* (1990), Donna Haraway embraces the machine/human pairing and sees it as offering new possibilities in constructing human identity that might free people at least partially from the sense that certain gender role characteristics are inevitable. By contrast, P. Jamison (1994) is profoundly concerned with the social and relational ramifications of having the source of human pleasure be a machine. In order to participate in the pleasure of cyborg discourse, a cyborg must give up other pleasures and relinquish some sense of embodiment. Jamison contends that when females become cyborgs, that which is relinquished is the women's womb. Because it fails to embrace the body as a source of experience, cyborg discourse separates women from a critical source of their social reality.

We do not disagree altogether with Jamison's diagnosis, but we would add a dimension to this diagnosis which modifies and perhaps reverses her rejection of technology. Although cyborg consciousness may, indeed, encourage bodily alienation due to the sustained illusion of disembodiment, this reduction in the importance assigned to the biological components of individual identity in cybernetic communicative acts opens a space where a rare form of creative identity play across the bodily signs of sex and race can occur and new formulations of identity can be explored.

Still, all freedoms have costs. The technologizing of humanity assumes a different character when seen, in the context of the historical relationship between the sexes, as both a mode of oppression and a mode of empowerment. Thus, while Hans Jonas argues that "the triumph of *homo faber* over his external object means also his triumph in the internal constitution of *homo sapiens,* of which he used to be a subsidiary part," with the result that "man himself has been added to the objects of his technology" (quoted in Gronbeck 1990, 10), one could productively complicate Jonas's thesis by adding that the external object of "man" has traditionally been symbolized as female, so that *woman* is and always has been the object of male technology. Seen in this light, Jamison's concerns about the price paid for women's entry into cyberspace do merit consideration. It is true that many denizens of cyberspace will on occasion speak of the pleasure of cyberdiscourse as a feeling of power that enables the computer user to transcend the limitations of the body and hover effortlessly over the ethereal web that connects millions of users and information sites. Yet, since cyborg discourse reduces male as well as female bodies as sources of meaning, Haraway ultimately may have the more winning argument. The reduced value attributable to sex identity enabled by cybernetic communication opens up the creative possibility of "forgetting" one's identity as something substantively sex/gender determined, and engaging in malleable exchanges with others significantly free from gender role factors. Yet caution is warranted, for the degendered play of cybercommunication opens up the oppressive possibility of "forgetting" that conditions outside cyberspace (job hiring patterns, socialization biases, and unequal distribution of economic resources) militate against equal participation of the sexes in cyberspace itself. Finally, while the sensation of disembodiment is an illusion—we cannot escape our bodily tie to the machine—cyborg discourse does have the potential to equalize the status of women and men as actors, and not merely objects, in the technological world.[9]

When the complex phenomena of human/computer cyborg discourse is considered against the evolution of human communication that we have described here, additional aspects of the cyborg come into view. In the postprint era, telegraph, radio, telephone, and television each altered communicative possibilities and power differentials between communicative participants in ironic ways. The telephone was largely a populist invention that took the power to communicate out of the hands of telegraph agents. Radio and television, by contrast, created dualisms comprised of speakers and hearers, giving the power to establish the discourse totally to speakers while forming audiences of listeners and spectators whose role was not to speak back, answer, or change the subject but simply to listen and watch. These technologies did not generate communicative, social cyborgs. They generated, as has been so aptly perceived, human potatoes. Thus, it may be a mistake to judge "technology" as if it were a unified whole that we could weigh in a moral balance to decide whether its cumulative effects were good or bad. Perhaps it is more productive to think of multiple technologies (like multiple rhetorics) which constitute audiences in very different ways, some beneficial to human communities and some with pernicious effects. An important ethical criterion for evaluating any new technology, then, is the quality and the degree of sociability that it makes possible (Rheingold 1993).

If our judgment is to be based on this standard, then (speaking for ourselves) we have already made our decision. We, the authors of this essay, met and became friends on the Internet; and the mutually stimulating conversations that bore fruit in this essay are evidence enough for us of the value and potential of this new medium. Given the permeation of technology in contemporary Western life, we side with Haraway in thinking that for our high-technology society, the computer cyborg—while neither ideal nor something for everyone—is a desirable merging. We find the communicative, social cyborg a fascinating and desirable addition to human community precisely because it permeates the nearly reified boundaries between the human and the material and brings into being people who can speak from experience about the ethics of human/material interchanges. While fears of machine domination of human conditions are worth taking seriously, it is also possible that the intimate interactions that create cyborgs hold the potential of a heightened appreciation for the spirituality of the material—a religious insight that, as contemporary ecofeminists insist, is in serious need of cultivation, given our precarious approach to the limit of global resources (see Adams 1993; Plant 1989; Diamond and Orenstein 1990; Primavesi 1991; McFague 1993).

The religious practices of cyborgs challenge sacred/profane distinctions between humans and machines. In this, they do not sacralize machines but make impossible an antagonistic dualism between human and machine that declares either sacred or profane. Instead, CMC gives rise to unique opportunities for the development of thick connections between physically disparate, technologically embedded contemporary people. This reverses the long, slow trend of technology-abetted one-way communications. The ethical challenge of cyberspace is the extent to which entry into this relationship will be commodified, packaged, and sold.

We do not wish to give an unqualified endorsement of the discourses we have presented here. One issue raised in CMC that we find particularly troubling is the extent to which the new media reduce all discourse to information. This can result in a contemporary analogue of Gnosticism, the mystical quest for the knowledge that saves. Physicist Heinz Pagels puts the problem succinctly:

> Some intellectual prophets have declared the end of the age of knowledge and the beginning of the age of information. Information tends to drive out knowledge. Information is just signs and numbers, while knowledge has semantic value. What we want is knowledge, but what we often get is information. It is a sign of the times that many people cannot tell the difference between information and knowledge, not to mention wisdom, which even knowledge tends to drive out. (1988, 49)

If our traditions cannot keep knowledge and wisdom alive, these distinctions will disappear as all is reduced to information. The cyborg's spiritual quest would become an endless search for the information that saves—a quest doomed to failure, an endless and eternally restless manipulation of signs and numbers that, like the search for the philosopher's stone, can never produce the gold or the semantic value we seek. When the ambitious dream described by Richard Lanham in *The Electronic Word* is realized, and the whole record of human culture is digitized and available on computer databases connected to each other by a global web, our spiritual crisis will remain and even intensify, for we will be forced to confront the fact that no electronic alchemy can turn information into knowledge or into the wisdom that will teach us how to live.[10]

Western culture is material and technology driven. The challenge that confronts our generation is how to live responsibly, or, more precisely, how to understand the meaning of responsibility, on the cusp of the technological millennium. A major step toward this goal could be achieved by an acknowledgment of the intricate human/machine interdependencies that delineate modern life and the making of careful, informed decisions that actually reflect this status. As people who take language seriously, we think an important part of this process of global maturity is the use and perhaps even playful exploration of metaphors that reflect the plethora of human/machine matings already underway. In the computer, humanity has discovered a machine it can mate with, and, through that mating, connect and interact with other human/machine mated pairs. A cyborg consciousness, formed by the synthesis of the human and the material, may be the necessary existential precondition to cultivating alternative habits of being that will move us closer to a sustainable ecosystem. Ultimately, we think coming to terms with the cyborg will be more helpful than alternative paradigms that encourage the flight of human consciousness from the conflicts of modernity through an embrace of archaic metaphors that lead to the tropic labyrinth of a mythical, reconstructed past. Thus, we cast our lots in favor of the cyborg. Retooling the offbeat, poetic salutation Haraway coined for the close of her famous *Manifesto,* given the way we perceive the present and conceive the future, we'd rather be cyborgs than God/-desses.

The emergence of cyborg theology parallels and is propelled by the development of new rhetorics which theorize and guide the communicative practices of the citizens of cyberspace. As the ancient polis was constituted by the practices of oral communication, and its ideal of citizenship first articulated in a theoretical conception of character as revealed in public speech, so today new conceptions of identity and new forms of community are being formed through the practices and the theories of electronic communication. We will not speculate here about the forms the new rhetorics will assume as the transition to CMC continues and is finally completed, but we note that recent works by Jay David Bolter (1991), George Landow (1992), Richard Lanham (1993), and Mark C. Taylor and Esa Saarinen (1994) provide useful introductions into the discourse conventions and theoretical implications of cybercommunication, each in his or her own way supporting the thesis that postmodern approaches to discourse theory make considerably more sense when applied to electronic communication. Bolter's observation regarding the changing nature of textual construction by writers and readers in cyberspace is surely pertinent to any imagination of the future of religious discourse as conducted through the new media: "An electronic text is a network rather than the straight line suggested by the printed book, and the network should be available for reading in a variety of orders. Texts written explicitly for this new medium will probably favor short, concentrated expression, because each unit may be approached from a different perspective with each reading. Electronic writing will probably be aphoristic rather than periodic" (Bolter 1991, xi).[11] Having reached the limit of our attempt to encapsulate the characteristics of these new media in periodic prose, we close with a brief indulgence in aphorism.

A Peroration: The Cyberpunk's Prayer

We conclude by quoting an example of the new folklore of the electronic age, the Cyberpunk's Prayer, which we first read on our computer screens. A contemporary analogue of Paul's appeal to the "unknown God" of ancient Athens, the prayer presents a deliberate and sincerely devotional transformation of traditional spirituality into the terms of technical reason. We believe that such hybrid forms are or will be characteristic of the virtual religions of the future.

> Our Sysop,
>   Who art On-Line,
>   High be thy clearance level.
> Thy System up,
> Thy Program executed
> Off-line as it is on-line.
> Give us this logon our database,
> And allow our rants,
>   As we allow those who flame against us.
> And do not access us to garbage,
>   But deliver us from outage.
> For thine is the System and the Software
>   and the Password forever.[12]

The unknown God may be a sysop (systems operator) or a cyborg; the spirit bloweth where it listeth, whether the Logos is embodied and apprehended as oral speech, as printed text, as bread and wine, or as ethereal, evanescent, phosphorescent flashes of insight on our computer screens. With all due caution, then, we celebrate the manifestations of divinity in the era of the electronic Word, and invite our readers to join us in the quest for human connection and spiritual meaning through cyberspace.

Notes

The authors wish to thank each other, the editor for his helpful comments, and their friends and colleagues at the University of Southern California and on the scholarly Internet community, including Walter R. Fisher, John Gresham, Sigrid Peterson, Michael Strangelove, Jeffrey Kaplan, and many others who responded to queries regarding online religion that we posted to computer networks. Portions of this research were made possible by a generous grant to the first author from the James H. Zumberge Research and Innovation Fund at the University of Southern California and by sabbatical leave time from the College of Letters, Arts and Sciences at USC.

1. The term "cool" as applied to media is borrowed from McLuhan (1964), who expounds his usage as follows:

A "hot" medium is one that extends one single sense in "high definition." High definition is the state of being well filled with data. . . . Telephone is a cool medium, or one of low definition, because the ear is given a meager amount of information. . . . Hot media are . . . low in participation, and cool media are high in participation or completion by the audience. (36)

2. This account is largely based on Conley 1990 and Bizzell and Herzberg 1990. Other sources consulted for the historical summary that follows include Wilder 1971 and Kennedy 1984, 1972. Those interested in the philosophical issues raised by our account of the rhetorical tradition should consult Grassi 1980 and McKeon 1987.

3. This is obviously a polemical reading of Plato, one that necessarily collapses many subtleties in the ancient conflict of rhetoric and philosophy. Considerations of space make it impossible to defend the interpretation of the classical traditions sketched here; for a more nuanced account of cultural conflicts in classical Greece, we refer the reader to Jaeger 1943. The classic discussion of Plato's political elitism is Popper 1966; for a spirited and polemical analysis of Plato's treatment of rhetoric that places it in a political context, see Vickers 1988.

4. We refer in particular to Ong 1988, although the concepts discussed here appear throughout Ong's long series of books and essays. See also Ong 1981. For a summary of Ong's theories that considers but finally absolves him of the charge of technological determinism, see Gronbeck 1990.

5. For a dissenting view, see Conley 1990, 59–62.

6. For an excellent historical introduction to the evolution of liturgy, see Thomson 1961. Ong (1981, 277–83) draws attention to the linguistic and symbolic dimensions of sacramental and liturgical theologies.

7. There are a number of lists devoted to the academic study of religion, such as RELIGION and SSREL-L, which we do not dwell on here since our focus is explicitly religious activity; however, we mention them since conversations on these lists are occasionally interrupted by cryptic postings from misguided mystics or appeals for help by members of marginalized religious groups, as when in 1993 a member of the controversial sect known as the Family (aka the Children of God) with Internet access bombarded the list SSREL-L (sponsored by the Society for the Scientific Study of Religion) with requests for help in the group's legal conflicts in Argentina. Thus, these lists constantly face controversies over the discourse conventions that proscribe explicit religious appeals on a list devoted to academic study.

8. For information about sacred texts online as well as many of the electronic groups and services described here, see Strangelove 1993. For an academic study of communication on religious networks, see Beaulieu 1993.

9. [See, however, Adams and Herring, both in this volume, for examples of real oppression of women in contemporary cyberspace—examples that serve as powerful counterarguments to these more optimistic claims.—Ed.]

10. [A similar point is extensively developed in Bill McKibben's *The Age of Missing Information* (New York: Plume, 1993), which powerfully contrasts the information made available through a plethora of cable TV programs and the knowledge and wisdom for living derivable from more traditional sources, including attentive observation of the natural order.—Ed.]

11. [The next essay in this collection, by Phil Mullins, in fact takes up the suggested connection here between Bolter's observation and religious discourse.— Ed.]

12. Quoted with permission of the author, Bill Scarborough of Austin, Texas. In private e-mail correspondence to one of this essay's authors (O'Leary), Mr. Scarbrough wrote:

> I had seen a rendition of The Lord's Prayer in the (Texas)_Baptist Standard_a few years back. It was done in sports dialect. It seemed that, if the Word could be helped by putting it in sports dialect, it could also be witnessed in computer dialect. "The Cyberpunk's Prayer" is not copyrighted. Anyone is free to quote, repost, or reprint all or part of it. . . . I hope that some sort of witness can say that one can be a Christian without being racist, homophobic, etc.

References

Adams, C. J., ed. 1993. *Ecofeminism and the Sacred*. New York: Continuum.

Beaulieu, H. 1993. Observing Unobserved Computer Networks as a Source for the Study of Religion. *North American Religion* 2: 11–34.

Bizzell, P., and H. B. Herzberg. 1990. *The Rhetorical Tradition*. Boston: St. Martin's Press.

Bolter, J. D. 1991. *Writing Space: The Computer, Hypertext, and the History of Writing*. Hillsdale, NJ: Lawrence Erlbaum.

Card, O. S. 1985. *Ender's Game*. New York: Doherty.

Coate, J. 1992. Cyberspace Innkeeping: Building Online Community. Reproduced in CRTNET (Communication Research and Theory Network), ed. Tom Benson, 905 (4 January 1994). [Back issues available from LISTSERV@PSUVM archives, CRTNET.]

Conley, T. M. 1990. *Rhetoric in the European Tradition*. New York: Longman.

Descartes, R. 1987. *Discours de la méthode pour bien Conduire sa Raison and Chercher la Vérité dans les Sciences: plus, la Dioptrique: les Météores: et la Géométrie: Qui Sont des Essais de Cette Methode*. Lecce, Italia: Dipartimento di Filosofia dell Universit'a Degli Studi di Lecce.

Diamond, I., and G. Orenstein, eds. 1990. *Reweaving the World: The Emergence of Ecofeminism*. San Francisco: Sierra.

Dick, P. 1982. *Do Androids Dream of Electric Sheep?* New York: Random House.

———. 1969. UBIK. New York: Doubleday.

Duhamel, P. A. 1949. The Function of Rhetoric as Effective Expression. *Journal of the History of Ideas* 10: 344–56.

Durkheim, E. 1915. *The Elementary Forms of the Religious Life.* New York: Macmillan.

Ellspermann, G. L. 1949. *The Attitude of the Early Christian Latin Writers toward Pagan Literature and Learning.* Catholic University of America Patristic Studies, vol. 82. Washington, DC: Catholic University of America Press.

Grassi, E. 1980. *Rhetoric as Philosophy: The Humanist Tradition.* University Park, PA: Pennsylvania State University Press.

Gronbeck, B. 1990. Communication Technology, Consciousness, and Culture: Supplementing FM-2030s View of Transhumanity. In *Communication and the Culture of Technology,* ed. M. J. Medhurst, A. Gonzalez, and T. R. Peterson, 3–18. Pullman, WA: Washington State University Press.

Haraway, D. 1990. A Manifesto for Cyborgs: Science, Technology, and Socialist Feminism in the 1980s. In *Feminism/Postmodernism,* ed. L. J. Nicholson, 190–233. New York: Routledge.

Ihde, D. 1983. *Existential Technics.* Albany: State University of New York Press.

Jaeger, W. 1943. *Paideia: The Ideals of Greek Culture.* Trans. G. Highet. New York: Oxford University Press.

———. 1961. *Early Christianity and Greek Paideia.* Cambridge: Harvard University Press.

Jamison, P. 1994. Contradictory Spaces: Pleasure and the Seduction of the Cyborg Discourse. *Electronic Journal of Virtual Culture* 1. [Electronic document available from EJVC-L@KENTVM.BITNET.]

Kennedy, G. 1972. *The Art of Rhetoric in the Roman World.* Princeton, NJ: Princeton University Press.

———. 1984. *New Testament Interpretation through Rhetorical Criticism.* Chapel Hill, NC: University of North Carolina Press.

Kinneavy, J. 1987. *Greek Rhetorical Origins of Christian Faith.* New York: Oxford University Press.

Kurtz, Gary, producer. 1977. *Star Wars.* Los Angeles: TCF/Lucasfilm.

Lactantius. 1964. *Divine Institutes.* Trans. M. F. McDonald. Washington, DC: Catholic University of America Press.

Landow, G. 1992. *Hypertext: The Convergence of Contemporary Critical Theory and Technology.* Baltimore: Johns Hopkins University Press.

Lanham, R. 1993. *The Electronic Word: Democracy, Technology, and the Arts.* Chicago: University of Chicago Press.

McFague, S. 1993. *The Body of God: An Ecological Theology.* Minneapolis: Fortress Press.

McKeon, R. 1987. *Rhetoric: Essays in Invention and Discovery.* Ed. M. Backman. Woodbridge, CT: Ox Bow Press.

McLuhan, M. 1964. *Understanding Media: The Extensions of Man.* New York: Signet.

Mitcham, C. 1986. Computers: From Ethos and Ethics to Mythos and Religion: Notes on the New Frontier between Computers and Philosophy. *Technology in Society* 8: 171–201.

Murphy, James J. 1974. *Rhetoric in the Middle Ages: a History of Rhetorical Theory from St. Augustine to the Renaissance.* Berkeley: University of California Press.

Nayfack, Nicholas, producer. 1956. *Forbidden Planet.* Los Angeles: MGM.

Ong, W. J. 1981. *The Presence of the Word: Some Prolegomena for Cultural and Religious History.* Minneapolis: University of Minnesota Press.

———. 1988. *Orality and Literacy: The Technologizing of the Word.* London: Routledge.

Pagels, H. 1988. *The Dreams of Reason.* New York: Simon and Schuster.

Plant, J. 1989. *Healing the Wounds: The Promise of Ecofeminism.* Philadelphia: New Society.

Popper, K. 1966. *The Open Society and Its Enemies.* Vol. 1. Princeton, NJ: Princeton University Press.

Primavesi, A. 1991. *From Apocalypse to Genesis: Ecology, Feminism and Christianity.* Minneapolis: Fortress Press.

Rheingold, H. 1993. *The Virtual Community: Homesteading on the Electronic Frontier.* Reading, MA: Addison-Wesley.

Rieff, P. 1987. *Triumph of the Therapeutic.* [1966]. Reprint, with a new preface. Chicago: University of Chicago Press.

Schuman, B. 1993. Interreligious Dialog in a Global Electronic Context: An Introduction to the Bridge across Consciousness. [Archived at LISTSERV@UCSBVM. BITNET; sending the LISTSERV command "GET RELIGION DIALOG" will retrieve the file to your e-mailbox.]

Scott, Ridley, producer. 1982. *Blade Runner.* Los Angeles: Warner/Ladd/Blade Runner Partnership.

Strangelove, Michael. 1993. *The Electric Mystic's Guide to the Internet: A Complete Directory of Networked Electronic Documents, Online Conferences, Serials, Software, and Archives Relevant to Religious Studies.* Ottowa. [The *Electric Mystic's Guide* is available on many gopherservers; those with access to a gopher can try UNA.HH.LIB.UMICH.EDU. It is also available via ftp from: gopher.uottawa. ca.]

Tacitus. 1946. *Dialogue on Oratory.* Trans. W. Peterson. Cambridge: Harvard University Press.

Taylor, M., and E. Saarinen. 1994. *Imagologies: Media Philosophy.* London: Routledge.

Tertullian. 1956. *De Carne Christi.* Ed. E. Eecy. London: SPCK.

———. 1957. *De Praesriptione Haereticum.* Ed. R. F. Refoule. Paris: Editions du Cerf.

Thomson, B. 1961. *Liturgies of the Western Church.* Cleveland, Ohio: William Collins.

Vickers, B. 1988. *In Defence of Rhetoric.* New York: Oxford University Press.

Wiener, N. 1964. *God and Golem, Inc.: A Comment on Certain Points where Cybernetics Impinges upon Religion.* Cambridge: MIT Press.

Wilder, A. 1971. *Early Christian Rhetoric: The Language of the Gospel.* Cambridge: Harvard University Press.

Weber, M. 1964. *The Sociology of Religion.* Trans. E. Fischoff. Boston: Beacon Press.

Zuboff, S. 1988. *In the Age of the Smart Machine: The Future of Work and Power.* New York: Basic Books.

11

Sacred Text in the Sea of Texts: The Bible in North American Electronic Culture

PHIL MULLINS

Introduction

Nothing will draw the monk more closely to active perfection than giving himself, for love of neighbor, to the copying of divine Scripture. (Trithemius 1974, 57)

One need not agree with McLuhan that the age of the printed book, the Gutenberg era, is over, to recognize that with the astronomic number of new books being published every year the age of a very special book, treated differently from all others psychologically, metaphysically, sociologically, is changed. (Smith 1971, 25)

The first statement above is from a German Benedictine, Johannes Trithemius, writing at the close of the fifteenth century. Abbot Trithemius's *In Praise of Scribes* is an effort to assure his brothers that the vocation of scribe remains a necessary, important, and pious vocation, despite the emergence of printing. Much of Trithemius's case seems extraordinarily quaint to persons living at the end of the twentieth century. In an electronic culture, where duplication usually means pushing a button or two, it is hard even to imagine the claim that copying—even copying the Bible—can be edifying in any way. Although he was mightily resisting it, Trithemius, writing at the close of the medieval world, seems to have sensed a sea change in whose early phases he was already immersed (he had a later edition of his work printed!). Familiar conceptions of scripture and of monastic life as it was bound up with the production of scripture were soon to be fundamentally reshaped.

The second quotation comes almost five hundred years after Trithemius; it is a passing comment in an important 1971 essay by Wilfred Cantwell

Smith, an eminent Islamicist and historian of religion, a scholar who has taken great interest in the power of scripture in the human imagination. Smith, however, makes surprisingly little of his insight; it is merely a peripheral element in a larger discussion of the limitations of historical-critical approaches to scripture and the need for broader approaches in academic institutions. Smith, of course, was keenly aware of the influence of broadcast media and the ways in which modern printing and mass marketing work. But his essay was written before inexpensive microcomputers, electronic writing, and easily accessible international networking had taken us a step deeper into electronic culture.[1] Smith, like Trithemius, seems to sense a coming sea change. At the end of the twentieth century, we seem poised not only for some new attitudes toward scripture but also perhaps for some new ideas about our lives insofar as human lives are bound up with certain images of sacred text. The following comments are preliminary thoughts about the ways in which our cultural presuppositions about the Bible as a sacred text may subtly be transformed in the evolving electronic culture of North America.

My account unfolds in three components. The next section provides a rough attempt to locate the late twentieth century in terms of the media that shape culture, and, particularly, attitudes toward the Bible and religious sensibility. Simply stated, I suggest that the alphabetic letter press, from its humble beginnings, develops into a dynamo; in this century, broadcast media begin to modify the culture shaped by the book. Now, at the end of the twentieth century, computers have become major tools used to generate, preserve, and manipulate cultural lore. We are now entering an era of integrated, interactive media, and the mental habits of book culture seem destined for further transformation. The study of the Bible has, of course, persisted through the age of print and into our own incunabula phase of electronic culture; in the second section, I outline and examine two dominant approaches to the Bible, the approach through critical scholarship and the literalist approach, which have prospered and remained in tension for about a hundred years in North America. I argue that both critical scholarship and literalism are responses to the Bible which are heavily invested in the presuppositions of book culture. Finally, the last section of this essay offers some speculations about the dynamics of life and the fate of the Bible in the communicative excess of the information age. I analyze ways in which our approach to knowledge seems to be changing in this environment; I suggest ways in which the computer as a tool for reading and writing subtly changes our notions of reading, writing, and text as well as book-culture ideas about authors and authority. Surely such changes, I suggest, will offer new challenges to communities intent upon using the Bible to shape human lives.

An Environment of Abundance

The mechanical press, seen against the backdrop of manuscript culture, was a technological organ of abundance. The Reformation was a time in which theological treatises, polemical cartoons, Bibles, and other religious literature came into the hands of the masses.[2] Mass literacy, of course, did not emerge overnight, but being able to read revered texts like the Bible and being able to own such a document are not necessarily ideas that always strictly belong together in early print culture (Cole 1972, 98–99). Nevertheless, the Bible must be regarded from the beginning of print culture as a document with symbolic weight or momentum. At least in North America, making sense of the biblical text has always been an exercise of interacting with a public deposit of overtones and nuances that powerful symbols leave in the common air.[3]

As we enter the last part of the twentieth century in the United States, the abundance of early print culture and even that of the last century pales into insignificance. Our sophisticated printing technology and mass marketing truly allow profligacy. An Associated Press article in the mid-1980s indicated that there were 15 million Bibles sold in a single year and this was only a part of the 130 million volumes of "religious" books sold (Cornell 1986). Survey research indicates that most Americans consider themselves "religious" (Ladd 1986, 15–30): Whatever else this means, it certainly indicates that we voraciously consume (i.e., purchase, whether or not we read) literature that somehow acquires the label "religious." A recent article covering the 1993 trade show of the Christian Booksellers Association in Atlanta, Georgia, reported that annual sales for Bibles are more than $400 million. There are now approximately 450 versions of the Bible available in English; sophisticated publishers now produce "niche Bibles" tailored for highly specialized audiences (athletes, working women, pregnant women, environmentalists, recovering alcoholics, to name a few). Bible study aids—which these days are available not only in print but also as audio tapes and software—are also mass marketed (White 1993).

For a majority of Americans during this century, the commercial broadcast media have been an important source of culturally valent images, knowledge, and pleasure. Broadcast media have shaped religious sensibilities for many, perhaps only a little less than face-to-face interaction, and as much as reading. Some religious institutions have bitterly challenged those who capitalized on broadcast media to create their own electronic religious institutions, institutions with practices adapted to the medium but different from those offered by local religious institutions. More interesting than this controversy about the efficacy of electronic religion is the symbiosis between print, audio, and broadcast media in American religion and, more generally, in American media. Novels and plays have long been adapted for television, although writing for screen or television is also an established vocation in its own right. Best sellers quickly become films or television movies; also, however, televised or film material often inspires the production of printed products (Ong 1977, 82–91). This sort of interaction between media is at its height in the world of religion. Religious broadcasting very frequently has something quite tangible—tapes, books, pamphlets, special Bibles—to sell as an aid for viewers/listeners and as an additional support to the enterprising broadcaster.

In the last decade, the media environment in North America has become immensely more complex, and promises to become even more so. Television, as the dominant broadcast medium, is rapidly changing due to technological innovations. Cable television has expanded; the number of specialized channels targeted for micro-audiences is soon to mushroom. Digital compression techniques will allow 500 channels; future fiberoptics innovations will allow even more options. All sorts of questions about the impact of such changes in television remain unanswered: Will the fracturing of the power of the mass networks mean that television will have less power as a shaper of cultural values? How will more options affect religious broadcasting? Will future program content become any more diverse than it presently is (Waters 1993, 75–76)?

Perhaps more important than developments in broadcast media are the recent changes that microcomputers have brought to American society.[4] By the mid-1980s, the computer had become a modestly priced, efficient writing tool. Now computers are daily used throughout American society to create, manipulate, store and transfer the written word as well as images and numerical data. The computer provides a somewhat different kind of writing environment than earlier writing technologies (for the most thorough discussion of the electronic environment, see Bolter 1991). It combines vast, compact storage and almost instant retrieval; the computer can feed print distribution systems (generating hard copy) or it can consolidate, through networking, creation and distribution functions. Electronic writing offers contemporary culture some genuine alternatives to the book and to broadcast and film media. This doesn't mean that any of these powerful communication tools are likely quickly to disappear, but it means that they will be supplemented and modified by the emergent products of electronic writing.

What is even now in process in our electronic culture is the digitization of whatever can be digitized. Translation into the codes of other media becomes possible with digitization (Thorp 1991, 106). Thus we are embarking on the first phase of an era of integrated media. We will increasingly see image, print, and sound technology brought together (termed "integrated media''), often in interactive forms. Hypertext and hypermedia are forms of electronic text that capitalize on the large storage capacity and quick random-access potential of the electronic medium; they are (or can be) integrated and interactive forms. The ''hyper'' in ''hypertext'' and ''hypermedia'' really refers to another or additional dimension of text beyond the presently obvious, just as in mathematical physics ''hyperspace'' refers to space with more than three dimensions (Heim 1993, 30). The text you have before you at any moment on the screen is a text that always offers extension to other texts seemingly close at hand. Technical definitions and discussions of hypertext and hypermedia usually focus on information nodes and associative links that carry the user (i.e., writer or reader) almost instantaneously from one locus for making meaning to another (see, for example, Conklin 1987, 18; Jonassen 1989, 7; and Shneiderman and Kearsley 1989, 3). From a more literary perspective, Moulthrop (1989) calls hypertext simply ''distributed textuality'' (266) which allows writers to offer and readers to choose a variety of particular realized constructions of text. Hypermedia is an extension of these principles of distribution and construction to anything that can be digitized.

From another vantage, one can argue that modularizing knowledge gives users the option, in the electronic medium, of selecting personalized constructions of text (Jonassen 1989, 7). Manageable units of meaningful text can be sequenced according to choice in a medium that fetches inscriptions almost instantly and offers almost infinite space for textual assembly. Electronic textuality is a network of modules, each quickly consumable, from which a particular permutation is concatenated as an occasion for meaning making. Meaning making is a cumulative human process of working through the particular tapestry of modules that has been woven.

John Slatin offers yet a third image of hypertext in his suggestion that hypertext is intertextuality writ large:

> Intertextuality can very generally be defined as the notion that a text (any text) is really a collectivity of texts, so intimately and intricately bound to one another that they have to be described as mutually constituting each other; the text one is looking at is composed of and by other texts. (1988, 115)

Hypertext is thus quite literally an ''embodiment of intertextuality'' which Slatin sees as analogous to poetry:

> One implication of this analogy, I think, is that there is likely to be an irreducible element of difficulty about hypertext, as there is in poetry, neither form being *meant* to be easy. (1988, 115)

While Slatin's figure of hypertext is on the mark, it is important not to portray the present incunabula phase of hypertext too exotically; academic humanists who are not aware of the longer tradition of philosophic, religious, and literary reflection on language may be tempted to do just this.[5]

The digitization of resources perhaps provides some warrant for the habit of contemporary intellectuals, influenced by French literary theory and philosophy, to regard nearly everything as a text. Admittedly, the term "text" has now become overworked, but it does point out a fact about digitized resources that we are increasingly aware of: They can be altered, edited, and reconstituted. In fact, they are made for this. The images of text as an unchanging edifice and a bulwark of authority are reifications of book culture. Printing makes texts quite tangible and objectifies our sense of their meaning-making potential. Images of electronic text are only distantly tangible; they are also more fluid. The new images of texts produce subtle shifts in our mental habits which are undoubtedly beginning to have some impact not only on traditionally text-concerned domains such as literature but also on religious ideas and practices concerned with a sacred text (Mullins 1988, 1990).

Resources electronically available are growing at what could be considered an alarming rate. This is the case both because older print culture resources are becoming accessible as digitized electronic texts and because new resources are being generated with such abandon. Some of the gatekeeping functions related to social definitions of "knowledge" in print culture seem to have dissolved in the culture of electronic writing. Factors such as economics and hierarchical organization in print culture combined to limit, to at least some degree, the legitimization and distribution of knowledge. Electronic networks, unlike print culture, diversify and diffuse notions of author-ity (i.e., being an author in the sense of speaking as a knowledgeable authority). Internet, Bitnet, Usenet, and similar grand networking schemes give their users access to an enormous number of sites which offer resources that can be retrieved for local use or can function as conversation/cooperation sites for joint endeavors. In sum, the emerging culture of electronic writing is quite unregulated and chaotic when compared to the broader culture shaped by print and broadcast media.[6] Put more positively, network culture is nonhierarchical and recenterable, as I discuss below.

Presently, access to emerging culture created by electronic writing is not open to all, since connectivity is expensive (although not directly to the academics who are major users of Internet and Bitnet) and some new skills are required. Nevertheless, it seems likely in the next decades that access will progressively broaden while resources and capabilities multiply beyond the imaginable; with this will come revised social presuppositions about authoring and textual authority. Such presuppositions will inevitably reshape some of the book-culture attitudes about the Bible as a sacred text. How will a powerful symbol of the sort the Bible has been in Western culture fare in the environment of digital excess? How will receptive communities (i.e., those communities in which the Bible was heretofore regarded as a sacred text) function to provide legitimation in the coming era? These are the questions of interest in the present age of the electronic incunabula. As a prelude to approaching such questions, the next section offers ideas about the interpretative dilemmas of the present.

Late Print Culture and Early Electronic Culture Responses to Sacred Text: Literalism and Critical Study

> The very familiarity with which we move among books and handle the ubiquitous printed page has bred in us its own kind of contempt; we have some difficulty empathizing with persons for whom a copy of a text was or is a seldom and wonderful thing, perhaps a magical and awesome thing, before which the proper response is fearful veneration or fervent worship. The power of scripture as holy writ is, however, very much a part of most traditions past and present in which scripture has figured at all prominently. (Graham 1989, 134)

William Graham is certainly correct that in a time that is dubbed the "information age," most people have difficulty imagining awe before the written word. Nevertheless, contemporary North American culture is one in which, within some religious institutions, great battles still rage over such matters as "inerrancy"; many who identify with religious traditions nurtured by a sacred text seem today self-consciously to opt for literal-minded approaches to scripture. Although it is sometimes mistaken for it, this phenomenon does not represent the sort of veneration of the sacred text described by Graham as present in cultures in which the printed page is not ubiquitous. Modern literalism instead represents some of the fears and nostalgia of modern literates as well as the dynamics of imagination in the lifeworld of late book culture. Below I reflect briefly upon biblical literalism as a posture deeply indebted to some of the dynamics of late book culture. But not only literalism is nurtured by the soil of book culture: In an environment of textual proliferation, critical approaches to writing develop and prosper. Critical study of the Bible is thus also a second offspring of book culture. Critical approaches to writing can eventually undermine a particular text insofar as they produce questions about meaning and often shift attention from the text to the social context of writing and ultimately to the interpreter. Havelock (1963, 1982, 1986), of course, argues that critical thinking per se develops with the development and spread of writing. Critical approaches to texts and especially to the Bible seem to mature in late print and early electronic culture; along with this development comes a literalist reaction against the uncertainties introduced by critical approaches to texts. Ultimately, there remain irresolvable tensions between critical responses and predominantly honorific responses to texts; below I consider both responses as the natural product of the development of print and then electronic media.

Critical Biblical Scholarship and Its Pilgrimage

Bolter explores the tensions between critical and honorific responses to texts with respect to attitudes toward contemporary literature and the new electronic writing:

> A great book is less likely to be worshipped when it can be bought in paperback for a few dollars and when it is so flimsy that the pages come away in the reader's hand as he or she turns them. The critics of worshipful reading are still reading books in print, but their attitude is appropriate to paperbacks rather than editions bound in leather. Indeed, the radical literary theories . . . including reader-response criticism and deconstruction, still assume that readers will be reading printed books. But in fact, the electronic medium is a more natural place for the irreverent reading that they suggest. (1991, 152)

What is called "scientific," "critical" or "historical-critical" biblical scholarship (which certainly isn't new, but dates back to the book culture of the nineteenth century) is the primary domain of Bolter's "irreverent reading" in modern religious circles. In an environment of many texts, it becomes plausible or reasonable to make sense of texts by linking them with their earliest social context (and, more recently, to the changing social contexts in which such texts are valent). Readers come to distinguish and value "original meanings" (i.e., those meanings likeliest in the earliest context) in texts, including the Bible.[7] To make this move in biblical study, of course, is to read "irreverently" in the sense that it injects historical sensibilities (with awareness of the differences among cultures and cultural epochs) into the hermeneutics of the sacred text. Irreverent reading has its own interests and partisans, namely, those who accept (consciously or unconsciously) many of the suppositions about history and its artifacts which emerge in the Renaissance, Enlightenment, and nineteenth century. For many, if not most, modern people, irreverent reading eventually becomes not irreverent at all but merely sensible reading. Recently, however, biblical scholar Tom Boomershine rather bluntly described the course of sensible irreverent reading (i.e., Bible reading informed by mainline biblical scholarship in the twentieth century) as follows:

The promise of the historical-critical paradigm was that it would render the past alive and would result in illumination and vitality for the religious community. The religious communities that have accepted historical criticism since the 19th century are in decline and the educational enterprise of critical study of the Bible has been massively reduced in theological curriculums since the 1930's because it did not produce spiritual vitality and life. (1993a, 210)

Boomershine and other scholars concerned with interpreting the Bible are beginning to recognize not only the practical problems (in religious communities) spawned by historical-critical study but also that the appeal for scholars of a narrowly construed, historical-critical paradigm is declining:

The collapse of Biblical theology as a strong and viable hermeneutic, the emergence of narrative theology and literary critical methods of exegesis, the impact of semiotics and deconstruction, the development of social science methods of analysis—all are connected by a common epistemological thread which moves away from the distinction between the phenomenal and the noumenal to the phenomena of sense experience itself. (1993a, 220)

Boomershine is rather clumsy here in mimicking Kantian distinctions, but he is certainly on the mark in insisting that there is now a broad array of post-historical-critical approaches to the Bible. It is important to distinguish the members of this scholarly array (some of which are enumerated above) from noncritical (literal) approaches (discussed below), but it should also be clear that such approaches do not necessarily fit seamlessly together. Those without a high tolerance for ambiguity will likely remain troubled by tensions among different scholarly interpretative approaches. As the Kantian language at the end of the quotation above implies, Boomershine addresses such tensions by positing a cultural paradigm shift whose fallout is seen in biblical scholarship:

In electronic media and its cultures, what is known is what is seen and heard. That is, the theory would suggest that the declining impact of historical-critical scholarship is a symptom of a change in the culture. These developments in Biblical scholarship are responses to that new culture and its ways of knowing. (1993a, 220)

Whether Boomershine has correctly analyzed all of the particulars of the plight of contemporary biblical scholarship is not the major issue here. His general thesis is, however, a provocative one worth reflection: Print culture is declining and electronic culture is emerging, and this is surely felt in the responses to the Bible as well as in scholarship about the Bible. The declining grip of the old historical-critical paradigm reflects the changing understanding of knowledge which is emerging in electronic culture. Many scholars today find it less interesting (or less truthful and viable) to engage in scholarly projects that historicize meaning as biblical scholars routinely did until twenty years ago. To put matters as Neil Postman recently has, "every epistemology is an epistemology of a stage of media development" (1985, 24). The shift to electronic culture is a sea change which figures such as McLuhan, Bolter, and Ong, as well as Postman, recognize in terms of the fragmenting of univocal Enlightenment rationality.[8]

It is worth noting that the venerable American Bible Society (ABS) has a project underway which implies at least a limited acceptance of the idea that North American culture is immersed in a significant shift to electronic media. The ABS is a group committed to translating and distributing the Bible; an organization approaching two hundred years old, the ABS has a history of taking excellent advantage of developing technology.[9] ABS currently has underway an expensive, experimental multimedia project that produces state-of-the-art hypermedia software for a PC platform with a video motion card and a laser disk. The ABS experiment is creating an integrated, interactive electronic rendering of sections of the Bible (e.g., the Gerasene Demoniac story in the fifth chapter of the Gospel of Mark). Some scholars associated with this project call their work a "functional equivalent" multimedia translation, one having the same legitimacy and scriptural authority as a traditional text translation in print (Boomershine 1993b, 179; Harley 1993, 176).[10]

Proscriptive Biblical Study and Its Psychodynamics

> A fissure runs through communities that take the Bible seriously, especially within American Protestantism. "Literalism" marks the divide between the two camps, the two spiritual regions, the two political forces. Listen to the two factions fighting for the spoils within a single denomination—as in the recent case of the Southern Baptist Convention or the Lutheran Church-Missouri Synod—and you will hear them fighting over biblical inerrancy and a literal approach to Scripture. As battle lines are drawn between the "evangelical" and the "mainline" churches, no concept is used more frequently as the divider than literalism, by whatever term it is called. (Marty 1994, 38)

For those who watch contemporary American religious institutions, historian Martin Marty[11] here sounds a familiar note. Marty makes clear that in fact the tensions between literal and nonliteral responses to the Bible play through American religious history in the eighteenth and nineteenth centuries. Nevertheless, the lines seem to be very sharply drawn at the end of twentieth century, just as American culture moves decisively into an era of electronic writing. As we move more deeply into this culture, perhaps we will be better able to understand biblical literalism and its connection with print. Even on the front edge of electronic culture, two dynamics of biblical literalism seem clear: Literalism is a naive but perhaps understandable response in the life-world of print, for it is an extension of a more general literal-mindedness that print nourishes. Also, biblical literalism in the twentieth century is a deeply conservative reaction. It is possibly grounded in fear before complexity in a world where texts have social contexts and remain ambiguous and social change is rapid. To explore these propositions, I turn again to Bolter.

Bolter's notion of "irreverent reading" is primarily linked to the approaches to contemporary literary critical theory which have undermined, in literary circles, notions of an established canon of great authors and what he terms "worshipful reading" (1991, 152). "Worshipful reading," he suggests, is a phenomenon linked to printing:

> Printing also fosters the ideal of a single canon of great authors, whose works should be distributed in thousands of identical copies to readers throughout the world. By its technique of mass production, printing has helped to make such texts available to every reader in a culture. At the same time, by ensuring that the reader cannot enter into the space that the text occupies, printing encouraged worshipful reading. (1991, 152)

Because printing standardizes and objectifies the written word, it helps create a certain sort of reader, namely, one whose response to the text may be quite naive. All readers in print culture always already tacitly assume a world in which texts are a normal feature used to function in the world; further, there is always already the assumption that many texts are identical (standardized editions) and the suggestion at least that a hierarchy of value can be established identifying the merit of particular texts in some life domain (e.g., the literary domain). No doubt, the fact that printed texts are quite tangible, material objects lends credence to the notion that texts can be compared and value can be determined in almost the way that differences and preferences can be noted for other objects affecting the senses. Standardized printed texts in print culture thus become, in a sense, self-evident artifacts that can never be fundamentally strange. Phenomenologically, it is fair to say that, at some level, printed texts are already meaningful to the properly socialized reader. For some readers—namely, those likely to be dubbed naive—printed texts are always already almost full of meaning. That is, printed texts for such readers are, in principle, transparent even when they are problematic, for problematic texts simply must be "decoded." Extreme literal-mindedness about textual meaning, biblical or literary, seems to be but a compounding

of the naiveté found in an orientation to the printed word concerned with
"decoding."[12]

In the domain of religion, if historical-critical and postcritical biblical
scholarship are "irreverent reading," Bolter's "worshipful reading" might
be linked to the partisans of "inerrancy" and all conservative reactions against
critical scholarship. Although worshipful reading, at least in its extreme literalist version, is (by historical-critical standards) naive, it often seems self-
consciously and committedly so; thus it might be regarded as a proscriptive
form of biblical study that has sprouted and prospered in the soil of print
culture. It is, in part, an outgrowth of the literal-mindedness that print fosters.
But also, particularly in Protestant circles, the Bible has been regarded as the
authoritative arbitrator of all religious concerns. Luther's *sola scriptura* (the
principle that turns all attention to the text to resolve religious controversy)[13]
in the North American context has produced a truly astonishing narrowness
of vision; the Bible has become, in some cultural enclaves, almost a fetish
object of veneration and a rallying point for resistance to all the forces compli-
cating modern life. Marty speculates that fear lies deep at the heart of biblical
literalism in America:

> No one will understand the hold of biblical literalism who cannot work
> her way into the mind of the fearful. What Lippmann called "the acids
> of modernity" do threaten people. Unsheltered, these people feel that
> they will be deprived of the authority they need in the face of relativism,
> the experience they crave in the face of scientism, the identity they
> would lose if they blended into the humanist, secular or, as they see it,
> moderate and liberal religious landscape. (1994, 42)

As Marty also suggests, close inspection of biblical literalist proclamations
reveals strikingly different literal meanings held by proponents of literal reading of the biblical text: "The idea of literalism turns out to be more important
than a consensus based on its yield" (1994, 43).

Literalism has appeal and plausibility for a variety of reasons. It becomes second nature in an environment of many printed texts merely to
assume that most (and, in principle, all) texts can be understood straightfor-
wardly. As a text, the Bible simply gets linked with most other printed texts
frequently encountered, many of which are, in fact, designed to be quite
transparent (e.g., newspapers, which must sell and advertise products for sale).
The presumed transparency of the Bible is also the result of assuming that
whatever is the revealed word of God should be directly accessible and available to all. Stanley Hauerwas is correct (see note 13, above) in pointing out
that, at least in Protestant America, the peculiar link between the Church and
the Bible functioning as the Church's scripture is not well understood. The

Bible is taken by many to be "free-standing" scripture, available to anyone interested, rather than a text which a community takes as its guide for common life.[14] Finally, in North America it is also sometimes a matter of resolve to retain a literalist approach to the Bible. Such resolve is a combination of personal piety, antiintellectualism and general reaction against all the debilitating forces of modernity which get politically focused around questions about the Bible in contemporary culture.

Bolter and scholars such as Richard Lanham persuasively show how print inevitably legitimizes a canon, while a culture that shifts to electronic writing/reading tools will just as certainly initiate forces that delegitimize a canon.[15] Of course, in one sense, the material included in the Bible had already been selected by the time the printing press was invented (i.e., canonization as a historical process had been largely completed much earlier). But certainly several centuries of printing has served to solidify and reify the biblical canon; a printed canon is one that emphasizes the distance between the human experience of the great mothers and fathers of the past and those experiences of the present.

The Bible has, for many modern literates, become what Bolter would term an "objectified writing space" (see quotation above), that is, one that excludes the reader and therefore elicits a curious sort of adulation. With the Bible, such adulation is magnified because the Bible in North American culture has always been a powerful symbol woven into our civic heritage. The reader is excluded in the sense that reader involvement and the tradition of texts and reading are matters about which the reader is not mindful. In book culture, the printed word is often presupposed to be an unmediated representation of what is. The Bible is thus taken to be clear, direct, and from God by the literalist worshipful reader, and to honor and more deeply understand the Bible requires only better quality attention.[16] Worshipful responses to the Bible, as they have emerged in modern discussions and political movements, usually omit any careful examination of the nature of modern literacy and the ways in which print has shaped human consciousness.[17] Worshipful responders in most of the twentieth century have rushed to work out theological rationales concerned with the Bible as inerrant, inspired, or as revelation.[18] Worshipful readers see no need to address in philosophical terms serious questions about signs and symbols and their function in human communities; they rarely work out a phenomenological description of "faith." In sum, worshipful literalist reading of the Bible is a child of modern print culture in very much the same way that modern mainline biblical scholarship is.[19]

Is worshipful reading of the Bible, like reading informed by historical-critical perspectives, to be transformed in the transition from book culture to a culture in which electronic reading and writing play a more dominant role? It seems that this is likely, although this transformation will probably be more subtle than the squabbles of self-aware scholars. The transformation will be one reflecting primarily the new tacit mental habits, discussed below, that are emerging in electronic culture.

Text, Authority, and the Bible in Electronic Culture

North American culture at the beginning of the twenty-first century will likely be an electronic culture featuring the kind of expansion described above of the broadcast media along with the emergence of integrated media and greater reliance on electronic writing and electronically accessed resources. In what ways are dispositions and habits of thought about human creation of and response to communicative artifacts going to shift in this environment? How will this shift likely be reflected in responses to the Bible? At least in part, these large questions can be explored by reflecting upon the roles and responses of message senders and message receivers in our present information age, an incunabula phase of a fuller electronic culture.

Contemporary culture is a communicative environment which inhabitants frequently experience as rapidly changing and very quickly developing and promulgating information. It is a domain of geometrically proliferating communication artifacts, an environment of excess in that it offers to overstimulate those who allow it to do so. Such an environment is a dynamic one in which inhabitants adopt reactive (protective) strategies and, at the same time, develop rhetorical styles designed to penetrate the reactive strategies of those with whom they desire to communicate. The word *information* and its soulmate *data* are rather neutral, technical terms that often have superseded the term *knowledge* as referents for our preserved cultural lore in the contemporary era. These terms also suggest our ambivalent attitude toward many of the symbolic artifacts produced in the late twentieth century. ''Information'' and ''data'' imply symbolic artifacts without mooring;[20] such uncontextualized material seemingly floats and accumulates and serves as a reservoir (largely untapped) for the individual inhabitants of electronic culture. Of course, human beings remain knowers in much the same fashion they have in earlier eras. To be a knower is a social endeavor that involves contextualizing such that one becomes an effective agent. A knower recognizes significant relationships among domains of information. Nevertheless, individuals in electronic culture perceive a certain distance between personal life and the larger environment; they sense a disconnectedness within the larger framework of expanding information. In part, this is to say no more than that the suppositions about reason and the edifice of knowledge developed in book culture seem to be collapsing. We have at least imagined that there were a finite number of appropriate classificatory schemes within which to locate ourselves and our experience; but now we seem to be relinquishing this hope for at least a map of maps. The world of information seems to have lost its human scale; its vastness leaves us unsteady even if we remain excited about its prospects.

In an environment of communicative excess, message senders adopt a rhetorical posture that exploits the medium and is preoccupied with the task of enhancing the visibility of the message. Bruce Gronbeck suggests that North American political discourse must now be understood in terms of "electronic rhetoric":

> The electronic revolution of the twentieth century, however, has done to political oratory what the great humanists could not accomplish: remold it into a different sort of discursive practice. Especially in the United States where 99 percent of the households have television and where computer technology has permeated all major economic-political institutions, we have witnessed the coming of electronic rhetoric, of forms of rhetorical political discourse adapted to technologically conditioned uses. (1990, 142)

Gronbeck shows that the image of gentrified politicians rationally debating issues is no longer an appropriate vision of American political discourse. The most obvious face of electronic rhetoric in politics is political ads on television. Such ads are carefully crafted, slick constructions designed by those who have used polling and computer analysis to assess target audiences. Provocative images and sound bites are the order of the day. Gronbeck suggests that in the environment of contemporary broadcast media, Americans are conditioned to absorb "condensed communications encounters" (1990, 148).

Rhetorical condensation seems to be present not only in broadcast media but also in other important media in an electronic culture. Even printed documents are structured to allow readers to absorb information very quickly. Provocative images, mnemonic devices, and all sorts of gimmicks are regularly used as components of books as well as audio and video tapes. Those who use e-mail quickly learn the prudence of "netiquette," which requires tagging memoranda with a subject line and limiting important messages to one screen of prose. In sum, condensation is an important way to make messages visible in an environment of excess.

However, it seems also to be the case that the multiplication of condensed messages in our culture makes people somewhat cynical about many communicative efforts available to them. In an environment of excess, messages themselves become commodities to be consumed or not consumed. Those with the option of responding to messages become very time-conscious figures. Time becomes a valuable commodity in its own right and must be managed. People become mindful about wasting time and using time wisely. People become rather self-conscious about devoting their attention. Not only is attention valuable: people further have a sense that their attention span is short but that it is possible (perhaps because of the predominance of rhetorical condensation) quickly to absorb what is important.

In an environment of excess, made both possible and more complicated by sophisticated technological tools, it may be the case that the general approach to knowledge changes. Joshua Meyrowitz suggests that

> our advanced technological stage allows us to hunt and gather information rather than food. Like hunters and gatherers who take for granted the abundance of food "out there" and therefore only hunt and gather enough to consume immediately, we are increasingly becoming a "subsistence information society." (1985, 317)

A "subsistence information society" is one in which, because there seems to be so much information and it seems so readily available, people thoroughly assimilate and self-consciously carry with them very little available information:

> Rather than engaging in long-term storage of knowledge in their memories or homes, many people are beginning to believe that information is available "out there" and that individuals do not need to stockpile it. Our children sing "we don't need no education," and even many scholars have begun to steer away from collecting and storing in their minds the long, linear arguments of literacy that linked new discoveries to old and that pointed to the future. Instead, the computer is increasingly used as an abundant jungle of bits and pieces of "data" (albeit, a jungle created and stocked by us). Some data are hunted, gathered, and analyzed when an appetite for correlations arises. The connections found are often consumed and digested immediately without being painstakingly linked to other knowledge and ideas. (1985, 317)

It is precisely this "appetite for correlations" that aptly characterizes a writer's or reader's habits of thought about communication in an environment in which the computer is the primary tool. Those who work with these tools come to consider text creation and use as acts of "making connections," although none are lasting. Connections are interesting but temporary.

It seems likely that electronic culture's emerging notion of literacy will focus on skills for manipulating electronic resources necessary to make such correlations. The late print-culture notion of literacy as individual expression and critical thinking, the ability to articulate informed judgments based on a global, internalized, coherent framework of knowledge, is being subtly reshaped.[21] Authoring now frequently means manipulating materials or mining resources available rather than creating out of nothing.[22]

Perhaps the image that best captures the urgency those in contemporary electronic culture feel shrewdly to steer their own lives among the communicative excess is the image of the television watcher deftly managing his or her fate with a remote control device. Unwanted messages are simply zapped with the controls. The exercise—termed variously "grazing," "channel surfing," or "channel hopping"—is one in which the depth of immersion in a broadcaster's selection is sacrificed for breadth of exposure to several available offerings. It seems likely that the rhetorical condensation which is central to television and other media promotes grazing. In essence, the channel surfer is taking over the responsibility of constructing what he wants to devote attention to. He is playing a more active role "reading" what the television has to offer than the conventional passive couch potato. It might be argued, as a final ironic twist, that commercial television is implicitly already an interactive medium, given the dreadful quality of programming which provokes channel surfing.

The notion that a message receiver actively constructs the text from communicative resources available turns attention again to the ideas discussed earlier about hypertext, hypermedia, and the character and potential of electronic writing. Those who use the computer as a writing environment in even the simplest sense as a word processor are aware of how easy it is, like the channel surfer, to construct a document by borrowing and reassembling parts of other documents. Those who exploit the resources available on the Internet also readily see the aptness of John Slatin's notion of text as a collectivity of texts; resources available through networking are resources available to be reconstituted in terms of the particular needs of the user/receiver. Particularly interesting material can be downloaded, edited, and combined with other interesting, useful material (if a "personal" copy is desired). Text production is a process of reweaving modules, a process that the reader often largely controls. These two rather simple and common experiences of using the computer as a tool for reading and writing hint at the direction in which electronic culture is moving.[23] It is clear that in a culture more deeply committed to electronic writing, a reader/user's active involvement in the process of text construction will come to be seen as quite acceptable and perhaps normative. The notion promoted by book culture—that message reception is largely passive and strictly distinct from active message construction—is eroding; it is a notion that the physical status of printed texts reinforced. Those who use the computer as a writing and reading environment are encouraged to see a text as a temporary selection of material from a larger body of available resources; the sense of a text as a final and inviolable whole was largely a by-product of earlier print technology. As Landow and Delaney put the matter,

> Particularly inapplicable are the notions of textual "completion" and of a "finished" product. Hypertext materials are by definition open-ended, expandable, and incomplete. (1990, 13)

Literate persons in electronic culture will eventually accept responsibility for the reader's active role in negotiating the electronic medium; concomitant with this acceptance of responsibility will come a sense of the fluidity of text. Notions of text as fluid or unstable will, in turn, more and more challenge the long-held notions of textual hierarchy which have operated in Western culture and especially in print culture. Canons fracture in electronic culture where the computer is a primary tool for reading and writing.[24] Bolter aptly describes the fate of canons in the culture that already is emerging in North America:

> In the world of electronic writing, there will be no texts that everyone must read. There will only be texts that more or fewer readers choose to examine in more or less detail. The idea of the great, inescapable book belongs to the age of print that is now passing. (1991, 240)

The status of great and inescapable books, even sacred texts like the Bible, depends in part on the physical discreteness and solidity of texts (which existed in print culture and its predecessors) as well as the self-perceptions as passive receptors (common in print culture) of those who use them. Richard Lanham, a scholar interested in rhetoric, insightfully shows how notions of canon, a noninteractive view of writing, and a largely Cartesian metaphysical scheme for conceiving text and reader are bound up together:

> The traditional idea of an artistic canon brings with it, by the very "immortality" it strives for, both a passive beholder and a passive reality waiting out there to be perceived, the best that has been thought, said, or painted perhaps, but unchangeable in its perfection, a goddess we can adore but never ask out to play. (1993, 38)

Lanham recognizes that reading and writing in the electronic medium not only make text malleable, but in doing so it also changes the tacit attitudes toward texts of readers and writers, making them much more flexible: "The intrinsic motival structure of electronic text is as comic as print is serious" (1993, 38). The ludic mode invited by the electronic medium for writing and reading may itself contribute to the undermining of schemes of textual hierarchy.

The destabilizing of canons which ensues in the interactive electronic medium does not imply that electronic readers and writers somehow fail to be appreciative. Perhaps it is best to view this change as a democratization (see Fowler 1994, 7); in part, canons always mask exclusions, but the electronic writing medium does not offer very effective ways, as did print and manuscript culture, to enforce such choices. Fowler suggests that, although the electronic medium for writing does decenter, it is best to view this as an opportunity rather than a threat; centers or canons are necessary, and what the electronic medium does is remind readers/writers that persons and the politics of community are involved in establishing canons and that the process of recentering is and should be ongoing:

> Nonetheless, centers are crucial; humans cannot live for long without a center. The danger, perhaps, is the *fixed and permanent* center, *imposed tyrannically.* Hypertext, however, offers the possibility of a shifting center, a "multicentered" or "infinitely recenterable" textual universe, with the center to be determined by an empowered, liberated reader. Centers come and go; the act of establishing a center, however, is an ongoing necessity, to be repeated again and again. (Fowler 1994, 6–7)

Certainly, readers and writers using the electronic medium do recognize and articulate particular values about particular texts; but a medium that merges reading and writing, making the user primarily responsible for text (i.e., an interactive medium), is a medium in which the dynamics of interpretative communities cannot work as they did in manuscript and print culture.

Not only are our images of reading and text recast in the electronic medium, but writing also will acquire new associations. At the risk of caricaturing the ethos of earlier book culture, we can now see that visible linguistic signs have had a shocking priority in cultural expression and especially in the scholarly world. Speaking of the era of print, Richard Lanham offers the following satirical jab at the narrowness of our print culture's vision:

> In a literate culture our conception of meaning itself—whether of logical argument or magical narrative—depends on this radical act of typographical simplification. No pictures; no color; strict order of left to right then down one line; no type changes; no interaction; no revision. (1993, 33–34)

Lanham suggests that integrated media brings with it a fundamental reorientation of the sensorium:

Concomitantly with the explosion of the authoritative text, electronic writing begins a complete renegotiation of the alphabet/icon ratio upon which print-based thought is built. We can detect this foregrounding of images over written words most clearly in the world of business and government communications, but it is happening everywhere. When the rich vocal and gestural language of oral rhetoric was constricted into writing and then print, the effort to preserve it was concentrated into something classical rhetoricians called *ecphrasis,* dynamic speaking-pictures in words. Through the infinite resources of digital image recall and manipulation, *ecphrasis* is once again coming into its own, and the pictures and sounds suppressed into verbal rhetorical figures are now reassuming their native places in the human sensorium. (1993, 34)

In an era of digitization, we are now beginning to understand that you can "write" with anything that can be digitized. Linguistic signs no longer have priority in communication. You can now "write" by stringing together pro-vocative images, audio, and conventional written language. Each of these venues may have its special grammar and rhetoric, but now hybrid grammars and rhetorics are imaginable. Of course, you cannot necessarily spin out syllogisms in audio or video or a mixture. But you can make or design unfolding meaning.[25] It is this broader sense of "writing" possible in the era of integrated media that leads some biblical scholars working on the American Bible Society's multimedia experiment to use descriptors such as "functional equivalent" multimedia translation (Boomershine 1993b, 179; Harley 1993, 176) for their work. As the ABS experiment shows, a persuasive strategy which integrates different media is possible, and it is this sort of integration that the future in electronic culture likely will explore more and more.

This essay began with Wilfred Cantwell Smith's prescient comment some twenty years ago that the age of the very special book is fundamentally changed in an era of communicative abundance. In ways that Smith did not anticipate, the sheer bulk of information generated in the computer age has fostered protective, reactive postures in the citizens of electronic culture. We may be moving into a "hunter and gatherer" approach to knowledge in the information age. Perhaps more important than the communicative excess of the computer age is the fact that the electronic medium as a tool for reading and writing is slowly shifting our tacit notion of text from a stable, discrete body to a fluid network format. There are no permanent borders or boundaries for electronic materials, at least as such boundaries exist to set off one hard copy from another.[26] In the same way, there are no final distinctions between reading and writing in the electronic world; reading often involves authoring in the sense of constructing what is of interest; reading invites writing in the electronic medium in a way that it did not in print. The Romantic image of the author as inspired genius is not much reinforced in the context of electronic writing. The solemnity of print culture is also challenged by the fundamental playfulness of the electronic medium. It is quite difficult in a fluid electronic environment to conceive of texts in terms of lasting textual hierarchies. Canons fracture in the electronic writing medium, but this may serve to make us mindful of the political process of canonization in interpretative communities. Finally, it is worth noting that the electronic medium, in a digitized world, is a communicative locus in which sound, sight, and sign come together. Writing is apt to become an endeavor not so dominantly aniconic as in the era of the book.

Surely all of these changes will be felt in some ways in the common responses to biblical literature. It is not possible at this incunabula phase of the era of electronic reading and writing to chart out the course of such responses with any precision. Religious institutions certainly will continue to cultivate interest in sacred texts, but the tacit mental habits of participants will be different from those that earlier book culture fostered. Textual communities will come under new pressures, but pressures themselves are not new, nor are they necessarily a bad thing. Religious communities will have to be more aware than they were in earlier eras of the dynamic social process through which a text becomes and continues to be scripture. In an era of electronic reading and writing, the biblical canon may not stand apart so prominently (as it does at least in Protestant circles) from other literature, whether ancient or modern. It seems likely that in an era of integrated media, a more iconic sensibility may flourish even in text-shaped communities. Finally, it seems likely that more interpretative diversity in religious communities will be acceptable (or at least more visible) since the objectifying influence of print is already being mitigated.

Notes

1. Smith's very recently published book, *What Is Scripture?*, follows up and greatly extends the discussion of issues he touches on in his 1971 article. His book is certainly a substantial contribution to scholarship about the cross-cultural study of scriptures. What is surprising about *What Is Scripture?* is that there is no treatment of any of the matters concerned with scripture and electronic media. Smith does seem to recognize that contemporary culture is in a situation strikingly different than most earlier cultures influenced by traditions of sacred literature, but he does not link questions about sacred text and the particular tools or technology operative in a culture. Smith senses a certain potential for shallowness that modern secular culture has:

With the lack of a common scripture or of something counterpart to play its role, modern secular culture is in danger of finding itself without a shared vocabulary to enable it corporately to live well, or even to talk and think about doing so, or its members to encourage each other to aim so. (1993, 239)

2. See the essays by Andersson (1986), Jouhaud (1987), Cole (1972), and Wall (1986), as well as Graff's comments (1987, 108–173), for illuminating discussions of the role of the press in the Reformation.

3. Frerichs (1988) begins his introduction thus: "The Bible in America, judged by typical American success criteria, is assured of a prize. Viewed variously as a monument, an icon, a living presence, the Bible has continued to inspire and inform American life" (1).

In the same volume, see also John Alden's interesting historical reflections on the production and dissemination of English Bibles in the United States (Alden 1988).

4. There, of course, has been much written about broadcast media and its impact on society, as well as the way the "electronic church" works. I agree with scholars such as Richard Lanham who, in *The Electronic Word,* suggests that McLuhan to some degree mesmerized cultural analysts and this led to great interest in television but that, in fact, the computer as a reading/writing tool may be a more important force shaping culture:

> We have been preoccupied, ever since Marshall McLuhan made "media" a household word, with the much sexier world of broadcast television. It was TV that was creating the global village full of couch potatoes with minds to match. It was TV that dramatized politics. It was TV that created a special channel to reenact rhapsodic sexual foreplay on a round-the-clock basis. Thus bemused, we failed to notice that the personal computer had presented itself as an alternative to the printed book and the electronic screen as an alternative to the printed page. Furthermore, in the last three or four years, that alternative page has been enhanced so that it can present and manipulate images and sounds almost as easily as words. (1993, ix-x)

Lanham's final note here certainly understates the direction in which North American culture is headed; as I discuss below, the computer is the vehicle that is being touted for producing an integrated, interactive media. Soon broadcast media will not be regarded as a subject separate and distinct from discussion about computers as tools for reading, writing, and preserving information.

5. This essay focuses primarily on contrasting print culture with electronic culture; it is important to appreciate change and difference. It is also important, however, to see the continuity between print and electronic culture. Some hypertext "prophets" such as Ted Nelson overdraw the contrast between print and electronic writing (see, for example, Nelson 1992).

6. Heim insightfully comments on "the artificial information jungle" (1993, 104) that is spreading over the world: "The electronic world, unlike the traditional book industry, does not protect its readers or travelers by following rules that set up certain expectations. Already, in the electronic element, the need for stable channels of content and reliable processes of choice grows urgent" (104). And a bit later, he

observes that "cyberspace without carefully laid channels of choice may become a waste of space" (105). [See also John Lawrence in this volume.—Ed.]

7. Stanley Hauerwas, drawing on the work of other scholars, puts the matter thus for biblical scholars:

Most scholars trained in biblical criticism still seek to recover the "original" historical context of the text, the original intention of the author, and they regard the exegetical tradition prior to the development of historical criticism as an obstacle to proper understanding of the true meaning of the text. (1993, 34)

8. In the last section below, I make some suggestions about the ways in which the nature of knowledge is being reconceived in electronic culture.

9. ABS is very much an organizational outgrowth of committed Christianity and the commitments of book culture. So far as I can discover, Richard M. Harley (1993, 159–178) has published the only available official description and discussion of the ABS multimedia project that I briefly discuss here and below; Tom Boomershine and Gregor Goethals provide interesting responses to Harley. Boomershine (1993b, 179–184) outlines the history of the ABS, its scholarly commitments and its long-standing interest in biblical translations, and the challenge of a multimedia project. Goethals is an artist and scholar with interests in art history and contemporary media. Her recent book, *The Electronic Golden Calf* (1990), shows how religious authorities in earlier periods in Western culture used the visual arts to represent social realities and religious vision; she explores the ways in which, in contemporary American popular culture, electronic images have preempted the traditional role of art. Goethals's response (1993, 185–191) to Harley and the ABS project draws on her earlier scholarship and is a very thought-provoking reaction, pointing out both difficulties and the potential of the ABS multimedia venture.

10. This subsection is no more than a brief comment on the evolving course of biblical scholarship, showing that this course is intertwined with the evolution of book culture and the emerging culture shaped by electronic media. Boomershine (1993a, 209–230) does something similar. Although I several times refer to Boomershine's work, I have many questions about the prospects for multimedia "translations" of the Bible. At the 1993 Society for Biblical Literature annual meeting (Mullins 1993), I presented an initial response to the ABS pilot hypermedia software "Out of the Tombs" (on the Gerasene Demoniac material). Boomershine and others affiliated with the ABS Bible and electronic media experiments are committed to the historical-critical presuppositions of book culture, presuppositions which may not, in fact, survive (at least in their present form) in the new electronic world of integrated, interactive media. What has been written about the ABS Bible and electronic-media project does not imply that ABS has done much exploration of the ways in which the electronic writing medium is reshaping the tacit commitments of those in the culture. ABS seems to conceive its multimedia translation largely in terms of the problems of a culture saturated with electronic broadcast media; that is, the project has a very McLuhanesque ambience but is not informed by much of the growing post-McLuhan literature on electronic culture which focuses on the computer as a communications tool.

11. Recently, there has been a resurgence of interest in "fundamentalism" among scholars in religious studies. This includes not only Christian "fundamentalism" but also certain movements in Judaism, Islam, and Hinduism. Marty is perhaps the best known scholarly figure at the helm of The Fundamentalism Project, a major scholarly study focused on these movements.

12. For suggestive reflections on the seemingly inevitable literal-mindedness that socialization in print culture creates, see Sam Gill's discussion of the problems that literate interpreters of nonliterate native American religious cultures often confront (1982, 39–58). Living in a print culture produces literal-mindedness to a degree, but, as I suggest below, the sort of ideological biblical literalism found particularly in some contemporary Protestant circles seems to be an exaggerated and self-conscious form of literal-mindedness. Nonetheless, such an orientation could have taken the shape it has only in print culture.

13. Stanley Hauerwas (on whose recent work I comment below) contends that *sola scriptura* is conjoined with other tacitly held principles in print-rich America (where Bibles are everywhere) and that this alliance functions in both fundamentalism and biblical scholarship to withdraw from the church the project of interpreting the Bible:

> Indeed literalist-fundamentalism and the critical approaches to the Bible are but two sides of the same coin, insofar as each assumes that the text should be accessible to anyone without the necessary mediation by the Church. The reformation doctrine of *sola scriptura,* joined to the invention of the printing press and underwritten by the democratic trust in the intelligence of the "common person," has created the situation that now makes people believe that they can read the Bible "on their own." That presumption must be challenged, and that is why the Scripture should be taken away from Christians in North America. (Hauerwas 1993, 17)

Luther's famous principle, according to Hauerwas, invited a distinction between text and interpretation which becomes a foundation assumption in both critical scholarship and fundamentalism:

> When *sola scriptura* is used to underwrite the distinction between text and interpretation, then it seems clear to me that *sola scriptura* is a heresy rather than a help in the Church. When this distinction persists, *sola scriptura* becomes the seedbed of fundamentalism, as well as biblical criticism. It assumes that the text of the Scripture makes sense separate from a Church that gives it sense. (1993, 27)

14. See note 13, above, as well as further comments on Hauerwas's perspective below.

15. Lanham, like Bolter, is attuned to debates in literary circles and in academic culture; he is not particularly aware of or interested in discussions about the Bible. The following comment succinctly summarizes the cultural impact of using computers

as a major writing/reading tool as the "volitizing" of text. Lanham offers a nascent cultural epoch theory placing contemporary discussions about the literary canon in a broader context:

> To volatilize text is to abolish the fixed "edition" of the great work and so the authority of the great work itself. Such volatility questions the whole conception of textual authority built up since the Renaissance scholars resurrected Alexandrian textual editing. The "Great Books" view of Western culture that depends on these great fixed texts thus becomes imperiled. Not only does electronic text dissociate cultural greatness from the codex book form but, as we shall see, it threatens a reappraisal of that greatness. (1993, xi)

I discuss the matter of electronic text and canon further below.

16. This is a point that seems to distinguish truly precritical (i.e., readers living before printed materials saturated the culture) biblical interpreters from the literalist worshipful readers in late print culture. Precritical Bible readers such as Augustine are not literalists in the modern sense of the term. Such figures fervently seem to hold that the biblical text is true, but they do not hold it is simply and transparently so. Augustine has this to say about difficult figurative passages:

> Therefore in the consideration of figurative expressions a rule such as this will serve, that what is read should be subjected to diligent scrutiny until an interpretation contributing to the reign of charity is produced. (1968, XV)

This is hardly literalism.

17. Walter Ong, in works like *Orality and Literacy* (1988), has done much to show the ways in which writing and print shape consciousness. Ong's work plays off the contrast between primary orality and literacy. A more nuanced set of contrasts would be helpful. In his introduction to a book on computers and literacy which he edited, Myron Tuman argues that literacy itself has meant quite different things in different periods in America:

> In preindustrial America (and in most of the preindustrial world even today), reading was defined largely in terms of the ability to recite socially important (often religious or nationalist) texts; and writing, when it was taught at all, was defined in terms of the ability to transcribe texts (hence the emphasis on penmanship and spelling). It is only with the great tide of industrialism that the now-pervasive definitions of reading and writing as the abilities to comprehend and to create new material was established. At the heart of this new model is the ability of readers to arrive at—and writers, in turn, to express—a new understanding based solely on the silent, solitary contemplation of written language. . . . Even more important than process in the modern model of literacy is the crucial role afforded the notion of ever higher (or deeper) levels of understanding, an understanding most often defined by the adjective *critical*. (1992, 6)

What I am describing as a worshipful literalist reading of the Bible in some ways correlates nicely with Tuman's preindustrial sense of literacy.

18. Modern literalists are not, of course, the only ones who have taken an interest in "revelation" and the status of the Bible. From the earliest period in which a text began to function to represent tradition and guide the evolution of community ideology and practice, Christian theologians have been challenged to work out a rationale for the Bible's authoritative role. Modern literalists, however, often seem to use theological rationales to avoid addressing the complexity of an ancient text. But it is also true that modern theologians who accept the historical-critical approach to the Bible have sought clarity about the status of the Bible. Historical and cross-cultural studies in the nineteenth and twentieth centuries have often pressed such questions about the status of the Bible upon them. H. R. Niebuhr, for example, is an interesting twentieth-century figure wrestling with the problems of historical relativism in *The Meaning of Revelation* (1941).

19. Stanley Hauerwas's recent book *Unleashing the Scripture* (1993) comes to conclusions somewhat similar to those reached here. Hauerwas is not, however, interested in changes in media, but is a steadfast critic of the Enlightenment. Enlightenment bashing is in great fashion these days; we may come, as we move more deeply into electronic culture, eventually to take a kinder view. Hauerwas is too ready to blame modern problems on the Enlightenment's emphasis on reason. I suspect that a more careful account of the roots of modern attitudes toward the Bible would need to consider not only the Enlightenment but also changing attitudes toward history in the Renaissance and nineteenth-century scholarship shaped also by Romantic thought. Hauerwas suggests that historical-critical scholarship and fundamentalist Bible-reading practices both represent Enlightenment visions of rationality that privilege particular interpretations:

> Fundamentalists and biblical critics alike fail to acknowledge the political char-
> acter of their account of the Bible, and they fail to do so for very similar
> reasons. They want to disguise how their "interpretations" underwrite the
> privileges of the constituency that they serve. Admittedly, such realities may
> also be hidden from themselves, convinced as they are of the "objectivity" of
> their method. Accordingly, fundamentalism and biblical criticism are Enlighten-
> ment ideologies in the service of the fictive agent of the Enlightenment—
> namely, the rational individual—who believes that truth in general (and particu-
> larly the truth of the Christian faith) can be known without initiation into the
> community that requires transformation of the self. (1993, 35)

Hauerwas, of course, wants to relocate the project of interpreting scripture in the church; his agenda is, in fact, very similar to and sympathetic with the Roman Catholic process of using scripture in the life of the Church. Hauerwas's bitter but insightful claims against both biblical literalists and historical-critical scholars nicely comple-ment some of the insights of Boomershine (see quotations above), who laments the fact that historical-critical scholarship seems to have impoverished the church:

By privileging the individual interpreter, who is thought capable of discerning the meaning of the text apart from the consideration of the good ends of a community, fundamentalists and biblical critics make the Church incidental. (Hauerwas 1993, 25–26)

20. John Slatin (1990, 156), drawing on Gregory Bateson and Christopher Dede, suggests several ways to think about the connection between data and knowledge. [Cf. as well O'Leary and Brasher's discussion of knowledge and wisdom, in this volume.—Ed.]

21. See Tuman's interesting discussion of the changing meaning of literacy (1992, 3–8). In the era of electronic writing, North America has almost completely lost what Tuman characterizes as preindustrial notions of reading and writing as the ability to recite and transcribe socially significant texts (1992, 6). Critical literacy already has undermined this earlier notion of literacy, but the information explosion, the fluidity of electronic text, and tricks like scanning text now make preindustrial notions appear merely quaint. Tuman is correct in his conclusion that "how the new postindustrial technology (and computers in particular) will affect our practice and our understanding of literacy" (1992, 8) is the most significant question in literacy education today. Bolter puts this matter in a way that perhaps better speaks to the tendencies of scholars (those living today are all the children of book culture): "This shift from print to the computer does not mean the end of literacy. What will be lost is not literacy itself, but the literacy of print, for electronic technology offers us a new kind of book and new ways to write and read" (1991, 2). [Cf. David Kolb in this volume.-Ed.]

22. As John Slatin shows, the emerging notion of writing in electronic culture is not necessarily less complex than that which dominated in late print culture:

"Writing," in the hypertext environment, becomes the more comprehensive activity called "authoring." Authoring may involve not only the composition of text, but also screen layout and other things that fall under the general rubric of interface design; it may also involve a certain amount of programming (as in Apple's HyperCard, where complex navigational and other processes are scripted by the stack's author). Perhaps more importantly, authoring involves the creation and management of links between nodes. (1990, 160)

The last suggestion here is perhaps the most significant. Exploring the rhetoric of hypertext and hypermedia is an extraordinarily complicated and significant new area. Slatin (1990) is working in this area from a more literary perspective. Gronbeck (1990) is interested in "electronic rhetoric" in terms of broadcast media and political culture. Richard Lanham, as I note below, is interested in electronic rhetoric as a rebirth of the iconic:

Through the infinite resources of digital-image recall and manipulation, *ecphrasis* is once again coming into its own, and the pictures and sounds suppressed into verbal rhetorical figures are now reassuming their native places in the human sensorium. The complex icon/word interaction of oral rhetoric is returning, albeit *per ambages.* (1992, 225; see also the revised and expanded version of this essay in Lanham 1993, 29–52)

Electronic or digital rhetoric will undoubtedly have important bearing on the way in which those who use a sacred text like the Bible respond to it. We know that the rhetoric of print (determined by the physical character of printed documents) is tacitly internalized by readers, and, therefore, in print culture, reading is assumed to be a sequential and continuous process. There are beginnings, middles, and ends, and reading materials are organized to take readers along a path to a conclusion. An electronic rhetoric is not so sensitive about beginnings, middles, and ends; furthermore, it "jumps" from idea to idea and may introduce the aural and visual. The American Bible Society "multimedia translation" of the Mark 5 story of Jesus healing the Gerasene Demoniac (discussed above) is thus an interesting experiment in digital rhetoric.

23. A third example which is only slightly less rare in the present developmental stage of electronic culture is the type of experimental, electronically accessed "prose" (i.e., it is not just prose) fiction called "interactive fiction," which Bolter discusses (1991, 121–47). Eastgate Systems, Inc. (134 Main Street, Watertown, MA 02172, (800) 562–1638), now offers a whole line of such fictions. Readers are jolted into awareness of what it means for the reader to construct the text with such fiction. In this type of fiction, the reader's choices are what determines the unfolding plot.

24. Major theorists speculating about the character of a culture that uses the computer as a major reading/writing tool seem to agree on this point. For a succinct statement of the case which synthesizes work of several theorists, see Fowler 1994.

25. Actually, with the advent of digitization, Western culture is only rediscovering this larger sense of "writing" which was an important part of the tradition before printing. The work of scholars who study illuminated manuscripts richly documents this "writing." Robert Calkins's criticism of the narrowness of much of art historical scholarship nicely suggests the dynamism of the medieval book:

Art Historians tend to examine miniatures as paintings—as isolated images to be arranged like photographs or excised folios in a row in order to demonstrate stylistic affinities and development, or like canvasses hung on a museum wall to be contemplated in isolation in their own right. Only passing attention is paid to their context in the book or their relation to the text they illustrate; and almost none to their placement on the page and their relation to such secondary decorations as may accompany them such as decorative borders, and to the sequence in which they reveal themselves as one turns the page. In its proper environment—as part of a book—an illuminated page is rarely seen one at a time, for it usually is seen in conjunction with its facing folio. That is the way a book presents itself to the viewer, and frequently the designers of a book took this presentation into account. . . . [A] medieval book is not a static object as one sees it in exhibition cases, presenting only two folios at a time to the viewer. It possesses a fourth dimension, for it requires a sequential experience, like music through which one must circulate to fully receive successive impressions of the relationship of its exterior volumes and interior spaces. As the context of the text reveals itself through time, building the narrative by word, sentence, and paragraph, so time is a factor in turning the pages so that the layout of the page and the sequence of illustrations and decorations of the divisions unfold *ad seriatim.* (1984, 16)

See also Calkins's more general treatment of illuminated books (1983), as well as his detailed discussions of particular manuscripts (e.g., 1986), for insight about the construction of what we are now beginning, in the age of digitization, to term "integrated" media.

26. Landow and Delaney comment on this characteristic in an interesting way that shows its double edge: "Since it weakens the boundaries of the text, nonsequential reading can be thought of as either correcting the artificial isolation of the text from its contexts or as violating one of the chief qualities of the book" (1990, 12).

References

Alden, John. 1988. The Bible as Printed Word. In *The Bible and Bibles in America,* ed. Ernest S. Frerichs, 9–28. Atlanta: Scholars Press.

Andersson, Christiane. 1986. Popular Imagery in German Reformation Broadsheets. In *Print and Culture in the Renaissance: Essays on the Advent of Printing in Europe,* ed. Gerald P. Tyson and Sylvia S. Wagonheim, 120–50. Newark, NJ: Associated University Presses.

Augustine. 1968. *On Christian Doctrine.* Trans. D. W. Robertson, Jr. Indianapolis: Library of Liberal Arts.

Bolter, Jay David. 1991. *Writing Space: The Computer, Hypertext, and the History of Writing.* Hillsdale, NJ: Lawrence Erlbaum.

Boomershine, Thomas E. 1993a. Biblical Megatrends: Towards a Paradigm for the Interpretation of the Bible in Electronic Media. In *The Bible in the Twenty-First Century,* ed. H. C. Kee, 209–30. Philadelphia: Trinity Press.

———. 1993b. Response. In *The Bible in the Twenty-First Century,* ed. H. C. Kee, 179–84. Philadelphia: Trinity Press.

Calkins, Robert G. 1983. *Illuminated Books of the Middle Ages.* Ithaca, NY: Cornell University Press.

———. 1984. *Programs of Medieval Illumination* (The Franklin D. Murphy Lectures V: ISBN 0–913689–12–2). Lawrence: University of Kansas, Spenser Museum of Art.

————. 1986. Liturgical Sequence and the Decorative Crescendo in the Brogo Sacramentary. *Gesta* 25(1): 17–23.

Cole, Richard G. 1972. The Dynamics of Printing in the Sixteenth Century. In *The Social History of the Reformation,* ed. Lawrence P. Buck and Jonathan W. Zophy, 93–221. Columbus, OH: Ohio State University Press.

Conklin, Jeff. 1987. Hypertext: An Introduction and Survey. *Computer* 20(9): 17–41.

Cornell, George, W. 1986. Religious Books Show a Gain in the Market. *St. Joseph News-Press/Gazette,* 27 December.

Fowler, Robert M. 1994. The Fate of the Notion of Canon in the Electronic Age. Paper presented at the Spring 1994 meeting of the Westar Institute, Sonoma, CA. [Electronic document available from rfowler@rs6000.baldwinw.edu].

Frerichs, Ernest S. 1988. Introduction to *The Bible and Bibles in America,* ed. Ernest S. Frerichs, 1–8. Atlanta: Scholars Press.

Gill, Sam. 1982. *Native American Religions: An Introduction.* Belmont, CA.: Wadsworth.

Goethals, Gregor. 1990. *The Electronic Golden Calf: Images, Religion, and the Making of Meaning.* Cambridge: Cowley.

————. 1993. Response. In *The Bible in the Twenty-First Century,* ed. H. C. Kee, 184–91. Philadelphia. Trinity Press.

Graff, Harvey J. 1987. *The Legacies of Literacy: Continuities and Contradictions in Western Culture and Society.* Bloomington, IN: Indiana University Press.

Graham, William A. 1989. Scripture as Spoken Word. In *Rethinking Scripture: Essays from a Comparative Perspective,* ed. Miriam Levering, 129–69. Albany, NY: SUNY Press.

Gronbeck, B. E. 1990. Electric Rhetoric: The Changing Forms of American Political Discourse. *Vichiana* 3(1): 141–61.

Harley, Richard M. 1993. New Media for Communicating the Bible: The Potential and the Problems. In *The Bible in the Twenty-First Century,* ed. H. C. Kee, 161–78. Philadelphia: Trinity Press.

Hauerwas, Stanley. 1993. *Unleashing the Scripture: Freeing the Bible from Captivity to America.* Nashville: Abingdon Press.

Havelock, Eric. 1963. *Preface to Plato.* Cambridge: Harvard University Press.

————. 1982. *The Literate Revolution in Greece and Its Cultural Consequences.* Princeton: Princeton University Press.

————. 1986. *The Muse Learns to Write.* New Haven: Yale University Press.

Heim, Michael. 1993. *The Metaphysics of Virtual Reality.* New York: Oxford University Press.

Jonassen, David H. 1989. *Hypertext/Hypermedia.* Englewood Cliffs, NJ: Education Technology Publications.

Jouhaud, Christian. 1987. Readability and Persuasion: Political Handbills. In *The Culture of Print: Power and the Uses of Print in Early Modern Europe,* ed. Roger Chartier, 235–60. Trans. Lydia G. Cochrane. Princeton: Princeton University Press.

Kee, Howard Clark, ed. 1993. *The Bible in the Twenty-First Century.* Philadelphia: Trinity Press.

Ladd, Everett. 1986. Secular and Religious America. In *Unsecular America,* ed. Richard John Neuhaus, 14–30. Grand Rapids, MI: Eerdmans.

Landow, George P., and Paul Delany. 1990. Hypertext, Hypermedia and Literary Studies: The State of the Art. In *Hypermedia and Literary Studies,* ed. Paul Delany and George P. Landow, 2–50. Cambridge: MIT Press.

Lanham, Richard A. 1992. Digital Rhetoric: Theory, Practice, and Property. In *Literacy Online: The Promise (and Peril) of Reading and Writing with Computers,* ed. Myron C. Tuman, 221–44. Pittsburgh: University of Pittsburgh Press.

———. 1993. *The Electronic Word: Democracy, Technology, and the Arts.* Chicago: University of Chicago Press.

Marty, Martin E. 1994. Literalism vs. Everything Else: A Continuing Conflict. *Bible Review* 10.2 (April): 38–43, 50.

Meyrowitz, Joshua. 1985. *No Sense of Place: The Impact of Electronic Media on Social Behavior.* New York: Oxford University Press.

Moulthrop, Stuart. 1989. Hypertext and "the Hyperreal." In *Hypertext 89 Proceedings,* 259–67. New York: Association for Computing Machinery.

Mullins, Phil. 1988. The Fluid Word: Word Processing and Its Mental Habits. *Thought* 63(251): 413–28.

———. 1990. Sacred Text in an Electronic Era. *Biblical Theology Bulletin* 20(3): 99–106.

———. 1993. Multimedia as a Theoretical Tool. Paper presented at the annual meeting of the Society for Biblical Literature, 23 November, Washington DC. [Electronic document available from mullins@griffon.mwsc.edu].

Nelson, Theodor Holm. 1992. Opening Hypertext: A Memoir. In *Literacy Online: The Promise (and Peril) of Reading and Writing with Computers,* ed. Myron C. Tuman, 43–57. Pittsburgh: University of Pittsburgh Press.

Niebuhr, H. Richard. 1941. *The Meaning of Revelation.* New York: Macmillan.

Ong, Walter J. 1977. *Interfaces of the Word: Studies in the Evolution of Consciousness and Culture.* Ithaca, NY: Cornell University Press.

———. 1988. *Orality and Literacy: The Technologizing of the Word.* London: Routledge.

Postman, Neil. 1985. *Amusing Ourselves to Death: Public Discourse in the Age of Show Business.* New York: Viking Penguin.

Shneiderman, Ben, and Greg Kearsley. 1989. *Hypertext—Hands On!: An Introduction to a New Way of Organizing and Accessing Information.* New York: Addison-Wesley.

Slatin, John M. 1988. Hypertext and the Teaching of Writing. In *Text, Context and Hypertext: Writing with and for the Computer,* ed. Edward Barrett, 111–29. Cambridge: MIT Press.

———. 1990. Reading Hypertext: Order and Coherence in a New Medium. In *Hypermedia and Literary Studies,* ed. Paul Delany and George P. Landow, 153–69. Cambridge: MIT Press.

Smith, Wilfred Cantwell. 1971. The Study of Religion and the Study of the Bible. *Journal of the American Academy of Religion* 39: 131–40.

———. 1993. *What Is Scripture?* Minneapolis: Fortress Press.

Thorp, E. David. 1991. In Video Veritas: The Mythic Structures of Video Dynamics. In *Video Icons and Values,* ed. Alan M. Olson, Christopher Parr, and Debra Parr, 97–108. Albany, NY: SUNY Press.

Trithemius, Johannes. 1974. *De Laude Scriptorum.* Edited with an introduction by Klaus Arnond. Trans. Roland Behrendt. Lawrence, KS: Coronado Press.

Tuman, Myron C. 1992. First Thoughts. In *Literacy Online: The Promise (and Peril) of Reading and Writing with Computers,* ed. Myron C. Tuman, 3–15. Pittsburgh: University of Pittsburgh Press.

Wall, John N. Jr. 1986. The Reformation in England and the Typographic Revolution: "By this printing . . . the doctrine of the Gospel soundeth to all nations." In *Print and Culture in the Renaissance: Essays on the Advent of Printing in Europe,* ed. Gerald P. Tyson and Sylvia S. Wagonheim, 208–21. Newark, NJ: Associated University Presses.

Waters, Harry F., with Lucille Beachy. 1993. Next Year, 500 Channels: Can the Global Village Survive TV for Every Taste? *Newsweek,* 1 March, 75–76.

White, Gayle W. 1993. Publication of the Bible Goes Forth and Multiplies Versions Targeted at Specific Groups Helps Push Sales above $400 Million. *Atlanta Constitution,* 15 July, F1.

CONTRIBUTORS

Carol J. Adams's recent publications include *Woman-Battering* (Fortress Press) and *Neither Man nor Beast: Feminism and the Defense of Animals* (Continuum). She edited *Ecofeminism and the Sacred* (Continuum), and has also written for *Ms., The Christian Century, The Utne Reader,* and *The Women's Review of Books.*

Brenda E. Brasher is Assistant Professor of Religion at Thiel College (Greenville, Pennsylvania). Her most recent publications include *Reinventing Protestantism* (co-authored with Donald E. Miller) and "Life in Multiple Worlds: An Archeology of a UCC Congregation Alive and Well in the Modern/Postmodern Divide," in *Religious Communities in Changing Times,* edited by Arthur Farnsely.

Donald Cunningham (Indiana University) has just completed a two-year appointment as Professor and Head of the Department of Learning, Development and Communication, University of New England, Australia. His recent journal publications focus on hypertext and semiotics in education.

Peter Danielson is Associate Professor of Philosophy and Senior Research Fellow at the Centre for Applied Ethics, University of British Columbia. He is the author of *Artificial Morality: Virtuous Robots for Virtual Games* (Routledge) and the editor of *Mcdeling Rational and Moral Agents* (Oxford University Press). He is a co-investigator in the Canadian Applied Ethics Research Networks project.

Dag Elgesem is Director of the National Committee for Research on Ethics in the Social Sciences and the Humanities, Norway. He has worked and published in the area of philosophical logic. His current research deals with informational privacy as a moral and a legal right.

Charles Ess is Professor of Philosophy and Religion, Drury College (Springfield, Missouri). He has received awards for outstanding teaching, as well as an EDUCOM award for his work with IRIS Intermedia. He has published articles, book chapters, and reviews in the areas of computers and education, feminist biblical studies, philosophy of technology, and the history of philosophy.

Susan Herring is Associate Professor of Linguistics and Humanities at the University of Texas at Arlington. She is editing a cross-disciplinary volume entitled *Computer Mediated Communication* (Benjamins Publishing), co-editing (with Pieter van Reenen and Lene Schoesler) *Textual Parameters in Older Languages* (Benjamins), and writing *Tense and Aspect in Tamil Narrative* (Benjamins).

David Kolb is the Charles A. Dana Professor of Philosophy at Bates College (Lewiston, Maine). He is the author of *The Critique of Pure Modernity* (University of Chicago Press), *Postmodern Sophistications* (University of Chicago Press), and *Socrates in the Labyrinth* (a collection of hypertext essays, published by Eastgate Systems). He has published essays on Greek philosophy, German philosophy, architecture and planning, and hypertext writing.

John Lawrence is Professor of Philosophy at Morningside College (Sioux City, Iowa). He is the author of *The Electronic Scholar* (Ablex), and co-author (with Robert Jewett) of *The American Monomyth* (Doubleday). He co-edited (with Bernard Timberg) *Fair Use and Free Inquiry: Copyright Law and the New Media* (Ablex). He has also published hardware and software reviews and served as list moderator for H-PCAACA at H-Net.

Phil Mullins is Professor of Humanities at Missouri Western State College (St. Joseph), where he teaches in an interdisciplinary studies program as well as in religious studies and philosophy. Mullins has published articles in a variety of journals, and is currently editor of *Tradition and Discovery: The Polanyi Society Periodical.*

Stephen D. O'Leary is Assistant Professor at the Annenberg School for Communication, University of Southern California. He is the author of *Arguing the Apocalypse: A Theory of Millennial Rhetoric* (Oxford University Press). He has published essays in various scholarly journals, and currently serves as book review editor for the online *Journal of Computer-Mediated Communication.*

Gary Shank is an Associate Professor of Educational Psychology at Northern Illinois University (De Kalb). He has published in such journals as *Educational Psychology Review, Contemporary Educational Psychology, The American Journal of Semiotics,* and *Contemporary Education Review.* His work on abductive reasoning and CMC has been published in *The Electronic Journal of Virtual Culture.*

Sunh-Hee Yoon teaches in the Department of Communication, Sogang University (Seoul, Korea). He has co-edited (with Mashoed Bailie and Dwayne Winseck) *Democratizing Communication: Comparative Perspectives on Information and Power* (Hampton Press) and (with Deanna Robinson and Woo-Hyun Won) *Making up a Nation's Mind: South Korean Communication in Transition* (Ablex).

INDEX

abduction, 35–36. *See also* semiotics

abductive inference, 37. *See also* semiotics

abductive multilogue, Internet communication as, 37–38

abstraction: as characteristic of literate culture, 245

access: economic barriers to, 249; egalitarian, in Internet, 37; gender, as barrior to, 248; lack of, accelerating sexual objectification, 162–63; to network culture, 276; to scholarly texts, 106–7; as a right, 220; rules of reason and, 216; unlimited, problems of, 218

accountability, instituting in cyberspace, 163

act/speech distinction, 163

adversariality: combined with freedom of speech, 138–39; good vs. bad, 129; tolerance of, 139; women's response to, 129

adversarial posting style, 118–19; as male, 120–21. *See also* agonistic ritual; anarchic/agonistic; anarchistic value system; anarchy; ethic of agonistic debate, 117; flaming; male

aesthetic attitude, vs. argument, 19

Age: of information, 262, 277; of Meaning, vs. Age of Science, 40

agonistic ritual: dialectical disputation as, 244

Alexy, Robert, 205–6, 209

alienation: as characteristic of literate culture, 245

American Bible Society, 9, 280, 293n. 9 (280)

American Culture Association, 98

anarchic/agonistic: ethic, 130 (*see also* ethic of agonistic debate, 117); problems of, 139–40; value system, 126–128. *See also* adversariality; adversarial posting style; agonistic ritual; candor, debate as anarchic values, 128; face, 124; male; politeness (negative)

anarchy: 139; as valued in Usenet, 135; Usenet and, 71; Internet and cyberspace, 126

anomie, global network responds to, 248

anonymity, 75 (*see also* pseudonymity); prohibited in lists, 99; vs. accountability, as accelerating sexual objectification, 162–163 (*see also* accountability, 163; gender inequality)

anonymous e-mail: credibility of, 75; vs. cooperation, 74; vs. responsibility, 71

antipornography analyses, feminist, 147

Aquinas, St. Thomas, 244

argument, 19–20; electronic publishing and, 111; hypertext and, 22; linear, vs. Hegel, Nietzsche, 22; linear, associated with literacy, 11, 237, 286

argumentation: rationality and (Habermas), 208

Aristotle, 20, 204; conception of rhetoric, 236; critique of Sophists, 235–36

ASA-L (American Society for Aesthetics), 100–103

Athenagoras, 242

audience/director duality, 20–21. *See also* author/reader distinction, 21, 287–88

Aufhebung (Hegel), CMC revolution as, 11–12

cyberspace, 1; as amplifying gender inequality, 7, 162–163; commodification of as ethical challenge, 261 (*see also* commodification of messages, 285–86); economic barriers to, 249 (*see also* access); and the limits of harm, 86; philosophical approaches to, 3, 12; as public space, sexual harassment in, 158–59; sexism in, 7; utilitarian concepts of harm in, 86–87

cyborg, 254–263

cyborg disembodiment: ambiguities of for women, 259–60. *See also* disembodiment, 161

cyborg theology, 258–63

cypherpunk remailers: anonymity and, 75. *See also* anonymity; anonymous e-mail

cypherpunks, 69

Cyprian, 240

Data Protection Commission, 59. *See also* privacy protection

debate, as anarchic value, 129. *See also* anarchic/agonistic; anarchy; candor

decentering of text, 19. *See also* author; authority; author/reader distinction; text, fluidity of in electronic culture, 10, 288

decentralization: and communication technology, 173; and computers (failure of) in Korea, 8, 189; and democracy, 173 (*see also* democracy, democratization)

deconstruction, 22; and print, 278; as undermining historical-critical approaches, 279

deduction (semiotics), 35–36

deindustrialization. *See* communication technology, deindustrialization and, 173

democracy: communication and, 198; communitarian (*see* communitarian democracy; decentralization and,

173); definitions of, 198–202; electronic discourse and, 100 (*see also* listcourse); electronic publishing and, 100; Enlightenment conceptions of, 203 (*see also* Enlightenment democracy); Internet as biased towards, 88; Internet lists as examples of, 218–19; Korean definition of, 186; as localization of information (Korea), 187; MUDS and, 20; Panopticon and, 179; plebiscite (*see* plebiscite democracy); pluralist (*see* pluralist democracy); two-way communication as condition of, 189

democratic discourse, perspective-taking and, 217

democratic process: example of Usenet groups, 251–52.

democratic spirit: cooperation and the ethics of e-mail, 85

democratization: bureaucracy and technology vs., 186; CMC and, 4, 8, 11, 197; communication and (Habermas), 215; computers and, 184; computers and: Korean example, 184–190; destabilization of canon as, 289; discourse and (Habermas), 205; Lyotard's conception of, 214; PEN as example of, 199; social context of use, as condition of, 220; undermined by technological discourse, 186

democratization claim: as ideological, utopian, 201

demographics of the Net, male, 151. *See also* male

Demon Seed (movie), 150

Derrida, Jacques: Habermas's critique of, 213

Descartes, René, 11, 27, 36, 40, 222n. 7 (203), 256. *See also* Cartesian; reason; reason, technical conceptions of, 247, 263

de Solla Pool, Ithiel, 107

developmentalism (theory of technology), 172

Dewey, John, 20